SEMPER ODYSSEY

Conflicts of a Marine Reservist

John M.M. Caldwell, Sr.
Colonel, USMCR (Retired)

Semper Odyssey
Conflicts of a Marine Reservist

Copyright ©2021 John M. M. Caldwell, Sr.

ISBN 978-0-578-90405-4   Paperback
ISBN 978-0-578-90406-1   eBook

Library of Congress Control Number 2021909166

Book design by StoriesToTellBooks.com

Published by John M. M. Caldwell, Sr.
Paid for by Friends of John Caldwell
PO Box 167, Nesbit, MS 38651

SEMPER ODYSSEY

Conflicts of a Marine Reservist

John M.M. Caldwell, Sr.
Colonel, USMCR (Retired)

Dedication

*To my wife Lee, my children
Jennifer, JC, Cannon and Daniel,
and to my grandchildren and the families
of those with lost stories never told or forgotten,
and finally, to Marines, especially reservists
who live rich history but hesitate to share.*

Contents

"Only take heed to thyself, and keep thy soul diligently, lest thou forget the things which thine eyes have seen, and lest they depart from thy heart all the days of thy life: but teach them thy sons, and thy sons' sons;"

Deuteronomy 4:9

PRELUDE

Daddy introduced the Marine Corps to my four sisters, my four brothers, and me. Momma introduced us all to church. Like most couples of their era, he and Momma had their young romance interrupted by "The Big War," as Daddy nearly always referred to it. Their wedding and soon-to-be family of nine children had to wait.

In 1942, at the age of 17, Joseph "Joe" W. Caldwell Jr. joined the Marine Corps. Elizabeth Ann "Lib" McCalman, like most women of her generation, supported the war effort from home. Years passed. The war ended. Joe and Lib were married.

"Loads of Love, Joe" A message for Lib to remember him while the war raged.

Not many details were shared with us of his ominous stops on the Marine Corps' island-hopping campaign, but we all had an idea of what took place there; Tinian, Iwo Jima, and Saipan would be part of Daddy's legacy and part of our family's pre-school vocabulary. Most of his recollections to us were tales of liberty in Hawaii between combat operations or a few amusing stories from his boot camp experience.

Daddy embodied the spirit of the Marine Corps. He was especially proud of being promoted to the rank of corporal and his expertise as a machine gunner. Machine guns "had the power," he would brag.

Ironically, I was already an active-duty Marine Corps artillery officer before I realized that he manned that machine gun in an artillery unit—Battery L, 4th Battalion, 14th Marine Regiment, 4th Marine Division.

War details—or lack of them—aside, his love for God, Country, and Corps was evident in everything he did and said. Decades later, Daddy revealed only a few more glimpses of his World War II combat experiences. Sometimes, it seemed that he intentionally or unintentionally erased them from his memory. Now it is more apparent than ever that he simply spared us the clarity of deeply etched details of an immeasurable horror he lived through in order that we wouldn't have to.

After the war, Momma and Daddy enjoyed farming in North Mississippi. He loved it. They filled the simple wood-framed farmhouse with my four sisters.

An outbreak of disease killed a large percentage of their hogs. It cost them the farm and house, but it didn't diminish their resolve. After moving the family to the suburbs of Memphis, Tennessee, Daddy began operating a service station. It was all full service back then. He had a magnetic personality and was a natural entrepreneur and an auto mechanic with a great professional reputation.

My four brothers and I were born and raised in the shadow of his tireless work ethic and his contagious sense of humor. Daddy worked 12- to 15-hour days, 7 days a week as a rule. He taught us early that 12 hours was "just a half day" of work, and that Saturdays, Sundays, and holidays were also workdays.

Until our early teens Momma ensured church came ahead of work, at least on Sunday mornings. As we aged we were scheduled to be at work by seven o'clock each morning. The station's television was already tuned to one of the early morning gospel music shows by the time we arrived. The Lewis Family and the Gospel Singing Jubilee were Daddy's favorites.

Daddy is gone now. He shared jokes, most of his thoughts, and opinions freely but carefully guarded the indelibly embedded accounts of his World War II combat experience. Those stories are now lost to time. Somehow, I understand why but still wish I could hear the ones he chose not to tell.

Marines in general are normally quick to share the funny side of events but reluctant to reveal the personal struggles within their Corps odysseys. Exceptions inevitably expose internal conflicts, painful vulnerabilities, and human imperfections. That kind of heightened consciousness can silence anyone.

Each leatherneck's tale is different. Only after my father's passing did I become acutely aware that only one was uniquely mine. Foreseeable strains of family and career are woven into the less-predictable elements often linked directly to the military experience. Reservists can complicate storylines further by blending the Marine Corps with civilian careers, even politics. In due course, international conflicts escalate into armed conflict, and activation orders impact all of the above.

My first impulse is to keep it all inside, but then I think of Daddy and the untold stories. Silence is no longer an option.

A love-hate relationship with the Marine Corps is fashioned by most who have ever earned the title of Marine. Even the wives cannot help but love some parts of Marine Corps life. Even Marines cannot help but hate some. In between there are good times and bad.

As the Marine Corps family experience revolves around relationships and events, it would seem communion with God would be almost automatic. Yet there is the haughty predisposition to keep God shelved until we finally realize He is needed.

It's been well said that "there are no atheists in foxholes." Marines cannot leave that popular axiom well enough alone. Marines are taught early not to dig "foxholes" because "a foxhole is where little animals run and hide." I was taught that Marines dig "fighting holes." There tends to be no atheists in fighting holes, either, but that is still a far cry from knowing God and nurturing a relationship with Him.

Life before, during, and beyond the Corps is inextricably linked, and the common adage, "Once a Marine, always a Marine," is real. By the time these writings are published, nearly a decade will have passed since my retirement. Active-duty colonels have enough guaranteed retirement income to enjoy their well-earned retirement . . . if they so choose. Reserve colonels, not so much.

This is my story, although it bothers me sometimes that memories fade with time. Trying to present the facts, the feelings, highlights, and life lessons seems a little dishonest, as I purposely avoid narrating some real blunders and embarrassments. Some of them are so egregious they would completely derail the book's original intent and diminish any underlying value of this effort.

So things are omitted that might be more suitable to a confessional, unnecessarily ugly, or especially hurtful to other people. Sometimes, names are changed with similar thoughts in mind.

Unintentionally, details are surely skewed and even questionable by those with better memories. A friend of mine who wrote a book about his childhood recounted his siblings being his worst critics. He finally had to tell them to write their own version if they remembered it so differently. That likelihood remains within these pages, and the advice remains the same.

Throughout the good times and bad, immeasurable joy, laughter, heartbreaking pains, tears, boredom, random depression, anger, resentment, pride, and fears life goes on. Oddly, the emotions and feelings did not always match the circumstances.

Just as life is impossible to fully capture on a bumper sticker, it is nearly as hard to completely chronicle several decades within any number of pages in a book. Some things, even important things will be short-changed, glossed over, even omitted . . . maybe, subject matter for another book someday. For instance, because this literary journey began *for* and not *about* my children and grandchildren, many experiences with them are not included.

JAPAN QUITS! Corporal Joe Caldwell holds the news that makes all the Marines happy.

Love of God, family, and friends provides the order and stability that balances an otherwise messy assortment of events and times. Within the chaos, faith rises, family prevails, duty calls. Patriotism and service to others continue to stand fast as functional intangibles for all of us. It is how to impact our world while looking back and moving forward.

Kay joins Jan, Beth and Pam on the farm in Nesbit, Mississippi.

Caldwell Farm feeding the swine garbage from Memphis' finest restaurants and hotels.

Jan, Beth and Pam join Daddy on the tractor in Mississippi.

Cotton Sacks: Jan and Beth get their fill of picking cotton while Pam plays.

Tom, Jim, John, Daddy, Joe and Frank manned the 24/7/365 full-service filling station over a 30-year period of success, thanks to Daddy's work ethic and leadership.

Caldwell Family: Momma and Daddy had 9 children and saw their family grow with sons-in-law, daughters-in-law and a growing number of grand-children and great grandchildren before their passing.

"I returned and saw under the sun that the race is not to the swift, nor the battle to the strong, neither yet bread to the wise, not yet riches to men of understanding, nor yet favor to men of skill; but time and chance happen to them all."

Ecclesiastes 9:11

...1
Conflicts of Youth

Handfuls of old spark plugs from Daddy's service station lined up like cannons. Opposing defensive lines carefully placed in the backyard grass simulated epic gun battles. That imaginary war came to an abrupt end when the push mower sent one of the spark plugs careening across the patio and through Momma's sliding glass door.

1968 *Growing up in the suburbs*

"Playing army" meant building forts out of everything from cardboard to pine needles and fighting with everything from green apples, crab apples, and persimmons to magnolia "grenades" and dirt clods. The neighborhood wars were always in good fun—at least when they started. In addition to my siblings, there were two dozen other kids within a couple of blocks.

The Whitehaven suburb of Memphis, Tennessee, in the '60s and early '70s was about as good as it gets for middle-class kids. My four brothers and I had plenty of friends in the neighborhood. My four sisters did too, but they were nearly grown and out of the house by the time I began first grade at Graceland Elementary. The neighborhood school was just a few blocks behind Elvis Presley's Graceland Mansion.

The mile or so trek home each afternoon was a steady stream of elementary-age school children. Numbers diminished as we got farther from school. The sidewalks and lawns allowed for the usual play, roughhousing, and even a few fistfights along the way.

Once, in fourth grade, a girl I had never met pointed me out to her sixth-grade boyfriend. I never knew what was said, but I took the blunt of several punches to the face in the aftermath of that whispered provocation. I will never know why it occurred, but I learned to always be ready for a fight and not wait for the first punch. I also learned there is not always a suitable explanation for everything.

A little over halfway home, we reached Hillcrest High School. Normally, we passed slightly ahead of the rush of big kids and teenage drivers. Muscle cars were the craze. If we timed it right, we could get on the other side of the parking lot just in time to watch a cool, wheeled exodus as we walked.

Just two doors from home was the inconspicuous residence of an elderly widow. One summer I finally met the homeowner, Mrs. Evans, when she hosted a one-week neighborhood Bible class called the "Good News Club."

Enough of my friends attended to fill the living room of her small house on the corner lot. The 70s-era décor of an old lady seemed strange to us, almost reverent. Everything was in its place. Everything was very clean. Breakables were in reach rather than tucked away or elevated to a safer place. The plush, wall-to-wall carpet was almost white.

We sat on the carpeted floor and listened while two energetic, teenage group leaders taught us Bible stories. Colorful cut-out illustrations would adhere to a soft felt board propped up in the upholstered living room chair. We also learned a few songs, including one of my favorites: "I'm too small to march in the infantry, ride in the cavalry, shoot the artillery, but I'm in the Lord's army." (Years later I would not be too small.)

It was amazing how exciting and compelling such a simple message in a simple setting could be. The message each afternoon focused on God's love, everyone's sins, and the good news of forgiveness.

Kool-Aid and store-bought cookies closed out each day. One afternoon I stayed late. In the quiet of another room, away from the snacks and laughter, we were getting serious. The reality of my own sin, even as a child, was coupled with conviction and a burning desire not only to be rescued from its consequences but to follow Christ. I had been introduced to Jesus at home, but I had never sought to know Him and truly trust Him until then.

In a few short minutes, my life and my eternity changed forever, but I wasn't old enough to fully understand. In fact, I have since learned that I might never be old enough to fully understand.

For years Momma drove us to a country church near my parents' old farm in Mississippi—New Bethlehem Presbyterian. Just minutes from dirt roads and cow pastures to our south, we were also less than half an hour from the congestion of both midtown and downtown Memphis in the opposite direction. Later, the family moved to Whitehaven Methodist, a huge suburban church closer to our home.

Vietnam was raging, but as a child with protective parents, I hardly knew about it. Seems like I remember some talk about the older teenagers and a draft, but it was a blur. Somebody said something about somebody they knew being killed. Some of the kids at school would mention watching some of it on the news. I rarely saw the news, but I would listen in disbelief to gory versions told by my friends and classmates. Then I heard it was over. To this day it is hard for me to imagine the total loss of American lives during my early years.

War to me was still John Wayne, Glen Ford, and Henry Fonda. Television shows with a military setting like *Gomer Pyle USMC*, *F Troop*, *Hogan's Heroes*, and later, the TV series *MASH*, were shows that made us laugh.

The city's three network television stations and one public broadcasting station signed off at night with patriotic music. Mornings began on our one black-and-white television set with a devotional introduction to the day's regularly scheduled programming. We hardly ever stayed up late enough to watch the TV channels go off the air. However, a few times we fell asleep on the floor just to wake up to the continuous beeping sound that indicated the broadcasts were over until morning.

• • •

Shielded from TV news and the realities of war in Southeast Asia, it was court-ordered busing that temporarily interrupted my fairytale existence in Southwest Memphis. Suddenly, my four brothers and I were removed from our neighborhood schools and scheduled to catch five different buses at five different times to take us to five different campuses in different areas of the city.

Until then, minority interaction had been minimal for me. I always remembered my oldest sister having us over to her house, which was in a minority neighborhood. I remember playing football in the streets in the 'hood, using a basketball. The quarterback told the center, "When I say boom, hike the ball." A minute later, he dropped a lit firecracker down his friend's pants . . . Never saw anything like that before!

Once, my brothers and I got into a fight with a few of the neighborhood kids. I don't recall what started it, but I know how it ended. Within minutes of the fight starting, older black youths dropped what they were doing at a nearby school park and ran over to beat up the white kids.

We were getting slapped around pretty good when my brother-in-law burst out of his house and everyone scattered. I was crying mad, still wanting to keep fighting even though I was not getting a lick in at the time. With that experience firmly etched into my memory, I was a little anxious about attending a school filled with predominately black students.

My parents reluctantly and somewhat under protest planned for us to participate in the integration effort. When my mom saw and smelled piles of summer garbage rotting at Mitchell High School, where my oldest brother was scheduled to attend, she began looking for options.

My oldest brother Joe got the first reprieve with an opening at an expanded Citizens Against Busing (CAB) School: Oakhaven Baptist Academy (OBA). Frank and next oldest was next in line, escaping from a volatile school situation at Corey Jr. High early in the initial semester of the failing busing experiment. My little brothers and I remained bused out of our neighborhood to three other public schools for the rest of the school year and one additional year before the five of us could reunite at a single school.

During sixth and seventh grade, I could count the number of white students in my class on one hand. The racial tension was not as bad as I had feared, but there was some. Fighting in sixth grade was nameless. Almost daily, someone would turn the lights off in the boys' room. No windows. Pitch black. Everyone would start swinging. One black friend and I would fight standing shoulder to shoulder, away from the wall to avoid hitting each other. When the lights came back on, everyone was all smiles. I never knew why the teachers didn't hear it, but it probably relieved tensions enough so that real fighting was rare.

Seventh grade included a locker room fight with a black friend of mine named Yule. Again, I don't remember what started it, but I remember the rest. Once the fight started, I was surrounded by other black students who hardly knew that the two of us were just two friends, like brothers fighting. All they cared about was that he was black and I was white. They took cheap shots at me from all angles and hurled racial slurs like "cracker," "honky," and "white boy." The PE coach finally heard the commotion. We both were paddled but remained friends. That was the second time that I learned that fights as a white guy in a black community meant I better be ready to fight more than one at a time. I witnessed that again several more times over the remaining months. In the white community where I was raised, fights were nearly always a 1:1 ratio. I'm not sure that was a lesson the courts expected me to learn from their integration experiment.

In the eighth grade my parents helped me avoid getting bused to yet another school. I could now ride to school with my brothers. Life settled down. School was fun again, and now it even taught Bible classes and held chapel services.

Brother Boots' Bible class in eighth grade was the setting of a fistfight between my friend Glen and me. We were fighting over some reason I didn't even remember the next day. Instead of a typical intervention and paddling, Brother Boots took another approach. He instructed the entire class to move desks against the wall, clearing the floor for us to fight. The other students provided a buffer between our flailing and the hardwood edges of the desks. Winded and tired, Glen and I looked up as if to ask, "Now what?"

"Are you done?"

"Yes, sir."

"Then let's put the room back together and have class."

I never saw that technique repeated at school, but it proved very effective. I don't remember any tensions or flare-ups between the two of us or anyone else for the remainder of the year or the years that followed.

Winning and losing high school ball games or wrestling matches seemed to establish a rightfully inflated importance at our small, close-knit Christian school. Competition and team sports taught me countless life lessons. Losing is never fun, but competing, succeeding, and even failing helped me begin to understand that the sporting events themselves were not such life-and-death matters after all.

Football took precedence over my old favorite, baseball. Track entered the picture next, mandated by the football coach. Wrestling began as an "off-season" sport to stay in shape, and it soon became my new favorite. The adrenaline rush when the referee slapped the mat was like nothing I had experienced in other sports as an average athlete with average foot speed and a small frame. Instead of competing against the bigger, stronger players, wrestling allowed me to compete in a sport with athletes who were my size.

The Fellowship of Christian Athletes chapter at my high school helped me keep a better perspective of sports and their place in life. Still, I had to learn some things the hard way.

After only one defeat early in the wrestling season as a junior, I entered my senior year championship tournament unbeaten and favored to win a second championship. I was more self-confident than ever . . . no better time for a humbling experience.

Fever of 103° F could not be overcome with a first-round bye or the 17-second breeze match that followed in the second round. Three complete overtime rounds with my fiercest competitor in the championship match ended with his victory, my reality check, and renewed perspective. Life and my ego returned to normal.

As a high school teenager, thoughts of joining the Marines began to surface. Those thoughts gradually became more frequent. None of the other services crossed my mind. It would be the Marines or nothing.

In fact, I was seriously considering going to see a recruiter about the same time that I got a date. It was one of only a few real dates for me in high school. Most outings were just groups of friends. This time, however, just two of us were going to a movie.

Obviously, I wasn't experienced at this thing called dating. She was nice, but the movie I chose was not. It was *The Deer Hunter*, one of the first notable war movies that did not glamorize combat. It was no John Wayne-style movie focused on glory with a fairytale ending; rather, it tempered my desire to see a recruiter, and it virtually killed any chance for romance that night. It would be a couple of years before serious thoughts of becoming a Marine returned— and nearly that long before any meaningful romance. I would no longer pick the movie.

Letting my date pick the movie—*The Champ*—proved to be just as much of a bust the next year. The first signs of trouble came while we were at the theater, waiting in line. The usher handed everyone Kleenex tissues. When the early show released, all the men, women, and children walked by us with red eyes, sniffling or openly crying. Surely, dating would get better with experience.

• • •

As high school ended, an unsupervised graduation trip to Daytona Beach was exactly what I had in mind. Graduation meant leaving the comforts, protection, and influence of a small Christian high school. Family values were temporarily shelved.

Time and distance from such a sheltered life would provide a new level of freedom. Carloads of friends, great weather at the beach during the day, wild times at night, and "10-cent drink specials" all came together on the popular Florida strip that week. It was hard to imagine we had graduated from a Baptist high school. We didn't act like we knew right from wrong or, if we did, that we cared. At least I had enough sense to avoid the drug scene. Or did I?

One night, back in Memphis, walking across the parking lot of a popular night club with my friend Sam, a custom Chevy van pulled up to us. When the van door slid open, a group of great-looking girls asked us something interesting.

"Do y'all have any pot?"

So much for our strong, anti-drug conviction. Although neither of us had ever used drugs, Sam and I immediately checked our pockets. As they drove away, we looked at each other.

"What were you checking your pockets for?"

"You were checking yours too!"

Much more of my time and attention was now focused on girls and good times. Those priorities almost cost me my college education and a whole lot more. It was the unofficial beginning of what I commonly refer to as my "stupid years." I spent them working and partying my way through school at Arkansas State University. Those first few semesters were nearly an academic waste, although life lessons piled high.

Derrick, an OBA classmate and friend, had made the graduation trip to

Daytona and the trip to college with me. While I was prepared to work my way through school, his talents on the court and his 6' 9" frame had landed him a four-year athletic scholarship.

It was a freedom ride for the two of us. The sun was shining. My 1963 Buick Wildcat was washed, waxed, and loaded with everything we owned. The music was loud. We were indestructible. Nothing could stop us. Nothing, that is, except blue lights.

"Man, I can't believe I got a ticket. What a rip-off!"

"You know that speed trap is set up just for new students like us."

"Chalk one up for experience."

Twin Towers, a nine-story, yellow brick, men's dormitory, was coming into sight. The narrow, white, cinderblock halls had low drop ceilings, white institutional tile floors, and were crowded with guys moving into their new homes-away-from-home. The cramped dorm rooms looked bigger when no one was in them.

"I just hope I don't get a gay roommate."

"You shouldn't have anything to worry about. You're in Arkansas."

"That's easy for you to say. You're living in the athletic dorm."

We opened the door to find that someone had already moved into my room. Derrick immediately dropped the load he had been carrying and began rummaging through the absent roommate's effects.

"What are you doing? Man, you're gonna get caught. What if he walks in on us?"

"Uh-oh."

"What?"

He held up a picture of my roommate-to-be in ballet leotards. There was also a girl in the picture, but all I could think was that my fears had come true.

"Wait a minute. He can't be all bad." Derrick held up a stack of *Playboy* and *Penthouse* magazines.

He continued to dig, and now I was helping with no more concern of being caught. This was too important to be shy.

We located a black bag in the closet that looked like a doctor's kit. It was full of drug paraphernalia. One tall, plastic bong had an oxygen-style-mask attached to it. The items looked well used. What had I gotten myself into? There was too much chaos in the halls and at the dorm office to worry about any immediate room-change requests. I would just have to deal with it for at least a few days and maybe find a way out.

The first night in the dorm there was a door-to-door collection taken for a beer run. Heavy, binge drinking was rampant. It was a sign of things to come.

The next afternoon a small group of us avoided the cafeteria and went to the local Pizza Hut. The waitress asked for my order last.

I looked at my friends around the table. "I'm surprised after last night that none of you ordered beer with your pizza."

"Man, Craighead's a dry county."

"A what?"

"You have to go to the next county to buy beer, and you have to be twenty-one years old anyway."

I had never heard of a dry county, so I never thought to ask about it. "Dry" referred only to the prohibition of the sale of alcohol and didn't seem to affect the consumption rate, at least from what I had witnessed so far. A 30-minute round trip to the county line became a familiar routine. Never mind that none of us were of legal drinking age.

Everyone on the eighth floor where I lived seemed friendly and stayed in the partying mood. Education seemed secondary to everyone I met. In addition to the Arkansas, Missouri, Tennessee, and Mississippi crowd, I quickly met friends from as far away as Massachusetts and upstate New York.

Dave "Josh" Joslin from Rochester, New York, introduced me to more than a little trouble along the way, and I was always quick to return the favor. Josh also introduced me to someone who immediately got my attention.

Lee Perkins was a tall, beautiful, Arkansas brunette returning for her sophomore year. While I had always been partial to short blondes, this country girl could make anyone change their preferences. Unfortunately, she was already dating some lug. From her Ozark Mountains home to the Miss Arkansas pageant to the university campus, Lee could and did turn every head in a room.

I was a scrawny, incoming freshman with wide eyes and big dreams. She seemed so out of my reach that I felt an instant easiness around her. (It was the girls I thought I had a chance with who made me nervous.)

Good times seemed to be my focus, and my grades were showing it. Just about anything that crossed our minds, my friends and I would be willing to try.

"Hey, John, you want to jump a train?"

"Sure. Who's going?"

"I don't know. I just thought of it."

"Hey, Josh, Nettles wants us to go jump a train."

"I'm in. Where are we going?"

"Wherever the train takes us. We'll try to catch one heading to Memphis. We may spend the rest of the weekend trying to catch one back, but if we can't, I'll leave my keys with Sull and he'll come pick us up."

Steve "Sull" Sullivan was a student resident assistant on our floor in the dorm and somewhat of a father figure. How he arrived there from Framingham, Massachusetts, is still a mystery. Nevertheless, he fit.

Revelry and foolishness were not part of Sull's routine. In fact, our irresponsible festivities usually stood in direct contrast with his serious-minded approach to college and life. Although he more than tolerated us, as a friend he also at times chastised us. He soberly accepted the keys as would a typical, designated driver.

"Hey, Murph and Jerry 'Teke' are coming with us."

"Great. The more the merrier."

The trains near campus seemed to be traveling too fast to board, so we walked up the tracks toward town. One went by slowly enough but in the wrong direction. As the train cars passed us, the sun began to go down.

"We can't go back to the dorm and not have jumped a train after telling everyone we would."

"Okay, we jump on the next one going slow enough to board, no matter which track or direction."

It wasn't long until the five of us were running alongside a grain car, reaching for an external ladder and pulling ourselves up. We all boarded like we had done it all our lives. It was a huge adrenaline rush as the train picked up speed. We waved at the cars stopped at each crossing. We even climbed up to the catwalks on top. We had done it. We had jumped a train—but to where?

"I don't think this train is going to Memphis."

"It's probably headed to Paragould."

We arrived quickly at the small town 30 or so miles up the track, but we weren't ready to get off yet.

"Let's stay on."

"Okay."

Nobody was ready for it to end. The adventure was just beginning. After Paragould there was no sign of stopping until well after the sun had set. Then a cold front passed through, and we weren't dressed for the change in temperature. The cold steel of the external platform was getting uncomfortable. The speed of the train blew wintry night air that cut through our clothes with dreadful ease.

Sounds of the hard wheels rolling over the rail seams were an exciting sound at first. Every screech and squeal had been an awesome testament of the train's power and an audible endorsement of our choice to experience something new. Now, it was just noise. Loud and relentless noise.

The train stopped a few times, but each time it was in the middle of nowhere. We couldn't get off and walk up to a strange farmhouse in the middle of the night, so we continued our journey into the darkness. At one point we realized we were crossing the Mississippi River. Our best estimate put us near the boot heel of Missouri, but it was a dark, moonless night, and we couldn't tell if we were headed north or east after we crossed.

The fun, nearly lost in the intense darkness, was now being forced into submission by the bitter cold. On the verge of frostbite, we longed for our next opportunity to get off. This time we would jump from a moving train if it would just slow down a bit.

Then it happened. We could hear the tension shift on the couplings. We could feel the force of the winter blast subsiding as the train slowed. We saw streetlights as we entered a new town. In the dark, Jerry "Teke" recognized the town names. Letters were barely legible by the ambient light dimly brushing the water towers ... DUPO. We were in Illinois, just south of the city of East St. Louis. The train continued on a steady but much slower pace.

"This is where we get off. Either it stops or we jump before it picks up any more speed."

We were in total agreement. It had been over nine hours since we left the dorm and almost that long on the train. We were cold, tired, hungry, thirsty, and ready to close out this adventure.

Chi-Clang! The renewed tension on the steel couplings and the faster beating of the wheels across the uneven rail seams told us the train was speeding up. Ready or not, Murph and Jerry made short work of their exits.

Nettles was next, but as he hung from the ladder, his feet touched the ground. Before he could let go, he was tossed like a rag doll under the train. He held onto the ladder for dear life. Josh and I were helpless. We couldn't grab him and weren't real sure that was what he needed. I reached for him anyway... just in case he needed a hand.

The train continued to pick up speed, and Nettles tried to regain control. His feet touched the ground several more times, and each time he hung on tightly as the force pulled his legs and body under the train. He had to push away and let go. Finally, he did it.

Almost instantly, I jumped. My intentions to hit feet first and roll were noble but naïve. The speed of the train had now reached at least 30 miles per hour. Once my feet touched, I was airborne, catapulted forward into a two-point landing on my chest and face. I lay there, dazed for a minute, trying to assess my aches and pains before I moved.

I also looked up and watched the silhouette of the train rolling into the night. I wondered if Josh had jumped or not. As the train clattered out of sight, I hollered a few times for Josh and then went back down the tracks, looking for Nettles.

"Hey, Nettles, are you alright?"

"Yeah, but I think I broke my hand. How about you?"

"I'm alright. Just a little banged up."

The cool night air touched the fresh blood on my face. Scrapes on both palms were beginning to sting a little. I had learned the difference between pain and injury during high school athletics. I was in pain.

"I'm not sure if Josh jumped or not. We need to go look for him and then find Murph and Jerry."

It took a few minutes to link up with Murph, Jerry, and Josh. We had been scattered down the tracks like litter as we jumped. Josh had a pretty good bump on his head, but Murph and Jerry were relatively unscathed.

"I guess we're in Dupo."

"Dupo? Where in the heck is that?"

"We left Dupo a while back. We're in Cahokia."

"Well, where the hell is Cahokia?"

"Near East St. Louis, Illinois."

"Is there somewhere that we can eat or sleep?"

"Probably not at two thirty in the morning."

"What's up ahead?"

"It's a motel."

"Alright."

"Whoa. That sign says 'hourly rates.'"

"I'll pass. Let's keep walking."

"That doesn't sound so bad right now."

"They probably don't even change the sheets."

"Gross."

"Let's go to the police station and see if they'll let us sleep in the jail."

"Where do you think we are, Mayberry? We can ask Sheriff Taylor if Aunt Bee will fix us breakfast."

"I'm serious."

"I'm too tired to argue or think."

"Let's do it."

"Lead the way."

"You do the talkin.'"

We had their attention as soon as we walked in the door. One of the uniformed policemen got up from his roost.

"Good morning," I said politely. "We're looking for a place to stay. We saw a motel back that way, but it was hourly rates."

"You boys didn't want to stay there, that's for sure. What happened to you?"

"Well—"

We hesitated to confess.

"Was it something that we need to get you tetanus shots for, or what?"

"It was rocks."

"Rocks?"

"You see, we sort of jumped from a moving train. We go to Arkansas State and our fraternity made us do it."

That was a lie. Jerry was the only one of us who had joined a fraternity, but we did know that it was illegal to jump a train. Plus, we didn't want to admit our stupidity up front. It worked. They took pity on us.

"Those fraternities are going to get someone killed. Let's get you bandaged up. There's also a decent motel just up the road, but how will you get back?"

"Oh, I left my keys with a friend to come pick us up."

After a brief, first aid session and few lighthearted jokes, they sent us on our way. As we walked through town, we noticed a small roadside inn. It was a '60s-vintage, single-story, L-shaped building with about a dozen or more rooms facing the parking lot. There were only about three or four parked cars, so we knew there had to be vacant rooms.

We rang the door buzzer. The old lady who answered the door would not open it. Through the glass she shouted, "No Vacancy." Then she pulled the shade down so we wouldn't argue the point.

The look on her face made us take a good look at ourselves. No wonder she wouldn't open up. We had dressed in the most ragged clothes we owned to jump the train. The five of us still had visible signs of our abrupt encounter with the rocks that lined the tracks. We must have looked like we were fresh from a gang fight that we had lost. My face was covered with cuts and scrapes and still bleeding slightly. Nettles had a bandage spotted with blood on one hand. Josh had a good-sized knot on his head. Jerry and Murph were relatively unscathed. The five of us were haggard, dirty, unshaven, with tired red-eyes.

We were getting ready to sleep on the side of the road but decided to go back to the police station one more time and beg for a bed in the jail.

"Hey, we're back again. The clerk at the motel wouldn't rent us a room."

"I can't blame her. You look rough."

"Can we spend the night in your jail?"

"We have to keep the doors locked even if nobody's in them, so you'll be locked up."

"That's fine with us. We just need to get some sleep."

In the morning they woke us and fed us donuts. There were three or four cops at the station that morning. Fortunately, they had a great sense of humor and helped us laugh at ourselves. One of them drove us to a payphone at a nearby McDonald's.

Our pre-arranged ride home backed out when he found out where we were. We called our most trusted friends. The girls—including my not-yet-girl-friend Lee—agreed to come get us, so we arranged to meet them at the base of the St. Louis Gateway Arch.

We hitched a ride in the back of an open top garbage truck. The refuse was piled to the top, so we could easily see and be seen over the sideboards. It was pretty humbling but better than walking.

When the girls arrived, they realized that five, dirty, smelly boys would have to crowd into the small car with the four girls who had generously offered to come get us.

• • •

By the end of my freshmen year, Lee and I had started dating steadily, and we continued dating through the summer.

That summer I went back to Memphis to work for Daddy. It was a hard, hot job at the station, but it provided decent pay, plenty of hours, and great job security. It was good to see some of Daddy's old friends and customers I had come to know over the years of working during high school.

"Hey, John. Back from college already? What are you majoring in?"

Before I could get a word in edgewise, Daddy would interject loudly and forcefully. "Good times! He's majoring in good times."

That wasn't too far from the truth, so we'd all usually laugh and leave it at that.

Lee and I seemed to be getting serious. Neither of us was ready for that kind of relationship. The distance factor was difficult enough, and my heavy work schedule didn't leave much time for fun in the sun. We finally found time for a night out. I was going to make the long drive after work to pick her up at her dorm. She was expecting me to call to let her know I was on my way. I got off work early enough to arrive at her dorm lobby about the time she was expecting my call. She answered the phone three stories above me.

"Hello?"

"Hey, Lee. This is John."

"Are you off yet?"

"Yeah, but I don't think I'm going to make the drive from Memphis to Jonesboro tonight."

"Ah, I understand. You must be tired."

"No, I'm not tired."

"Well, do you just not want to drive up here."

"That's it."

"Well, fine then. Bye."

By the time she hung up on me, I had disregarded the girl manning the front desk and bolted up the dormitory stairs. When I reached her door, she was

still giving her roommate an earful about me canceling our date. Her roommate opened the door.

"Uh, Lee."

"What?"

"You might want to come to the door."

"Hey, honey, I wouldn't ever do that to you. I got off early and called from
downstairs."

"That wasn't funny."

"I know. I'm sorry."

I really thought it was funny. As we hugged, I just smiled over her shoulder.
She was too beautiful and sweet for me to carry a joke very far with her.

A late date, a long trip home and back to work.

A quick summer and back to school.

• • •

My second year of college began with me getting dumped. Lee had decided
she needed some space. I was never one to fight with girlfriends and their
mood swings, etc. Either everything would work out or it wouldn't. It looked
like our relationship wouldn't. It must have been too good to be true. Lee and
I remained good friends and saw each other off and on at campus events and
parties. Although we dated other people, we still had a unique bond and a lot
of mutual friends.

As I continued into my second reckless year, I began to realize I had better
get serious about school and life. Several of my friends had already been added
to the dropout rate, and I wasn't far behind. I was just surviving academically
and wrapping up a semester of disciplinary probation. Surprisingly, the probation was unrelated to our many shenanigans because most of those did not
reach the dean.

Coercion and assault were among the list of charges the campus leadership
wanted to levy on a small group of us who had taken a friendly prank too far.
It was similar to hazing, which was very common in the Greek life on campus
in those days, but we weren't part of a fraternity. I knew right from wrong but
was lacking the self-discipline to make better choices. Wasting money and
time seemed to come naturally.

Thankfully, our friend and victim of the prank would not file charges, even though the university was pressing him to do so. Dr. Denny, the Dean of Students, let us know in no uncertain terms that we should thank our friend, because the university wanted to make a public example out of us. We did thank him.

• • •

It was only May of my sophomore year, but it was already hot in Jonesboro, the small but vibrant college town in Northeast Arkansas. Time had come for greater independence. After moving out of the dorm and into an apartment near campus, it didn't make any sense to go back home and work for Daddy for another summer. Working for Daddy wasn't independence. I also needed to change my "major" from "Good Times" to something that came with a degree.

Job hunting began in earnest. Everything died down in the area when school was out, and the summer of 1981 wasn't looking to be any different. This job hunt was going to be difficult.

Friends were making plans for reconnecting on summer excursions—road trips—to one of several lakes or any other excuse to get together. Usually, my friends and I preferred all-day canoe trips down Spring River. When we got together, we always had about as much fun as we could stand, but all this fun cost money, and I was running out.

A few too many parties and a couple of bad choice romances had convinced this college sophomore that he had better get his head on straight and soon!

• • •

Consider the Marines. Since *The Deer Hunter* had squelched my initial desire to enlist, a lot had changed. Years had passed. Ronald Reagan was elected president. His assassination was almost played out on dormitory TV sets, but instead, he walked into the hospital. He faced his gunshot wound with the optimism and sense of humor he had restored to the nation. Now it was time for me to face some personal decisions.

A job hunt was first and foremost. Without a paycheck, my mostly self-funded college career would be over. My grants and loans didn't amount to enough on their own. I had been working part time, but I needed more hours.

One humid morning I began on my old Free Spirit 10-speed. While slowly pedaling past the military recruiting offices, thoughts of what might have been were almost audible. *What if I had joined the Marines when it first crossed my mind?*

WHAM!

Before I knew it, my head impacted the blistering asphalt. With all the weight on my right pedal, the white racing bike had slipped out of gear, sending me headfirst over the handlebars. Ironically, a U.S. Navy recruiter saw me wreck and treated my wounds—my first corpsman.

He took me into the recruiting office and cleaned the abrasions and cuts. We laughed about the whole episode as he carefully finished bandaging me. He even did a little recruiting. After such hospitality, I was very receptive but not persuaded.

Thoughts of joining the Navy never really entered my mind, but I began thinking seriously again about the Marine Corps next door. Maybe my head had hit the pavement a little too hard. Maybe it was divine intervention. Select phone calls to a few family members and friends received mostly negative yet predictable reviews that day. None swayed me from the decision already in progress.

The next morning was a Tuesday. It was just like any other day, but thoughts of the Marine Corps were as fresh as the knot on my head. I went back to the recruiting office, ready to join.

"I want to be a machine gunner, but I want to join the reserves so I can finish college. Can I be back in time for school this fall?"

A quick glance at the calendar and one phone call and the recruiter answered, "Yes, but you'd have to leave next Tuesday."

For the first time my good times with my friends at the lake or on the river were now taking a back seat. "Okay, let's go for it."

A pre-packaged folder was placed on the desk. A black government pen was placed in my hand. Signing was the easy part.

Momma's unhappy reaction was predictable. Coldly discarding the fact that I had freely volunteered to go in, she focused her energy on how to get me out.

"Maybe we can get you out of this enlistment contract."

"I don't want out. I signed it because I want to be a Marine."

"There's still got to be a way out."

"You're not listening."

Daddy was transparently excited and proud, but he remained uncharacteristically quiet—obviously to keep peace with Momma. She had already given the recruiter a piece of her mind.

The final decision prompted a myriad of reactions from friends and family alike. One of the friends I had called at the outset was Lee Perkins. Following our brief dating relationship and a gentle break-up, we had rekindled our friendship. We had also made plans to get together with other friends during the summer.

She didn't like the idea of me becoming a Marine. She spent our time on the phone telling me why I shouldn't do it. "Do you know what you're getting into? I've known people who've joined, and they weren't the same when they returned."

"That's the idea, Lee."

"I'm serious, John. You really need to think more about this."

After we ended the call, Lee wrote me a three-page letter detailing reasons why I shouldn't join the Marine Corps. While missing the mark somewhat in her analysis, she proved eerily prophetic in some ways. One of her insightful questions pondered the possibility of me going to war and leaving a wife and family at home. She couldn't foresee that the wife would be her and the kids would be ours.

I had been living on the edge, both literally and figuratively, for the first two years of college. I knew I needed some help. I needed discipline. The Marine Corps would be a big part of my answer.

Tuesday came quickly. It was time to go. As I embarked on my first airplane ride, I wondered how many recruits took their first flight on the way to a Marine Corps Recruit Depot (MCRD). Excitement was tempered by apprehension. Maybe I should have asked questions of the recruiter. I had been so sure of myself that I refused to hear any "recruiter lies" and, therefore, missed out on any truthful insights that might have accompanied more conversation.

The plane landed. It was a beautiful, temperate night in Southern California. Because of my time constraints and because I enlisted west of the

Mississippi, I was shipped to MCRD San Diego instead of MCRD Paris Island. Paris Island, South Carolina, is typically for recruits who enlist east of the river.

Rude responses at the San Diego International Airport woke me to the realization that the recruiting process was over. I boarded a nearly full bus of equally enlightened recruits. The silence on the bus was deafening.

After an hour or so spent sitting on the bus and waiting quietly as others boarded, the short ride from the airport began. It was a strange one. One side of me was looking out the bus windows as a tourist. I was in a new place and was intrigued by the house lights shining like stars across the low hills. My imagination tried to picture what I would see once the sun came up.

The other side of me was all business and could see boot camp coming into view on the other side of the bus. I was confused, tired, and ready for a good night's sleep. I'd just get oriented in the morning.

Suddenly, hell boarded the bus, screaming, barking, and bellowing something about "yellow footprints." Hell was a receiving barracks drill instructor. He rattled the script off so fast that very little could be understood except the last few words. "Get off my bus. Do it now!" The intense barrage of commands that followed was relentless and perverse. As we were herded like cattle through a stockyard, I looked for an American flag or at least an eagle, globe, and anchor for reassurance that I was in the right place.

Within minutes our hair and civilian clothes were gone. Then we were cramming everything they issued into our sea bags. About the only personal item that remained was a Bible that my sister Beth had given me for a graduation present from high school. My fully stuffed duffle must have weighed more than I did. I could only carry it a short distance without a painful pause and quick, awkward adjustment. The double-shoulder-strap version hadn't been made yet. We had a single strap and one carrying handle. It didn't take long until the strap cut into my shoulder. The carrying handle only served to steady the bag over alternating shoulders. Although frustrated with the logic of the design, I saw a few others having even more trouble than I was. The "sea bag drag" lasted for days as we worked our way out of the receiving barracks.

The first stop in the receiving barracks was to "Shit, Shower, and Shave." I quickly learned there were other rhythmic phrases and rhymes that flowed strangely in this new vocabulary.

"Five Minutes!"

Most elements of the new language were easy to understand, but timing was seriously flawed. Almost immediately after a cold shower with 10 seconds of water, I tried to shave. Just as I brought the razor to my face, the DI came from behind and screamed in my right ear.

"One Minute!"

Flinching with my razor in a quick downward motion, I cut myself deep enough to bleed all over my pillow that first night. The slash was superficial, but it stirred real fears of getting caught bleeding without permission.

One minute was allotted for just about everything, and a quick "3, 2, 1— You're Done" came about 20 seconds after each one-minute notice. I'm sure I didn't quit bleeding fast enough.

The second night wasn't much better. A recruit upstairs began to hysterically laugh non-stop. From the downstairs barracks we saw the MPs arrive. We heard the scuffle coming down the stairs, and we could see the MPs push the recruit into the wall. There was a loud thud and no more laughing. The next morning on the way to the chow hall, we saw the head-sized hole in the wall where the recruit had impacted.

Tensions were high; something I had never experienced. There wasn't time or inclination to even say a word, much less smile or laugh.

The receiving barracks drill instructors were about the meanest on the depot. Ours took his place at the top. If he wanted us to be fearful of him and the consequences he could bring to bear, he succeeded.

Besides wreaking havoc, the DI had some basic duties to perform to bring his new recruits into the system. One of his first tasks was to teach us how to mark our clothing. First, he showed us how to put our stamp pad together. "I need a volunteer. Recruit, what's your name?"

"Sir, Private Delgado, Sir."

He showed us how the last name comes first, followed by the initials: DELGADO RJ. Of course it had to be done backwards so the stamp would read properly when applied.

Once the stamp pad was functional, he went into excruciating detail at lightning speed as to where and how the name should be placed. On the boots, flap down, left side: DELGADO RJ; on the skivvies drawers, left leg, 2" above the seam: DELGADO RJ; on the skivvies shirts, back collar behind the tag; on the socks, left side below the ribs, toe turned to the left: DELGADO RJ; on the cover, left inside head band, upside down: DELGADO RJ; on the camouflaged trousers, left inside waistband: DELGADO RJ; on camouflaged blouses, inside back collar: DELGADO RJ, on the shower bag . . . The list went on and on, and he went so fast it was impossible to keep up.

When finished he asked, "Any questions?" Sure, we had questions, but all of us had learned not to ask anything or bring any attention to ourselves—all of us except Romano.

Private Romano was a little too intense, even for the Marine Corps. He sometimes tried so hard that he couldn't get things right. This time was almost his first and last. With bulging neck arteries, a red face, and a loud, demonstrative tone, Romano boldly addressed the drill instructor.

"Sir, the private has a question, sir."

"What do you want?" the drill instructor growled.

"Sir, how do you spell *Delgado*, sir?"

All at once the tension broke. The whole room burst into laughter with no thought of consequence. Even the drill instructor couldn't hold his composure completely, so he left the room with a few choice words in the best huff he could muster. I almost split a gut at the thought of Romano getting ready to put "DELGADO RJ" on his clothes.

One day later, Romano spoke up again. This time the drill instructor had explained to everyone in no uncertain terms to have a pen and paper by the time he returned to the barracks, even if we had to "beg, borrow, or steal" (a phrase everyone added to their Marine Corps vocabulary).

The drill instructor returned to continue our processing. A few minutes into his class Romano raised his hand.

"What do you want, Romano?"

"Sir, the private doesn't have a pen, sir."

Instantly, Romano went from sitting Indian style on the floor to lying flat on his back with a drill instructor's boot on his chest. There was no shortage of words, and this time there was no laughter. Even after watching it, I'm not real sure how the DI did that so fast. Romano took it in stride, and eventually adjusted in order to successfully complete the coming weeks that made up Marine Corps boot camp.

Each night, minutes before taps, or "lights out," recruits stood at the position of attention on line in front of each rack (bunk). White skivvy shirts (T-shirts), skivvy drawers (boxers), and shower shoes were the uniform for the nightly ritual. Recruits remained motionless until the drill instructor stepped in front of each recruit. As the DI executed a perfect right face centered on each recruit, each of us raised our hands, bending the elbow at a 90-degree angle with forearms parallel to the deck. Palms were facing up, fingers outstretched and together, then rotating palms automatically and returning sharply to the position of attention.

"Sir, the private has no medical problems at this time."

The DI inspected for close shaves, clean fingernails, nose hair, etc.

"Open."

At that time, he would spray Listerine in each recruit's mouth.

"Close. Swallow."

The DI would move the next recruit and repeat each step until he came to me.

"Open."

As the squad leader for first platoon, I would get more. He would squirt Listerine into my mouth until it was so full it was just about to run down my chin. There was always a long pause and then, "Swallow."

The next recruit was the last. He was our platoon guide, Private Slatt. Slatt was from Oregon. He was tall and broad shouldered and lived up to his visual image. A no-nonsense natural leader, Slatt was the company honor man and won the company pugil stick competition known as the "bridge over troubled water." The losers fell into the water, and the winner was the last man standing.

The shortest and skinniest DI, Sergeant Primer, loved to goad Slatt about being an Oregon lumberjack with a blue ox named Babe. But I think it was the nightly inspection that Sergeant Primer liked best. After his little fun with me and the Listerine, there was usually about a third of the bottle or more left for Private Slatt.

"Open."

A new command, "Lean your head back," was added.

Drill Instructor Sgt. Primer unscrewed the top off the spray bottle that he had filled with Listerine that evening. He would just about have to get on his tip-toes and stretch in order to pour the remains down Private Slatt's throat.

"Swallow.

"Prepare to mount."

"Sir, prepare to mount. Aye-aye, sir."

Recruits would leave their position at the center of the squad bay and stand at the position of attention beside their racks.

"Mount."

"Sir, mount. Aye-aye, sir."

Immediately, we would lie on our racks in the position of attention without moving the covers. Sometimes, we laid at the position of attention a long time. Sometimes, there was enough time for the drill instructors to ask questions and play mind games. Other times, it was swift. There was no sweeter sound in the evening than to hear the bugle call for lights out.

"Aaaaaaaaadjust."

The command to adjust allowed us to get comfortable and out of the position of attention. Sometimes, it wasn't worth the effort, and I woke up the next morning without ever breaking the attention position. Usually, the next sound I heard, other than a few planes taking off from the nearby San Diego International Airport, was reveille.

"Good morning, recruits. You are all hired killers for Mr. Ronald Reagan."

"Oorah."

Early in training we went to our first hand-to-hand combat class. Although we weren't officially Marines, it was beginning to at least feel like it.

They taught us how to kill. Self-defense would not be good enough. In hand-to-hand combat, it's not about trying to keep from getting hurt but about killing as many as possible, as fast as possible, until the threat is gone.

You don't have to like it, but you might as well be good at it. So whether you need to break the neck of an enemy sentry, or cut the throat of an attacking adversary, this is a training session you don't want to miss. I especially appreciated the knife-fighting techniques that were taught. They seemed to be practical, and I couldn't imagine getting caught without my K-bar. It has been the Marine Corps' knife of choice since World War II.

Organized physical training (PT) was my favorite part of the training cycle, but years of track, baseball, football, and wrestling in high school hadn't really prepared me for this. This was different and certainly made a little more difficult after two years of slacking in college.

In addition to running in shoes and running in boots, there was hand-to-hand combat, pugil sticks, rappelling, obstacle courses, and more running. It all seemed to have a clear purpose, and there was more motivation and positive reinforcement.

Also, with PT you can feel the progress. When I arrived in the receiving barracks on that first dreadful night, the sea bag drag was almost more than I could stand. By the time I graduated, I could throw a sea bag on each shoulder and walk wherever I wanted.

There was one kind of PT, however, that I didn't like. It was Incentive PT, also known as going to the "Pit" or the "Classroom." The pit was just the outdoor version of the classroom in the patches of sand all over MCRD. The classroom was the indoor version of the pit on the open floor area at the end of the squad bay.

Push-ups, sit-ups, mountain climbers, bend and thrusts, leg lifts, etc. were some of the usual classroom events—usually with no end in sight or goal in mind except to make us suffer. That's when the drill instructors had the most fun. They would have us lie on our faces in the sand and tell us we were dead because of our stupidity. Then they would remind us we really weren't dead. They demanded to see some sand coming up to prove that we were still breathing. With rivers of sweat pouring from us, the hot sand would stick to our faces.

One day PT took a turn I had never imagined. We recently had an "alligator" put into our platoon. An alligator is a recruit who has made allegations of abuse against a drill instructor. Our alligator arrived with a large, dark bruise on his sternum, but we soon felt the same frustration that had led his previous DI to cross the line and left that bruise.

We quickly saw that the new recruit was struggling when it came to PT. Some would say he was a non-hacker. He couldn't run a mile. What's worse is that he didn't seem to make much effort to try. One morning we were about a half mile ahead of him while running in formation. The drill instructor had us circle back to get him. Then we ended up about a quarter mile ahead and we circled back again. The alligator was walking. We tried to encourage him to keep up, but we saw no real effort. Again, we ran ahead. Again, we circled back. I lost count. Eventually, we returned to find him walking as before. The whole platoon ran over him with a survival-of-the-fittest animalistic mentality. Everyone had had enough. It was ugly and mean in retrospect but seemed so natural at the time.

He continued to whine and make excuses, and we continued to pay for his shortcomings. One of the recruits suggested a blanket party. Reluctantly, it was agreed.

In the still of a recruit depot night, a green wool blanket was held over him to keep him in the rack while everyone took their turn hitting him. There wasn't a roll call, so I'm sure some did not take their turn, but the message was clear: Shape up or ship out.

When it was over, recruits scattered for their own racks in the ambient light of the squad bay. Now, with the low rumble of planes taxiing at nearby San Diego International Airport, the squad bay was strangely silent. With no visible or audible clues, it still seemed as though some recruits had enjoyed the blanket party while it had made other participants extremely uncomfortable, even remorseful. I was one of the latter.

Everyone wondered if the alligator would blow the whistle on the whole platoon. When he didn't, the whole platoon made an extra effort to make it work for all of us. The alligator succeeded in becoming a Marine. Some of the help he received from other recruits along the way was surely a combination of guilt and gratefulness. He graduated with us. He was one of us. Recruit-on-recruit violence was not totally uncommon in close quarters under stress, but it seemed to always have a way of working itself out.

When Carter and Clark finally came to blows during a head cleaning detail, Clark was hit in the eye. It was nearly swollen shut. The senior drill instructor was the first DI to notice. "What happened to you?"

"The private dropped his toothpaste. When the private reached down to pick it up, the private hit his head on the sink."

Clark's lie came in properly canned, third-person form.

"Do you expect me to believe that?"

"Sir, yes, sir."

"Are you going to stick with that story?"

The drill instructor could tell that it was probably the result of a fight, and he also knew the company staff, and the officers in particular, would see it and try to dig the truth out of the recruit.

"Sir, yes, sir," Clark reaffirmed with both his good eye and his bad eye facing forward at the rigid position of attention.

"Very well, carry on."

The two recruits had worked out their differences, and nothing ever came of the incident.

A similar excuse was necessary when Private Ramano put another recruit's head into a window for goofing off during field day. The official story was that the window was cracked when a swab handle was pulled back into it while cleaning the barracks.

On a typical day, stress could rise to great heights for individuals and the platoon as a whole. We had now been weeks without anything remotely civilian. The programmed life of a recruit was taking its toll. Normal feelings were all but completely shut down as a defense mechanism. There was no need to let girls and parties back home cross your mind. They would just be a distraction and, thus, a weakness.

But just when all my defenses were in place, I was told to run to the drill instructor's room—normally off limits—and rewrite the next day's training schedule on 3 x 5 cards for him. He carried them discretely in his campaign cover and referred to them as needed throughout the day.

A strange voice could be heard as I walked into the room. The voice was provocative and alluring. I hadn't heard a song on the radio in over a month—and what a song to walk-in on for the first time in weeks. It was Kim Carnes' new release, "Betty Davis Eyes." The voice, the lyrics, and the imagery in the song were a special touch from the outside world. When the song ended, I had to regroup and refocus. I had let my guard down to enjoy the "roll you like you were dice" moment. Thankfully, no one else was around.

A much better mental, physical, and spiritual escape was chapel service, thankfully afforded to Marines each week. If I weren't already a Christian, I think I would have faked it just to get away.

The second phase of boot camp included basic infantry training in the field and rifle qualification at Camp Pendleton's Edson Range. The hills just an hour's drive north of San Diego saw no rain in the Southern California summer, and there was plenty of hot sun and dust. We walked across dry creek beds and up the steep trails that followed the ridgelines.

One special hill was referred to as "Mount Mother F-----." Everyone who ever hiked up it knew why. It was then that my squad leader fell out during the climb, and the drill instructor put me in his place for the remainder of recruit training. That was a compliment and a curse. Squad leaders often paid the price for mistakes of other individuals. Many times, I went to the pit with, or sometimes in place of, individual fellow recruits who messed up.

One recruit who wasn't a squad leader spent more time in the classroom than any other. Private Juarez was either the only one I saw totally broken by the Corps, or he was already broken when he arrived and recruit training just exposed it.

An openly friendly manner and a strong Hispanic accent marked Juarez. He seemed to be an early target of Drill Instructor Sergeant Jefferson. Normally, Sgt. Jefferson was a DI who motivated more than he disciplined, but he had a strange punishing connection with Juarez. Over and over, he would call him to the classroom.

The last time was the worst. Juarez was the only one in the classroom. He did sit-ups until he was flat on his back with no energy to get up. He did leg lifts until he couldn't get his feet off the ground. Then he rolled over and tried push-ups until his hands slipped out from under him in his own pool of sweat on the tile floor of the squad bay. He was wringing wet and in tears. I felt the most pity I have ever felt for a fellow recruit. The drill instructor finally had enough. He sent Juarez back to his rack. Juarez struggled to get to his feet. Crying and sweating, he arrived at the position of attention.

On the first step toward his rack, he skipped. He began to laugh and skip along like a schoolgirl on the playground. That was the beginning of the end. He was placed on meaningless guard details for the platoon until his paperwork was complete. We were told that he was discharged under "Section Eight," meaning he was mentally unfit for duty. We didn't know if it was true, but it seemed plausible.

Two recruits decided they could just quit together. They were "being thrashed," or "digging," or "in the classroom," which simply meant they were getting individual incentive PT. They just stopped and stood at attention. The drill instructor screamed and ranted, but they just stood there. They did their best to explain that they were just not going to do it anymore.

"Sir, the privates are quitting, sir."

"Quitting? You can't quit. Get on your face."

"Sir, no, sir."

"What? I don't think I heard you."

"Sir, the privates are quitting."

"Are you refusing to train?"

"The privates—"

"—Are you refusing to train?"

"Sir, yes, sir."

"Let me hear you say it."

"Sir, the privates are refusing to train."

The drill instructor broke out into evil laughter. He jumped for joy and told them to wait there. He ran to get the Series Gunnery Sergeant. Several minutes later, they returned together.

"Recruits, tell him what you just told me."

"Sir, the privates are refusing to train, sir."

"Are you sure you want to do this, recruits?"

"Sir, yes, sir."

The next day we saw them in the correctional custody platoon (CCP). Those CCP misfits wore shiny chrome helmets and loaded rocks into a trailer. They would pull the trailer around MCRD like a team of mules and unload the rocks. Then their drill instructor would have them re-load the rocks and pull them somewhere else. I think that's all they did all day long. A couple of weeks of that may or may not have helped the ones doing it, but it sure as heck got the attention of any other recruits thinking of quitting.

Recruits weren't the only ones who fell victim to attrition. Drill Instructor Sergeant Jefferson was the platoon's best motivator. He was a great encourager and got the most out of us on the drill field. He was a natural. We understood that he was close to getting promoted to senior drill instructor on the next cycle.

Then one day he was gone. We saw him with the receiving barracks recruits without a campaign cover and knew he had been fired. All we could pick up through the recruit grapevine was that the company commander had over-reacted to some situation. It fed our distrust and even disdain for officers. The drill instructor we looked up to the most had been sent to the receiving barracks.

His replacement was hell on wheels. He was shorter than almost everyone in the platoon, and he felt he had to prove he was tougher than any of us. He screeched his drill commands and had no rhythm. It was almost impossible to understand his commands, so we regressed at close order drill. As we did, he flat out let us know about it. We wanted to tell him the cause, but we could not.

He was on a tear one afternoon. As he screamed and screeched and jerked around, I had a vision. He looked like the little Martian character on Bugs Bunny cartoons. Just about the time that vision entered my mind, he turned his attention to the other squad leaders and me to his left. I burst into laughter. I had made it this far without laughing at the wrong time. Some of my family and friends had worried that it would happen, and it finally did.

The drill instructor couldn't stand it. As I was getting my composure, he threw a Listerine bottle at me. As it whizzed past my ear, I stopped laughing. Of course he made me pay for it in the "classroom" with incentive PT. He still looked like the Martian. I just didn't laugh about it.

Rifle range was next. It was a good time, a quiet time, with primary marksmanship instructors (PMIs) running the show instead of DIs. They were focused on one thing—teaching us to shoot. All that screaming and yelling that had defined boot camp up until this point at least had to wait until we got back to the barracks in the afternoon.

During the rifle range training, three recruits who joined together on the buddy plan from Little Rock, Arkansas, went UA (uauthorized absence), more commonly known as AWOL (absent without leave). They jumped the short fence that ran along the interstate. After hitching a ride all the way back home, their parents turned them back in to the Corps.

That's the story we heard, and by the looks on their faces as we passed them in the CCP, it was probably at least partially true.

The calmness of the rifle range was shattered on the day we fam(iliarization)-fired pistols. I had just completed my string of shooting and a head call. I was not yet back on my gear in a waiting area when the next string started firing.

"Cease fire. Cease fire."

The recruits on the firing line were quickly rushed off the line and back on their gear.

"Somebody just blew his head off."

"What?"

"Some recruit just shot himself."

It wasn't hysteria, but there was a lot of chaos. Apparently, there was nothing that could be done for the recruit. The range was immediately shut down so an investigation could begin.

"Was it an accident?"

"I don't know."

"Nobody's able to ask him."

Some recruits in my platoon saw it up close and personal, and they couldn't tell if it was accidental or not. It was hard to imagine either scenario. Instantly, the seriousness about what we were training to do—"close with and destroy the enemy by fire and maneuver"—sank in deep. This was a dangerous business.

Immediately, the drill instructors went into their best "fatherly" role. They wanted to check on our reaction and make sure the recruit's death didn't derail us psychologically or emotionally. After that, they really downplayed it, and it was hardly mentioned again.

That week our platoon won the rifle range competition, which meant maintenance duty during the following Mess and Maintenance Week. It was great to avoid mess duty.

While the mess duty platoons began their days at zero dark thirty, we had normal reveille and lights out. Our days were filled with head cleaning details and extreme amounts of polishing "brass." Not just brass; any shiny metal was brass for our purposes. We even polished exposed copper plumbing anywhere we were assigned across MCRD.

Work details were so scattered across all areas of the base that the drill instructors could not be with all of us. That level of independence was temporary, but that didn't matter to us. Even polishing copper pipes in the head was a welcome task.

The Series Field Meet, an assortment of contests, signaled moving from the second phase into the third and final phase of training. Platoons competed in a number of games from fireman's carry relays to tug-o-war.

We thought it was supposed to be fun, so we got as many involved as possible. Little did we know that DIs made bets on this, and it would be a serious competition. We put a wide range of recruits into the games but not necessarily our best in every event. We lost, but we really didn't care. To us it was just a fun day off—until we got back to the squad bay.

Drill Instructors Sergeant Corbett and Sergeant Primer began throwing things, swearing, and raving like we hadn't seen since early in the first phase. It took us a minute to understand what had triggered them. Our performance in the field meet had embarrassed them, and they were letting us know about it.

About the time Sergeant Primer was gathering more steam, Private Whitfield began a tirade of his own. He interrupted our DI by throwing his towel to the ground, then venting some pent-up frustrations. The rant began with a line of expletives.

"—so some recruit blows his head off and no one gives a sh*t, but we lose a f-*-ing relay race and it's the end of the world—"

Before he could get another word out of his mouth, he was whisked away for some individual counseling. He wasn't hit or yelled at immediately, so I think there was some legitimate concern that he wasn't coping well with the Marine's death on the pistol range just days earlier. By the time Whitfield came back to us, we were showered and dressed for chow.

Drill instructor-on-recruit physical contact was almost expected, although we all knew it was against the written rules. Most contact was referred to as, "adjusting your position of attention"—usually, a hand forcefully around our face or throat. The adjustment I especially hated was the swift kick in the shin. It was DI Sgt. Primer's favorite because it was less visible, and he could do it openly on the parade deck without getting caught.

The last time I felt the hard toe of his boot, we were just days away from graduation. We were told to have seven recruits help pass out the civilian clothes we had packed away upon our arrival. We were counting to see if we had the seven requested when we were called down for "running our sucks."

After sending me back into the formation with a bruised shin, Sgt. Primer took a swing at Private Whitfield. Private Whitfield had the company high PFT (physical fitness test) score. There was nothing they could do to wear him out. They sometimes stood on his hands when he did push-ups to keep him from smiling. They tried everything to break him, but they couldn't.

As Sergeant Primer went for the face, Whitfield coolly rocked back on his heels and the sergeant missed him. Primer's embarrassing swing at the air was short satisfaction for Whitfield.

"Oh, you want to dodge it, huh? Dodge this!" Primer reached back and slapped Whitfield so hard with his open hand across the face that even I could feel it. Private Whitfield didn't flinch, and he told no one. He took it like a man—no, he took it like a Marine. Private Whitfield could have had his revenge. The whole platoon saw that one. One word and Sergeant Primer would likely have lost a stripe and never come near another recruit. Instead of finishing that Marine's career, Private Whitfield was more determined to get his own started.

Another one of the more interesting evolutions took place in the squad bay as training was concluding. The senior drill instructor was announcing each recruit's MOS (Military Occupational Specialty) and duty station. There wasn't much anticipation for me as a reservist. I knew exactly where I was going and what I'd be doing. For most of the others, however, it was a surprise. Even the ones with a guaranteed MOS didn't know their duty station, and most of them didn't know where their MOS School was located. Others were surprised like lottery winners, and still others were so disappointed they couldn't believe their ears.

Nothing was going to keep us from graduation. Then rumors of the air traffic controller's strike heated up. During the week of graduation, we looked up and realized that no airplanes were taking off from the San Diego airport. The runway was clearly visible. We had paid homage often during PT all summer by singing chants to those big steel "freedom birds." Today, the freedom birds sat idle at their gates for what seemed like an eternity.

We knew it wouldn't affect our graduation, but a Greyhound bus ride to Memphis didn't sound all that appealing. Later that same day, a few jets took off, giving us some relief. However, it was clear from our vantage point that normal operations at the airport had ceased.

Graduation day did come as scheduled. Tickets and many flights were messed up. Several of us had late flights with several connections. With time on our hands, a number of us decided to have a few cold ones at the bowling alley at the depot. I didn't count how many we had, but they sure were good at the time. We even had one of our drill instructors, Sergeant Corbett, join us.

When I found my way back to my sea bag, I had to wait on a taxi. The next thing I knew I was passed out on my sea bag at the corner of the parade deck. The unknown drill instructor who woke me just pointed me to a taxi without much fanfare. I was grateful, to say the least.

The trip home included layovers in Phoenix and Dallas. The stop in

Phoenix was extended, which allowed for my second beer call in one day. I first joined what appeared to be Marines, but they were washouts who still had the haircuts. They were loud, unruly, and embarrassing, so I found an empty seat away from them at the airport bar.

An attractive, mature woman was also at the bar. The conversation was light and refreshing after weeks of screaming in boot camp. She was relieved to hear that the others were not *real* Marines because she also was getting a bad impression of them.

An older gentleman in the place paid for my drink in appreciation of my service. I explained that I had only become a Marine that day. He said then I needed it more than ever. He must have been a veteran.

Over the years I have always accepted drinks and meals bought for me on behalf of all veterans. It remains a gratifying yet humbling experience to accept such generous offers. (I carry on the tradition from time to time when I see a junior Marine or serviceman in an airport.)

When I stepped off the plane in Dallas, I heard the last call for my flight to Memphis. There were nearly 20 gates between my arrival and departure gates. I sprinted the whole way and barely made it. I figured my bags didn't make it, but I didn't care. I was going home.

1981 MCRD San Diego Boot Camp Graduation

1982 First Christmas together with Lee Perkins Caldwell

"And his mercy is on them that fear him from generation to generation."

Luke 1:5

...2
Conflicts of Change

The final days of boot camp meant the summer of 1981 was coming to an end. In a matter of days, I would be back on a college campus. Returning to my friends and family—now known as slimy civilians to those of us indoctrinated to Marine Corps jargon—would be a personal self-test. Had I gained the level of maturity I had been seeking? Could I apply the lessons learned in the Corps to help me complete my degree and tackle life as an adult?

Thankfully, I wouldn't be alone in my endeavor. My family was a big one and extremely close by most measures. I could always count on my entire family for support when I needed it most, and I always hoped each of them felt the same.

Now that I was "back on the block," Daddy was a little freer to show his approval of my enlistment in front of Momma. She also was much more accepting of the Corps now that I had returned apparently unscathed.

My brothers and sisters and my extended family treated me no differently. They harassed me as usual, and we debated world, national, and local issues with evangelistic fervor. Members of my family have never had simple opinions; everyone has deep-seated convictions. No one ceded any ground to me just because I had the new title of Marine.

My friends were also a big part of my life-support system. I had a lot more of them than anyone deserved. I had missed them and our good times together.

One friend I wanted to see was Lee Perkins. She had abruptly ended our dating relationship over a year before, but during my time away, I thought of her often and was determined to rekindle our relationship when I returned.

Her original letter had strongly discouraged me from enlisting, but she kept in touch anyway. Her correspondence with me in boot camp had been a big encouragement, but how would that translate upon my return. How would she react? Had the Marine Corps changed me in some way—for better or worse—in her eyes?

One of my first tasks upon arriving back in Jonesboro for the fall semester was to find out where Lee Perkins was and go see her. She had moved into an apartment that was, regrettably, on the other side of town from mine, but that was a minor inconvenience.

It wasn't long before I knew I wanted to spend every day of the rest of my life with her. But wait! The United States Marine Corps owned me one weekend a month and two weeks in the summer. Plus, I needed to convince her . . . and I needed a job.

Good-paying jobs were scarce, so when an opportunity arose to make $4.35 per hour as a "scab" working for Riceland Foods, I jumped at the chance. I was too young to appreciate unions, but I soon learned some working conditions were extreme for any amount of money.

For eight hours per night, seven days a week, I wore a basic dust mask, a bump cap, and some cheap plastic goggles. With a shovel in hand, I boarded open-topped tractor trailers being filled with ground rice hulls. My purpose was to shovel, stomp, and walk in the sawdust-like substance to pack in more of the product. Otherwise, the settling process during transit would leave customers with less than a full load.

Dust particles filled the air and penetrated my goggles and my mask. Each morning I would leave my shift at seven, shower, and make it to class by eight. Usually, I would sleep through the class. The fine dust from each previous night would make my lungs feel like I had been smoking cigarettes for years. Sometimes, the dust and my tear ducts would join forces to literally glue my eyelids shut. I would have to plead for the one weekend off per month to be a Marine again.

Arriving at the Reserve Training Center in Memphis for my first drill weekend may have been the most anti-climactic moment in my Marine Corps career. With all the pride of a Marine, and confidence in my fellow Marines, I reported for duty. I was nervous and excited. I had earned the title Marine and wanted to live up to it.

The first thing I noticed was that the place was dirty, not the spit and polish I had seen at MCRD. Next, I noticed the Marines I saw were not as focused as drill instructors or recruiters. While it was relaxing in some ways, it was also disconcerting. What had happened to the Marine Corps that trained me and inspired me over the summer?

On the first weekend drill, we just cleaned rifles. There's no fun or challenge in that. We cleaned every rifle in the armory. We stood in line to draw weapons. We waited in line to turn them in. We stood in line for bad chow. We stood in lackluster formations. We stood in more lines and cleaned more weapons. I cleaned about 7 to 1, compared to some others. Several just bided their time and worked on the same rifle all weekend. During the next drill, we cleaned rifles out in the parking lot again. Morale was nowhere.

This time I smelled marijuana smoke while cleaning the rifles. I had a general idea where it was coming from, but I didn't really want to know and be ultimately responsible. Where was the NCO leadership? Where were the officers? Where was my Marine Corps? It was going to be a long enlistment.

Although I had enlisted to be a machine gunner, I was put into a rifle platoon instead of a weapons platoon. I would have to wait until I went to ITS (Infantry Training School), now known as SOI (School of Infantry).

Just one weekend per month doesn't sound so bad, but I learned to count on it being the least opportune weekend every month for the duration. It started almost immediately.

The next drill weekend was homecoming at ASU. I worked a deal with my recruiter to be a recruiter's assistant on that weekend. He kept me longer than I had hoped, which made me late for the football game, but the Marine Corps paid me, so I didn't complain. When I finally made it to the homecoming game, I couldn't find Lee. It hadn't occurred to me that she was at her apartment, waiting on me to pick her up. I figured she simply chose not to come to the game.

After the game I went by to pick her up. She wasn't happy and had heard reports of me being a little too happy at the game and being with other girls. The reports were factual but misleading. The girls in question were just acquaintances. Maybe I should have just gone to drill.

For reservists like me working their way through school, working weekends is the norm. Part-time employers really think they're doing you a favor by giving you a "weekend off." What those employers don't seem to understand is that drill weekend is just another working weekend.

Back to college as a full-time student, 16 hours of overtime each week at the rice mill and about 4 hours of sleep every evening was the routine. There wasn't much time for fun.

Physical limits and sleep deprivation were taking their toll. That blunt realization came to me at the edge of a catwalk one night. As I sat above the truck to observe the early stages of ground rice hulls filling the big rig, I reached to rub dust from my eyes. Like a time-lapse movie sequence, I blinked away at least 30 minutes of my life in an instant. The next thing I knew, rice hulls were pouring over the sides of the trailer and piling up on the outside, burying the wheels. Falling asleep like that could have meant being buried alive. It was time to quit the rice mill. I had saved enough money by then to pay for another semester of tuition and put a down payment on a small engagement ring.

Lee stayed with me through those times. The closest thing we had to a date during those months was her cooking dinner at her apartment. She was definitely the marrying type, and I knew I'd better not mess it up this time. I asked her to marry me in November, and she said yes.

Daddy laughed when I told him. He quickly reminded her that if the Marine Corps wanted me to have a wife, then they would have issued me one. For his sake she pretended that his comment bothered her a little.

Even with extra overtime and another job, it took until Valentine's Day three months after the proposal to pay off the ring. I drove her out to the lake in my '63 Wildcat and parked near the campus pavilion to propose again, this time *with* a ring.

Jobs would come and go. Working nights and most weekends at Chuck's Meat Market paid less than the rice mill but better fit my schedule. Drill weekends were constantly interrupting my somewhat regular routine of work and school while providing less than $100 each month in take-home pay.

The highlight of my initial enlistment was my promotion to lance corporal. My disappointment was that I left the unit before making corporal. I had wanted to be a corporal like Daddy was in WWII, plus I loved the NCO sword that I never earned.

An officer selection officer (OSO) called. The OSO had heard I was in college at ASU and had recently finished boot camp. ""Have you ever thought about the officer program?"

"Not really."

My drill instructors had painted a picture of officers as the enemy—or at least as a disconnected group hardly qualified to be real Marines. But the more I thought about it, the more it interested me. I had seen in my reserve unit that somebody had to get involved if things were going to get any better.

The Corps already had plans to ruin my summer again by sending me to ITS (Infantry Training School), so why not OCS (Officer's Candidate School)? It couldn't be any harder than boot camp, I thought, and I was already getting disenchanted with the reserves.

There was no pre-commitment with the PLC (Platoon Leaders Course) Program. I could change my mind in the middle or even after completing the 10-week, summer course. I would only need to make my final decision by the time I graduated from college. If I chose not to continue as an officer, I could revert to enlisted reserves. If I accepted my commission, it would mean nearly four years of active duty.

The option almost vanished when the Jonesboro PD answered a complaint call at Lee's apartment building. Some friends of ours were having a lovers' quarrel in the parking lot. Just as we arrived to try and calm them, the police rolled in like a TV show. They had me and some other friends sprawled against the car like criminals. We were placed in the back of the squad car and hauled downtown. My plans for a career as an officer were in jeopardy.

It was a dry county. We were intoxicated and underage at 20. As they administered the breathalyzer one by one, I saw our chances of getting out of this diminish. It was my turn.

"How 'bout we don't test you?"

"That's great with me." But I didn't know what prompted the shift in protocol.

"Follow me. These girls are here to pick you up."

Lee and her friends had come to our rescue. Apparently, the police had put on an enforcement show for the apartment manager. They had predetermined that if we were nice and cooperative, they would release us, but if we smarted off, they would book us. A younger me would have smarted off. Thankfully, we were all growing up.

• • •

Decisions abounded. Our wedding date was still pending. After an egregious response to my enlistment, Lee had warmed up to the Marine Corps. She even supported my interest in the full-time officer corps.

Wedding plans were made for after OCS but before school started back up in the fall. Orders then arrived with later dates than we anticipated. OCS was going to start later and run later into the summer. We moved the date up and married before I left for Quantico.

We were already learning to be flexible in a Corps that demands it of all their Marines and families. In a few short weeks, we planned and put together our own wedding in Jonesboro. It was a few hours northwest of my family and a few hours southeast of hers.

I never thought I'd get directly involved with wedding planning. It just happened that way. The church we had attended was booked, so we shopped churches. I never knew that was so complicated, but it was.

After sorting through the available dates, rules, fees, and limits from church to church, we just about gave up in frustration. Then we found the ideal church. That may have been a sign of things to come for us as a family: nothing simple, never exactly according to plan, a lot of work and persistence, a perfect finish. From our wedding day forward, it seemed destined to be that way in everything from finding Christmas trees to having babies.

The wedding went without a hiccup. I should have tipped the preacher when he left the "promise to obey" in Lee's vows. She almost choked, but she said, "I do" loud and clear.

A short honeymoon and a move to the campus trailer park for married students preceded my trip to Quantico for OCS. The mobile homes weren't much larger than campers, but we didn't need much.

Facing an OCS summer, I knew a little more about what I was getting into than I had before boot camp. I'm still not sure that's a good thing. With memories of boot camp fresh on my mind, I couldn't help but compare everything from the PT to the chow hall. Similarities were everywhere. Close order drill, uniform inspections, general orders, principles and traits of leadership were all the same.

Differences were minor. There was little to no incentive PT, but the additional organized PT more than made up for it. Drill instructors were called platoon sergeants and sergeant instructors. They cursed a little less when they screamed at us, but that may have just been differences between individuals.

Inspections were nothing new, so I felt like I had a leg up on those who hadn't been through boot camp. It didn't take long to realize that I could still blow an inspection with the best of them.

I stood confidently as Platoon Sergeant Staff Sergeant Ristivo faced me. "Oh my God, what is this?" He reached and pulled a thread from my camouflage utilities, "An Irish pennant! No, this is not an Irish pennant. It's a Russian rope! You can hang yourself with this thing!"

Everything else was a blur as I faced the onslaught of verbal attacks while he inspected my rifle and my gear with a vengeance. I didn't feel like an experienced Marine at that point. I felt like any other new candidate.

Chow was worse at OCS than at boot camp. One night I witnessed for the first and only time in my career when the chow hall was emptied and the cooks were made to re-cook the meal because it was unfit to eat. The chicken had not been fully cooked. Most of us had either already eaten part of it or avoided it and filled up on vegetables, bread, and milk. We were marched back to the chow hall to eat the new dinner, whether or not we were hungry.

Developing individual leadership skills and thinking outside the box was emphasized more at OCS. At boot camp, everything was definitely inside the box.

One big difference was that we could quit or DOR (drop on request). In boot camp they would recycle you until you finished. At OCS they would just send you packing.

One friend of mine from Klamath Falls, Oregon, Tom Bocchi, had told me he would DOR, but he doesn't quit anything he starts. He said he would finish OCS, but he would probably not see us after that. One year later, he was the first familiar face I recognized at TBS (The Basic School). A year or so after that, he was flying F-18 Hornets.

Perhaps the biggest difference between OCS and enlisted boot camp was that six weeks into OCS we got a day off. I would have done just about anything for a day off during boot camp. RHIP—rank has its privileges—seemed to hold true, at least that day.

With the extra pay allowance for being married, and the low cost of married housing on campus at only $100 per month, we had plenty of money to fly Lee out on one weekend off. It was actually for half of Saturday, Saturday night, and most of Sunday.

After almost two months at OCS, I met Lee at the airport. She was gorgeous on any normal day, but I think even the soles of my shoes melted when I saw her arrive. It was all I could do not to just gawk at her in amazement.

Besides getting reacquainted, there was also the business of washing my clothes to get ready for next week. While loading the washer, we met a nice older lady. She noticed that I was in the Marines and kindly shared some of her experiences with us. She told of travels around the world with her military husband. It didn't dawn on us as she spoke that, with all those years, he must have gained some rank. It was just very interesting conversation for the laundry room.

With no desire to stand in the laundry room very long, we decided to trust that our clothing would not be stolen in such a nice hotel. We almost completely forgot about the clothes. Rushing back, we were surprised to find that not only was everything still there, but it was dried and folded neatly on the table. We surmised that the nice lady we met had probably done it. A little while later, we ran into her in the hallway of the hotel.

"Thank you so much. You really shouldn't have, but we really appreciate you taking care of our clothes."

"Well, if you decide to accept your commission as a second lieutenant, always remember that a major general's wife folded your clothes."

"Yes, ma'am."

Our mouths dropped open as she casually continued along her way, and we never forgot it.

The last few weeks of OCS went quickly. It was becoming clear that I was going to accept my commission and that Lee and I would be giving the Marine Corps a few good years.

Returning home from OCS was a huge relief. No drill weekends were required. I just needed to successfully complete my senior year at ASU.

Although Lee and I still needed part-time jobs to get by, life was good. It looked like it would be summer before Lee could complete her graduation requirements, and the Marine Corps agreed to begin my active duty following her graduation in August instead of mine in May.

Then, only weeks away from my graduation, the Marine Corps changed its mind, as it has a tendency to do. I would need to leave almost immediately. When those orders arrived, I was just days away from commissioning as an officer. It was not too late to change my mind. I knew it and the Marine Corps knew it. I called my OSO.

"I thought all of this was already worked out."

"It was."

"What's going on?"

"I don't know, but I think we can fix it with a simple letter. I'll help you write it."

"I sure hope so, because it will really mess up our plans. If they'll do this to us before we're in, what will they do after we're in? I'll write a letter and tell the Marine Corps never mind."

I wrote a letter explaining my position and let my OSO take a chop at it.

"You don't want to say that."

"But it's the truth."

"Yeah, but there's a better way to say it that will still get you what you want."

I listened to my OSO and let him edit my letter tactfully requesting a delay. It was approved.

Lee and I both graduated in 1983, and we packed up all our belongings in our red-and-white, 1963 Buick Wildcat. It was the same car my dad and I had fixed up for my high school graduation present. It was long and sleek with a lot of chrome. It wasn't ready for a car show, but it could have proudly ridden in any parade. It had all the amenities of its era: A/C, power steering and brakes, electric windows and seats, and even an electric antenna. The AM radio sufficed for me because country music was always easy to find. We placed our most expensive possession, a new, 19-inch Magnavox color TV, in the backseat but saved enough room by the passenger's side window for our dog, Bogey.

Bogey was a grayish, medium-to-shorthaired mixed breed with some brindle markings and a German Shephard build. He sported an almost human personality. Even people who don't normally like dogs would take a liking to him. More than a few times we would hear someone say, "If all dogs were like Bogey, I would like dogs." Those are the ones who saw him on his best behavior. Bogey would be part of our family for nearly 12 years of our Marine Corps experience.

Good fortune smiled on us when we arrived at TBS. (The Basic School is where all newly commissioned Marine Corps officers are taught the basics of being an "Officer of Marines.") The housing office had a house for us on base. We wanted to move in quickly in order to quit paying for a motel room and driving into work. However, we basically had no furniture except for a bed that was being shipped.

The first night on base we slept on the bare linoleum floor. Sharp pains and aches the next morning told us we needed something fast, but the bed in route was our only furniture. We didn't want to buy one or wait on the one being shipped. It dawned on us to purchase a hide-a-bed couch.

We didn't know the names of stores yet. Just driving up and down the street didn't help much. Driving in and out of shopping center parking lots, we finally found a furniture store in Woodbridge, but they couldn't deliver it for another day. With no desire to sleep on the hard floor again, we made the purchase and carried the fold-out mattress and couch cushions back home in the Wildcat with us.

• • •

Lifelong friendships were born at TBS. There's something about shared misery that brings people close.

Years after TBS, Lieutenant Beal and I were recalling the good times we had. The bad, as usual, faded with time, and the good memories remained.

"But you know, there were relatively few good times for a six-month period of our lives."

I had to agree.

According to my OSO, TBS was a lot like college. I don't know what college he went to, but it must have been close to hell. My college days were nothing like I experienced at TBS. Just as life differs from college to college, TBS differs from company to company.

Eric and I were in "Artic Alpha," which referenced our luck with weather in the field. It seemed that every time we went into the training areas we saw snow, sleet, or freezing rain drop from Virginia's winter sky. It was also my first time to see lightning and snow together.

In the quarters adjacent to us was "Breezy Bravo." If we had only arrived a week or so later, we would have been in B Company. Breezy Bravo enjoyed several weeks of basket leave at Christmas because their billeting was being renovated. We constantly watched those lieutenants get into their cars while our staff platoon commanders (SPCs) added more and more to each day's schedule. We even had extra training on weekends. Meanwhile, most other lieutenants from TBS were on liberty in Georgetown.

What they couldn't add in the evening, they added in the morning. It was not uncommon for our SPC, Captain Stan Gray, to schedule a uniform inspection at 0500 in the morning. Then he would arrive at 0630 and realize he had forgotten.

"Gents," he would say. "We'll just have to do the inspection this evening."

Gee, thanks. Again, we watched the other companies and even the other platoons within our company drive away. We were destined to stay for hours.

Captain Gray scheduled our platoon to clean someone else's pistols one random morning. Of course it wasn't on the regular training schedule, so we had to do it at zero dark thirty. He had us march in formation to the armory, but not until he lined us up single file under the streetlight to check the spit shine on our boots. It was pure harassment, but there was nothing we could do about it except learn from it—*what not to do* to our Marines when we arrived in the FMF (Fleet Marine Forces).

Another thing we learned was that cold weather training without cold weather gear sucks. Even our rifle range experience was interrupted by cold rain and high winds. We always hiked to the range in the dark, arriving just before daybreak. Pre-qual Day, the wind was howling. When we saw the soft, wet ground beneath us at each firing position, we thought we could at least lie on our ponchos, but that was not allowable. So we laid in the prone position in the near-freezing temperatures while the wind blew and the rains fell. Our cammies soaked up the mud puddles from below us and the rain from above.

Hot coffee arrived on the roach coach (slang for food truck). The commercial vendor had a mob of lieutenants swarming around his truck.

"Eric, I thought you didn't drink coffee."

"Who's drinking it? I bought it to pour on my hands," he abruptly explained as he slowly began the process.

We were the first string of shooters, and it looked like it was going to be a long day. Some were nervous enough about qualifying that they were still trying to adjust their sights in all the wind and rain. I, on the other hand, determined there was no way to do it, plus I was pretty sure my dope (combined settings on the front and rear sight) was good from the day before. Calmly, I loaded each round, pointed safely down range and, with frozen fingers extended awkwardly onto the trigger, fired each round without adjustment. Firing with clumsy arm motions seemed ridiculous.

The old saying, "You don't have to train to be miserable," came to mind. We could be as miserable as anyone without working at it.

The pre-qualification day was finally cut short when the soggy cardboard targets refused to stay in their carriages. In the middle of firing, our targets would take flight. Some just shifted or fell without much fanfare, but others looked like kites and sailed effortlessly across the dreary sky.

Why did it take so long for common sense to prevail? We policed the range by picking up the brass cartridges from the puddles and hiked back to clean our rifles. There was no productive training that morning, but it was another ugly reminder to get used to it.

The three-day war was the culmination of a series of basic field exercises while the Virginia winter punished us. We had at least learned to bring all the gear we had. The forecast included rain, with the possibility of turning into freezing rain, sleet, and snow.

One of the early stops was combat town. The rains were hard, even loud, as they splashed through the trees and on our green, rubberized outer garments.

"Take off your Gumby suits."

"Ha. That's funny."

"I'm not kidding."

"Why would we take off our rain gear in a driving rain? That's why the stuff was made."

Then the captain joined the student commander in the unwelcome order and loudly reiterated that we were to take them off. Looking through the water dripping off the rim of my helmet, I couldn't believe my ears. Didn't they realize it was about 38° F?

Bits and pieces of warped logic circulated. Supposedly, the staff didn't want us ripping the Marine Corps' wet-weather gear when we went through the barbed wire and concertina wire of combat town. By the time we got our rain gear off and stashed away in our packs, we were soaked to the skin and cold to the bone.

Combat town was a blur, literally and figuratively. Soon it was over, and they told us to put our rain gear back on. You've got to be kidding me. Now that we're drenched, we're going to put it back on? They reckoned that the rubberized material would hold some body heat inside. It was a little late for that. Our body heat was downstream somewhere in Beaver Dam Run.

That night they allowed us to build a fire in hopes we would warm up. I burned the top two eyelets off my boots, trying to dry them. It was no use. Although we had a fire, the rains continued, and the temperature continued to drop.

It was no longer training; it was survival. Boy, was I thankful I wasn't one of the student platoon commanders! Imagine trying to write a five-paragraph operations order while the sleet bounces off your platoon commander's notebook.

Tired, wet, cold, and disgusted with the whole thing, we put one foot in front of the other. Motivation was long gone as we stoically went through the motions.

We were on the move, traveling through the dark woods as the freezing rain and sleet turned to snow. With no ambient light, we could see no more than a foot or two in front of us. Lieutenants meandered like pack mules, reaching out to touch the man in front of them just to be sure he was still there.

Extreme cold coupled with a lack of sleep was beginning to take its toll on all of us. I was hallucinating and imagined that I could see clearly beyond the night. Then reality would set in, and I would be in the pitch-black darkness again. I was shivering and wet but not quite as miserable as those who fell into the creeks as we crossed them.

Slowly, the dawn came. The pace quickened slightly as we moved toward our objective. You could hear and feel the relief from the lieutenants as everyone could now see in front of them. Well, nearly everyone. Lieutenant Campbell was behind me as we walked.

"I can't see anything."

"It's beginning to get light, just give it a minute."

"I still can't see."

"Move your hand in front of your face. You should be able to see that."

"I'm telling you, I can't see. I can't see."

There was some real agitation in his voice. He was concerned that it seemed like everyone could see where we were going now except him.

I turned toward him to respond but couldn't help laughing as I did. "I bet you can't see. Your glasses are covered with an inch of ice."

As the sun rose behind the snow clouds, we could see the ice clinging to all of us. It covered all our gear, including our rifles. Even patches of snow stuck to us, and small icicles hung from some of the lieutenants.

Heavy snow had replaced the freezing rain and sleet, and the woods were white. We finished one attack, but when we set up our defensive perimeter, some lieutenants did not get up. They were in early stages of hypothermia.

For the next 360° perimeter we set up, we were instructed to remain standing. The last time we had gone into the prone position, some lieutenants and even some staff had to be carted away.

About 70 of Alpha Company's 200-plus lieutenants were diagnosed with hypothermia, and that doesn't count the ones like me who probably should have been.

Completion of the three-day war was one of the milestones that meant TBS was coming to a close. Another training highlight that neared the end was our final inspection.

2nd Lt. Beerman was approached by the inspecting officer. He noticed that 2nd Lt. Beerman was a "double expert," meaning he shot expert scores with both the M-16A2 rifle and the M-1911 .45-caliber pistol. Curious as to how good 2nd Lt. Beerman's scores were, the inspecting officer asked a common question. "What did you shoot on the range, Lieutenant?"

"A rifle and a pistol, sir."

Every surrounding lieutenant heard that answer, and the rest of the formation also heard the inspector's response. It took extra effort not to lose our bearing and laugh out loud. "Well, no sh*t, Dick Tracy. I meant, what were your scores?"

Lieutenant Beerman still denies he said it like we and the inspector heard it. We never gave him a chance to try to explain to us what he thinks he really said. By then the scores and the rest of the inspection were irrelevant and unmemorable.

Another culminating event, our company mess night, which most classes enjoyed thoroughly, was intentionally planned to be dull for us. It was.

The company mess night that preceded ours had apparently been *too* remarkable. Stories of the traditional carrier quals with drunken lieutenants sliding over tables and on the floor were overshadowed by the inclusion of a paid stripper for entertainment. It had been an embarrassment to the top brass. We followed that debacle by our predecessors with a stuffy event that must have made the general proud.

• • •

Training had concluded . . . or so we thought. It was early April and six cold months in Quantico were nearly done. We were fresh lieutenants hungry for our first FMF (Fleet Marine Force) assignment.

An unscheduled addition to the last days at TBS should have been readily accepted as par for the course. After all, our staff platoon commanders and company commander had well earned a reputation of adding extra training to an already hectic schedule. But this addition was different. Our course was supposed to be complete. Our time was done. Months had shrunk to weeks. Weeks had turned to days. The last training highlight before graduation, a 15-mile forced march, was finished.

As much as any forced march could be enjoyable, that one had been. Our packs were light. The course was along the gently rolling hills of the historic Chancellorsville battlefield. Spring had sprung near Fredericksburg, Virginia. A slight breeze and a soft sun paired with the scent of new life. Flowery highlights marked the landscape.

Our pace was textbook: not too fast, not too slow. Breaks seemed frequent and were punctuated with interesting Civil War history lessons on early maneuver warfare.

The final leg was upon us before we knew it. The pace quickened. Almost instantly, we were marshaled on an uphill approach to a defensive line of Napoleons. These and other era cannons appropriately accented the battlefield.

As if choreographed and rehearsed, the spontaneous charge began. First, it was a jog. Then it was a run. Even rebel yells, mine and others, could be heard.

For a brief moment I was a Confederate soldier filled with enthusiasm, conflict, and confusion. Eventually, we reached the top. The cannons were silent, manned by ghosts who knew the solemn reality and immeasurable brutality of close fight.

The enemy had been us—brother vs. brother. Just as iron sharpens iron, surely, we as a nation were better in some intangible way so that no one on either side had died in vain. That was my solace.

Thoughts of the past melted as quickly as they surfaced. Winded by the sprint and worn by the miles, the wonder of an uncertain future as a military professional filled my head. It was a quiet bus ride back to TBS.

What a great finish to an otherwise miserable six months! Aviators had already been assigned their flight schools. The rest of us had our MOS (Military Occupational Specialty) school assignments and our first duty stations. We would have and should have been in the party mode—if it weren't for one man.

Major Brooks, a quiet, shadowy figure in our midst, was the quintessential infantry officer and seemed to remind us of his presence as our company commander when we least expected it. And in his last act as commander, he went too far. Instead of letting us enjoy our last few days in the Commonwealth of Virginia, he was determined to ruin them.

Apparently, so inspired by our motivational performance during our 15-miler, he decided we would be the first TBS company to complete a 20-mile MCCRES (Marine Corps Combat Readiness Evaluation System) hump, also known as a forced march. That hardly seemed like a reward for a job well done.

Blisters from the 15-miler were still fresh for most. The new gear list must have included about 40 additional pounds added to our packs, and the new course included the muddy, rutted, up-and-down, off-road TBS trail commonly known as "The Washboard."

Our motivation hit rock bottom. In less than a week he wasn't just adding five miles. He was adding 20! Disgust, anger, and resentment were coupled with dread and even some self-doubt in our physical ability to complete the task under the circumstances. No one wanted to finish on a sour note, but no one dared to turn away from the challenge, no matter how unwelcome.

To make a bad situation worse, Major Brooks commanded us to "Cammie up" prior to stepping off. That meant full face-paint camouflage. Now the harassment package was complete.

We stepped off as we had in times past. We had now generated about enough adrenaline to carry any Marine for 20 miles. There was no cadence—no songs, no motivational chants—just an unhappy silence broken by the sound of boots against the deck.

Then we stopped. Less than a mile from the start, Major Brooks commanded, "Halt."

In plain sight were the makings of a party. Food and drinks were piled high, and a long, fat rope suitable for tug-o-war into the all too familiar and cold waters of Beaver Dam Run lay on the ground.

"Before we begin the party, I want to say something," Major Brooks explained. "When you arrive at your first command in the fleet, there will be some things you like and things you don't. Some things in the Marine Corps you have control over and some you don't.

"Some of you made yourselves sick over the last few days, worrying about this hike that you had no control over. There is no need to worry about things you have no control over. They will be miserable enough when they happen, *if* they happen."

I didn't fully appreciate the lesson that day. It was, however, one of the most valuable and applicable life lessons I would learn in the decades of duty that followed.

• • •

For six months we had been focused on our mission to successfully complete TBS, but another period of completion was at hand. Lee had come to full term with our first child.

It was time to leave Quantico, but our baby wasn't born yet. Our friends had followed the process with us. They called Lee's stomach "Chesty" in honor of Chesty Puller, one of the most decorated Marines in history.

"What if it's a girl?"

"Then she'll have a head start in life with that nickname," they would say.

My parents had come to graduation. At the graduation reception, the general noticed that Daddy was wearing a 4th Marine Division lapel pin. "You were in the Fourth Marine Division?"

"Yeah, but that was in the Big War. You were nothin' but a boot then."

I retreated. I didn't need any attention—good or bad—from any senior officer, but Daddy and the general visited for a while and seemed to have a good time.

After graduation my parents left early to pick up my great aunt in Newport News, Virginia. We were to rejoin them in Roanoke, Virginia, to spend the night. We were ready to be on our way to Memphis, but our plans were about to change. Before we could leave, we had to clear base housing. Lee and I had to get our quarters on base inspected so we could be released. As soon as we turned in the key to our house . . .

"Honey, I think I'm having contractions."

Now, we had been through false labors in the last few weeks. She was overdue, but the timing here was unbelievable.

"Well, honey, what do you want to do? Do you want me to drive to the hospital at Fort Belvoir."

"I don't know. We don't even have any place to stay?"

"How hard are the contractions?"

"Not too bad."

"How often are you having them?"

"Maybe every fifteen minutes or so."

I couldn't believe we were having this discussion. I had been worried about her going into labor while I was out in the field, but I never imagined her going into labor on the road. We really had nowhere to go. The hospital and doctors we had been working with were north. The route home was south.

"What do you think about driving to Fredericksburg for lunch and deciding after we eat?"

"That's fine. Let's just go."

Lamaze classes would have come in handy, but with our schedule at TBS, it had been impossible. I'd just have to wing it. It's not like *I* was in labor. Hopefully, Lee would guide me through it.

Lunch was over. Decision time was here.

"Well?"

"Well, what?"

"Do we go or stay?"

"I don't know. What do you think?"

"You're the one in labor. I sure don't know."

"What do *you* think?"

"You're the one in labor."

"I don't know."

"Do you want to go for it?"

"I don't know."

"Let's go for it."

"Okay."

"You let me know when I need to pull over."

The trip started with mild labor pains 13 minutes apart. Like clockwork, they dropped to 11 minutes, then 9, then 8. I drove hard, but we had stayed up late the night before getting the house ready for inspection. I was getting sleepy at the wheel.

"How are you?"

"I'm fine."

"How are the contractions."

"Not too bad."

"Can you drive?"

"I'm not that fine."

"Well, you have to let me know. I can't feel what you're feeling, and I'm too tired to keep driving. I've got to pull over."

"There's a rest area. Pull over and take a nap, and I'll take Bogey for a walk."

Bogey had been with us since we were married. He was a mutt, but he was our mutt, and seemed unfazed by the labor and delivery at hand. The nap was short lived but effective. It seemed like an instant before she was back with the dog, and Lee was barking at me to get on the road.

As we passed the historical markers along the road, I asked her if she wanted to have our baby where Stonewall Jackson was born.

"Keep driving."

I could tell she had all but lost her sense of humor. The time between pains reduced to seven minutes, then six, then five. We decided that when intervals dropped under five minutes, we would find a place to pull over. Two hours later, they were still five minutes apart.

We arrived at the motel at Roanoke. My parents hadn't arrived yet from picking up my aunt. Lee just wanted to stop long enough to shave her legs and go. Her sense of humor may have been gone, but her pride was intact.

We left a note for my parents: Headed to Memphis. Pains five minutes apart. We really didn't expect to make it that far but didn't know what else to write.

Once on the road again, the pains quickly dropped below five minutes. I drove harder and faster, hoping a Tennessee state trooper would pull me over. We arrived in Knoxville with hard labor pains three minutes apart.

I looked up an old friend in the phone book and asked directions to the nearest hospital. The directions were simple, but when we arrived they informed us that they didn't deliver babies. They sent us back on the road again to the University of Tennessee Medical Center. It was only a few more minutes, but it seemed like an eternity.

Arriving in a panic apparently wasn't enough. It took the hospital a little time to decide if they would keep us. Labor pains had remained at three-minute intervals. They kept her under observation for more than an hour before we were admitted.

Finally, we were settling in for the delivery, or so I thought. Contractions were harder and more frequent. Delivery time was getting close. Then the nurses walked out on me—on us. I lost my composure like some TV sitcom.

"Hey, where are y'all goin'?"

"Don't worry, the doctor's not even here yet."

"Well, the baby is!"

"We've got to get her into the delivery room anyway."

"The delivery room? Where in the heck are we?"

"You're in the labor room."

On TV they always seemed to stay in one room. How was I supposed to know? They finally came to get Lee. They left me outside, waiting for a hospital gown before they would let me in the delivery room. I about lost my composure again.

After a few short hours at the hospital, Lee delivered our daughter Jennifer. I could feel and see my life change before my eyes. Now I wasn't just a husband and Marine officer—I was also a father.

Jennifer was a year old and there was stack of paperwork 12 inches high before the hospital bill was finally paid by the military medical plan. It was only our first experience with military dependent medical care. I found out the hard way that things could get worse. In the meantime, we took a few weeks of well-earned leave.

Next stop, Fort Sill. The field artillery officer's basic course (FAOBC) was four months long at the U.S. Army base on the outskirts of Lawton, Oklahoma.

"Does the wind always blow like this?"

"In four different directions."

The store clerk was friendly, not very funny but right on the money in answering a question from me that she must have heard a hundred times. That Okie twang and wit spoke volumes. The wind blew hot all summer, and it didn't seem to matter which way you turned. It was inescapable.

An unplanned stop along the turnpike was forced upon us when our old '63 Wildcat ran hot. It always had that tendency to overheat, and it seemed to always pick times like this to remind us that it was over 20 years old.

Facing our new life adventure together, we simply pulled off the road. We were hot, tired, and more than a little frustrated. It wouldn't have been as bad if we weren't travelling with our newborn baby girl. Nobody wants a new mother and daughter sweating in the Sooner State sun while steam rises from under the hood of the car.

I walked away from the car, which had the dual purpose of getting a little distance from Lee and finding an improvised container and water from the roadside ditch. Eventually, the engine cooled enough to start and get us to a service station. Of course, running the air conditioner would make us run hotter, so it was windows down. We limped into Lawton, ready to put the roadside stress behind us and enjoy the air conditioning of a motel.

Our friends had arrived ahead of us and had scouted us an apartment with a nice pool for the brutal summer. Temperatures regularly topped 100° F that year.

FAOBC was much more enjoyable than TBS. There was actually time off in the evenings and on weekends.

The first things we noticed were the Army officers. There wasn't a lot of visual difference at the lieutenant level, but we guessed they must promote by weight. We were quickly able to tell an Army officer's rank from the rear view. The wider and heavier an officer was, the higher rank he seemed to be.

Army lieutenants looked at us funny too. We overheard a few of them talking about us. They had decided that Marines never smiled. We liked that observation, so we intentionally fed the image.

The Army Reserve officers were more relaxed and easier to get to know than their regular counterparts. The class was comprised of about one third Marines, one third regular Army, and one third National Guard or Army Reserve.

Time there really helped me to understand the differences between them and us. One thing that still rubs me wrong was the requirement for us to attend their leadership classes.

The U.S. Army seemed to teach everyone to question orders before following them. The Marine Corps taught us that the only illegal order might just be, "Shoot that prisoner," but we had better think twice before questioning it. That difference in philosophy was nearly irresolvable. We had six months of TBS and Marine Corps leadership before arriving. The Army lieutenants only had OCS and college.

Another notable difference was the staff non-commissioned officers (SNCO) panel discussions. We had them at TBS and we had them at Ft. Sill. The Marine Corps had the most squared-away group of senior SNCOs it could assemble. It made you proud to serve with them. They respectfully answered our questions and taught us a lot in a short time.

At Ft. Sill the spokesman of the panel was a greasy, overweight sergeant first class. He slouched in his chair with the front pockets of his dirty utilities bellowed open. They were open so he could reach in and grab sunflower seeds. He would suck and crunch and smack on a mouthful of them as he talked down to all the lieutenants in the room. It was good to find out later in my career that he was not the cream of the crop but, rather, an ugly exception. It made me wonder if the Army itself even respected lieutenants. How could they send someone like that for us to see as an example? They have so much better!

From that point on, we Marine Corps lieutenants collectively made up our minds not to pick up any of the teachings that conflicted with what we had learned at TBS, and we would not let borderline disrespect slide just because we were on an Army base. That created some friction along the way, but it cleared our conscience.

One day while shopping with my wife and some friends at the mall in Lawton, we ran across a female soldier in cammies, or as the Army calls them, BDUs (battle dress uniform). They were not allowed as liberty attire for Marines, but the Army didn't seem to care. It irritated us as intolerant 2nd lieutenants, but we usually didn't let it show.

This day was different. Did the Army wear their covers (caps) inside? Some did and some didn't. The female soldier we saw not only had her cammies on and her cover on her head, but she had it on backwards as she shuffled through the other shoppers. I almost came unglued. I stepped into her path and corrected her sharply. I was ready to get to a Marine Corps base.

In the meantime, we did enjoy Lawton. We went out to a restaurant almost every night with friends. It was El Chicos, Red Lobster, or Chuck E Cheese. All of the lieutenants and our wives used our three-month old daughter as our excuse to go to Chuck E Cheese, but we really enjoyed it ourselves.

We went out to a park with our dog, Bogey, too. It was mostly prairies and a few rock formations around a few ponds, but there were buffalo and prairie dogs galore. Bogey always swam in the pond until he was exhausted. On those hot summer days, we would let him sleep while we swam at the apartment's pool upon our return.

One night between our swim and our trip to whatever restaurant, we heard a lover's quarrel. Apparently, the Oklahoma boy was heartbroken and was making his plea to his former sweetheart. We leaned over the balcony so we could hear a little better. As we stretched out, we could see our friends Eric and Cindy eavesdropping like us. The poor boy's appeal was seared into all our memories.

"I ain't your baked potato. You can't just eat my insides out and throw away the peel."

Leaning back quickly, we tried to keep from laughing out loud and getting caught. I don't know if they ever made up, but if he was a country music song-writer, he might have at least made a little money with that line.

There was life outside the military, but elements of the Marine Corps some-times seeped into everyday life. Sometimes, the Marine just comes out, like the time an employee at the corner Texaco charged Lee $5 for putting air in her tire. It was only $5, but I wasn't going to take it.

My Daddy ran a service station for 30 years. I worked there enough to know the Texaco attendant was taking advantage of Lee. Here she was with a three-month old baby, no air conditioner, and a low tire, just looking for enough air to get the car home and out of the heat.

"Can you help me get some air in my tire?"

"That tire's too flat to air up. We'll have to fix it."

"Well, okay."

The guy strained and pulled until he broke his wrench trying to loosen the lug nuts. The '63 Wildcat had left-handed threads on that side, and he didn't realize it. So he gave up and put air in the tire, which he had earlier said couldn't be done.

"That'll be five dollars because I broke my wrench."

"Okay, thank you."

She drove away and told me the story when she got home. If she had expected my reaction, she wouldn't have told me. The Marine in me wouldn't let it alone.

"I'll be right back."

"Where are you going?"

"To the Texaco. I won't be long."

The car had barely stopped, and I was already in the office.

"Where's the guy who charged my wife five dollars for air? I want her five dollars back . . . now."

"You can have the five bucks back." He disgustingly flung a five my way. A few choice words and I was out the door.

"What did you say to him?"

"Not much. He knew he was wrong."

"You really didn't have to do that."

"I know. I just couldn't stop myself."

Sometimes, Marine wives see their husbands treat the rest of the world like they're Marines. It may be at the movies, at the mall, or at their child's ball game. It's not an excuse; it's a fact of life. Sometimes, it works out, and sometimes, it doesn't.

• • •

Completing FAOBC meant it was time to move again. Both the summer and artillery school were coming to an end. The move to California lay ahead. We packed our car like it was a U-Haul and headed west.

We had moved from Jonesboro, Arkansas, to Quantico, Virginia, a little over a year before. We moved from Quantico to Lawton, Oklahoma, with a stop en route in Tennessee to have a baby. Now it was time to move from Lawton to Oceanside, California.

Family came first. My brother Frank and my sister-in-law Carolyn lived in Longmont, Colorado, so our path to California was pre-determined. Along with many other "firsts" I was going to experience in the Marine Corps, my first trip to the Rocky Mountains was memorable.

The views were breathtaking as we left the plains of Kansas and approached the majestic Rockies. At first I thought I was seeing a line of white clouds. As I stared, I noticed the blue below them was slightly different than the sky above. It was my first glimpse of snowcapped mountains. As the road ascended the aspens were in full array, and everywhere we turned looked like a postcard advertisement from the state's tourism department. I wanted to stop the car and just look. I did a few times, but we had to keep going.

A short visit with my family members and then we were on our way again.

From Colorado we traveled to the north rim of the Grand Canyon. It was a different breathtaking view of color and space, rock formations, and canyon walls. It was nearly impossible to mentally grasp it. I had seen it in books and movies and on television ever since I could remember, but this was different.

In some ways it made my eyes hurt just trying to soak it all in. After a few short minutes of crystal clear view, clouds rolled in from behind us. A soft, beautiful snow began to fall as we drove out of the national park in Southern Utah.

We enjoyed it so much that we drove the long way around to the south rim for a different view. The sun was shining there, and the perspective was not at all like the north rim, but it was equally awesome. Instead of the ever-green-covered mountains on the north rim, Arizona's south rim had more of an arid desert feel like I had originally envisioned. The urge inside me was to go to the bottom of the canyon and look up, but we were out of time.

Driving into California was an experience all its own. First, the agriculture agents' version of border patrol met us at the state line, as if we were entering a foreign country. In more ways than I'd like to count, we were.

"Do you have any fruits, vegetables, plants—"

It struck me a little funny that we were getting checked out going from state to state. I think it was around the time of the national fruit fly scare. Illegal aliens seemed to have an easier time entering California from the south. The agent was very unfriendly and seemed to be going a bit overboard, so I played along.

"Nope, but we got a dawg!" I ensured that I used an exaggerated southern drawl with a little hillbilly twang for emphasis. I was being sarcastic, but with Arkansas license plates on our 1963, four-door hardtop, he couldn't tell. He didn't crack a smile.

Next, it was on to L.A., unique in its own right. It was larger and more crowded with traffic and people than we could have imagined. Dirty, too. We drove through the heart of it for the experience instead of taking the by-pass. It was the last time we'd do that by choice.

Then it was down the coastal interstate to Camp Pendleton. Dry brown mountains were on our left. The great expanse of the Pacific Ocean was on our right. It was quickly apparent that anywhere a sprinkler system reached was lush and even tropical. Where no water was, nothing but scrub and a few pitiful trees survived.

Neither of us had ever lived this far from where we had been raised. About the only familiar things we saw in California were fast food chains and things directly related to the Marine Corps. It was time we learned the old adage, "Home is where the heart is," and ours was together—Lee, Jennifer, and me.

We missed the rest of our immediate family and old friends, but we were making new ones at the same time. We had walked parallel paths with our friends the Beals since TBS, where our houses had been around the corner from each other. We had lived in an apartment they found for us at Ft. Sill across the pool from theirs. This time we arrived first and located an apartment complex for us all. They lived across the parking lot until we both got base housing and lived on opposite sides of a small playground.

A well-organized base housing office had facilitated our apartment search. They had a list of apartments that showed exhaustive lists of amenities and restrictions. That was important to us because we had Bogey. Most apartments did not allow pets. The ones that did limited their size by weight. Most of them excluded our big dog.

The McVarishs, a couple we knew from TBS and FAOBC, joined us in the search. The phone calls we made together side by side saved a lot of time and legwork.

You could hear the frustration in her voice when Kathleen answered questions from the apartment managers.

"What kind of dog? Uh, terrier."

I'm sure it was an innocent omission when she didn't specify that she meant their loving, "pit bull" terrier.

We all laughed.

Outside Camp Pendleton's back gate on a street with a name we could not yet pronounce—Calle Monticetto—we found our new home at Libby Lake. New and clean and nearly filled with military families, the apartments seemed nice enough during the day. The frequency of police search helicopters at night told a different story. It was a good place and time to have a big dog like Bogey.

1984 Ready for the FMF (Fleet Marine Force)

1983 The Basic School

1984 Jennifer arrives altering our primary assignment to that of parents.

"He hath made everything beautiful in its time.
He has also set eternity in the human heart; yet
no one can fathom what God has done from
beginning to end."

Ecclesiastes 3:11

...3
Conflicts of Timing

Within days of arriving at Camp Pendleton, several friends and I were assigned to separate batteries in 3rd Battalion, 11th Marine Regiment. Our battery offices at Las Pulgas were in the same metal building. Eric went to Golf, Vance went to India, I went to Battery H, or "Hog" Battery, more properly called Hotel in the military phonetic alphabet. Other friends from TBS and FAOBC were scattered across the regiment, division, and base. It was hard to keep in touch with those in other units. We just enjoyed bumping into them off and on.

Hotel Battery was the last remaining 105-mm howitzer battery in the Marine Corps. We felt like we were following in the tradition of our predecessors who had arguably fired the last round of the Korean War. In the Old Corps the "H" stood for "How" Battery.

Hog Battery had earned a bit of a renegade reputation before I arrived. It thoroughly enjoyed and promoted that image from within. The leading instigator was the battery executive officer (XO) 1st Lt. Dave Landersman.

Landersman was taller than just about everybody and, generally, had more positive energy than anyone I'd met to date. I'll never forget his welcome aboard to me. He was never short for words and believed to his core everything he freely espoused.

"Lt. Caldwell, our duty is to make this fun . . . oh yeah, yeah, we'll do the 'mission accomplishment' thing. But everybody does that because we're Marines. The challenge is to make it fun for our Marines. Do you understand?"

Oddly enough, I did. After experiencing a TBS from hell, I knew exactly what he meant. That was a challenge that I gladly undertook.

Then it was back to a certain measure of reality. I had to check in with the CO. My commanding officer, Captain Pearson, was well liked by everyone in the battery, but he was short. In the Marine Corps, being short had nothing to do with stature and everything to do with your time remaining in your current unit. He only had weeks left as the battery commander.

"Well, Lt. Caldwell, are you checked in?"

"Yes, sir."

"Have you gotten housing locked on and your family moved in?"

"Yes, sir."

"So do you see any undue hardship that would be caused by us sending you to Twenty-nine Palms next week for twenty-nine days? The rest of us just got back, and they need a lieutenant."

Undue hardship? *What's that?* I thought. It sounds like I'm the logical choice. I don't guess I could claim any exemption status.

"No, sir. No undue hardships here. I'm checked in, moved in, and ready for whatever."

"Good. The XO will get you all the details."

Going home and explaining my assignment to Lee and our five-month-old daughter was no fun. It would be 29 days, exactly. If we crossed the 30-day mark, we would rate additional pay and allowances. I think it was about a dollar more a day, but the Marine Corps didn't want to pay it.

A short time ago we thought the seven-day war at Ft. Sill, or even the three-day war in Quantico, was hard on us. What would she think? It didn't faze her, or at least she didn't show it.

It was a sign of things to come. It seems the Marine Corps Air Ground Combat Center (MCAGCC) at 29 Palms is the training area of choice for 11th Marines and 3/11, particularly.

High desert training areas spanned seemingly countless acres. Those training areas were ideal for artillery training or just about any size combined-arms exercise (CAX).

This seemingly God-forsaken land was about to become my home away from home. Three-week trips, one-week trips, four-week trips, and two-week trips were commonplace.

Rattling our way along in a slow convoy of vintage jeeps and trucks, we passed through the Mojave Desert and its unique assortment of highway towns. The desolate, harsh environment was not inviting in the least. In fact, after growing up in the lush green country of the Southeastern United States, I wondered how and especially why anyone would live out here.

Reddish-brown rock formations jutted from the colorless sandy soil. Even the mountains stood barren, seemingly void of life. A few of the distant peaks had small snowcaps, which looked out of place. Very little vegetation grew, and absolutely no natural shade was anywhere to be found.

Sunsets were swift and beautifully serene. My favorite time of day in the desert was immediately after the sun fell below the horizon. It was a common time for a break in training for chow, and it provided welcome relief from the glare and merciless heat that the sun forced upon us each day.

On the edge of the maneuver and impact areas was a remote base camp. Known as Camp Wilson, it was miles from other permanent military facilities at 29 Palms. Less than a mile square, it primarily consisted of rickety, A-frame buildings. Each A-frame was a wooden skeleton with weathered, corrugated metal covering. The floors were just desert sand unless some previous unit had laid down boards or pallets to keep the dust to a minimum. Most had electricity for three or four bare lightbulbs hung loosely from the frame. Makeshift plywood doors flapped in the wind, as did some corners of the dented sheet-metal exteriors.

Aluminum cots were placed in a line from one end to the other on both sides of the room. Officers and staff NCOs shared their own A-frame, and the rest of the Marines were housed in like fashion. The cots were beat up and difficult to get just right.

"Sir, how many people does it take to put up a cot?"

"I don't know."

"One lance corporal . . . or four lieutenants."

Sadly, that was too close to the truth to be very funny. Besides, new lieutenants were usually left with the worst, even unserviceable, cots. Those aged cots were impossible to use as they were intended.

A-frames were sometimes an improvement over sleeping under the stars in the training areas. They were better protection during sandstorms and rain, and some basic head and shower facilities were within a hundred yards or so.

A field chow hall also operated at Camp Wilson. Based on the food quality. it's debatable whether that was an advantage, but there was outdoor seating under the partial shade of camouflage netting.

On my very first trip to the high desert at 29 Palms, I was eager to soak up every experience. Some were more enlightening than others.

What was that hanging on nearly every jeep and truck mirror? It looked sort of dysfunctional. It was a rectangular, desert water bag. It was made of thick, natural-colored canvas. It hung loosely by a rope handle and had a simple cork stopper in its metal spout at one of the bag's top corners. The most noticeable thing about them was that they all leaked. It was a slow drip that required them to be placed outside the vehicles. This must have been a tradition carried over from the good ol' days. It sure seemed like more trouble than it would be worth, but my curiosity got the best of me.

"Hey, what's the deal with the desert water bags?"

"They cool the water."

"Really?"

"Oh, yeah! They work by evaporation."

"So how and how well do they work?"

"Just keep the canvas wet so the evaporation is continuous, and it works like a charm. Here, try some and find out for yourself."

By the looks of things, wasps and yellow jackets liked them especially well too. They took turns drawing water from the bag. I hesitated as I held what seemed to be just a wet, dirty bag. After all, dry sand and dust blowing in the wind would stick to the wet canvas. Then I sipped the water. It was remarkably cool—cold in fact—compared to water from any other available source. The water in my canteens was hotter than bath water. I was sold.

"Where can I get one?"

"They sell them here at Camp Wilson, if they're not sold out."

They weren't, and I didn't waste any more time.

"Thanks for the scoop. I'm buying one right now."

The next morning I arrived at a large sand-table brief. A sand table is a miniature re-creation of the area of operations on the ground. It's large enough to walk around but small enough that the entire staff could gather, hear, and see. It was the time and place where primary staff would present their portion of the operations plan to the commanding officer, in this instance, the regimental commander of 27th Marines and his company commanders.

The brief began with the orientation to the sand table and how it related to the map and surrounding terrain. The group was informed to hold all questions until after the brief was completed. That helps the process flow. Plus, many times questions are answered during the course of the brief.

"Hold on."

The colonel stopped the first briefer in his tracks. I listened intently, thinking this must be important.

"Do we have shitters?"

"Sir?"

No one quite knew if he was joking or serious at first. Did he have to go? There had to be a point in asking at this juncture of the sand-table brief. But he restated the question without a smile.

"Do we have shitters?"

"Yes, sir, I believe we do."

"Very well, continue."

It was a strange distraction, and I almost laughed out loud. I couldn't believe what I heard, and I was trying to focus on the briefer, who didn't seem too rattled. He continued.

"Stop. Wait another minute. Are they four-holers or two-holers?"

"I'm not sure, sir, but we can send someone to find out for you."

"That's not necessary, but get back with me after the brief."

"Yes, sir."

Thank goodness that was not really the norm, but those types of exceptions are certainly memorable. I can't remember one other thing said in that brief on that day, but I'll guarantee you that everyone there still remembers that little exchange nearly word for word.

• • •

Prior to tactical operations in the field, I assisted the liaison section with target planning on Mainside. Mainside of MCAGCC 29 Palms was much more civilized than Camp Wilson. There were typical base amenities that gave us a few hours away from the confines of Camp Wilson.

Eventually, it was time to leave Camp Wilson and move to tactical positions out in the rugged training areas. I was assigned as a naval gunfire spotter and located with the STA (surveillance and target acquisition) platoon. An eight-inch artillery battery was firing to simulate naval gunfire. The desert floor to the east was the simulated ocean.

STA platoon consisted of two infantry corporals and a sergeant. The four of us were dropped in by helicopter on the backside of a mountain that we were going to use as an OP (observation post).

An arduous trek up the rough and rocky slope was made more difficult by our need to tote several five-gallon water jugs with us. When we reached the top, it was like the world opened. After staring into the rocks on the face of the slope all the way up, we could now easily see across the open desert, past the shorter ridgelines, and well beyond the limits of the military installation. The view was picturesque by any standard. We took a few moments to soak it all in as we caught our breaths from the climb.

We set up our radios and our living area on the only flat piece of real estate. It was about 6' x 12' and dropped off sharply on all sides, especially, the front slope, which faced the impact and maneuver area. We would enjoy a bird's eye view of the Corps' first Marine Amphibious Brigade (MAB) CAX.

During our wait for the CAX to start, we had time to get to know each other a little better.

Sgt. Smith was on his last trip to the desert. His enlistment was up and he was ready to get out. I was a new lieutenant on my first trip to the desert and had several years before I could think about getting out. I was looking forward to my time in the Corps.

"It just doesn't get any better than this."

"Sir, you can have it. I'm getting out in a couple of months."

"Why are you getting out? Don't you like the Marine Corps?"

"Oh, yes, sir. I love the Marine Corps. It's just the infantry; if you're not stupid when you get here, they'll make sure you're stupid by the time you leave. I'm getting out while I still have some sense."

How could I argue with that? We've all laughed about the "grunt mentality." I had seen it beginning in boot camp. It was there at OCS and TBS, and I had already witnessed it in the fleet.

Finally, the four, long weeks were over. It was time to get home, see the family, and take some time off.

• • •

"Lieutenant Caldwell, you've got duty Saturday."

"What do you mean I have duty? I just got back from twenty-nine days of duty at Twenty-nine Palms."

"While you were away, I had to stand duty once a week."

"Let's see, that's four times in garrison verses twenty-nine in the field. I'm not following your logic."

Basically, the rationale was that I was a 2nd lieutenant and the adjutant who controlled the duty roster was a 1st lieutenant. When he had been a 2nd lieutenant, his predecessor screwed him, so he continued the stupidity.

Standing duty wasn't difficult, it was just bad timing. It involved reporting at 0700 on the morning of duty. If it was a regular workday during the week, the officer of the day (OD) could carry out his normal duties and report back as OD at the close of business, usually around 1700. On a weekend or holiday, it was literally a 24-hour duty from 0700 to 0700 the next day.

It was a sleeping post, which meant you could go to sleep at night as long as you got up a few times during the night to walk the area and check with the subordinate battery duty personnel.

Most nights there was very little to write down in the duty log. Fights, drunken marines, phone calls . . . Sometimes, it was entertaining to read the other log entries from previous duties.

One stormy, rainy night, a creative OD decided the requirement to tour the battalion area was up to some interpretation; thus, the following entry: "Toured the area—telephonically."

The goal was to not have any entries in the OD logbook concerning your own battery. Those items were always addressed harshly the next morning at the battalion XO's meeting.

We hit the blotter a few times in succession on similar incidents. That's even worse.

Two botched, half-hearted, drunken "suicide attempts" hit the blotter. The last one—over a failed romance—sent the battery XO into a spin. The Marine involved had gotten drunk and jumped off of a second-floor balcony on base and broken his arm.

Lt. Landersman called a battery formation. "Marines, I'm sick and tired of being on the battalion blotter with suicide attempts. I think you could screw up a wet dream. If anyone here is going to try suicide, you better at least get it right. This is the last failed suicide from this battery. If anybody needs to know how to kill himself, come see me! Any questions? Gunny, take charge of the battery, and carry out the plan of the day."

Some could argue the value of his short tirade, but we did not have any more suicide attempts.

Planned social events were the flip side of the Marine Corps coin. Contrary to weeks in the hot desert training areas with no showers, these sporadic occasions encouraged you to bring your wife.

My first social event as a 2nd lieutenant in the fleet was a "Calls made and received" at the regimental commander's house on base at Camp Pendleton.

Arriving on time is a must. In order to arrive perfectly on time, a battalion of lieutenants will congregate on the street to synchronize watches and approach the front door in an orderly fashion. The formal greeting with host and hostess is painfully endured.

The next step is to find the plate, bowl, or whatever in which we are to place our calling cards. It is easily spotted. Then the plan to discretely leave our cards begins in earnest. How many cards do we leave? Is it one for the host and hostess and another for adult males or female children? And what is the age cut off? We determine that if we get it wrong, we'll get it wrong together just to be safe.

The reception spilled into the backyard, where my battery CO's wife proved to be too tipsy to navigate the turf in high heels. Her narrow spikes sank deep. She would lose a shoe with each step and struggle to keep it on her foot. She was providing excellent aeration for the ground but needed a little fresh air for herself. In all of our preparation at The Basic School, this sort of duty wasn't covered. I escorted her as gentlemanly as possible from the yard.

One of the social events that came more naturally was a Battery Officer's Call at the Red Rooster, a small bar with a greasy grill for cooking "Rooster Burgers." There were peanuts and beer, a few pool tables, and a dart board. It was our battery's favorite spot for officer calls.

The Red Rooster was a warm host for unverified sea stories and long-winded advice from Lt. Landersman.

"Choose your torches carefully. John, you'll find a lot of things wrong with the Marine Corps. You can't fix it all. If you carry a torch on everything, you'll be labeled a malcontent and get nothing done. Fix what you can and keep quiet about the rest."

It's amazing how much you can learn by listening if you're sober enough to sort through all the tripe.

There wasn't much time spent in garrison for 3/11. If we weren't at 29 Palms, we were just getting back, performing maintenance and recovery, or getting ready to go again.

It's a wonder Lee and I had time to conceive our second child. It had to happen in the short window between 29 Palms and Camp Roberts.

Camp Roberts was a California National Guard Base near San Luis Obispo. The out-of-the-way base was nearly deserted and ideal for a two-week command post exercise (CPX).

I think they had to un-board the windows and doors of the old, two-story wood-framed barracks to use them. Stepping into the whitewashed structures was like a step back in time. The hardwood floors were still solid, years of character etched into the wood grain. The bunks were nearly as aged as the floor. Thankfully, the mattresses were not quite as old as the electrical wiring.

The 24-hour operations—broken down into 12-hour shifts—tell only part of the story. Each 12-hour shift had every hour divided into 50 minutes of planning and 10 minutes of gaming on a tactical table that nearly filled an old gymnasium. That 10 minutes of gaming was supposed to replicate one hour in "real time" in the exercise.

Junior lieutenants occupied the night shift. It began at 1900 (7 p.m.) and ended at 0700 (7 a.m.). The full intent of the senior officers on the day shift was that nothing should happen overnight while they were sleeping. That made for uneventful, quiet, boring nights. Why were we even there? We could have and should have stayed home, and they could have simulated our shift.

My theory was confirmed when something actually happened one night. The guidance was to move each unit in the multi-pronged attack at their maximum movement rate. One of the units had a higher movement rate and made enemy contact well before morning. We fought the units for several hours with measurable results. The 24-hour aspect of the training was beginning to have meaning until . . .

Senior division staff officers arrived the following morning with coffee in hand. The screaming started. The lieutenants on the night shift were well into a high-pitched battle they had wanted to start themselves. All the talk about learning from "real-time" training went out the window. After staying up night after night for two weeks, trying to simulate "real-time," they punted. We moved all the units arbitrarily back to where the general and his staff wanted them to be and re-cocked. Two wasted weeks. It was a miserable trip with a disgusting finish.

I try to learn from all my experiences. There were just two takeaways from this one. First, a new respect for two weeks' restriction and EPD (extra police duty) as a punishment for Marines was gained. Before this, that seemed an extremely light non-punishment. Following our time in Camp Roberts, I thought better of it. Second, I learned that I wanted out of the Marine Corps at the end of my initial obligation. I had bought into a philosophy espoused at TBS by the staff company executive officer, Captain Neller (eventually, commandant of the Marine Corps).

One of our lieutenants had asked him when he was getting out of the Marine Corps. His response: "Whenever I have two bad days in a row."

I'd buy that. I'd never had two bad days in a row myself, and I saw no reason that should change. The CPX at Camp Roberts was two bad weeks in a row! Sold.

• • •

I broke into the fleet quickly and was somewhat salty for a 2nd lieutenant. I was getting into a comfort zone, and I knew my job as well as any. Confidence and MOS knowledge became more important as I began to serve as a liaison officer to an infantry battalion.

My first CAX as a liaison officer was spent in the back of a C-7 (amphibious assault vehicle set up as a command track). It enlightened me even more on the pitfalls of being attached to a grunt unit. Often, liaison officers and forward observers were treated poorly when attached to the infantry.

On the first day, communications were poor in the C-7. Other than the prep and pre-planned fires, I wasn't able to get any fire missions cleared on the fly. There was so much chaos in the C-7 that the grunts didn't notice, but my battery did. Artillerymen want to shoot!

On my way to check with my liaison chief in our communications jeep, I was cut off at the ramp.

"Where are you going?""

"I'm going to my jeep to see if they have comm."

"Who's watching the radio in here?"

"Nobody, but there's no one on the other end anyway. That's why I'm going to my jeep."

"I'm the radio watch officer, and somebody's got to man that radio."

"Did you hear what I said? It's not working."

"I don't care. Somebody's got to be on it."

"Well, then, put somebody on it, or you can do it yourself, but I'm getting out of here."

"I said you need to man that radio, and I'm a first lieutenant and you're a second lieutenant."

Now I was mad. The jerk hadn't been cooped up in that cramped, stuffy C-7, inhaling diesel fumes and fighting with a busted radio for the last four hours. I was getting off that ramp if I had to go through him.

The FSC (fire support coordinator), who was also a 1st lieutenant, stepped between us and defused the situation, allowing me space to get off.

I had always subscribed to the popular saying, "Rank among lieutenants is like virginity among the whores," meaning there isn't any. All lieutenants are basically equal.

After a brief break, and with the re-establishment of communications with the battery, I had time to find the radio watch lieutenant alone.

"Hey, if you ever talk to me like that again, I'll knock you off that track."

"Are you saying you'd hit me."

"I didn't stutter. You'll be pulling rank from your backside. Don't ever pull a stunt like that with me again."

It was time to walk away without saying any more. I really wasn't looking for a fight, but I think I would have felt better if I had just hit him in the first place.

The next day I had worked out the communications issues. When we rolled out, we were able to shoot. The C-7 had so much chaos that the fire support coordinator had more than he could handle. When I saw that he was approving my missions without even checking the map, I knew it was all on me and I quit asking him. I verified and approved all the missions as if I were the FSC. The battery was pumped to get so many back-to-back missions. As fast as they could call good, safe missions, I was giving them approval. The "Fido" or fire direction officer, Terry Zeille, was like a little kid he was so excited. The grunts didn't know any different.

The battalion S-3 operations officer proved to be less than tolerable and made me glad I was an artillery officer. We had pulled over and dropped the back hatch to shift from the lead battalion into a reserve position. Major Moore had already proven to be a jerk to several others, and now it was my turn.

"Lieutenant Caldwell, who is our direct support battery for this phase?"

"Sir, we don't have a battery in direct support."

"Like hell we don't. They don't put us out here without any fire support, lieutenant."

"Sir, the artillery battalion is firing in direct support of the regiment, and now we are in reserve."

"We've got to have direct support artillery out here. Somebody's got to be firing for us if we need artillery."

"We can always request it. We just won't have priority because we're not the focus of effort."

"Lieutenant, I'm not arguing with you. I want to know who *our* direct support battery is *now*. So get on that radio and find out who it is, then come tell me."

He stormed off. I picked up the radio handset to call. I was hot, tired, and mad, and a little embarrassed that he had screamed at me in such a derogatory tone in front of everyone.

I put the handset down. I didn't need to call anybody. I was right and I knew it. I wasn't going to ask a stupid question when I had the answer it front of me. I grabbed the major's own copy of the operations order.

Unlike his public display, I chose to set him straight with more class. I walked up to him when no one else was around.

"Sir, here's the fire support annex of the op order showing the battalion's direct support relationship to the regiment and who has priority of fires when. I've got nothing else to the contrary. If you know of any frag orders that might have changed this, just let me know. All I can do is advise you of the facts as they are published, and this is spelled out clearly right here in your own op order."

"Well, then, go look for any changes."

Of course I knew there were none, but it gave him an out, and I was glad to get some distance between us.

"Yes, sir."

I had my fill of tagging along with the infantry. Instead of a welcome addition, they often treated artillery liaison attachments like redheaded stepchildren.

●●●

Another trip successfully completed, then back home to Camp Pendleton and the daily routine of maintenance and training. We had collateral duties, additional duties, and assigned tasks, like the time I was assigned to be the safety officer for a day at the pistol range.

"Gentlemen, we can't begin firing without a corpsman present. I'll check over on the rifle range and see if he ended up at the wrong place."

Great. I'm placed in charge of a pistol range as a 2nd lieutenant, and I have a bunch of senior officers, including my battalion executive officer, waiting on me to find a corpsman.

The rifle range shooters and, hopefully, my corpsman, were a healthy distance away from us. It was hot and the pressure was on. I literally ran to several locations across the range complex with no luck. On my way back to the pistol range, I chose to take a shortcut over a grassy berm. Bad idea.

I didn't hear anything but felt a hard slap across my shin. Although no one was with me, it felt like someone had released the tension from a tree branch, causing it to strike my leg. Instinctively, I bent down to rub it and saw one of California's prized Western Diamondbacks quickly disappearing into the tall weeds. It must have been 5-6 feet in length. Although there was no doubt it had struck me, I wasn't sure yet that he had injected venom. It was starting out to be a really bad day.

As I surveyed the area on my leg only an eighth of an inch above my boot line, I could only squeeze out a small drop of blood from my shin. My first thought was that he didn't get a good bite. I was frustrated and still missing a corpsman for the pistol range.

Almost immediately, I got a bad taste in my mouth. It was a medicine-like, poison taste . . . metallic even, like the taste of losing a tooth filling. The snake must have injected at least some venom. Within seconds I could feel my face begin to tingle. With all my running around prior to getting bit, my blood must have been pumping pretty quickly.

It was time to get some help and forget the pistol range. I never found a corpsman and now I needed one. The rifle range was in sight but hundreds of yards away, and they were firing in the opposite direction, so no one could see me or hear me. The pistol range was closer, just on the other side of the berm, but this time I'd walk around it. I didn't see any sense risking another bite in the high grass.

When I rounded the berm, I located my battalion XO.

"Sir, I've been bitten by a rattlesnake."

"Where?"

"Around the corner of this berm in the grass."

"No, I mean where on your body."

"It's my left leg, just above the boot."

"Let's get you to some help."

Briskly, we walked to the parking lot, and he drove me to the regimental aide station. It had only been a few minutes, but I could already feel myself losing muscle coordination, and I was feeling slightly numb all over. I was really hoping that I wouldn't get sick to my stomach.

Past training had taught me that snakebites themselves weren't supposed to be so bad. The point was not to cut the bite open and bleed the poison out, because so many people caused even more harm trying to do that.

Our regimental aid station at Las Pulgas was just a mile or so down the road. It seemed like a logical place to go. They did nothing but place me on an examination table and wait for an ambulance, which seemed to take forever to arrive.

As I waited, I felt my leg start to swell. Then it began to feel like my whole body was swelling like a balloon. I couldn't control my arms, and they slid off the bed on both sides. Someone raised the rails to keep my arms up. Everyone was calm and trying to keep me calm, but they didn't do anything except ask me my name and age over and over.

Finally, the ambulance arrived. Again, I was asked my name and age over and over. They first began giving me fluids intravenously. They debated the seriousness of the bite as they communicated with the hospital.

Once at the Camp Pendleton hospital, I thought they'd give me shot and send me home. Not so. Before I knew it, I was in intensive care.

I would never have guessed that a snakebite would be so serious. Neither did my fellow lieutenants and friends. They arrived at the hospital shortly after the bite with a rubber snake. 1st Lt. Keith Flamer cut them off at the waiting room door and explained that I was in intensive care, and my wife, Lee, had better not see that rubber snake.

Keith wanted to go back to the ICU to check on Lee and me. A hospital staff member stopped him at the door with the usual instructions.

"No one can come back here except immediate family members."

"I'm his brother."

"Okay, go ahead."

He didn't seem to notice that he was black and I was white. In many ways we *were* brothers but probably not what they meant.

One of my real brothers dropped everything and flew out to California to be with Lee and check on me. It comforted Lee and helped her with Jennifer. Most of all I think it comforted our momma. She wanted to fly out, but Frank being there put her mind at rest. It also put the rest of the family at ease.

The hospital ordeal is a fuzzy blur. I was slipping in and out of consciousness, but I can remember sweating profusely. Two IVs couldn't keep up with the perspiration. They were constantly changing the sheets as I soaked them with sweat.

I remember the irony of the nurses trying to keep a privacy rag on me after placing a catheter. I continually discarded the rag because it felt like a heating pad. My body temperature was extremely high, and I was begging for a cold drink. I even offered one nurse $50 for a Sprite. He wasn't impressed.

I remember Lee by my side, offering me shaved ice and a wet rag to let me suck the water out. It doesn't sound like much, but I had never been thirsty like that in my life.

I knew the swelling was bad, and they were discussing cutting the swollen areas of my lower leg to relieve pressure. They were also discussing the pros and cons of anti-venom. Anti-venom was not a preferred treatment, because humans tend to reject the antitoxin, which is made from horse serum. In addition to the normal difficulties with anti-venom, a quick test had showed that I was allergic to it.

Unbeknownst to me, they were sending telegrams from the commanding general to my parents to keep them updated on the seriousness of my condition.

As a last resort they chose to administer the anti-venom in multiple, small doses and follow it with Benadryl each time to reduce the allergic reaction. The rash must have looked awful, because the nurses kept asking me if it was itching.

By then I was tired—tired of hard breathing, tired of sweating profusely, tired of being hot, tired of fighting. My muscles had been twitching for hours and hours. At one point I determined I'd had enough. I told Lee that I was just going to exhale my last breath, but I would involuntarily inhale every time I tried to quit. Only two days in intensive care and I was ready to give up. My new regard for those who tough it out through cancer, painful hospital stays, or lifelong infirmities would remain with me for the rest of my life.

Consciousness came with an acute awareness that I was not alone. Not only had my wife been by my side, accompanied by medical attendants, but there was obviously more. God's presence had been close enough to touch. Even long-distance prayers that had been offered up for me from friends and family seemed to be almost tangible throughout the ordeal.

Finally, they wheeled me into a regular room. It just so happens I was sharing it with another snakebite victim; he had no troubles and was in and out in a day or so.

The nursing staff was very attentive, but the quality of care came into question several times.

"Lieutenant Caldwell, we need to get your permission to let this corpsman perform his first IV."

"That's funny."

"No, we're serious. We have to have a patient's permission for a corpsman's first IV."

"Go try somebody else first and tell me how it went. I can't believe we're having this conversation. Are you for real?"

"Now, you wouldn't want his first IV to be on some little old lady where we can't find the vein, would you? You've got great veins, and I'll be here to supervise."

"Okay, but I'm coming out of this bed if anything goes wrong, and somebody's going to pay."

"Don't worry. It's going to be over in a second."

The nervous corpsman did a yeoman's job. I hardly felt a thing, but I didn't want to let them know that just yet. After a few minutes of good-natured ribbing, I let them go about their business.

I was feeling well enough to joke with the corpsmen and was feeling better about the level of care I was receiving until an older nurse walked in and began examining my leg. She looked it over from my knee to my ankle. "It looks much better today," she said.

"That's because you're looking at the wrong leg. The snake bit the other one."

"Oh," her flustered voice squeaked.

I quietly watched every move she made until she left the room.

Lee broke out laughing.

Her laughter kept me from getting mad. "Can you believe that nurse?" I puffed.

"That wasn't a nurse, honey. That was a hospital volunteer."

"That makes me feel a little better."

Nearly a week in the hospital had just about driven me crazy. I was feeling better and wanted to get out of there. My left leg was mostly black and blue and purple, with a few other colors mixed within the humongous bruise. The extreme swelling in my lower leg had actually created enough pressure to burst the vast array of blood vessels. I couldn't put any weight on that foot without severe pain.

After two days in the ICU and another week in the hospital, I left the hospital on crutches, having been given 30 days' convalescent leave. Then I spent several days of it running back to the emergency room.

As the swelling left the leg, the anti-venom, which had caused such an allergic reaction while in the ICU, would release back into my bloodstream and I would break out in hives. The allergy medicine would work for a day and then stop. The next day we would be back to the emergency room for an alternate allergy medicine. This happened three separate times.

Eventually, it was time for a trip home to see family. It was a short-notice trip for us, and we thought we would surprise everyone. I knew Daddy would be working at the station, so I found a payphone at the Memphis Airport. When Daddy answered, he almost didn't believe me, but he was quickly convinced. We piled into his old Chevy pickup, and he drove us to the house.

A crowd had already gathered for the usual family gathering to celebrate family birthdays for the month. It was great to see everybody, but that was enough surprises for one day.

Lee and I also suspected she was pregnant again. During the snake ordeal, she began to feel that way and experience some of the usual signs. But those signs could have been related to the stress or the change in diet and sleep revolving around the snakebite ordeal. We didn't want to announce anything prematurely.

• • •

Shortly after we returned to California, the pregnancy was confirmed—not by some off-the-shelf drugstore test but because the baby began to kick. Lee needed to see a doctor to help establish a likely delivery date and begin basic prenatal care.

The baby was due in November, but we waited until mid-September to let the family back home know she was pregnant.

"Hello?"

"Hey, Jan, this is John. I wanted you to be the first to know that Lee and I are going to have another baby."

"Oh my! When?"

"November."

"Of this year?"

"Of course, it better not be next year."

The initial visit to the OBGYN section of the base hospital let us know immediately that we wanted to do whatever it took to have the baby out in town with a civilian doctor.

This time we were going to have a normal delivery, at a hospital we knew, with a doctor Lee knew, and I wasn't as green as the first time.

We still had a labor room *and* a separate delivery room, but it took us a while to get there once the contractions started.

It was a normal night at home watching *The Cosbys* on TV. Lee decided that she was having contractions.

"Are you ready to go to the hospital?"

"Not yet. I'd hate to get there and have the contractions stop. Let's go for a walk first."

"Okay."

The November California night was very pleasant. Our plans were to walk around the block a few times, but by the time we got to the sidewalk, she had us turn around. It was time to go.

The 10-minute trip to the hospital was uneventful compared to our first time, driving for hours between Quantico and Memphis.

"Slow down. They're not progressing."

"I'm just going the speed limit."

"But I don't want to get there too early."

"Fine. I'll slow down."

As we pulled into the parking lot, I looked for a parking place close to the door.

"I'm not ready to go in yet."

"What now?"

"I don't want to get in there too early, and the contractions are still about the same. Ooh, there's one now."

"What do you want to do?"

"Let's walk around the parking lot."

"Okay."

"That's far enough."

"We've barely started walking."

"I said that's far enough."

Once inside the hospital, she was determined to walk around on the ground floor for a while. Finally, she agreed to get on the elevator.

"Let's don't go up to the desk."

"Now what?"

"Can we just sit here in the waiting room for another few minutes?"

"Sure. You let me know when it's time."

"It's time."

"Are you sure?"

"Yes."

"Are you sure you don't want to walk around or up and down some steps before we bother the nurses and the doctor?"

"I'm sure."

Finally, she was ready. I could tell because her sense of humor was fading. I was more prepared this time than last time. So was Lee.

As we watched the monitors in the labor room, there was a screamer in a labor room down the hall, drowning out the sound on our TV. I was glad when that woman finally delivered. Next, it was our turn.

The monitors indicated that the umbilical cord was wrapped around the baby. The doctor was concerned but took steps to reduce any risks during birth. Just like his sister, JC waited until the last minute to get into position. Now it was time to push. The delivery went relatively well, and we had our first son and Jennifer had her first brother.

We took a few days to enjoy it. Thanksgiving came quickly... then Christmas ... then back to work.

1985 JC enjoys the sunshine at Camp Pendleton.

Only a handful of days in a uniform other than camouflage utilities.

*"Now the Lord had said unto Abram, Get thee
out of thy country, and from thy kindred, and
from thy father's house, unto a land that I will
shew thee:"*

Genesis 12:1

...4

Conflicts of Duty

Off-road tires create a constant whine of road noise that is occasionally interrupted by unexplainable clatter from a questionable old engine. Engine heat pierces the well-aged hot steel panels. Our convoy of trucks and vintage jeeps far beyond their reasonable service life struggle slowly down the concrete interstate.

The seemingly lifeless desert terrain on all sides is littered with miles of billboards trying to attract shoppers and golfers to popular vacation hot spots. Soon, we will turn off the expressway that leads to Palm Springs. Our convoy will climb the two-lane roads to the high desert training area. Conversations are short and loud to hear each other above the noise.

A jeep and trailer pass to break up the monotonous journey. The standard wave and nod from the passing jeep are accompanied with more eye-to-eye contact and a larger than usual smile.

From the canvas-covered trailer in tow, my driver and I see why. Another face, inflated with bright red lips, peeks from the drab canvas. An air-filled leg and arm are also carefully positioned to advertise their deviance. What could anyone do but smile and wave?

Convoy briefs prior to hitting the road and counseling afterwards never seemed to completely register with the Marines. It was not unusual to find unclaimed, dirty cardboard signs in the back of trucks. The most common one—"Show us your tits"—was a timeless and apparently effective one.

"How many times do we have to tell you, Marines?"

"Sir, it's not mine."

"I'm sure no one wants to confess."

Silence.

"Why would you do something like this? It makes us look bad, and it would never work!"

"Oh, yes, sir, it does."

"You've got to be kidding me."

"No, sir. We get flashed several times during every convoy."

All I can do is just shake my head in disgust and walk away, although part of me envies the carefree youthfulness of the junior Marines.

Recurrent trips to 29 Palms over the next two years would be within the battery with all its ups and downs, but I wouldn't trade it for any other place in the Marine Corps. Battery life was generally pretty good.

There was one downside, however. As an officer in a firing battery, you could bet on not eating evening chow in the field the first few days. Food would always run short and officers ate last.

Either by increasing the amount of chow delivered or decreasing the portions served or both, by the third day we all could eat. As lieutenants, we regularly served the chow. It had a two-fold purpose. First, we showed a little humility and sense of humor, which the other Marines appreciated. Second, we made sure there was chow for the Marines at the end of the line—namely, us.

Evening chow was a time to socialize with your fellow lieutenants and swap a few experiences you had lived through that day. You could also make some personal contact with almost every Marine and conduct some cursory supervision.

"Corporal Richards, what's on your helmet?"

"It's a lizard being crucified on a cross. It's for good luck," he boasted.

"Get rid of it and leave the animals alone."

"Yes, sir."

You'd think we just took all his fun out of being a Marine. He moped a bit but complied, nonetheless. The desert made people crazy like that, and when you consider we were all a little crazy to join the Marines in the first place, the combination can get dangerous at 29 Palms.

One Marine from Headquarters Battery played with a little sidewinder on another trip. When it bit him, he in turn bit the rattlesnake's head off.

The story would have probably ended there, but the snake bit the Marine's tongue in the process. The Marine was rushed to the hospital; his tongue was so swollen they had to perform a tracheotomy for him to breathe.

All of God's creatures are protected on military bases as if on game preserves. It is a strict violation for Marines to even bother them, much less kill them. It can put a crimp in your training, but we learn to work around it most of the time.

"Nick, get me a shovel."

"Get your own shovel."

He had assumed I needed the shovel for the usual reason—to dig a cat hole. When you think of why cats dig, you'll understand why it's called a cat hole.

"Just get me a shovel, and hurry."

Nick could tell by the tone of my voice that the shovel wasn't needed for a cat hole.

With one swift stroke, the rattlesnake's head was separated from its body. Sometimes, you just have to do what needs to be done, whether it's a game preserve or not.

"Endex! Endex! Endex!"

The culmination of every exercise was the anticipated ending of it. Once those words sounded almost simultaneously over every radio in the desert, and every headset in fire direction centers and along the gunlines, a huge explosion of activity began. Packing up to return home was fast and furious.

In addition to typical repacking and loading was the signature artillery powder burn. Excess powder bags from the charges cut during fire missions had to be safely burned. The bags were lined up to burn upwind in sequence. The flames were bright, loud and intense.

Everyone was scrambling to be the first ones to rollout. Desert range roads would soon be filled with speeding vehicles and dust headed for showers, equipment maintenance and more importantly, a beer call. The official limit would be two beers per Marine, although you could count on some friendly cheating.

Convoys eventually returned to Camp Pendleton.

Old jeeps and 416-trailers were returned to the motor pool. Standard shift, M813, 5-ton trucks were being replaced with the new 900-Series 5-tons with automatic transmissions. It wouldn't be long before a strange-looking new vehicle called a "Humvee" would force out the jeep and trailer.

My first active-duty tour wasn't up yet, and we were already seeing several new models of the M-16 rifle and the Berretta 9 mm replacing the military's .45-caliber pistol. New Kevlar helmets and flak jackets, even new woodland utilities with smaller collars, were a few other changes. It seemed that everything but our underwear was changing. Eventually, it changed too.

Most dramatically for the artillery community, the lightweight 105-mm howitzers were being sidelined. We couldn't stand to see them go. Besides all the tactical and technical reasons for wanting to keep them, there were sentimental reasons, too.

Marines loved shooting them. It wasn't unusual to shoot over 500 rounds in one day. With larger, more expensive, 155-mm munitions, the whole battalion wouldn't shoot that many rounds in a week or more.

When the new, M198, 155-mm howitzers arrived, there weren't enough to equip the whole battalion; only Golf and India batteries received them.

We, on the other hand, transitioned to the much older M114A3 howitzers. Formerly considered a general support weapon, it also fired 155-mm rounds, but the two cannons looked drastically different.

M198 howitzers have a much longer painted tube and longer trails. It is a much different look than the fat, stubby, silver-tube artillery piece commonly referred to as the "Pig". Ironically, the Pigs were headed to Hog Battery.

The old howitzers grew on me. They had stood the test of time well enough, and frankly I hadn't. It was just another opportunity to learn for a young lieutenant like me. In the years ahead it became almost natural to transition from weapon system to weapon system. Change was inevitable. How to respond is up to each one of us.

Changes in equipment were secondary to changes in personnel. Marines are constantly adjusting to new billets, new orders, promotions, finishing tours, etc. That included those that worked for me and with me as well as those in command over me.

During the howitzer change we also had a new commanding officer assigned to our battery. His name was Captain Hug, affectionately referred to as "Huggie Bear." He was easy going and friendly, something I learned not to take for granted as the years passed.

While in garrison he would keep us entertained with stories of his personal arsenal and tales of shooting varmints in Oklahoma. If you didn't want to get the long version, you'd better come up with an escape plan.

Our Executive Officer, Keith Flamer had an uncanny way of walking out in the middle of his stories or finding a way to redirect the boss's energy.

"Keith, I can't believe you just walk out on the CO."

"He was driving me crazy. I can't get any work done with him around telling stories about shooting gophers. One of us needed to leave, and I have a lot of work to do."

That didn't last long. The XO soon checked out for the "1st Civ Div." A short time later Captain Hug was promoted out of his command billet. As a new major, he went to the battalion staff as the S-4 logistics officer. That seemed to be a natural fit for him. I stayed in the battery purposely avoiding assignments to battalion staff billets.

Commanding officers are all different. I worked for four, distinctly different personalities during my time in the battery. I learned something from each one, but the best teacher by far was the next one, Captain Christie.

As the battery commanders rotated, several batches of lieutenants also worked their way through Hotel Battery. The physical make-up of the battery changed, as did its strengths and weaknesses. Changes could be seen and felt nearly everywhere.

We moved our O-calls from the Red Rooster to the San Clemente pier. Of course, there was still beer, but huge prawns replaced Rooster Burgers, and the ocean breeze replaced the sound of second-rate pool players taking too many shots to finish a game. It became more of what one would expect from a Southern California unit.

It was always a challenge to fully integrate back in the rear with everyone changing billets—not to mention all the collateral duties of an artillery officer. Garrison platoon commander billets, armory officer, motor transportation officer, and maintenance management officer assignments in the battery usually took up more time than tactical billets. Every local, division, and Marine Corps-wide inspection had to be squeezed between recurring field operations.

We were already feeling the pangs and the benefits of our new battery commander. Captain Rick Christie arrived with a fury. He made list after list and lists of lists of things for each lieutenant in the battery to do. We found out later that he had been tasked with breaking the renegade mold that had been our trademark. In the process he taught us a lot about artillery and ourselves. We stayed the best shooting battery in the battalion, but now we were challenged to be better team players.

Once, early in his tenure and with our heads still spinning and our workloads taking a toll, he stopped us in our tracks. At the usual morning meeting in his office, we thought he had snapped. As we sat expecting the usual additions for our lists, he leaned back, propped his feet on this desk, and put his hands behind his head.

"I expect soon to walk in and see each of you like this at some point."

That seemed especially weird and contrary to everything he had said and done so far. Then he explained. "I've been working you pretty hard, if you haven't noticed. You've all stepped up and you've gotten a lot done. However, you are paid to think and not work like that all the time. Sure, there's work to be done, but as officers you are paid too much to just work hard. You are paid to use your brains, too. I haven't left you time for thinking much, but as you delegate more, you should make more time to think. So, prop your feet up and put your hands behind your head. Then I'll know you understand."

It was a great lesson and very welcome relief indeed. He taught me a lot in a short time, and he became a mentor I could and would learn from throughout my career.

● ● ●

Las Pulgas was home to 3/11, but 29 Palms remained our home away from home. A DESFIREX— a battalion-level, desert, firing exercise—was added to the training schedule. Major Watson was the S-3 and had planned an aggressive week. We also picked up a new battalion commander and regimental commander who boldly fixed some of the overzealous safety policies that had evolved in the artillery community.

No one wants to compromise safety, but we had been compromising our training in the name of safety. It was getting ridiculous. Instead of a separate safety officer being responsible for safety, the battery officers and commanders were once again made responsible for their unit's safety. It was referred to as Chain of Command Safety. There was no need for a separate safety officer looking over the shoulders of commanders.

During a firing exercise without overhead fire—no infantry in front of the gun line—batteries could shoot from a firing position with hasty survey. That had been unheard of when I first arrived in the fleet.

As the AXO (assistant executive officer), I was on the advance party and was responsible for that survey. We shot from three-point resections and locations I was able to compute from the old TI-59 handheld calculator with a survey chip. Battalion Survey would come in later and verify our position. We were always well within 10 meters and once were only 3' x 1' off final survey. That level of accuracy is more than adequate considering that the casualty radius of just one 155-mm artillery round was many times that. Plus, the natural dispersion of a battalion's impacts on a target could easily spread over several hundred meters.

The pace was grueling. We could not allow the hot desert temperature to slow us. Our entire advance party moved at double time every time we got out of our vehicles. There wasn't much choice, because the main body was always so close behind us.

After the battery was laid and safe, I could take a breath until the first round was fired. Then it was, "Advance party up," and off to the next firing position. We didn't even have time to eat most meals.

In six days of firing, we averaged moving and shooting from more than two positions a night during the hours of darkness. (I lost count of the day moves.) Things really became second nature at night. Everything could literally be done blindfolded by the time we left for home.

Op tempo and success prompted the battalion commander to brag, "We own the night." At that moment I believed it . . . and still do. Never did I learn so much so quickly about battery operations or leave the field so physically exhausted and satisfied.

As we were making out our rosters for future field operations, we were always short of bodies, so creative solutions were in order. Captain Christie advised us to place all our sick, lame, and lazy as assistant drivers in our supply trucks and ammo trash trucks. When I did that, the battalion's head corpsman came into the office on the verge of disrespect. He told Captain Christie that he couldn't take them because they had been placed on limited duty by medical professionals.

Captain Christie cut him off at the knees. "Thanks for your advice, Doc. I really appreciate it, but you're an advisor—a medical advisor, but still, an advisor. You don't make the decisions around here. I do, and they're going. If there are any repercussions, I'm responsible, not you. End of discussion."

By stretching the envelope with personnel, our battery was able to excel in the battalion FIREX. The Marine Corps had recently reconfigured its artillery to promote split-battery operations with eight-gun batteries. However, the other two full batteries, Golf and India, could barely man three- and four-howitzer sections, respectively. Hotel trained with seven. My platoon manned and shot four.

I loved being a platoon commander. My section chiefs were always the best, and my Marines always shone, which made me look good in spite of myself.

A good platoon sergeant also helped. I can remember two occasions that at first looked similar, but they were not.

Another platoon commander in the battalion and I had wandered up to the gun park together to check on the day's maintenance effort of our Marines.

When we arrived on the first occasion, the Marines were "smokin' and jokin'" in the gun park. The lieutenant with me started yelling at his Marines. I quietly observed and went looking for my platoon sergeant.

"Hey, Staff Sergeant, did you know the Marines were goofing off in the gun park."

"Yes, sir. They've been working hard all morning, so I told them to take a break."

Boy, was I glad I didn't yell at them that day. The Marines would have thought I was nuts.

Not many days later, the same thing transpired on the front end, but when I found the platoon sergeant this time, it was a different story.

"Hey, Staff Sergeant, did you know the Marines were goofing off in the gun park."

"What? No, sir. I left them a few minutes ago, and they're supposed to be working."

Immediately, he sprang into action. He took it personally, as if he himself had been caught goofing off. I almost pitied the Marines.

I learned valuable lessons through that turn of events. It seldom pays for an officer to lose his temper, and the Staff NCOs are better at screaming at Marines anyway. I never liked it if my seniors bypassed me, and it was better if I didn't bypass my staff NCOs. It's not that I never corrected a Marine on the spot, but if at all possible, I employed my staff NCOs and NCOs. They seemed to appreciate it.

Sometimes, the job involved simply taking care of Marines 24/7. I remember the call when Lance Corporal Fegal wound up in Balboa Hospital in San Diego. He had been stabbed in the border town of Tijuana, Mexico. A curfew had been briefed to all Marines and the battery gunny had emphasized that the Marines had to be off the streets of Tijuana before dark.

My first concern was the seriousness of the wound. I checked in with the nurse on the ward. "I'm looking for one of my Marines, a Lance Corporal Fegal."

"He came in last night. He's in bed number six."

"How is he?"

"He's going to be fine."

When I entered the ward, I was a little shocked. The line of beds down each side of the ward felt like a step back in time. It was an aging hospital showing signs of wear. The ward appeared vintage 1960s, with old beds but more modern equipment surrounding them. Fegal was awake and alert.

"Lance Corporal Fegal, how are you doing?"

"I'm better, sir."

"Now that I know you're okay, do you want to tell me what you were doing in Tijuana, breaking curfew?"

"Sir, we weren't breaking the curfew. The gunny said to be off the streets by sundown, and we were."

"Then how did you get stabbed at night in TJ?"

"We were in a bar—not on the streets."

Marine logic. He was so sincere—and still laid up in a hospital bed—that I didn't have the heart to break it to him just how stupid that sounded.

"Does your family know you've been stabbed?"

"No, sir."

"Can you make a call from this ward?"

"No, sir."

"Do you want me to call your mom or someone when I leave here and let them know what happened?"

"Yes, sir. That would be great. Thank you, sir."

I thought of my momma. She would have exploded if I was stabbed and hospitalized without so much as a phone call for a day or more. So I was glad to do it. His mom and I had a wonderful conversation, and after the initial natural reaction, she seemed very grateful and at ease.

The next day I was called into the battalion XO's office.

"Lieutenant Caldwell, did you make a phone call notifying Fegal's mother that he had been stabbed?"

"Yes, sir."

"We don't do notifications. The general does."

"Oh, the general called?"

"No, the general doesn't call unless the Marine is in grave condition?"

"So who called, sir?"

"Nobody else called. I just had to tell you that you shouldn't have."

"Sir, he didn't have a phone in that ward, and it would have been a day or two before he could get to one. Besides, I asked Fegal first if he wanted me to call."

"I understand all that, and I don't blame you. I'm just obligated to let you know that it was technically wrong to do it."

"Aye-aye, sir. Is that all?"

"That is all."

It didn't seem like the words came from his heart. It was like someone had told him to counsel me about it, and he reluctantly obeyed. Obviously, it was the battalion CO. If it happened again the next day, I wouldn't change a thing. Mrs. Fegal even called the battery office to thank me again.

• • •

Back in the desert there seemed to be something new every day if only the time was taken to see it. A tarantula large enough for a zoo to be proud of, a flowering cactus, a dirty sidewinder making tracks in the sand, scorpions, turtles, dust storms, thunderstorms, or snow could break up the monotony.

Once, as I was orienting the aiming circle to lay the howitzers in position, I reached for a rock. The "rock-drop method" was a field substitute for a plumb bob. This time when I reached, the desert floor was covered with hailstones and more were still clattering on my helmet. I chose to be the only known lieutenant to orient his aiming circle with the "hailstone-drop method."

Several days into the FIREX, it was time for me to make a command decision.

"Gun Two, out of action."

"What's wrong, Gun Two?"

"Sir, it's the recoil again."

"Is it doing anything different?"

"No, sir, it's the same excessive recoil, but we have a different gun doc, and he's called us out of action."

"I'll be right down.

It was probably a good call for a first-time observer. The young gun doc saw a possible safety hazard and made an on-the-spot assessment. We had known about the excessive recoil in a previous shoot and had other gun docs and the battalion gunner look at it. They determined that it did not create a safety hazard, and I accepted their professional opinion. I also understood that there could be conflicting opinions.

As I walked under the net, Corporal Munoz' body language was already bad. He had apparently already had words with the section chief. I knew the Marines wanted to shoot.

"What's going on?"

"This gun is out of action for excessive recoil."

"I'll make that determination. As our artillery mechanic, you advise and I'll make the decision after hearing all the facts." I turned to the sergeant and asked, "What's it doing, Sergeant?"

"Sir, it's doing the same thing it's been doing."

"It's not any worse?"

"No, sir."

"Do you feel like it's safe to fire?"

"Yes, sir."

"Gun Two, you're back in action."

"No, sir, I've already called it out of action." The gun doc was getting a little disrespectful.

I liked him, so I asked him to step out from under the net if he wanted to discuss it further. If he crossed the line one on one, I could chalk it up to him being passionate, hot, and tired in the desert. If he crossed that line in front of the other Marines, I would have to deal with it more harshly—possibly a charge sheet.

We stepped about 50 feet from the edge of the gun's camouflaged netting. I knew he was upset, but I misjudged how upset. "Alright, now, Doc, explain your assessment again."

He went on a little tirade. He had some valid points and made a good case for taking the gun out of action. It's a good thing we took it away from Gun 2, because he was measurably disrespectful.

There were eyes and ears on the other side of the cammie netting, but I got what I asked for—his opinion. We were face to face in the hot Mojave sun. I responded in a low tone, partially to diffuse the situation, and partly because of the spectators.

"Are you finished? (Pause.) I asked, are you finished?"

He nodded.

"I've stood here and listened to you run off at the mouth, now it's your turn to listen."

The memories of the technical side of my discussions with the gunner and other gun doc were coming to me, and I was going to explain my rationale. I knew he wouldn't like it, but I thought it was the right thing to do.

As I began to speak, he began to roll his eyes up in his head like a child trying not to pay attention. That pushed my last button. I backhanded him across the front of his flak jacket. It made a loud pop . . . and a lasting impression.

"Look at me when I'm talking to you."

"Don't touch me! Don't ever touch me!" he screamed for the entire world to hear.

Now I really spoke under my breath and in his face. Up to this point I still thought I could reason with him.

"You know I didn't hit you. If I hit you, you wouldn't be standing right now. I just wanted to get your attention, but if you want to put on a show, we're done here."

By this time, Gun 2's Marines had cleared the net and stepped in to make sure it didn't get out of hand.

"Y'all go back to work. There's nothing going on here. Gun Two, you're back in action."

Before Cpl. Munoz calmed down, he spoke to the battery 1st sergeant about charging me with assault. I laughed out loud.

"He wouldn't know assault if it slapped him in the face."

"Sir, don't take this lightly. It could be serious."

"I don't expect to hear any more about it. There was nothing to it. I popped him on his flak jacket to get his attention. He was out of control. If he weren't a good Marine, I'd be writing *him* up."

"Sir, I'm going to try and settle this if you can just not say things like that."

"I don't think there's anything to handle, but I do appreciate your effort and concern anyway."

That was the last I heard of it, except for the Marines on Gun 2 asking me if they needed to testify on my behalf. They were a loyal bunch. I really appreciated their support.

● ● ●

I'll never forget one of my last trips to 29 Palms as a lieutenant in a firing battery. By that time I was working for Captain Cliff Simmons, Hotel Battery's fourth battery commander since I had arrived. I had been to the desert in nearly every billet in the battery and knew most of 29 Palms like the back of my hand. I always had success there, so there should have been no reason this trip would be any different.

As we planned our trip, the battery motor transportation chief and I discussed our shortage of drivers. Two new drivers had arrived that week from school, but he wasn't prepared to put them behind the wheel yet in the desert. I understood his concern, but we were running out of options.

"Sir, you know they can't drive a gun truck or an ammo truck. And these jeeps are held together on a prayer, so I can't put them out there driving the officers either."

"Why not? I'll take one of the greenhorns."

"No thanks, sir. That would be a disaster."

"I resent that. I can break one in."

"No, sir. I'll come up with something."

He left, knowing there wasn't a better solution. I guess the pressures of a new Marine just entering the fleet are enough without having him drive an officer. Most officers pick the best drivers anyway when they can. So we are used to drivers with experience, a little extra G-2, and initiative.

"Well, did you find me a driver?"

"No, sir."

"Come on, give me one of the new guys. How bad could it be? I've must have been there a hundred times. I can help break him in. Besides, what's your other option?"

"Okay, sir. You asked for it; plus, you're right. It's just about the only option we have."

PFC Jones was obviously uptight. I tried to get him to relax, with no luck. He was hard to communicate with. Either he couldn't hear me, couldn't understand my southern accent, or just couldn't understand, period. Whichever it was, I somehow knew I was about to regret this.

His poor communication skills and lack of initiative made for a frustrating first week. One dark night we approached a fork in the dirt road. The desert roads weren't much more than tire tracks in the sand, but they were visible to me, and he was the only one of us wearing night vision goggles.

"Turn right."

"Turn RIGHT?"

"TURN RIGHT!"

Bump. He totally missed the turn and drove into the virgin desert sand. Then he panicked and over compensated, effectively doing a donut in plain sight of the second vehicle in the convoy. They must have thought we were nuts. We righted ourselves and proceeded with little problem.

As fate would have it, the next move after dark was a long one. We had to go from one side of 29 Palms to the other. At night, in a convoy, it could take a while. Then I received my poorest route brief since entering the Marine Corps. The recipe for disaster was just about complete.

"Just fall in behind Golf Battery, and when we see you, we'll guide you into position."

What? That's not a brief. But if it's going to be that simple, I guess we'll manage.

"Where's our night vision goggles? They were right here between the seats."

"I don't know, sir. I guess the gunny has them."

"Forget it. I can see well enough."

One more ingredient in the recipe for disaster.

Golf Battery passed our staging position like a bat out of hell. By the time I got my convoy on the road, they were nowhere in sight. They had blackout lights on, but we couldn't see them through the dust at night. When the dust settled, we could barely even see the road. Then we got lucky. I spotted a vehicle. I drove up to it. It was the battalion commander for 2/11.

"Sir, I'm trying to get to this grid from here. Can you help me?"

"No problem. We're just here trying to figure out this new GPS system. It doesn't work, because it says we're *here*, but we're actually *here*. If you just take this road, it'll take you where you are going."

"Thank you, sir. Our radios can't pick up anyone from this position, so this really helps."

How was I supposed to know that the new-fangled GPS actually *did* work, and the Lt. Col. was wrong? We all found out soon enough as I led the battery into a box canyon. Turning around in the dark was an adventure in itself.

It was so dark on the way out of the canyon that I had to lead the convoy on foot. The motor-T chief walked with me. It was going to be a long night.

Wham! The next thing I knew I was on the hood of an out-of-control jeep. When the driver came to a stop, I rolled towards him and started yelling. "What in the hell are you doing?"

"I'm sorry, sir. I fell asleep."

When he did, he leaned forward on the accelerator. I was lucky I only got a broken watch out of the ordeal.

"And what are you laughing at?"

The jeep had barely missed the motor-T chief. After having advised me not to use the new driver, he was in the "I told you so" mode. I was trying not to give him the satisfaction for the moment.

"You have to admit that was funny."

"I don't have to admit anything right now except that I was run over by my own driver and I am pissed off."

I could feel him smiling in the darkness. I was so relieved that I wasn't really hurt that I had to smile too. The driver, on the other hand, was going to have to go. I didn't want to fire him, since he had been assigned to the fleet, so I gave it a few days separation then couched it as a training issue.

"You've spent enough time learning how to drive a jeep in the desert. Now you need to get behind the wheel of a five-ton truck."

By then one of the ammo trucks had been converted to a trash truck, so we swapped drivers.

Eventually, my last CAX at 29 Palms was over, at least for my active duty years. It was time to get back to garrison.

• • •

Deciding to leave active duty was an easy decision. Lee and I wanted a more stable environment than the Marine Corps could offer. We would complete my initial obligation and move back home to raise our family.

These had been good years. We had made some great friends for life. We worked hard, yet we were able to enjoy some special quality time as a family. Thanksgivings and Christmases away from our extended families in the Mid-South were unusually special times to grow closer to each other while missing the others. But we still wanted the children to know their grandparents and cousins and aunts and uncles better.

We loved the Marine Corps and our Marine Corps family, too. The reserve component would be a way to stay plugged into the Marine Corps family while returning to our roots.

At the time we were looking to leave, there were some outstanding officers who wanted to stay on active duty but who couldn't. Most Marine lieutenants enter full-time service on a reserve commission. It requires a formal request and approval of an augmentation board for a reserve officer to become a regular officer.

Augmentation rates fluctuate from time to time, and they had dropped dramatically in the 1980s. Only a handful of applicants were being augmented. It was not unusual to see only one lieutenant selected in a battalion. A dozen or so in the same battalion would be left bewildered. Some of the finest officers you'd ever want to meet were being forced out.

If anyone was selected, they had the option to decline, but the slot would not be offered to anyone else—effectively wasting a slot. Those who declined were not treated well, under the circumstances. On the other hand, those who applied but failed were encouraged not to give up.

My battery and battalion commander did everything but order me to put in an augmentation request. It was an ego boost like a recruiter's pitch. It's a good thing that Lee and I had discussed it in detail and our decision was so clear, or I may have succumbed to the onslaught.

My battalion XO had me come to his office for a personal interview. I was grateful that he cared.

"John, why don't you just put in a package and see what happens? I think you have a real chance at getting augmented."

"Thank you, sir, but it's not the competition. It's just that Lee and I have made up our minds to move on. Since we've come on active duty, we've had two children, and we want to plant some roots and raise the kids back home."

"The Marine Corps has a lot for families. It can be a great place to raise children. They'll do and see things they'd never have a chance to otherwise. They—"

"Sir, you don't have to sell me on the Marine Corps. I love it. But we've been at Camp Pendleton for two years now, and I've been in the field here and Twenty-nine Palms about half of that. A year in Okinawa is a sure bet when I leave here, which is another year away from home. That's a lot of time in a three-year stretch."

"If duty station is the issue, we may be able to work with you, or have you thought about an accompanied tour?"

"I really appreciate the thought, sir, but we discussed all the options before we made our decision. The Marine Corps just can't offer us what we're looking for."

The discussion continued for a while. I did a lot more listening, just to be respectful, but his words were falling on deaf ears.

"John, why not at least put in a package? You can always turn it down."

"Yes, sir, then the pressure really heats up, and if I turn it down, I'll be resented by those who didn't make the cut but would have loved to stay. Let somebody who really wants it have that slot."

"John, sometimes you need to look out for number one."

"Thank you, sir, but Lee and I are one hundred percent sure that we want out at the end of my tour." I don't feel like I dropped my pack, but it was a good feeling not to be in limbo. There was no turning back.

As our time came to an unceremonious conclusion, the required out-briefings with both the battalion and regimental commanders were left to attend. Among the lieutenants we would joke about what we would tell them on our way out. Serious, open-minded, and prepared to be candid, I reported as ordered.

If they were just going through the motions, it wouldn't matter anyway, but if they were sincere, some good might come from a brief meeting.

The first stop was the regimental commander. After a few pleasantries, he opened up the conversation to solicit some feedback.

"Lieutenant Caldwell, I have the out briefs to hear from you. I'd like to hear some of your observations from your time here. It can be something good or bad or somewhere between. Does anything come to mind that you'd like to share?"

"Yes, sir, now that you mention it. We like to brag that we take care of our Marines, but we don't back it up very well."

"Do you have any examples of what you mean by that?"

"As a matter of fact, sir, I have an excellent recent example. I have a staff sergeant who works for me. He has several meritorious promotions under his belt and is a superb staff NCO. He was told recently that he would fill the battalion's lone quota to Staff NCO Academy.

"That was fine until his circumstances drastically changed. There was already some stress in his marriage. His father-in-law died. The wife had to leave to help her family with arrangements that included keeping a family business afloat for an undetermined amount of time. To top it all off, Base Housing decided that because she wasn't living with him at the time, he would have to move off base before he left for Staff NCO Academy. I went to bat for him at the housing office, but you know how they are, sir. I even took it all the way to my battalion commander.

"I asked that if we couldn't work out a deal with the housing office, then could we have someone else fill the school quota and my staff sergeant could go at a later date. There were no takers. The next option I proposed was to let the school quota go unfilled. That was considered unacceptable, so we made him go under duress.

"He had planned to re-enlist soon, but we lost him. We didn't miss that all-important school quota, yet it cost us a fine staff sergeant who was about to re-enlist. Frankly, we put the school quota ahead of our Marine."

"Those school quotas are hard to come by, Lieutenant Caldwell. I can certainly understand why the battalion commander set such a high priority on filling it."

He had just reinforced my original premise. He rattled on about the importance of school quotas and passing inspections and never once mentioned the staff sergeant. He saw it as a numbers-management issue. I saw it as a leadership issue.

"Anything else?"

He opened the door, and I walked in.

"Yes, sir, one more thing. The medical care we provide to our dependents is substandard. We are not keeping a basic promise to our Marines and their families."

"I'd really like to hear this, because the CO of the base hospital is a good friend of mine."

I should have quit at that moment. After all, I was just a lieutenant on my way out the door. What did I know compared to a full bird colonel and his friend in charge of the debacles?

Several infamous examples were rattled off. Time wouldn't have allowed a complete accounting. From the poor bedside manner we received on multiple occasions to the way they herded pregnant women like cattle, I tried to squeeze a lot in without taking a breath.

I brought up specific examples, like when the base hospital sent us home with my 10-month old son's fever still over 103° F because they could not find anything wrong with him. He'd had some fever for days, and it had been that high for hours. We were so upset on the drive home that we diverted to a civilian hospital, which almost instantly identified a serious infection, treated him, and sent us home when his temperature dropped to normal.

By the time I was through listing examples, I expected a little bit of an empathetic response. But he basically looked through me like I wasn't there and hadn't heard a word I said. I knew then that I was through wasting my time.

"Thank you for your time, sir."

"Best of luck, Lieutenant Caldwell."

That little session was blessed assurance that our decision to leave was the right one. I'm sure he never gave it an ounce of thought after that. At least it was painless, and it was a good warm-up before meeting with my battalion commander, Lt. Col. Canario.

He was one of my least favorite officers, definitely my least favorite artillery officer.

"Lieutenant Caldwell, I always want to meet with those who are leaving. I'm curious about your decision to get out."

"No offense, sir, but I don't have any desire to stay in to become a field grade officer."

I knew that would pull his chain, but it was basically true, and I figured the entertainment value was about all I was going to get out of this.

"That concerns me since I am one. Would you care to explain?"

"Sir, right now I'm friends with nearly everyone I've ever met in the Corps. I've got no regrets. We all know that to keep from getting promoted to 1st lieutenant, we'd have to shoot the Pope on Easter Sunday. Captain is almost automatic. Beyond that I see field grade officers choosing sides, backstabbing, and jockeying for promotion. I don't want to be a part of any of that."

"It doesn't have to be that way, Lieutenant Caldwell."

"No, sir, it doesn't, but we both know that to a large degree it is. I'm ready to leave with a clean slate, good memories, and good friends."

He didn't ask me any more open-ended questions. We exchanged a few pleasantries, and that conversation was over.

In my last months at Camp Pendleton, there was a growing concern at the general officer's ranks about the culture of the Corps that promoted alcohol consumption. Considering the Marine Corps was born in a tavern in 1775, it's no wonder. Also, it's a warrior culture of extremes, and many naturally turn to alcohol without considering the consequences.

Shortly after the commandant's White Letter on alcohol at command-sponsored social events, our battalion had a beach party. The letter had stated plainly that any official function that served alcohol must serve an alternative as well. Upon arriving at San Onofre Beach, I asked about the new policy.

"Hey, I thought there had to be an alternative if we served alcohol."

"If you don't want a beer, eat a hot dog. There's your alternative."

I think something got lost in translation, but it was the beginning of a significant shift. Those Marines who didn't drink were a little less persecuted. At times I choose to be one of those. Social drinking is still a deep-rooted cultural element alive and well within today's Marine Corps; however, those who repeatedly abuse alcohol now are likely to be more of an outcast.

Somewhere between training Marines and living in the desert for weeks at a time, standing duty, extended hours of equipment maintenance, and endless inspection preparations, I needed family time. I wanted family time. My daughter was reaching milestones of walking, talking, and discovering the world around her. JC was 17 months behind her and changing every day. Soon, he was walking and talking too.

In the midst of it all, a serial killer identified by the press and police as The Night Stalker was leaving a trail of terror in Los Angeles, just a short drive north of our home. The Night Stalker crimes and clues led with a fever-pitched obsession on the local radio and television newscasts as well as print headlines.

Because of our close proximity to the crimes, and typical fears of the unknown, our friends, neighbors, and we would take extra precautions. One night during the height of the local fears, Lee was roused by a noise downstairs. She quickly woke me with a fright.

"John, I heard something downstairs."

"Well, Bogey didn't bark, so it was probably nothing."

I just wanted to roll over and get some sleep.

"The Night Stalker is still on the loose. You need to go down there and check it out."

"Well, if it's him, you go. He may rape you, but he'll kill me."

For some reason she didn't appreciate such morbid humor in the middle of the night, so the dog and I went downstairs. All was well.

• • •

San Diego Zoo membership offered our family a place to escape the stresses of military life. We came and went as we pleased. We could take short trips without worrying about "getting our money's worth" on a particular day or feeling pressure to experience it all each trip.

The children loved it, and we did too. We could enjoy each other without the Marine Corps interrupting us. It was a carefree time spent watching

Jennifer playfully chase the colorful roosters that wandered freely in the park. Even with all the exotic animals around, she seemed to like domestic roosters best. JC spent most of his time in a stroller, watching Jennifer.

Without notice I was dive-bombed by one of the exotic birds. It was a big bird with a sizeable payload. There was nothing exotic about trying to get smeared and smelly fowl feces cleaned off my chest, shoulders, head, and back. Ultimately, we had to leave. While it wasn't a pleasant memory for me, the rest of the family remembers it with a smile and a laugh, especially, Lee.

The Southern California lifestyle was not for us, but it was fun while it lasted. We could camp in the mountains around Julian one day and be back on the beach the next. The cities of Los Angeles and San Diego offered more than we could do. However, we were there living with young children and working—not vacationing—so we didn't experience as much as one might expect. When our tour of duty ended, we took the long way home.

"Battery Adjust. Aiming point this instrument."

Life in the battery is good.

*"But, beloved, we are persuaded better things
of you, and things that accompany salvation,
though we thus speak."*

Hebrews 6:9

...5

Conflicts of Job, Family, and Corps

Leaving active duty may have been the right decision for us, but it didn't make life any easier. Neither Lee nor I had a job lined up. Professionally, we were starting over, and the hope and plan was to allow Lee to stay home with Jennifer and JC.

It was hard to hunt for a job while working in the fleet, but that task was made more difficult because we limited our search to the Southeastern United States. We were leaving the Marine Corps to be closer to home and family. It didn't make any sense to look anywhere else. At least, a couple of months of terminal leave would provide some income during our transition.

Lee and I, Jennifer and JC moved in with Momma and Daddy in my boyhood home as a temporary fix. Jennifer was almost four and JC was two years old. The house was a little crowded with the four of us, our dog, plus my parents. It's hard to imagine my parents raising their nine children there.

We must have seemed like an invasion to them, but they never showed it. They made us feel welcomed and loved.

On the other hand, I was still their son, and Lee and I were subject to more advice than we had bargained for. It was almost like a regression because Momma started treating us like her children rather than like adults. We knew we had to make this as short of a stay as possible so we would keep fond memories. We did.

During the day, I hunted for a job, and Lee and the kids hunted for a house. In addition to the practical side of it, we felt like less of a bother to my parents that way.

Stress, humility, frustration, and plain old misery were everywhere. After being treated with respect as a Marine Corps officer, and being responsible for so much in the Corps, I was an unemployed nobody as a civilian. At least that's the way I was treated as I went from place to place.

Sometimes, I think the interviewers were just anti-military liberals who wanted a free shot at me because I was a Marine. Other times, it was a rude or even hateful receptionist who tested me. Some of them had to be glad I didn't become their boss, or they would be the next one unemployed.

Once, I even thought about working for the government. I stopped at the Defense Depot, a huge complex of Defense Department warehouses, in Memphis. I must have driven by it a thousand times as a teenager without even thinking about it.

The main office building was old but well kept. I entered, not knowing what to expect. There was someone behind a glass window.

"Excuse me, could you help me? I'm trying to see what to do about applying for a job here."

"Nineta 'leb'n, Tudeez-uh-Windeez."

"Sir?"

"Nineta 'leb'n, Tudeez-uh-Windeez ."

"Is this the right place?"

"Nineta 'leb'n, Tudeez-uh-Windeez ."

He never looked up or turned his head. I could roughly decipher that he meant, "Nine to eleven o'clock on Tuesdays and Wednesdays," but I needed more, and it was 11 on the dot on a Wednesday.

"It's just now eleven o'clock."

"Nineta 'leb'n, Tudeez-uh-Windeez ."

"Can I get an application I can take with me?"

"Nineta 'leb'n, Tudeez-uh-Windeez ."

I was just about to go through his glass and choke him out when I took a deep breath and looked around. This would be the last time I walked in there. I knew he was a federal employee with civil service protection, and I wouldn't fit into that environment.

Where would I fit in? My education was in graphic arts and marketing. My experience was in leading Marines. It seemed as if each of the jobs I found interesting demanded the opposite. Most wanted experience in graphic arts, giving little credit for my education. Others wanted formal education in management with no regard for my experience.

Opportunities were out there if I was willing to work just about anywhere in the country except near where we wanted. But the Tennessee-Arkansas-Mississippi region known as the Mid-South was home, and that's where we were determined to replant our roots and raise our family.

Through it all we were looking for a real church home, too. Although we were both Christians from our childhood, Lee and I had our spiritual ups and downs. We had visited a few churches and the Baptist Student Union in college. After that we had tried a few neighborhood churches from Virginia to Oklahoma and California, along with some base chapels.

We had experienced a variety of Baptist churches, other denominations, and non-denominational congregations. Our biblical understanding of what a church is and should be was tied to our past. We had finally learned that no church was or would be perfect. That was somewhat of a relief and took the pressure off as we followed our hearts, searching for a more permanent church home.

We settled on First Baptist Church in Nesbit. We had already visited several churches when a clown came by our house to invite the children to Vacation Bible School. The clown was our neighbor from across the street, Lynn Ford. It was the beginning of a dear friendship and a new extended family.

•••

In an effort to stay connected with the familiar, I gave the local Marine reserves a call. I knew that someday I wanted to join my old Marine reserve unit. The captain was conversational and initially glad that I had called until I told him I needed to get a job and a house before I joined.

"We're leaving for Twenty-nine Palms for AT this summer. You really need to make that trip, or you might as well not join here."

"Well, I just called to check in. I've got to find a job and a house, so I doubt I'll be on board for a trip to Twenty-nine Palms. You have a good trip."

He was not a reservist and obviously had no clue. My priority had to be establishing myself in a new career and finding a place for my family to live. I couldn't commit to taking two weeks off almost immediately to participate in annual training.

I already had enough active duty points for this to count as a good year for retirement, and there was plenty of time to worry about next year. Besides, I had spent more time in desert training at 29 Palms than he ever had. It was the last place in the world I needed or wanted to go.

Enough of the grunt mentality. I would call the closest artillery unit. That would mean several hours of driving, but I thought I'd test the waters.

The reception was nearly the same. The regular Marines must have been to the same hard-sell course. That captain told me that the billets could fill up before I decided to join, and if I didn't join soon, it would hurt my chances of being able to join at a later date.

Nearly turned off on the reserves all together, I also knew those two guys would transfer soon without remembering my name. Their successors would be more receptive when I called later.

Billet availability was the last thing I worried about as a lieutenant, although it would become more of an issue down the road as a field grade officer.

If I wanted to enter the civilian career field of my degree, Graphic Design, I would need to accept a huge pay cut. Looking at starting pay in my field didn't seem so bad when I was 19 years old and single. Now I was starting with no applicable experience at 26 years old, married, with two children. It was enough to make me investigate several other career options.

Since getting out, there was only one day that I ever seriously questioned my decision to leave the Marine Corps. After a hot, tiring, lonely day spent searching unsuccessfully for a job, I realized I had no prospects in sight. Had I done the right thing? I called my old friend Eric, who was still finishing his initial active duty commitment.

Within minutes of asking him how it was going back at Camp Pendleton, I knew I had made the right decision. His recollections of his last few days were enough to make anyone want to be as far away from that as possible. He was cleaning up someone else's failed inspection and working overnighters to do it. I hated that his last months there were going so poorly, but it was great reassurance to me nonetheless. The fleeting thought that I had made a mistake getting out never seriously crossed my mind again.

As I looked for work, Lee was looking for a house. When we had a chance to go together, it was obvious there wasn't much available in our price range.

By now I was about ready to live anywhere.

"Hey, Lee, do you see that shack?"

"Yeah."

"I could live there."

"There's no glass in the windows, and there's probably no floor. You can see through the walls to the other side of the house."

"I know, but we could fix it up well enough to get by for a while. I am sick and tired of looking, and I don't want to live with my parents for long."

"Me, neither, but I'm not moving into a shack."

"Well, you better find us something quickly."

Sadly, she knew I was a little too serious about accepting a shack, so she looked even harder.

Realtor after realtor discouraged Lee and told her what she was looking for did not exist. She proved them wrong when she found a small, nearly new, brick home on a 1.5-acre lot couched in 50 acres of soybeans and hay. It was even in our price range: under $50,000.

I accepted an entry-level job as a graphic artist at Riverside Press, a family-owned printing company in downtown Memphis. They were fine people, and I got some good experience there, but the pay was meager at $8 per hour.

It was a stark contrast to my time in the Corps. Instead of beer calls and coarse language in all-male surroundings, we had a weekly devotional on company time, and the ladies I worked beside talked about church and things of God.

The print shop was downtown in a dilapidated, single-story structure in the shadows of old skyscrapers. The building and our equipment were aged and worn. It was almost like learning and living the history of the commercial printing business from the ground up. Our '50s-vintage dictionary didn't even have the word "astronaut" in it.

I began as a simple paste-up artist. Soon, I was setting type, writing, editing, and doing a little creative artwork. Then I began stripping and plate-making to complete the pre-press cycle. Next, I was finishing by running cutters, collators, binders, etc. The only thing I didn't do was run a printing press, but the operators schooled me on their limitations. Some limits were just the nature of the type of press, but others were due to age, slack, and disrepair of the press.

When the owners started asking people if they wanted to take Fridays off, I knew I had to find something fast. They were apparently having trouble meeting their payroll. Lee and I could barely make ends meet on the pay from a 40-hour workweek. I couldn't afford to take Fridays off.

Reserve pay was getting more attractive. With weekends off, and flexibility on Fridays, it was the perfect time to give it a try.

Lee had found us a house and home, and we were settling in nicely. A worn, red-clay and gravel driveway curved slightly as it meandered about 300 feet up to the carport of a 1,200-square-foot, FHA "ranch-style" home. The yard was all weeds, but it was our yard. They were flowering weeds and prettier at times when they weren't cut. The trees in the yard were small enough to transplant to more preferable locations. So we moved them and began endless yard work with great satisfaction.

We had lived a lot of places in the previous four years, from campus housing and apartments to base housing. Now we were buying our first home as a young family. It was a great feeling. The first thing I added to our nearly perfect home was a concrete patio with a basketball hoop. My brothers and I had enjoyed basketball in our driveway while growing up, and I wanted our children to have one now.

The interior of the house was plain. We kept it that way. It had to be child- and pet-friendly for the foreseeable future. It's not that we didn't decorate; it just wasn't fancy.

The house and lot were a great find in the fastest-growing county in the mid-south and one of the fastest-growing counties in the country. It was nearly the only thing available in our price range that wasn't crammed into small-lot subdivisions.

But the satisfaction with the house and yard took a back seat to the country neighborhood and neighbors. Immediately, they befriended us and made us feel at home. It wasn't long before we considered our new neighbors as part of our ever-increasing extended family.

A monthly Neighborhood Watch meeting helped everyone keep in touch with each other. It was more of an excuse to get together and compare fishing holes and the like rather than to talk about the possibility of crime.

There was also the annual Neighborhood Watch picnic. It was there that I realized that national stereotypes of Mississippi were wrong. It was the healthiest racial harmony I had ever witnessed, including my time in the Marine Corps. About half my neighbors were black and half were white. There was genuine love and concern for one another, and we were blessed to be a part of it.

For once, we could relax and enjoy ourselves without concerns over rank structure. This civilian life was going to be all right. Why would I want to interrupt my civilian paradise with a commitment to the Marine Corps reserves?

Answering that question is best understood by first realizing that I had never totally left the Marine Corps. My calling as a Marine was still just as real as the first day I had answered it.

The Corps had been a place I could work through some inner conflicts about who I am and what I should do. It dealt uniquely with a personal restlessness that is hard to explain. Sure, I loved the civilian life I was now reacquainted with, but I also had a keen understanding of what made that civilian freedom possible. Part of it came with upbringing, part must have been hammered into me as a Marine, but mostly, I just knew.

There was a deep feeling that if I continued to put on the uniform, my children and maybe someone else's child would not have to.

• • •

Nesbit, Mississippi, fit us like a glove. As the sun rose at our new home, we could hear mourning doves cooing and bobwhite quail sounding off (Sadly, due to habitat changes, invasive fire ants and other predators the quail are gone from here). The soft, early light sparkled on heavy dew that had drenched the grass and flowering weeds that accented the landscape.

We had begun raising an assortment of chickens and turkeys. The hope was that they would keep the tick population down. Other than the convenience of always having eggs when we needed them, the yard birds weren't of any real monetary value. But they were great for the kids to learn about animal care and responsibility and the quintessential element to country-life atmospherics.

Chicken coups of any size need cleaning and defending. Chicken snakes, stray dogs, raccoons, and coyotes were recurring pests.

One morning Lee summoned me from the shower, telling me that the coyotes were back. I sprang into action. With only a borrowed shotgun and a pink towel wrapped around me, I stepped out into the middle of my back yard and scanned the area for a coyote. I got a quick glimpse, but he was well out of range and on the run. As I turned toward the house, still dripping from the quick shower exit, the daily Amtrak train passed on its way from Chicago to New Orleans. I could almost hear the passengers: "Honey, look out the window, we must be in Mississippi." All I could do was smile and wave.

Life was good, but there was still something inside that pushed me out of my comfort zone. Extra money on the weekends could have been earned any number of ways, but I missed the Marine Corps. Marines are family, for better or worse.

There were no regrets about our decision to leave, but there was always the thought of continuing my service with the reserves. It was time.

• • •

It was a little strange approaching the drill center. It still looked the same as when I had arrived as a lance corporal about seven years earlier. This time I was arriving as an officer. It was a good feeling to see and speak to Marines again.

It seemed like one thing that hadn't changed very much since I was a lance corporal was the repeated cleaning of rifles. There was never enough. It was the consummate time filler for a poor training plan—or a seemingly perfect cover for a lack of creative leadership.

No one could argue the need for it, because we never even met the minimums of the Marine Corps order. That required cleaning our weapons three consecutive days after firing. When weapons are fired Friday night, Saturday, and Sunday morning, it's impossible to comply when drill also ends on Sundays. However, there is a point of absurdity, and we not only reached it, but we well exceeded it.

In typical fashion, some Marines worked extremely hard to finish the task at hand on a Sunday afternoon in hopes of enhancing their chances of an earlier departure. Others more accustomed to the current unit's history slowly did the minimum, sure that no amount of effort would accelerate the final formation and departure.

The latter was the attitude I had seen in the reserves as an enlisted Marine; it was an attitude I wanted to break. I encouraged them all that I could. I had the NCOs take a more active role in the process, and I personally inspected their efforts as they worked. We started to send Marines to the armory to turn in their weapons.

The armorer rejected every weapon, one at a time. It began to create a huge line and discouraged those who had gotten their weapons ready early. The platoon sergeant and I went to the armory to see what was causing weapons that we passed to fail.

The armorer was going over each weapon with a fine-tooth comb. If he couldn't find carbon with his Q-tips or pipe cleaners, he would punch the bore with a dirty bore brush. Then he would follow that with a bore patch. The slightest hint of anything would cause him to reject it.

In response to our disapproval, the armorer explained that the rifles had to be spotless or he could not accept them. He had his orders from his boss. The active-duty armorer did not directly work for us; he worked for Captain McGill. Therefore, we took our protests to him. He would not listen.

Apparently, he had planned this in advance. He was ready for us and didn't even go down to the armory to see if our complaint was valid. I tried to explain to him that we had already inspected them, and while not perfect, they were more than adequate for a first cleaning after shooting blanks in them for two days.

Appeals to our company commander, Captain Williams, were better received, but the issue was not resolved. He was more laid back than just about anybody I knew and wanted to be supportive of the I&I (inspector and instructor). He had us try harder to meet the standard that was set.

The problem was that the standards changed as we met them. It became increasingly difficult to get a weapon into the armory as the evening wore on. Again, I think this was a deliberate power play by the I&I, with no regard for the Marines' morale or even safety.

Marines had already been deprived of adequate sleep while we trained late both Friday and Saturday nights. Now we were keeping them late on Sunday afternoon. A number of Marines had a drive of several hours to reach home and had early morning shifts at their civilian jobs. Conversely, the I&I and the active-duty Marines always took the Monday after drill off and, many times, the following Friday.

Tensions and near mutinous feelings grew with each passing hour. Harsh words were being exchanged all around the drill center between growing numbers of Marines—active and reserve. As it passed 2030, even Captain Williams had a few choice words with Captain McGill.

As 2100 approached, the discussion shifted to whether we would be paid for another day if we worked past midnight. The answer was "yes," but we still knew we had to be out of there in few hours.

Sometime around 2200, the commanding officer took the position that the other platoon commanders and I had encouraged him to take several hours earlier. He told the I&I that we were either stacking arms in the gym for them to pick up, or they could take them as they were into the armory.

They reluctantly took them, but they were still slow about it. By the time we held final formation, I had exfiltrated about half of my platoon. We left by 2300, well beyond what is reasonably required of most reservists on a typical weekend.

It was the Sunday drill from hell. It was bad enough that too many of our drill weekends went to 1900 or 2000. This one sucked any remaining life out of our incentive efforts, and motivation totally bottomed out. More significantly, a wedge had now been driven between *us* and *them* (reservists and regulars) that would not be repaired for years to come. Some Marines never got over it.

Marines already came up with a million excuses why they couldn't or shouldn't come to drill. Private First Class Minter was one who would try anything. The fact that he was still a private when most of his counterparts were corporals told its own story. The weekend we had a MORDT-and-go was one excuse to remember. The surprise mobilization operational readiness deployment test included a flight to Camp Lejeune, North Carolina, for a full weekend of training. That was the "and-go" portion.

PFC Minter, surprisingly, showed up on time. We had a high enough percentage of attendance to pass, and it looked like our paperwork was going to be adequate. It was just a matter of flying to Camp Lejeune for a weekend of training and evaluation in the field. That would be the easy part for us, but PFC Minter had other plans.

"Sir, PFC Minter wants to speak with you. It's an urgent personal matter."

"Very well, send him in."

"Sir, I can't go. My brother has been in a bad car accident, and I have to leave right now."

I can't say that I'm a mind reader, but something just didn't seem right. Of course this source was always questionable, but if it were true, I wasn't about to stand in his way.

"How bad is it?"

"I don't know yet. All I know is that it's bad."

"Do you have a car, or do we need to drive you?"

"I have my car here."

"What hospital are you going to?"

"I don't know where they've taken him."

"Well, let's call some family or friends who will know where he is. I'd hate to have you go on a wild goose chase, trying to find the hospital."

"Everybody has already left home to go to the hospital, so I can't call."

"Then let's call the hospitals. Where was the wreck?"

"I don't know that either."

"Well, if it was a bad one, they'd take him to The Med. It's the regional trauma center. We can start there. Staff Sergeant Broadnax, take PFC Minter to a phone and start calling hospitals. I'll call the city police, the county sheriff, and the state police of Arkansas, Mississippi, and Tennessee to check on recent accidents with injuries. They'll know where they've taken the injured."

It didn't take long to find out there had not been any recent wrecks or injuries of the sort. A few hospital calls later, PFC Minter was still not ready to give up.

"I can't believe you won't let me go, and my brother might be dying."

"I'll be glad to let you go, but I'd hate to see you waste critical time. The best place for you to be is with us in case your family calls. I'm sure they know you're at drill. We'll keep calling hospitals as long as it takes."

"I can't believe you would hold me here like this with my brother in the hospital."

The gig was up, and he knew it. But he would never admit to telling a lie as bold as that one. He was convincing, but it wasn't his first.

Getting a confession wasn't important to me. He got on the plane, and we never heard another word about it. He was usually okay in the field, but he couldn't seem to adjust well in a garrison environment. A lot of Marines are like that, but the ones in the reserves spend so much time "back on the block" that conforming them and keeping them focused is unlikely.

Leading, counseling, teaching, and working with Marines, even the problem Marines, was my favorite part of being an officer. I could see the good in every Marine. There was something inside each of them that made them join, and I don't believe that "something" ever completely dies. Sometimes, though, it gets buried alive, and we have to give them the boot. I have too much respect for the Marine Corps and the good Marines than to let the slackers and malcontents drag everyone else down.

The delicate balance as an officer is to challenge and help the good Marines excel while keeping any problem Marines from reaching the point of no return or infecting the others along the way.

There is no better rank for an officer to lead by example than as a lieutenant and no better billet for that than as a combat arms platoon commander. I enjoyed being an infantry officer, but I missed the artillery community.

I was ready for a change. Besides, I was very close to being promoted to captain, and I was getting a little concerned about my career path in the reserves. I had been out of artillery for just a little while. A battery commander spot was what I wanted and likely what I would have been if I had stayed on active duty.

Reserves were different. Every Marine officer in the reserves had served several years as a regular. A short time after entering the reserves, most lieutenants are promoted to captain. That leaves few if any lieutenants to fill lieutenant billets. Typically, captains and even majors filled those billets, while majors filled most captain billets. I would have to wait for a command opportunity with no guarantees.

There were two possible billets for me. One in Bessemer, Alabama was a few hours further from home than the battery in Jackson, Mississippi. Either way, I was opting out of my convenient thirty-minute drive for multiple hours on the road. Both options would most certainly include an assignment as a fire direction officer (FDO).

Charlie Battery, 1/14, in Jackson seemed to be an immediate perfect fit. I met and liked all the officers. The battery commander was a Presbyterian minister. Sunday drills were typically finished by 1630. That was two to three hours earlier than I was accustomed to. The three-hour drive home would put me home no later than I was getting home with the 30-minute drive from Memphis.

The battery's fire direction center was extremely competent, which reassured me. They reminded me of some exceptional regular Marines in my platoon in California but with southern accents.

I was looking forward to this tour with great anticipation. I was promoted to captain as expected. We were scheduled for a CAX at 29 Palms. By now I was ready to go back to the High Desert, and with all my experience there, I thought I had something extra to offer the Marines of my new battery.

Then things changed. The CO completed his tour and was replaced with a much less competent officer who felt he had something to prove ,but he had less ability to prove it. The XO had a job change and was scheduled to depart shortly before AT, but he committed to stay through the summer. Worst of all, the I&I had changed.

I had learned that the I&I was not only critical to the mission but also linked to my motivation level. The new I&I personified the worst of all possible combinations. He was aloof and arrogant, especially inept, and envisioned himself and his role as that of the battery commander.

The I&I/commanding officer combination was now worse than it had been in Memphis. There was no way I would keep driving three hours each way to put up with that. The only question I had was if I should leave before or after annual training.

AT is when you really get to know each other in the battery. It is important during that time to forge a bond with the Marines that will continue throughout the year and years ahead. It's difficult to do that in only one weekend per month.

Options were limited. To serve with the Marines I would be working with the following year, I had to make a change immediately. That change was the best for me and Golf Company. The best scenario for Charlie Battery would be for me to hang around through AT as their FDO. I was torn.

Making the decision to stay even more difficult, I learned that Company G was going to Okinawa, boarding an LST (landing ship tank), and making an amphibious landing in the Philippines.

That weekend's three-hour trip home late Sunday night cemented my decision to return to the Memphis unit. The previous leadership in Jackson normally had us on the road before dark, even after going on a live-firing exercise. Now we didn't get on the road until after dark even on an uneventful weekend at the drill center. The mindset had changed drastically with the new leadership.

It was the right decision for a lot of reasons, but I still hated leaving such fine Marines with poor officer leadership. On the other hand, I had a new challenge and new Marines who also needed a positive influence.

The regular counterpart to a Marine reserve CO is the I&I. I&Is have command over a small support detachment of active-duty Marines between drills and have day-to-day oversight of the unit's budget and certain between-drill decisions that affect the unit. Both are responsible positions.

In simple and clear terms, commanding officers are in charge. At the company and battalion level in the Marine Corps reserves, reservists fill the commanding officer (CO) billets.

Petty shouting matches on the tarmac between the Memphis I&I and the company commander began the AT period. It was one of the reasons I had left Memphis, and then Jackson, in the first place. The two strong-willed officers held billets that by their very nature forced friction upon any who filled them.

This public display was unprofessional on their part but not a showstopper. It was, however, only the beginning.

To make matters worse, one of the Marines was caught eating apricots on the plane. Our company gunny, Staff Sergeant Rinehart, exploded.

"Get those apricots off my airplane."

"What's the matter, gunny?"

"Apricots are bad luck! Every Marine knows that."

Rinehart was originally a tanker by MOS. Those in the tank community and many in the AAV (amphibious assault vehicle) and even the artillery community are convinced that apricots are bad luck, especially around machinery. This trip would only add to the legion of apricots.

We boarded the C-141 transport plane in Millington, Tennessee. Our infantry company was on its way to Okinawa, Japan, to train with the regular Marines for our two-week AT. Halfway between Hawaii and Okinawa, the pilot informed us of a hydraulic leak that would require us to return to the airfield in Hawaii.

"Apricots!"

We landed without fanfare and the plane was quickly fixed. However, the pilots would exceed their flight limits if they took off again without rest. So they went to a hotel room to get some sleep, and our Marines spread out across the floor of the hangar deck.

The gunny and I located a soft patch of grass that seemed more comfortable than concrete. That is until the USAF security detail surrounded us with weapons drawn.

"Freeze."

"Whoa! We were just looking for a better place to get some sleep."

"You are in a restricted area."

"Sorry, we didn't see any signs out here in the dark. We'll just go back to the hangar if it's alright with you."

After the required amount of sleep, the pilots returned. We re-boarded our plane and headed for Oki. Hopefully, the curse of the apricots would be limited to that single event.

Barracks were available for our one night at Camp Smith. The next day we boarded the USS *San Bernardino*, our LST, and sailed to the Philippines for an amphibious landing. Excitement and anticipation were high.

None of us had our "sea legs." We would need those to adjust to the constant motion of any ship in any condition, but we would soon discover that we weren't on just any ship on just any seas. We were on an amphibious ship with a flat bottom. That feature was great for pulling up to the shore and offloading personnel and heavy equipment, like tanks, but not for the rough waters we were about to encounter.

Skirting a typhoon between Okinawa and the Philippines was not in our plans. Pitching and rolling our way across the Pacific was nauseating. Our ship was tossed around like driftwood. Forget "sea legs;" most of us were having trouble keeping our food down. The ones who didn't lose their chow were having just as much trouble finding a place where they didn't have to walk in somebody else's.

It wasn't until the last minute that the decision was made to continue our planned assault. It would have been a shame if we hadn't been allowed to splash in our AAVs.

The bad weather finally broke. Rain and clouds were still everywhere, but the waves had subsided just enough. The day before our actual landing, the AAVs made a practice run with no infantry inside.

From the aft deck of the lumbering old LST, we anxiously watched and waited for the AAVs to splash. Light-gray clouds and dark-gray water nearly blended with the medium-gray ship's hull. Even the Philippine coastline was hazy and gray. The fresh salty taste and smell of the ocean mixed with the equally familiar smell of burning diesel.

Finally, the first AAV rolled out. It was reassuring to watch as one after another of the heavy steel chassis quickly resurfaced in the wake and maneuvered effortlessly into rehearsal formation. Tomorrow, we'd be crammed inside. In fact, standing there on the deck gives you much more of a sense of excitement than being aboard an AAV when it splashes.

Splashing into the ocean in an AAV was a little anti-climactic. However, when we steered to shore, my perspective changed. Excitement returned. I was able to look out of the commander's hatch as we approached a strange new land in early morning darkness.

With all the clouds, there was no moon and not much ambient light. Morning nautical twilight brightened the water's surface as we made our way to shore. I could just make out the outline of a few of the closest crafts to each side. I couldn't help but think about the Marines like my dad in World War II doing this for real in the Pacific Island campaigns.

Instead of being greeted with incoming artillery and machine gun fire, we were met by Philippine locals selling rice and *lumpia*, the Pacific island's variation of an egg roll. They even had bottles of Coca-Cola for sale. I couldn't believe it when the battalion halted our training for the Marines to make purchases. It was a common goodwill gesture that had become a custom.

Austere living quarters were scattered at random along our trek as we worked our way ashore. Homes were made with ammo crates left behind by or scrounged from previous units. The chickens in the yards reminded me of my home back in Mississippi, but chickens and Coke were about the only familiar items in sight.

I looked up through the monsoon rains dripping from my helmet rim onto steep volcanic islands covered with thick vegetation. There was less dense jungle than I had imagined and more open ground.

The battalion positioned us to the far right flank. That meant a steep climb up a grassy mountain. Oddly, the map indicated marsh on the rugged terrain. It didn't make much sense to me, but it was accurate. As the rain picked back up, we sloshed up to our objective. The training day went quickly. The first night, on the other hand, was slow and miserable.

No sleep was to be had on ground covered in eight inches of water. The misery continued the second day and the rains increased. The typhoon may have passed, but monsoon rains displayed their own fury. The second night, sleep was again not an option, but after staying awake for over 24 hours, we couldn't help but sleep some. We lay in the marshy grass in our cold, wet clothes and boots, our feet and bodies soaked to the skin.

Just as I would pass out from sheer exhaustion, my body would relax. That would send cold shots of water running down new areas that had absorbed what was left of my body heat. Awake again. This up-and-down process went on most of the night.

The next morning our battalion informed us that they would not re-supply us with chow and fresh drinking water. Strange how a Marine Corps infantry battalion couldn't feed its own Marines, but an old lady could walk up those same mountains, barefooted, with lumpia and rice, paper plates, and bottled Cokes in a box on her head.

"How much for a plate of rice and lumpia?

"Wun dallah."

"How much for a Coke?"

"Wun dallah."

"Hey, they were fifty cents at the bottom of the mountain."

"Dey still fiddy cent at duh bottom."

That's true American capitalism and worth every penny.

Our I&I and company commander ended up in a screaming match on top of that mountain. They both lost. Everyone is entitled to lose his or her temper, but preferably not in front of junior Marines. This was the second time, and it was uglier than the first. I had to get between them and remind them that they were being watched.

Eventually, a break in the weather allowed a SAR Bird (search and rescue helicopter) to drop us food and water. That settled some of the hunger and personal agitation in the air, but it didn't warm us up or dry us off.

All we could do was continue. We had a helo assault scheduled, so we humped to the bottom of the mountain to catch the helos. As soon as they touched down, the rains increased with a vengeance. We boarded in the driving rain and the CH-53 Sea Stallions took off as we watched solid, white sheets of water deluge the helo pad.

Huddled tightly inside the helo was the closest thing to warmth I had felt in two days. Even though I hate those rattling pieces of scrap metal, I was glad to get that ride.

We arrived at the mortar range for the next day's live fire exercise. By this time, we were sleep deprived, and the skin on our hands was mostly white and wrinkled.

Another company was finishing their shoot as we arrived. We noticed a few short rounds due to wet powder. It was an uneasy feeling knowing we were next.

That night the rains continued to fall. At our commander's directive, we had not brought shelter halves to make tents. We stayed wet another day and night with questionable sleep.

"Captain Brown, we don't need to shoot today. The Marines can't feel their fingers, and they haven't slept in three days. Besides, did you see those short rounds yesterday."

"Yeah, but you know the battalion CO is not going to go for that."

"He probably won't, but it's the right call. If he wants to show us reserves that we need to be tough, that's fine. We'll be tough. But I want to go on record and say I advised against it."

"Okay, you made your point."

The shoot started slowly. I checked and rechecked our safety procedures. When it was finally time to shoot, I ordered an illumination mission. It was broad daylight, and the Marines looked at me funny.

"Hey, we're not shooting casualty-producing rounds until I'm comfortable."

"Aye-aye, sir."

The first mission proved my point. The round fizzled out of the mortar tube like cheap fireworks. Even though it was only illum, everyone moved toward cover.

"I thought you said the powder increments were kept dry."

"They were, sir. It's just that the constant downpour and the water in the tubes is taking its toll."

"Repeat that mission."

This time it fired more like normal, but we really weren't too sure of ourselves or the situation. There were sporadic delays and short rounds for over an hour, no matter how hard we tried to keep things dry. The rain lightened up just a little and the illumination rounds were finally performing consistently.

It was time to try HE (high explosive) rounds. The first round was nearly on target. It seemed like the HE performed more consistently than the illum.

We were overcoming the elements, but the training was minimal. Everyone was just ready for this ordeal to be over. Then the forward observers on the OP (observation post) started getting into it. They were moving the rounds around the impact area at will. We could see the impacts from the gun line too. That had everyone motivated. It was going to be a good day.

"Check firing."

"Check firing."

"Corpsman up. Corpsman up."

Where were these commands coming from? Someone came running from the rain-soaked vegetation in front of our OP. As they briskly made their way toward the gun line from the impact area, we made our way toward them.

They were carrying an injured Marine. How could that be? We had visually swept the range before firing and no one was there. We were the only ones hot on the range.

I could see some Marines from another unit assisting their lieutenant, who had been wounded in the thigh by mortar fragments. We had seen the impacts. There were no short rounds. It just didn't add up. Where were they when they were hit?

The reaction from our higher headquarters was very negative and accusatory toward us as reservists. Finger pointing and verbal slurs were coming from everywhere in the battalion, from junior enlisted to the top brass. The comments were too prevalent to miss or ignore.

Of course we were defensive but also objective in our approach to the incident. I had been in artillery long enough to know how to investigate a possible stray round. We needed to do it thoroughly for everyone's sake. We also needed to know if we were safe to continue our shoot.

Each mortar tube checked out. Each round and powder increment checked

14 John M. M. Caldwell, Sr.

out. All the firing data checked out. The observers verified witnessing all the impacts within the sheath and safely on target. We finished our shoot and awaited further investigation.

I felt confident that no fault would be found with my Marines but was unsure if we, as reservists, would actually be vindicated by such a predisposed and accusatory higher headquarters.

But the mood quickly changed. After further investigation it was made known that the lieutenant and the Marines with him had entered the impact area unannounced and unnoticed while the range was hot. They had decided to check on some demolitions that didn't blow when they had the range the day before. They thought they were a safe distance away from the shooting. Obviously, they weren't. A shell fragment can travel well outside the effective casualty radius, and apparently this one did, lodging in the front portion of the lieutenant's thigh.

Their efforts were now focused on covering it up. There were no reservists to blame. If one of the lieutenant's Marines had been hurt, it might have been different, but they figured the officer's injury and embarrassment were punishment enough.

We didn't care how they handled it. We were just glad to have experienced the amphibious side of life in the South Pacific, even for a short time. Thankfully, it was about over.

The rains had finally stopped, and the summer heat and humidity immediately began taking its toll. Marines who had been wet and cold for days were now experiencing prickly heat. For some it was a mere inconvenience, but for others the rash was nearly intolerable. None of them let it keep them from libo (liberty).

One day and a night of liberty was plenty for me. The short taxi ride to Olongapo let us know it was close enough to walk back.

The first sergeant, the gunny, and I stuck together. We walked the strip and shopped for souvenirs. We tried one bar and one San Miguel. The beer was nothing special, but it was part of the local experience.

Scantily clad bar girls hovered around the tables. They were one part of the local experience that we chose to avoid. They would visit us in groups of three. We would wave them off and three more would show up. The girls were attractive and increasingly aggressive. It was time to leave.

Similar places lined the streets. Marines could find themselves in a lot of trouble in a town like that. Our Marines were scattered to the winds, and it made me wonder if they'd all be back the next day.

Everyone returned. There were stories to be told and others that should not be told. A few of our Marines even woke up with strange tattoos they couldn't remember getting. Some of us were ready for home.

Although it wasn't without kinks, the exercise accomplished its goal. It was an early albeit qualified success at integrating reserve units into training cycles with their regular counterparts.

I'm sure none of those involved on either side wanted to be part of the next integrated effort. With an almost audible and common chorus, it was agreed to "Let someone else do it from now on." Slowly and painfully, reservists and regulars began to work together more often.

•••

Lee was scheduled to deliver our third child in the summer of 1990. Our first two had arrived under their own unique circumstances with a common thread of steadily increasing levels and frequency of labor pains. There was no reason to expect any different with our third child. We already knew the baby would be a boy and we had already named him Cannon David.

Leaving for work one morning I kissed Lee goodbye as she slept. Less than half an hour later I was having my first cup of coffee in my office when the phone rang. It was Lee.

"Hey, I need you to come home. I've having contractions."

Knowing she had just been sound asleep and expecting the scenario to be like the last two, I thought I had plenty of time. I had just arrived at work and had things to do.

"So, how far apart are the contractions?"

"Either five minutes or two. It's hard to tell."

"What? Are you awake? How can you not tell? Call me back in five minutes if you've had another one."

"Okay. Bye."

It didn't make sense. I just left her sleeping quietly. Either way I was slowly preparing to tell my boss and leave work… still expecting a predictably long day of it. Then the phone rang again. It was Lee's phone, but the voice was our good friend and close neighbor Lynn, loud and urgent.

"You better get home right now! We're going to have this baby right here!"

"I'm on my way."

Like a new father on a TV sitcom, I flew into action with reckless abandon. Twenty minutes home and maybe ten to the hospital and Lee was ready to push. Hospital paperwork almost caused me to miss the delivery. Cannon arrived like a rocket.

In the rush Lee's epidural did not have time to help her with the pain, and even hurt by causing some sort of spinal puncture. That created severe head-aches that kept her on her back for weeks. We had about a week of help from family. Then they left. Then I left. Lee was still nearly bedridden with three chil-dren and I was scheduled for two weeks Annual Training (AT).

Paternity leave wasn't even discussed in those days and missing out on key training as a Marine officer wasn't much of an option. While reservists had not been activated since Korea, our training was for war... real war and the timing would not be ours to choose. Most importantly I believed in leading from the front. The inconvenient timing was immaterial.

As our family dynamics changed, so too our cadre of officers changed dra-matically. Most notably, the commanding officer and the I&I both left the unit. Additional work conflicts had expedited the CO's departure. The I&I was promoted to major and moved on as well.

The new I&I arrived with a more positive frame of mind. He was much more low-key than his predecessor.

Major Macklin, a motor transport officer, was chosen for command of our infantry company. Several other officers were recruited to round out the staff, including a colorful and energetic executive officer, Barry Mathews, a "tanker" by trade.

The following summer we arrived at the all too familiar Mojave Desert, but two weeks at 29 Palms would prove to offer some unusual experiences.

The Marines had left the bivouac site. The XO and I were walking the area, discussing our training plans and casually scanning the desert floor as we walked.

"Hey, an Oreo!"

Barry reached down and picked up an Oreo cookie that appeared unscathed, and he ate it.

"I can't believe you actually ate that. You don't know where that thing's been."

"It was still crunchy," he said with great satisfaction and a smile as he shrugged off any possibility that it should have been left on the ground.

For some reason that motivated me. I had always thought I was still a grungy field Marine until then. I knew I had to make a conscious effort to get reacquainted with that side of myself.

Later in that same trip, I yelled at my driver as we traversed the sandy desert trails beneath the Bullion Mountains.

"Stop!"

I hurriedly climbed out of the Humvee and picked up a piece of candy in the dirt. I had spotted it through the windshield, glistening in the sun as we approached. I ate that piece of candy in honor of Captain Barry Mathews and told the Oreo story to the driver. He laughed and was sure I was more than a little bit nuts. Although plenty dirty enough for me, it also had a clear wrapper around it, so I knew I was still a little less gungy than my XO.

Then things got serious. The battalion commander called the company officers in one by one.

"Do you know why you're here?"

"Yes, sir, I think so."

"Tell us what you know."

"All I know for sure is that most days our company commander, Major Macklin, is gone somewhere other than the training areas we are using."

"San Diego?"

"Sir, I have no idea. He could have been with you for all I know."

I thought it might be about the TEWT (tactical exercise without troops) but I wasn't going to volunteer that idea.

"Go on."

"He usually returns at night by twenty-two hundred. He hasn't been around for any live firing evolution that I can recall. I stood in for him as CO during the TEWT while the XO took the company to another training area. On the four hundred ranges, he showed up around twenty hundred the evening prior to the company assault. The XO had already taken the initiative to issue an operations order just in case the CO didn't show.

"When the CO did show, he sat us down for about twenty-five minutes and talked like a coach before a big game and made references to Memphis State University basketball. It was really weird. Then he asked if there were any questions. We were dumbfounded.

"He said, 'Okay, we'll kick off in the morning.' and then he walked away. We sat there completely dismayed. A couple of the other platoon commanders went ballistic. I know you've heard from them already. The XO calmly told us to stick with the operations order he had issued and things would be fine. They were. That's about it."

"Anything else?"

"No, sir."

"Thank you, Captain Caldwell. That will be all."

I knew the XO and especially the other platoon commanders had given our battalion commander an earful. There were plenty of other problem areas that I didn't bring up. He didn't need to hear me ramble. I said more than I liked. It made me uncomfortable, and it felt especially disloyal, but sometimes, the truth hurts. Something needed to be done for the sake of our Marines.

Even though we are reservists, this is serious business. We may be activated, and if we were, the thought of having Major Macklin in charge would have been more than scary, it would have been wrong.

• • •

Captain Mathews, our XO, took over the company as soon as Major Macklin dropped to the IRR. We didn't get any details of how it transpired. It just happened. About a month later, the Iraqi army of Sadaam Hussein invaded Kuwait. As I watched on TV with the rest of the world, we continued to train. Mobilization for war has always been a distant possibility; now, it was a distinct possibility.

Speculation was rampant. Fifty-year-old retired national guardsmen were on TV, wringing their hands about getting activated. It seemed ridiculous to me. My friends and family asked about my status.

"Are you on alert?"

"No."

"Why not? My brother's national guard unit is?"

"We don't have that type of alert system in the Marine reserve. We're just supposed to stay ready."

"Aren't you worried?"

"Things will need to get really bad for them to mobilize us. They're mostly looking for specific skill sets, and we're just grunts."

I had learned from TBS not to worry about things I had no control over, and this was one of them. Plus, I didn't see any need to alarm my family and friends.

The first sign that we may be activated was at November's drill. We had our annual Marine Corps birthday ball as planned. Naturally, we discussed the likelihood of being activated.

I voiced my opinion that it was a sure bet we wouldn't be mobilized. Our I&I, on the other hand, confidently said he would take that bet. When I looked him in the eyes, I felt he may know something I didn't. So I kept the wager down to a Coke for the winner. I lost.

Aboard the USS San Bernardino before an amphibious landing in the Philippines

1990 Prior to activation and deployment

Kill the enemy, but don't forget your paperwork.

*"Through Thee we will push down our enemies,
though Thy name shall we tread them under that
rise up against us. For I will not trust in my bow,
neither shall my sword save me."*

Psalm 44: 5-6

...6
Conflicts of Culture

It was Monday morning, November 19, 1990. The call from Captain Mathews was patched into my office.

"Hello."

"John, this is Barry. This is it."

He didn't elaborate. He didn't need to.

"You're kidding."

"No, this is for real."

I could tell by his voice that he wasn't fooling around, but I had to be sure. My heart rate was noticeably faster. I could feel the adrenaline rush begin. A thousand thoughts were running through my mind. I was at work and had to tell my boss and call Lee. What about the children? Was I as ready as I thought I was to lead Marines into combat? Were they ready too?

"When do we leave?"

"We report Saturday."

"This Saturday?"

"Yes, officers and staff NCOs on Saturday. The rest of our Marines will report on Sunday. We fly out Tuesday. You're the first one I've called. The recall is starting now at the drill center."

We had known it was possible. We had been watching the nation prepare to kick Iraq out of Kuwait. Discussions of the presidential recall of reservists had first centered on certain specialty MOSs or skill sets. Activation of combat units like reserve infantry was now upon us, but this was shorter notice than any of us had expected. As Marines we were ready, but our civilian lives weren't. It took a few more days to get in touch with the last of our Marines. A few found out as late as Wednesday and the next day was Thanksgiving Day.

Lee and I put together a quick Christmas for us and the kids. We began rushing around decorating our house for Christmas, and we went Christmas shopping so we could open presents as a family on Friday. It was too early for a fresh-cut Christmas tree, so we bought our first artificial one.

Our family gathered on Thanksgiving Day, and the day flew by with good-byes to family. It was hard to relax with so much on my mind. Football games, parades, and the like took a back seat to news of Desert Shield/Storm.

Our church family scurried to put together a fitting send-off and every-one committed to help Lee and the children while I was away. "Honey-Dos" would soon be completed—by friends, family and neighbors—in record time. Firewood was be delivered without charge, even before Lee had a chance to ask for it. Ceiling fans were installed. Lawn mowers were fixed. The acts of kindness and support were the only things stacked higher than the firewood throughout my activation and deployment.

Nine years earlier Lee had written me a three-page letter explaining why not to join the Marines. One of the reasons revolved around me marrying and having to go to war and leave my wife and children. At the time neither of us had any idea it would be her.

In our years in the Corps, Lee and I developed a new term of our own called "The Dreads." Marine families won't need any explanation. It's the heavy-hearted feeling when you know enough about what is certain to come. You can't ignore it any longer. It's not a feeling of fear so much as it is an acute awareness of the heartaches ahead.

I was especially proud of our children during all of this. Jennifer was six years old and in first grade. JC had just turned five and was in pre-school. Cannon was just six months old and already living up to his name.

Since leaving active duty, I had been home routinely every night of the week, with weekends off (except for drill weekends). Deployment would be a big adjustment for all of us, and we'd have to adjust quickly.

The severity of the situation was all over the television. Newscasts were filled with stories from U.S. military families and the growing number of deployments. Chemical weapons experts told anchormen of the worst possible scenarios we would be facing if the impending war followed historical and theoretical models.

The mood was somber but highly charged at the drill center. We had planned for mobilization, so we reviewed our plan. It was actually solid and doable.

First, our recall went well, and we had every one of our Marines arrive on Sunday. Even Marines who were unreliable for drill didn't hesitate to answer their nation's call.

Processing was immediate. The I&I had done an exceptional job getting the drill center prepared as a processing center. It followed a model we had developed through training over the years.

As soon as Marines stepped foot in the drill hall, they were at an administrative processing station. After a quick record book review and update, they stepped into medical review. Shots were given on the spot for everything that was required in order to deploy.

Field gear was issued and inspected by platoon leaders. Gas masks and protective hoods were issued. The hoods we issued were mostly unserviceable—hardly worth using for training with CS (tear) gas—but they were the best we had.

Talk of chemical warfare was all over the television. It was on everyone's minds, especially, the Marine families. It wasn't healthy to dwell on the negative possibilities, but preparation and training for it would be a necessary focus of effort.

Wills and Powers-of-Attorney were completed at a fast pace in the classrooms down the hall. The day went like clockwork.

Those of us who lived close enough could go home at night. Those few moments at home were sad and mostly sleepless— for Lee and me; the children slept peacefully, not quite understanding what was happening. Deep inside I wanted to wake them so we could share a few more minutes together.

One of the unexpected challenges involved direct deposit. At that time there was no Total Force system. Day Two was the one-and-only banking day between our activation and our departure. Every reservist was required to re-enroll in direct deposit. That was nearly impossible for Marines who lived outside the Memphis metropolitan area. Multiple dozens of our Marines did not have the ability to create a direct deposit account in banks 40, 60, or

90 miles away, so it simply did not get done like it should have. The meager hope was that we could close the loop from Camp Lejeune, North Carolina. It would become an administrative "check the box" at best.

We also got an immediate schooling when it came to higher education. Reservists have reemployment rights but no federally protected rights as college students. Every university seemed to have a different way of dealing with this, and none had a written policy in place. One of my Marines was even told by his liberal professor that if he reported for duty then he would fail the class. He was apparently bluffing, yet no federal law protects reservist from that.

With only two weeks left in the semester, some offered the existing grade. That was good unless you had counted on the last two weeks to pull your grade up. Some offered an option to receive an Incomplete (I) or Withdrew Passing (WP) mark, both of which would cost them all their semester's tuition. To this date there is still no minimum standard, even for federally funded universities.

There was no wasted time. Soon, we were on a chartered plane to Camp Lejeune. We had ridden charters before. Nearly every year, we scheduled planes for annual training. Our company had made the almost-identical trip to Camp Lejeune a couple of years earlier. In the past we would drop in after dark and be transported directly to a bivouac site in one of the training areas.

This time it was a little different. Crammed into unfamiliar quarters, the priority of effort shifted to finding enough mattresses to keep Marines off the floor. Up to four Marines occupied each two-man room. Days of processing were scheduled for things we had completed in a few hours back at the drill center. It was the same hurry-up-and-wait we had all experienced since our inception into the Corps.

Our battalion had conducted a successful desert CAX (combined arms exercise) a few months earlier. Some say that training in the Mojave cinched us being the first reserve battalion activated. In fact we would be the only one to deploy and fight as a battalion with an active-duty infantry regiment.

Training success did not translate into any type of respect. We were discredited and unwanted by the regular establishment. Not a lot could be done about it at the time; there was a job to do.

Shortages of critical and not-so-critical personal gear and equipment were commonplace. The shortage of desert camouflage utility uniforms was most apparent. We tried to scrape up at least one uniform per Marine, and sizes didn't seem to matter. Misfit covers, baggy, tight, short, and extra-long uniforms draped ridiculously on our country's most elite fighting force. Desert boots were nowhere to be found.

Serviceable gas mask hood covers were still in especially short supply. While dire predictions of chemical attacks provided an interesting series of news stories, the sobering possibilities were more than interesting to us. We identified a mounting number of protective hoods which had been damaged over time during training. Attempts to repair them or replace them were futile.

As more and more items were identified as missing, or in need of repair or replacement, the excuses mounted. The promises grew and the results remained the same.

The regular Marines in Memphis promised our needs would be met when we reached Camp Lejeune.

"You'll get it in North Carolina."

Marines in Camp Lejeune assured us those important items would be waiting on us overseas.

"You'll get it in Saudi Arabia."

At a tent city in the Arabian desert, we were told those items would be available soon, so we were to proceed to our tactical positions.

"You'll get it once you go north."

We again made our requests for necessary items, only to hear the discouraging although somewhat predictable response.

"If you don't have it by now, you're not going to get it. You should have gotten it back in the rear."

We did gain three new officers in the rear. The first, Captain Lyons, was an artillery officer reservist who had been at Camp Lejeune, looking for a ticket to the war. We found him one.

The second officer was 1st Lt. Allen. He was an infantry officer fresh off active duty, which made him especially valuable.

Last but not least, we picked up Captain G. Alan Meighen, also an infantry officer.

We were more ready than ever. Then something happened.

"John, let's talk."

"What's wrong, Barry?"

I could detect uncharacteristic doubt in his eyes and body language, and I could hear the uneasiness in his voice. Something wasn't right.

"I'm thinking of turning the company over to Alan."

"What? Are you crazy?"

"He's the next senior and an infantry officer, and I think he'll do fine. Besides, you know my knee is giving me fits. If Lieutenant Colonel Dawson finds out how bad it is, I think he'll make me stay home. I can hardly walk today, and I probably won't make the hump tomorrow. It's hard to lead from the front in a knee brace. I wanted to hear what you think."

"We don't know Alan. I'm sure he's a competent enough officer, but we don't really know anything about him."

"Don't you think it might be better for the Marines to have an infantry officer instead of a tanker like me?"

"Eh, it might be worse. Just leave him as your XO instead of being his. You can draw off his experience if it's any good, and you can discard the rest. If you're asking me, I say don't do it."

"I think my mind is already made up, but I did want to talk with you first. I do appreciate your input. Don't worry. It'll be fine."

My gut said this was not good, but I could live with it. Alan was less of a communicator but on the surface seemed to know what he was doing. Anyway, he had already done me a favor just by being here. I had been the XO and weapons platoon commander at the same time until he came along, and I'd much rather have only the one job of weapons platoon commander to worry about.

• • •

My platoon sergeant, Staff Sgt. Broadnax, and I were busy identifying areas of weakness that we wanted to address in our training plan while at Camp Lejeune. We began to work extensively on our mortar fire direction center and our knowledge of the effective employment of machine guns in a desert environment.

Most everyone had stayed in good physical condition, but we turned it up a notch now that we were activated. Unit PT, individual PT, and progressive forced marches were all on tap.

Tactical training areas were at a premium. Although we were activated and attached to the 8th Marines, we were still treated as a visiting reserve unit by range personnel. We were bumped off the ranges and training areas several times by "local" units given priority.

If we reservists were as ill prepared as the regular establishment thought, we should have been the ones with top priority for training. Thankfully, the naysayers were wrong; our Marines were well prepared for what we were about to face.

At one point in the process, my NCOs returned from a class on the machine gun in which they were spoon fed basics like they were civilians who had never seen an M-60. They were insulted and righteously indignant. When they began to try to squeeze a little more out of the class, it became apparent that the regular Marine instructor, who had been sent from Quantico to teach us, knew less about the subject matter than his reserve pupils.

Another incident took place at the officer's club. Two lieutenants—probably with reserve commissions themselves—were poor-mouthing reservists, with the natural assumption that everyone in earshot was a regular Marine officer.

As a captain I felt it was my duty to school them on reality as well as good manners and discretion. I may have enjoyed that a little too much. In their defense they were just a reflection of their own senior leadership.

The Total Force concept of the reserves and regulars being interlocking pieces of the same puzzle did not have complete buy-in from most regulars. It was painfully obvious throughout the 8th Marine Regiment that many openly resented us. Some felt like Headquarters Marine Corps didn't have enough confidence in the regulars' abilities without sending reserves to help. Others saw the reserves as no help at all, just a political pacifier they had to suck.

Our battalion had a huge obstacle to overcome to become accepted as an integral part of the regiment. Our Marines and staff were up to the challenge.

• • •

Momma and Daddy drove Lee and the kids to Camp Lejeune so we could see each other one more time before the deployment began. Talk of the impending war was on every TV channel. Excruciating details of the worst-case scenarios involving chemical warfare were replayed and discussed at length in every public medium. We minimized the obvious in our family so as not to alarm the kids. They knew, but we wanted them to see confidence in us and be encouraged by our conversations and actions.

It was hard to say goodbye. Up to this point we had always seen another visit in the not-too-distant future. This one was way too final. Orders defined the activation period as a minimum of six months but spelled out the likelihood of a six-month extension. We tried not to think about the latter.

The family returned home. My focus returned to our pending departure.

On Christmas Eve the entire battalion was sitting at Camp Lejeune, scheduled to catch buses to Cherry Point and catch a charter to Southwest Asia. I walked to the base chapel for the Christmas Eve service. It was a solemn service. Most of the families there were without their Marines, and there was a spattering of Marines like me in the congregation without their families.

The old chapel earned its keep that night. There was a lot of unity and prayer among so many who had never met. The service ended. It was time to find an open payphone and call home one more time.

The slightly cool December night air was the only thing that seemed remotely like Christmas now. The shadows and silhouettes of Marines along the sidewalks and between the buildings caused reflective pause of where they and we would be tomorrow—on our way to war.

The feeling of love and pain was palpable as I leaned into the payphone for a sense of privacy while others waited respectfully for their turn a few short feet away. Lee and I both tried to cheerfully encourage the other. Lee was trying to get kids ready for bed and Christmas morning, so the conversation had to come to an end.

On Christmas Day we staged at the airfield and at zero dark thirty the following morning, we were "wheels up."

Uncertainty was staggering. Focus on my Marines was stronger than ever. It kept me from thinking of home, and it was a lot more productive. I continually scribbled things in my notebook. My list of things to do grew rapidly.

Sizeable shortages of basic individual protective gear and essential desert gear remained. Almost everyone had one set of desert cammies, but many were still wearing the wrong size.

The plane ride allowed for much—maybe even too much—reflection.

Determined faces of the Marines told their story without words. Thoughts of home and family were nearly visible. Light-hearted conversation was more than welcome to break the obvious tension.

Our stop and brief layover at the USO tent in Rhine-Main, Germany, provided a very Americanized pit stop. Junk food, soft drinks, games, and movies were in abundant supply. Then it was back to the plane and on to Saudi Arabia.

Tent city, also known as Camp 15, presented us an unwelcome odor of open and poorly managed "pissers" and "shitters." The specific-use category was spray-painted awkwardly on the outside of their short plywood walls below their makeshift, screened windows. Corporal McCreight, a strong Christian, refused to join in the vernacular. He and a few others began to call the primitive structures, "urinaters" and "defecators," which is proof positive that every Marine doesn't swear like a sailor.

The stench was accompanied by the uneasy sound of Arabic chanting over loudspeakers from the mosque just outside our camp.

"What is that?'

"That's their evening prayers."

"Do they do that every evening?"

"Plus a couple of times a day, I think."

"I don't think I like that. What if they're Iraqi sympathizers saying to kill Americans? We'll never know."

"Unless they try it tonight. Now settle down and go to sleep."

Similar conversations were heard all over the tent city. Most of our Marines were from Arkansas, Mississippi, and Tennessee. Few had seen a mosque, and other than our feeble attempts to teach and learn basic commands like "halt" and "drop your weapon," few had ever heard anyone speak Arabic.

After two weeks in crowded canvas tents, we pulled out. The vast desert in front of us was a boundless training environment. It was January 10, 1991 Although there was no way to know it, we had just had our last shower until mid-March. For the next seven days, we would continue our preparation and training for a war that was about to begin.

Once President Bush set the deadline of January 16th, the bets were on. Moving from fighting hole to fighting hole, we all made friendly wagers on our own predictions of the day the war would start. We defined the start as "bombs on deck."

Five-ton tactical trucks hauled us to our first tactical position. Being infantrymen, it was natural to start digging in, and the sandy dessert was easier digging than most places we'd been.

We moved every few days, which enabled us to hone our skills at digging fighting holes. The fighting holes doubled as living quarters. Artistic license abounded; no two holes were alike. Some were more traditional, following the textbook model of a two-man fighting position. Others were built for more comfort. Some Marines extended the length of their fighting holes or even dug tunnels to offset sleeping positions. Shelves, cabinets and even stoves were dug into the sides of some. Others concentrated on better overhead protection from the elements. Everyone soon found out the importance of a sturdy cover, not just for shade but for rain—lots of rain!

Weather in January and into February had us wondering if this was really desert. The sand and stark landscape were obviously desert, but the buckets of water from the sky were somewhat of a surprise.

One hole that the gunny, the XO, and I dug for the three of us seemed fine . . . until the rains came. First, the rain soaked the ground around us. Streams of water poured into the sides of the hole under our improvised poncho roof, causing the walls and top edges to erode. The sandy bottom of our abode absorbed huge amounts of water.

Eventually, the ponchos became saturated and began to leak. The winds howled and began to dismantle our shoddily assembled cover. We sat, frustrated, holding it up the best we could. A little water here and there didn't require action, but mini waterfalls washed away the sides and further undermined our construction. We became our own emergency services.

At least with the three of us together, we were able to laugh about it even as it happened. We would have made a comical site if there had been any spectators. But there were only participants up and down the lines. Some struggled a little less or even a little more than we did. That was obvious when the rains stopped and we walked the lines.

The smell of rain and wet sand was a fresh odor compared to the dripping 782-gear we were wearing and carrying. We hadn't predicted the rain and cool temperatures we experienced. All the images we had seen on television were of the early arrivals in late summer heat waves.

Low-flying aircraft cruised north over Saudi Arabia, breaking the morning's silence on January 16th. Helicopters and fixed-wing aircraft were noticeably more frequent than days previous. Word of the air war did not reach us through official channels; we saw it from the ground and heard it on the BBC (British Broadcasting Corporation).

Marines spotted the sandy hillsides like roving human antennas. Each Marine held his Walkman radio high in the air in one hand, his other hand holding an earpiece to his ear. Each was trying to get better reception to hear BBC updates.

Although we didn't know the day, hour, or duration of the air war at the infantry platoon level, we had been briefed on the likelihood of the air war lasting some 30 to 60 days before a ground war would commence.

We were still without assigned vehicles. Our transportation always dropped us off and departed.

The regular Marine infantry battalions with the 8th Marines were in AAVs (amphibious assault vehicles) with reactive armor. We were typically in 5-ton trucks, but at one point we were moved tactically in white school buses with Saudi drivers. We affectionately called them Iraqi school buses, based on the demonstrated skills of the drivers. They seemed determined to get us killed. Several near-head-on collisions at high speeds had us convinced.

"How many people can you get on one of these Iraqi school buses anyway?"

"About thirty-five Iraqi sixth graders or eighty-seven, combat-loaded U.S. Marines."

That tale circulated as we lay awkwardly atop piles of gear and ammunition with our face only inches from the bus ceiling.

The driver finally stopped, but he wasn't at our destination. He had driven off-road as far as he was willing to risk. He refused strong encouragement to continue.

The last few miles would be on foot, more like reserve pack mules than infantry. We watched 2/4, our sister battalion of regular Marines, ride by us in their AAVs.

At night we could see the air war being executed. The attack aircraft were high in the air, but we could easily see their lights. The dark sky to the south over Saudi Arabia was lit up like a Christmas tree. We intently watched as planes peeled off for their bombing runs. Some left their lights on during the entire flight. We could watch those cross into Kuwaiti airspace. When flashing lights turned sharply in another direction, we would visually drop straight down and await the coming flash and sound of freedom.

From our position on the battlefield, we could take time to reflect on those who had gone before, and what those bombs meant for us, as well as for those on the receiving end. Night after night, day after day, the air war continued.

We continued to move every several days. Each time, we moved closer to the Iraqi army near Saudi Arabia's border with Kuwait. Each time, we would dig into ever-improved and less-creative defensive positions. Each time, we were left afoot.

Religion flourished before the ground-combat phase began. Bible studies were well attended up and down the lines. It was not uncommon when making my rounds to hear Marines in deep theological discussions. Of course, I enjoyed interjecting my opinion every chance I could.

Chapel services were a popular place, with some of the most unlikely characters showing up every week. We even had several baptisms. There's no way for anyone to know which Marines truly repented and which ones were checking on the spiritual equivalent of a fire insurance policy.

One staff sergeant who was attached to us from Weapons Company caused me some doubts, based on his actions between services and, especially, after the war. He cussed just as much, told the same, old, dirty jokes, and made plans for debauchery and drunkenness upon his return from the war.

On the other hand, one Lance Corporal Hester was more than likely a true convert.

"Sir, I'm not only saved, but I'm sure I'm called into the full-time ministry."

"That's awesome."

"I'm just not sure if I'm supposed to be a pastor, evangelist, missionary, or what."

"It'll be clearer with time."

"I don't even know what denomination I'm supposed to be."

"Maybe you need to be a Methodist and teach them to be a little more like Baptists . . . or even a Baptist and teach us how to be more like the Presbyterians. Either way, I'm sure God will lead you where he wants you to go. It'll be up to you to follow."

After the war the corporal went on to become a missionary to English speakers in Kuwait.

Spiritual concerns easily commingled with physical ones. On the night of a supposedly imminent gas attack, we were instructed to take our nerve agent pills. The pills came with a publication listing all the potential side effects, ranging from A to Z. The fine print that made up an entire booklet was almost comical. We read every word of it by flashlight, but many took the pills anyway. Some did not.

At one point we were put into MOPP-Level 4, (mission-oriented protective posture), which included mask and hood, NBC (Nuclear, Biological, Chemical) protective suit, gloves, and boot covers. We had trained in all of it so much that it never bothered me except in extreme heat. This night had been relatively cool, so I slept with my mask on as we awaited the "all clear."

Our last defensive position in Saudi Arabia was especially memorable. Several things happened. We had witnessed some MLRS (multiple launch rocket system) artillery firing their rockets into the night. The "ground war" had not officially begun, but apparently, there were some targets of opportunity that enabled them to help shape the battle.

We had heard of the Iraqi assault on the coastal town of Khafji. I knew that was in the 1st Marine Division's zone, which was home not only to my brothers-in-arms but also to some old friends and even my nephew. It was starting to get personal.

It was also about the same period that we heard of the horrific *blue-on-blue*, when our planes bombed our own positions, killing Americans.

The next day we heard of Iraqis walking across the border and surrendering, some of whom were mistakenly fired on as attackers. The fog of war was already producing tragic results. It sure sounded crazy, and we were getting ready to enter the chaos.

"Sir, we've got movement to our front."

"Show me."

The entire cadre of company officers took turns peering through the binoculars, trying to determine what the situation was. The longer we stared, the more confused I got. We could see possibly half a dozen to a dozen individuals moving on the edge of our horizon.

We knew there were no friendly units to our front, but we called higher headquarters to confirm it. We knew from the Khafji incident that it was not beyond the realm of possibility that Iraqis could be probing our lines. The other possibility was that they could have been surrendering but did not understand the surrender terms of how to do it. We didn't want to be guilty of waiting too late to react or shooting the innocent.

The mysterious figures seemed to always be moving but never getting any closer. We began to make an extra effort to hold the binoculars motionless for more extended periods—seconds, then minutes. Maybe they were farther away than we thought, which would have accounted for some of that. Sometimes, a few or all would even disappear from view. This was getting frustrating.

"I think they're barrels."

"What?"

"They look like fifty-gallon barrels."

"Let me see that."

"What would barrels be doing in the desert?"

One by one we looked at the figures in a different light. They *were* barrels! They still seemed to move and disappear and reappear due to the mirage effect coming from the desert floor. Everyone relaxed as we laughed at ourselves, but we all took another couple of looks just to be sure.

That night India Company reported two or three figures walking in front of their position from east to west. That would place them in our line of sight in several minutes. I tried to call down the line on the phone, with no response. Phones must have been down, or the Marines were asleep, or both. Marines were told to be on 50% alert, which means one sleeps while one watches. I finally got to a fighting hole of Marines on our right flank and warned them of the sighting. Then I began making my way down the line.

The more fighting holes I reached, the madder I got. Almost everyone was sound asleep. Although I must admit I was a little concerned about who might be out there in the dark, I was raising my voice and exposing myself while running from fighting hole to fighting hole to wake Marines. As I reached the far-right flank, those Marines were already up, scanning the darkness for any sign of the reported figures.

My blood was really pumping by now, and the adrenaline was pumping faster.

"What do you see?"

"I don't see anything, sir."

"Let me see."

I took the NVGs (night vision goggles) and scanned the gap between us and India Company first. Nothing. Next, I looked to our front to see if I could see the figures continuing from east to west. Nothing. I stared and I stared. There was little if any ambient light, so the NVGs were suspect.

"Wait a minute."

"I see something."

"It looks like two figures, low, crawling."

"See if you see what I see."

I passed the NVGs to the Marine beside me, and I stared into the black night, waiting to get confirmation.

"Sir, I can't see anything."

"Right there in front of us. Look again and be real still. Can you detect any movement?

"I still can't see anything, sir."

"I'm almost sure I see two people moving out there."

I braced myself so that I wouldn't move. I didn't want to make the same mistake we had made in the daylight with the barrels. Blurry images seemed to move slowly across my field of vision as I lay motionless.

"Well, I can't engage with these. Are you sure you can't see anything?"

"Now *I* can't see anything. We need an illumination round. Have the radio watch call battalion and explain I think I saw the same figures India Company Marines reported, but we need permission to shoot illum."

Permission denied.

I didn't understand why illumination had been made out to be such a big deal at the time. It had something to do with the overall plan. The idea was to make the Iraqis think others were conducting an amphibious assault closer to downtown Kuwait City. We, and the actual breech sites, were further west and trying not to draw attention to ourselves.

Literally and figuratively, we were in the dark, not knowing if we had seen anyone or anything that night. I ensured that the NCOs kept a closer eye on our lines and kept the appropriate 50% alert after that.

The next morning I looked for signs in the sand—footprints, dog tracks, anything at nearly every conceivable distance. There was nothing. So, had

146 John M. M. Caldwell, Sr.

there been anything or anyone out there that night? Probably not, but we'll never know for sure.

Training continued amid the tactical push northward. Rumors that our unit would be involved in a preplanned combat raid turned the intensity up a notch. Although we never saw the plan in writing, it was supposedly cancelled when a 10,000-pound dumb bomb was effectively dropped on our raid target from the back of a C-130.

Also prior to the actual ground assault, elements of our battalion were sent into the Iraqi-occupied territory of Kuwait to support an artillery raid. Our company remained in reserve at the defensive berm along Saudi Arabia's northern border. The 15-20 ft. earthen obstacle was designed to slow any Iraqi ambitions into the kingdom. We stood watch at the breach as our combat engineers easily cut through it.

Anxiously monitoring calls for fire was as close as we could get to the action. It sounded like the resistance was light, and in fact, a quick surrender of an Iraqi battalion followed a few accurate volleys of artillery.

Smoke from the oil wells and dust from the desert floor obscured our view as a convoy of 5-tons arrived with Iraqi prisoners. Eventually, we could see empty sandbags tied over their heads as they passed us.

Sliding down the berm and kicking through the sand, I worked my way closer to the spectacle of prisoners. A buzz of activity surrounded the Marines. Concertina wire was up. Sandbags were removed and prisoners were fed.

This was our first view of the enemy. Captured, unarmed, and restrained, the Iraqis looked relieved and much less threatening than I had imagined. They were almost jovial as MREs (meals, ready to eat) were generously distributed to them.

Shortly after their meal, they became noticeably solemn, even sad. What had happened? Only a few of the prisoners could speak broken English, and there were no interpreters around. Maybe we would never know what changed their frame of mind so drastically.

The prisoners needed to be rushed to the rear for more professional handling. Heads down, feet dragging, and deeper despair on their faces, they were escorted back to the trucks. As they passed the last stretch of concertina wire, the prisoners turned right. The trucks were to the left.

"Get on the trucks!" a Marine growled as he turned them back with his

M-16.

"Oh, the truck!" shouted an Iraqi as he quickly translated the directions to his fellow prisoners.

Gloomy faces and body language instantly transformed. Smiles and energy returned to the group when they discovered the hole they had dug was for their MRE trash. Somehow, they had fashioned the idea—probably told by a Marine—that they had been digging their own graves.

Also, our limited communications with them revealed there were more Iraqis left behind who wanted to surrender.

"Should we send anyone back there?"

"It's getting dark."

"I think we should."

"Who are we going to send?"

"We'll need to take some Iraqis with whoever we send. They can—hope-fully— translate and be litter bearers for the wounded."

"Let's send one truck with a couple of Iraqis and a half-dozen Marines."

"Who'll take them?"

"I will if someone can tell me where I'm going."

"Great. Captain Caldwell, if you'll do this, we'll finish things up here."

"I'll need a radio."

"No, you won't. It's just straight up that road past the forward CP."

"Okay, let's do it."

I had volunteered with overly ambitious optimism. After all, the forward battalion command post was still out front. We hurried back along the road as the sun set. Our directions to find the CP sent us an hour into the darkness.

Just as I began to question our directions, the black silhouettes of American vehicles came into view. Cautiously, we confirmed it was an element of who and what we were looking for. They sent us farther north along a set of wheel tracks that served as our road.

After another uneasy stretch with no light, no communications, no vehicles, and no other Americans in sight, we passed a Humvee going the opposite direction. It was a near head-on collision. Then, several other Humvees did the same. Another stopped.

"Hey, where are you going?"

"We were sent to pick up more Iraqis who intend to surrender. Some of them are suspected of being injured and need special assistance."

"There's nobody left up there. We're the last ones, and we were told by some of the prisoners that the Iraqis are preparing to shell that position. You need to get turned around too."

"Roger that. We're right behind you."

While carefully turning the 5-ton around in the dark, we lost sight of the road and the last vehicle.

"The road should be right here and heading in that direction. Try to zig-zag a little until we find it."

"It's no use, sir, I can't see a thing."

"Me, neither. So much for these NVGs."

"I don't know of any minefields in this area, but I can't be sure."

"Let's just drive our back azimuth."

Years of training in 29 Palms had taught me two things about driving in the desert at night: (1) Know the direction you are going, and (2) frequently check the odometer.

The oil well smoke had eliminated all ambient light, rendering our night vision goggles nearly useless. Luckily, the tactical blackout lights showed us the desert floor in front of us. At least we would not drive off into a hole or worse.

"With an odometer reading and a known direction, we should be fine."

With as much confidence as I could muster, I reassured the Marine driving us. The long night trek was especially slow off-road. Frequent stops to check our direction and illuminate our odometer made it even slower. The clock told us we should have been back a long time ago. The odometer reassured us we had not gone too far.

Turning toward the berm too early could roll us into an unfamiliar U.S. or coalition unit and the hazard of friendly fire, not to mention our lack of knowledge about enemy mines in the area. Nevertheless, that undesirable option of turning was looking more likely. The decision point was nearly at hand when we felt our truck rock smoothly into the original tire tracks that formed our road. Within minutes we were back through the berm and into friendly territory.

From our friendly position at the berm, we moved south and west toward tactical assembly areas. The next morning I accompanied Captain Meighen to the battalion CP.

After a painfully boring and mind-numbing, two-hour operations order by our S-3, Major Hayes, to the battalion staff and company commanders, Captain Meighen and I made our way back to the Humvee. This was it. We were going through the minefield in the assault.

Determined to take everyone with us, we packed Marines into limited space. With more than a dozen Marines and extra ammunition piled high in the back of every truck, we prepared to roll. The risk of loss from an enemy attack upon a single vehicle was reluctantly accepted to ensure we would arrive in combat with sufficient firepower.

While exiting the battalion CP, I began to mentally craft my weapons platoon op order from the notes I had taken. Then, before we could reach our Marines for a company or platoon order, we were given the command to move out. Our Marines were staged and ready but not briefed.

We simply drove by them, using hand and arm signals to indicate they should follow us. Thank goodness there was a brief pause that night before we crossed the LOD (line of departure). At least a quick frag order could be communicated to my Marines. The assembly area was an awful gaggle of vehicles. It's a wonder we made it to the right breech in the minefield.

Columns of our trucks drove through the minefield as dawn came. It stayed relatively dark due to the oil well smoke blanketing the daytime sky. Yet it was light enough to see anti-personnel and anti-tank mines just a few feet away from our wheel ruts as we rolled through the open desert.

Burning wrecks of Iraqi military vehicles were scattered across the vast terrain—remnants of an already-defeated enemy. The air war and initial assault led by armor had overwhelmed them. The fierce resistance we had anticipated was nowhere to be found. Whatever remained of the war was still ahead.

The first night in Kuwait turned out to be the darkest night in history. The pitch-black night was solidified by thick smoke from the oil well fires. As night fell and shadows faded into the approaching darkness, the Marines opened fire. The CO and XO were not yet back from a meeting at battalion headquarters, so I had command.

"What are we firing at?"

"I don't know, sir?"

"Well, call them on the radio and find out."

"Sir, they're not sure. Something or somebody was moving in front of the line."

"It was Hickerson setting out aiming stakes."

"No, it wasn't. I saw Hickerson."

"There were tracer rounds everywhere. Did anyone confirm any coming in our direction?"

"I think there was."

"I don't think there was."

"I think it was someone around that abandoned BMP out in front of us."

He was referring to a Russian-made infantry fighting vehicle often used by the Iraqi army.

"If someone was at it, then it wouldn't be abandoned."

"I still think we were shooting at Hickerson."

"Get Hickerson up here now."

"Yes, sir."

"Tell me what happened."

"I was putting some aiming stakes out when all the shooting started. I'm not sure if they were shooting at me or not."

"Did you see anybody else out there?"

"No, sir."

"Carry on."

"But, sir, I saw Corporal Hickerson. We weren't shooting at him."

"There was movement near the BMP."

Again, we needed illumination.

"We just need to shoot an M Two-oh-three illum round. Get me a Marine with an M Two-oh-three up here ASAP."

"Don't ask, but let battalion know we're shooting illum. We've already fired enough tracers to give our position away."

About that time Captain Meighen returned, and the darkness had really set in. I explained what had happened to the best of my ability and explained we were going to shoot an illum round to our front to see if we could spot any enemy activity.

He decided against it. We'll never know whether we were shooting at ghosts, Hickerson, or Iraqis. There is still debate among the Marines who were there that night.

With the thought of a lone Iraqi or more than one directly in front of us, no one dared turn on a flashlight. You could still hear digging as Marines improved their positions.

As Captain Meighen slept, I stood watch with a radio operator. The darkness was surreal. Even with night vision goggles, no movement could be detected. I couldn't see a hint of my own hand in front of my face in any direction. With a little battlefield humor, I commented on the darkness to the radio watch.

"I hope it's not the new Iraqi nerve gas that makes you go blind before you die."

It wasn't very funny anyway, but in the quiet blackness it must have been impossible to pick up the subtleties that showed I was joking. A few minutes later, I saw my radio operator in our fighting hole under his poncho liner with a flashlight.

"What are you doing under there?"

"I'm just making sure we're not blinded by that new Iraqi nerve gas."

"I was just kidding. Put your light out."

Chemical warfare was on everyone's mind, so it didn't seem too outrageous at the time.

The distinct sounds of tanks—hopefully, ours—were all around us. I knew they couldn't see either and hoped they weren't as close as they sounded. I was more than a little worried about us getting run over.

The sound of artillery firing overhead was strangely reassuring. Maybe it was the artillery officer in me, or maybe it was because I knew that much steel down range would keep just about anybody at bay. Thoughts of Francis Scott Key's words echoed—". . . bombs bursting in air gave proof through the night that our flag was still there . . ."

When Captain Meighen took his watch, I turned to leave our fighting hole and go to sleep. There was nowhere to go. It was just a dark abyss in every direction. To get out of their way, I basically rolled out of the hole we had dug and slept on the edge above. That way I was less likely to move in the way of a vehicle, and if there was incoming, all I had to do was roll back into the hole.

The next morning we moved out at first light. We began to pass fighting trenches that the Iraqis had dug as defensive positions. The trenches had been there so long that they had become nearly invisible parts of the landscape.

Most of them were not revealed until our trucks were right on top of them. Thankfully, they were unoccupied.

Formations of various sizes were route-stepping unarmed enemy soldiers in some semblance of order toward Kuwait. Clusters of Iraqis following the surrender terms seemed to be endless. Then someone above us had a thought: "What if they change their minds?"

We were bypassing the trench lines and the weapons that filled them. If the unarmed Iraqis changed their minds, they could easily rearm on their march south, creating havoc in our rear area of operations.

The order came over the radio to clear the Iraqi defensive positions of their weapons and ordnance. Quickly, we started to accumulate more weapons and ammunition than we knew what to do with. There were AK-47 automatic rifles, machine guns of varying calibers, mortars, RPGs (rocket-propelled grenades), pistols, and hand grenades. It's a good thing so many decided not to fight.

The order changed.

"Forget the weapons. We're moving out."

BOOM! Something exploded plainly in our view from the command truck. I heard the voice of someone behind me thinking out loud.

"I bet it was Hoffman or Dickerson."

Somehow, Marines knew that luck, both good and bad, is usually created. Oddly enough, Hoffman and Dickerson were both injured by that grenade. We really knew nothing about what happened except that the corpsmen earned their pay that day. Five Marines were wounded in the blast.

They were just following orders. "Go. Stop. Go. Pick it up. Put it down." The same old change of word we had heard in the Marine Corps every day since boot camp. This time there were consequences. Three returned to duty. Two didn't return to the fight, and one of those was permanently disabled.

No one knows if an Iraqi pulled the pin on a grenade, hoping for results like that, if it was intentionally booby trapped in some other fashion, just unstable, or what.

The Marines were denied their purple hearts because somebody at a desk somewhere determined that the enemy didn't pull the pin or rig it to blow. I personally would have given the Marines the benefit of the doubt. They were under orders in a combat zone, and they didn't pull the pin themselves. My assumption for the sake of argument is that the enemy did.

Following their CASEVACS (casualty evacuations), I had a rifle. Many had asked me why I carried a pistol. I always said, "When the shootin' starts, if I need one, there'll be one." Unfortunately, I was right.

The movement north was strangely similar to a combined arms exercise at 29 Palms, California. As we moved up, I could imagine moving along the Delta Corridor, Gypsum Ridge, Black Top, and Rainbow Canyon, well-known training areas for Marines in Southern California's High Desert.

Visibility continued to be diminished by smoke from the Kuwaiti oil well fires, creating a unique atmosphere. In some ways I felt like an unwilling participant in a surreal déjà vu experience. In other ways I was supercharged with more adrenaline and testosterone than is normally possible.

"Gas. Gas. Gas."

The strange emotions of the moment were interrupted with the most-feared words in our vocabulary. We knew that a biological or chemical attack was a last-ditch option. Our rapid movement had positioned us in such a way that if it were going to be used, using it now would be in line with Iraqi doctrine.

Everyone had their masks on and cleared well under the ten-second training standard. We couldn't see well into each other's eyes because the shadowy light of the sun was only partially making its way through the dark smoke. The expressionless face of each gas mask said more than our own faces could have said. No one knew what gas was being used, where it came from, or what to expect next. We searched the landscape, turning our heads from side to side.

"All clear. All clear."

The "all clear" was sounded as quickly and unexpectedly as the "gas-gas-gas" warning. I was hesitant to take my mask off. We had trained for years on the laborious procedures to establish an "all clear" after an attack. Apparently, this time had been a false alarm. Confidently, everyone in sight removed his hooded mask without consequence. It made me feel like I could take mine off too.

Veering from the open desert toward Kuwait City, our two tactical columns approached an agricultural area with more vegetation, buildings, and fences. I was in the left column. The word "ambush" entered my head like a flashing neon sign. There was a tree line to our right. Visibility was still restricted by low-light conditions. Then . . .

BOOM-BOOM-BOOM-BOOM-BOOM.

I knew it. I ducked a little, expecting that the booms were likely weapons being fired at us. There were flashes of light in my peripheral vision. However, it was our own, vehicle-mounted, automatic grenade launcher in the right column, splattering the tree line with MK-19 rounds. He had apparently seen some hostiles. Several Marines said they saw Iraqis in the tree line and within the agriculture complex just yards away.

We dismounted in support of the other column. We never saw a target of opportunity, so we lay in wait with our weapons oriented in that direction.

A quick call for air support was followed by the almost instantaneous appearance of two Cobra gunships. They arrived on cue as if we were in a Hollywood production. They, like us, saw no targets of opportunity. Their arrival couldn't have been more dramatic or appreciated if it had come with musical accompaniment. The sounds of rotor blades above us made a beautiful melody. After a quick survey of the situation, they left as quickly as they came. Cobras had never been more reassuring or motivating.

We moved out. Blood was pumping and senses were keen. The ones who hadn't shot a round yet were more ready than ever.

We were getting closer to Kuwait City, and we were approaching another fenced, agricultural compound. Our direction of movement was going to put us awfully close to the fence line. We would be vulnerable to an ambush again. Everyone was focused on our right flank.

Our 5-ton stopped suddenly. The truck in front of us had stopped and the Marines were dismounting. Then the shooting started.

At first I wasn't sure which direction it was coming from, but I knew it was a mix of theirs and ours. As I reached the edge of our truck bed, I could hear rounds cracking around me as they passed. As I jumped, I could see the dusty road below me reacting to small-arms-fire impacts. A magazine or two had been hastily emptied in our direction, but none of us were hit. I leaped from the truck just a little to the driver's side as bullets ricocheted below me.

Orienting toward the enemy fire, all of us lay in the prone position, searching for the shooter or shooters. I didn't cuss as a general rule, but I vented a little in no particular direction. Then I shot at my best guess as to where they were firing from, but I never saw them.

A Marine seeking cover lay beside me. He looked up, as bewildered as the rest of us.

"Did you just shoot?"

"Yeah."

"What are you shooting at?

"I don't know, but I know we're taking fire from around those trees, so I shot into the trees."

Sporadic fire continued from all around us, but we couldn't see from where.

"Are they shooting at us?"

"Do you hear the cracking and popping like you're pulling butts at the rifle range?"

"Yeah."

"That's them shooting at us. The rest of it is us shooting at them."

"Okay."

As we were having our conversation, we were motioned by the Marines behind us to take cover with them. We had lain low a little too much out in the open.

"I'll cover you, sir."

As I got up to run, there was no covering fire. I zigged and zagged and hit the deck. There was no enemy fire that time either. Once more I got up and made the final break for cover.

"I thought you said you were going to cover for me. Were you just going to wait for them to shoot me before you decided to shoot?"

He shrugged with an apologetic smile. It's hard to imagine, but we were keeping our sense of humor, even with bullets flying. Now it was back to business. Was the enemy still out there or had they run or been killed? No one seemed to know.

The lead truck confirmed seeing an Iraqi setting up to fire an RPG when they stopped and dismounted. When we started shooting, he ran. We then received small-arms fire from the same vicinity and from high on a water tower. I couldn't see anything from my new vantage point.

"What do you think, Captain Caldwell?"

"I would fire a SMAW through that fence so we can see, or get ourselves on the other side so we can see." I was referring to the Mk 153, a shoulder-launched rocket assault weapon for busting bunkers and other fortifications. It can also be effective in an anti-armor role.

About that time there was another exchange of small-arms fire. As if orchestrated, a machine gun to our right and another to our left opened fire. Their
converging, symphonic fire was directed at hostile figures firing from the water
tower. The Marines confirmed at least one kill, but that was blocked from my
view by a single tree. When they stopped firing, it got reasonably quiet.

Up to this point there had been no fire discipline. Marines were shooting
at will. As a matter of fact, nearly the entire battalion dismounted to help us
with an unknown number of stragglers. Our Marines' estimates ranged from
three to thirty enemy engaged and from one to four enemy killed or wounded.
Oddly, I understood the wide-ranging differences.

Hotel Company had maneuvered from the rear of our column to flank any
remaining Iraqis. Their Marines fired on an Iraqi ammo truck in the compound that blew a plume of fire and black smoke high into the Kuwaiti sky.

We moved out again. As night fell on the outskirts of Kuwait City, we
circled the wagons. Dead carcasses of sheep and dairy cattle littered the landscape. The smell of death and rotting animals was prevalent. Instinctively, we
began to dig in, but everywhere an E-tool scratched the surface, dead animal
parts were uncovered. It didn't take long before we determined to take our
chances above ground.

Our mission for the next morning was to attack an Iraqi headquarters
element inside Kuwait City. The operations order was disseminated and I
had time to ensure that all my NCOs knew the plan and that everyone was
prepared to execute. As morning came, the attack was delayed twice then cancelled. The war was over. We had won.

Although the attack into the city had been scrapped, we had unfinished
business. We were told to circle back to the first agricultural area where we
had called for the Cobras. There was more suspected enemy movement and
possibly remnants of the Iraqi Republican Guard or some sort of die-hard
special operations forces.

With our company in reserve, we watched from several hundred yards away
as the attack commenced. It was slow and mostly uneventful until a tank from
4th Tanks began engaging parked Iraqi vehicles in the compound. The explosions and plumes of smoke were motivating until we heard that a U.S. Marine
tanker was killed by the back blast of secondary explosions from one of the

vehicles that had been shot.

Tensions between Captain Meighen, the CO, and Captain Mathews, the XO, finally blew as we waited and watched. They were fighting mad, screaming at each other in front of the Marines. They were face to face, and punches were about to be thrown until I stepped between them. I quietly told them, "Not in front of the Marines."

They knew I was right, and cooler heads prevailed. To this day I don't know what set them off, but it had been building for months.

The two of them could not have been more different. Barry, the XO, was aggressive, animated, and related well with Marines of all ranks. Alan, the CO, related better to senior officers and was passive and more reserved than most. Alan was stoic and calculating. Barry had a keen intellect but was more impulsive. It was a volatile combination, and I had to play mediator whether I was adept or not.

Together for almost six months, we gathered around a campfire in Kuwait. Captain Meighen came out and visited for about 15 minutes. When he left, I commented, "Do y'all realize that's the most time he's spent with us talking about something other than work since we've been here?"

There was no debate. He was especially distant when you consider that he and three of his platoon commanders were the same rank. There are some schools of thought that support that approach and others that do not. The flipside of that is when Marines share more than maybe we'd care to hear.

"Sir, we met a Kuwaiti sheepherder down the road. He took us in his car all over Kuwait City and showed us his house and his sister's house that was ransacked by the Iraqis."

"That's not very smart. Where were y'all when he picked you up?"

"We had walked down by the agricultural area where we had that last fire fight. But it's okay, sir, he was a former colonel in the Kuwaiti army."

"At least that's what he told you. What else did he tell you while you were UA, Corporal White?"

He hesitated, not sure whether I would push the issue of his Unauthorized Absence (UA) status, then continued.

"He told us he was a big sheep exporter before the war, but the Iraqis used machine guns and slaughtered almost everything he had."

"That makes sense. We've seen enough dead carcasses since we entered

Kuwait."

"Sir, he also gave us a sheep."

"What are you planning on doing with a sheep?"

"That's why we came to see you, sir. We want to eat it. We'll roast it over an open fire."

"I'll have to think about this one for a minute."

The thought intrigued me. As much as my military side new the hierarchy would be opposed, I didn't ask the question because I didn't want to hear the answer. If it was going to be done, it had to be done right.

"Okay, but there are conditions. First, keep the sheep for a couple of days and make sure it's healthy."

"No problem, sir."

"Next, because there are so many flies during the day, don't slaughter it until dusk. Bury the guts and stuff immediately. Does everybody understand so far?"

"Yes, sir."

"Last but not least, you better scrounge enough wood to cook it all the way. I will inspect it, and if it's not done, you won't eat it."

"Sir, how do we do it?"

"You've got to be kidding. There are enough deer hunters around who have field dressed a deer. You have two or three knives per man. If you can't handle it—"

"Oh, yes, sir, we can handle it. Thank you, sir."

They made a hasty exit before I changed my mind.

Gunny, the XO, and I were probably more excited than the Marines. We really hoped it would work out, but we had no idea it would be *so good*. They roasted it in quarters and had the tenderloins wrapped in aluminum foil and seasoned with Cajun spice. Never let it be said that Marines aren't resourceful.

In Marine Corps mess night tradition, I pronounced the meat "fit for human consumption." It was one of the finest meals I've ever had, and I've eaten in the finest restaurants of New York City and Washington, DC.

The tenderloins were especially appetizing, and so hot you could barely hold a piece long enough to get it to your mouth. There was great debate whether the leg quarter, with just the right amount of slightly charred exterior, was best or if it was the highly seasoned tenderloins. Back and forth we sampled, savoring every bite. I hadn't been that satisfied at a meal since leaving home. Full as a tick, I made my way to my rack, content.

Corpsmen from headquarters battalion fussed like a bunch of old wet hens the next day. They did not think it was healthy for us to eat the sheep. I didn't mind. It was their job, and I was still satisfied.

Our mostly positive experience was about to sour. We had six-month orders, and we were prepared to execute them fully. There was even a clause that would allow a six-month extension that had been well briefed. No one was looking for a quick ticket home—until the Marine Corps promised us one.

Official word disseminated that once the very first Marines from 1st Marine Division went home for the victory parades, the reserves, including us, would follow. They gave us a tentative date somewhere around the second or third week of March. That was earlier than we expected, but we were glad to get the news. Several days later, we were told an exact date. The next day the date changed. The next day it changed again.

We decided not to pass any word unless we were sure. After convincing assurance, we passed another date in March, then April 6th, then April 10th, then April 13th. The dates changed as rapidly as they were passed. The morale diminished at a more rapid rate. Everyone tried to get dates out of their heads, but they kept being passed down from higher headquarters.

We began to shuttle Marines to a phone tent. That helped in some ways and hurt in others. The families back home were getting conflicting word and changing dates just as we were.

To top it all off, the secretary of defense made an announcement at a televised press conference that all reservists were out of Kuwait. When that statement was made, almost all of what was left of the 2nd Marine Division were reservists. The remaining tank company, artillery battery, truck company, recon, engineers, and one of only two remaining infantry battalions were all reservists.

I even had a Marine ask me to explain to his wife on the phone where we were. She was beginning to think he was telling her lies. She had heard again on TV that all reservists were out of Kuwait. I told her plainly that we were on the phone in a tent somewhere in the Kuwaiti desert on the outskirts of Kuwait City. Hopefully, she believed me.

The date of our pending departure continued to change in two- or three-day increments. Three. Four. Nine. Five. Seven. There seemed to be no rhyme or reason.

The longer we waited, the hotter it got. As mid-March turned to late-April, temperatures climbed to 115° F or more in the shade.

"In five days we'll be outta here."

"Are you sure?"

"Make it eight days."

"Seven."

"Six."

"Five."

"Four."

"Three."

"Change of word. We'll be leaving six days from today."

"Seven."

"You can't be serious."

Infantry training days after the war seemed a little silly, so we invited the artillery, tanks, and even pilots over to give the Marines some insight into their business.

We also had uninvited guests. Scorpions and mice were the most common intruders. Everyone seemed to have one or the other in their living areas. I had mice. They would have been my preference if anyone had asked me to choose.

Stray dogs and puppies found their way to some softhearted Marines. We had to make a special effort to keep the dogs and puppies away. They seemed harmless, but the risk of bites and disease was too great to allow pets.

Each living hole was covered with a shade tarp, well-dusted if not completely covered by the blowing sand. The flimsy, camouflaged roof over the hole worked like an old-fashioned animal trap when a donkey on the loose found his way to our camp. The startled Marine's reaction from beneath the ground was about to be harshly misdirected at his fellow Marines. He assumed they had intentionally done something. That is until he saw the leg of a strange animal by his face. He burst out from under the tarp to see an equally surprised donkey.

The battalion chaplain had Bible studies and reunion classes for single and married Marines. For physical training we tried a few things, including a field meet, but the favorite was softball. The most memorable game was never finished. It was memorable because the game was called on account of darkness about noon that day. The wind had shifted and the oil well smoke blew in and blocked out the sun.

Large GP (general purpose) tents were erected. Most Marines, but not all, moved out from our holes in the ground. Those who stayed in their holes did so by choice. Sometimes, it seemed less hot in a dug-out hole, and some just liked the privacy or the luxury of not moving.

Heat radiated from the tops of the tents but the tents provided shade. The wind blew like a furnace, day and night. Flies were a real nuisance during daylight hours and forced me to use some sort of face cover beginning at first light. The rising temperatures made me want to uncover; buzzing flies changed my mind.

Hydration had become second nature by then. I lost count of the amount of water I drank daily, but I remember drinking a 1.5-liter bottle every night before I went to sleep and another one as soon as I woke up each morning. We drank water out of habit and necessity all day long.

Time passed slowly, and our ability to keep Marines focused became increasingly difficult. Word kept changing. The battalion commander met with all the Marines and apologized. He explained that they never passed any dates until they were confirmed as solid dates from regiment and division, but they still kept changing.

While the CO was talking, I thought I saw one of my Marines being disrespectful and unsafe. There he was, sprawled out like he was back on the block on his Momma's front porch, complete with his cover pulled over his face.

His rifle was carelessly laid flat across his lap like he was a moonshiner in Kentucky, and although I didn't hear any snoring, he appeared to be sleeping soundly. I intended to jerk his rifle up out of his lap to get his attention. When I did, I discovered that he was attached to it. He had his sling around his head, so when I jerked, the rifle and the Marine came up as one.

I was already mad, so I just carried on like I had done that on purpose. I pulled the rifle in close so the Marine and I would be staring eye to eye. I quickly recognized that he wasn't one of my Marines, but it didn't matter at that point.

"When the colonel's talking, you sit up and listen like a Marine."

He didn't say a word. I let go of the weapon, releasing the tension from around his neck, and he sat down slowly. You could tell he was madder than a hornet but knew better than to show it too much.

The next morning at chow, I ran into that Marine's company commander in line.

"Hey, John, we need to talk."

"About what?"

"We'll need to talk off line."

"Now you've got to tell me."

"One of my Marines is pressing assault and battery charges against you. (Pause) Don't laugh. This sounds serious."

"Were you there?"

"No."

"Well, I was. He must be crazy. I'm not too worried about it. Let's eat."

"You know I'm a civilian lawyer, and it doesn't require much to qualify for simple assault. You need to take this seriously."

"Well, I was there, and it wasn't even close."

Days passed. Curiosity got the best of me, so I asked my company commander about it.

"Captain Meighen, did you ever hear any more about that assault charge against me?"

"Colonel Dawson mentioned it to me once. I told him I saw the whole thing, and there was nothing to it. You shouldn't hear any more about it."

I didn't.

• • •

Ad hoc trips into Kuwait City helped get our Marines out of the confines of our desert abode. It was just for them to see the city and the people. For the first time, some of them saw the smiles of the Kuwaitis and the friendly waves and gestures. Graffiti written in broken English praising President Bush was everywhere. Sometimes, it was even written backwards by the locals, who normally wrote in Arabic from right to left.

Chapel services were getting more and more solemn as morale dipped. The slump was noticeable enough to prompt a personal testimony from a local

American contractor who had stumbled into our midst weeks earlier. He had begun attending our chapel services each week.

"I know you're ready to go home and that this place is not where you want to be. I'm from Oklahoma and have lived and worked here before the war, and I'll work here long afterwards. Every week I get excited when I can drive out and see your vehicles come into view. You give me a spiritual and emotional lift for the week. I can't wait to come back here each week. Soon, I'll drive out here for church, and you'll be gone. I'll hit the brakes. That will be a sad day for me. I just wanted to say thank you before that day comes."

Perspective is always important, but it's especially important at times like these.

• • •

Some Marines from our battalion were in Kuwait City one day and ran into a CNN reporter. As they talked, their frustration piqued the reporter's interest, and in a matter of hours, it became a story aired nationwide—*The Lost Battalion.*

We weren't really lost, but we were at least somewhat forgotten when it came to the secretary of defense. His byline, which reiterated that "all reservists are home," fueled a storm of phone calls and letters from family members to congressmen, to press outlets, to generals, and just about anybody for whom they could find an address and/or phone number.

When CNN came to our position, our company laid low. We knew nothing good could come of it, and nothing did. Several Marines and Marine officers spoke a little too freely that day. It just caused heartache and hard feelings, and we didn't get home a day sooner. We were still one of the last Marine Corps battalions out of Kuwait.

Hard feelings and harsh comments by Marines were as understandable to us as they were unacceptable to our higher headquarters. Even our operations officer, a regular, who left and went back to the States early, had the audacity to tell Marine reserve families that they were misinformed about our conditions in Kuwait. Basically, he was calling their loved ones—our Marines—liars. Maybe he should have stayed long enough to experience it with us.

•••

Our March exodus became a mid-May escape. How can anyone explain the emotions of a return from combat and a six-month deployment? Some things you just have to experience to understand. This is one of them.

Smiling stewardesses welcomed us aboard a chartered airliner. There's no telling how many flights they had already made, but they treated us like it was their first and even an honor and a privilege to escort us home. The pilots thanked us again as we taxied. Our excitement could have fueled the impending take-off.

I was numb on the plane home, but the sight of Memphis International Airport made me weak. A feeling of vulnerability encompassed me. I was beginning to let my emotional guard down.

A police escort included a former company commander who had been the CO when I joined the unit as a PFC ten years earlier.

They met us on the tarmac. I thought the police escort was a good thing until they took the long way around the city to get us to the drill center, and they drove way too slowly. It seemed to take forever.

Finally, the drill center came into sight. A remarkable crowd had gathered for our 3 a.m. arrival. At first I thought I would cry. Then I felt like I could laugh out loud. Maybe I would laugh and cry. I knew I would explode. Family and friends from childhood, from school, from church, and just about everywhere in between were there. I can't imagine a better reception.

The buses were supposed to let us off behind the drill center. My family knew where the buses were scheduled to stop, and they were anxiously waiting. But when the buses turned in off Jackson Avenue, they were mobbed. There was no driving through that crowd. The driver stopped the bus and opened the door.

We exited the bus to cheers and hugs, but I was looking for my family. I knew I had to push through the rest to get to them. It was an electric atmosphere. As I weaved and ducked my way around one side, Lee and the rest of the family were working their way around the other side.

When I broke out on the other side of the mob, two old friends spotted me and one said, "Hey, there's a Marine with no one to greet him. Let's go welcome him home."

It was me. We had a good laugh and took a picture together, and they pointed me toward Lee.

At least the confusion had probably saved me from bursting into tears. I was so happy to see her and the kids. Then I looked around and saw dozens of my family with matching T-shirts that read, "Welcome Home Captain Caldwell." There were more friends and family there than I would have dreamed at that early hour.

Jennifer and JC were a welcome sight and made me feel great. Cannon had grown so much, and at 10 months old didn't quite remember me, plus I had a new mustache that gave him second thoughts about such an unfamiliar character. I had prepared myself for that and didn't force the issue.

When I found Daddy, I was able to return the New Testament he had loaned me before I left. He had told me he wanted me to bring it back. I knew that meant he wanted *me* back, but I also wanted him to know I hadn't forgotten.

The New Testament was a gift he had received from Momma when he was a Marine in World War II. It was a small, black, leather-covered Bible with a metal plate discolored with time. The pages were yellowed, but the note from Momma was as clear as the day she wrote it: "May this keep you from all harm. All my love, Lib." Daddy had carried it though combat across the Pacific. Now I had carried it through combat in Southwest Asia. I was proud to return it.

I hugged everybody, even some I didn't know. At some point during the middle of all this chaos, we turned in our weapons, accounted for everything, including our Marines, and dismissed.

1991 Gunnery Sergeant Keith Rinehart and I flew our state flag proudly.

1991 One lane under the railroad let me know I was about a 100 yards from home.

1991 Desert Storm accommodations.
"Home is Where You Dig It" per LCpl Sing.

1991 Media adds to the atmosphere as we were welcomed home by family and friends

1991 Homecoming at the reserve center

"Let every one of us please his neighbor for his good to edification."

Romans 15:2

...7

Conflicts of Community

Widespread expressions of appreciation greeted us. Desert Storm veterans were offered free hotel rooms, amusement park tickets, and discounts across the country.

Parades large and small were popular and there were frequent public displays of support. We encouraged our Marines to participate, first because they, as Marines and combat veterans, deserved it, and second because it was a way we could show our appreciation for the support we received. Even the Marines who had been reluctant to ride or walk in a parade were glad they did.

Celebrations and accolades diminished rapidly with time.

Involuntary personal reflections on the country's infamous reception for Vietnam veterans tempered my own celebration a bit. Twenty years before us they fought gallantly for the freedom and independence of others. Their well-deserved hero's welcome was denied them. Time might have healed many, but certainly not all, of their old wounds. A twinge of indirect guilt stayed with me, along with a personal commitment to always remember that group of underappreciated vets.

More sobering thoughts dampened my elation to be home. It was the underlying thought of those who didn't come home. The low number and percentage of casualties allowed too many to look away as if the casualty count were zero. It wasn't. Grief for those who lost loved ones was and is just as real and just as painful—their sacrifice just as great.

Invitations to speak at men's prayer breakfasts, elementary schools, church congregations, and civic groups allowed me to tell a piece of my personal story, including the spiritual side of the conflict. While questioning my own knack for speaking to groups, I felt an obligation to share, and I enjoyed sharing that side of Desert Storm.

How could there not be a spiritual side? President Bush had called on the nation to pray. We prayed. I prayed. In so many ways our prayers—my prayers—were answered.

"Lord, give our leaders the wisdom they need. Make it quick. Minimize our loss of life. Bring us home safe, and we will give you the glory."

Similar prayers were voiced across our nation and across the battlefield. The Lord answered in a mighty way, but too often we didn't keep our part of the bargain.

Before the short war ended, most Americans and our allies began to give credit to technological superiority. The image of a "smart bomb" entering the vent shaft of an Iraqi bunker was televised over and over and seared into the nation's memory.

"Weren't the air strikes amazing?"

"What about those Abrams battle tanks? They were awesome."

"Field artillery is still the king of battle."

Even after the successful bombing, it required boots on the ground to push the Iraqis out of Kuwait. Our infantry was better equipped than any force that has ever gone to battle. And don't forget the command and control. President George Herbert Walker Bush, his staff, and his generals got a lot of credit.

"What a brilliant plan of classic deception and modern maneuver warfare!"

When there were estimates of tens of thousands of casualties and legitimate fear of chemical weapons, prayers were not lifted to American technology. We may have prayed *for* the generals, but no one prayed *to* the generals. We prayed to God. We asked specifically for things that we received. Where were His credit and our humility? God could let us go to war in the future, counting on our own technology and military genius. It would be quite an awakening.

Now was not the occasion to gear up for the next war; it was the time to wind down. The whirlwind return included time off for some of us, but civilian employers were waiting.

It was time to go back to work. My boss, James Delgadillo, had already paid me one month's advance pay upon my activation. Upon my return he gave me a $500 bonus to spend on our family vacation before returning to work.

That's the kind of employer support I wish every Marine reservist had. It was a small company, like a family, which made it even more special. He probably doesn't remember his own generosity. Lee and I will never forget.

During the initial activation, a few of our Marines were actually fired. At least one employer reconsidered after a simple letter from our company commander explained the law.

Many other Marines responded to their nation's call with little real assurance that their civilian jobs or careers would be intact upon their return. Some weren't. The law hadn't really been tested, and it had its limits.

According to the law, part-time employment is not protected, even if it is the Marine's primary or sole source of income. Insurance salesmen and those working in other commission-based positions were hit hard and sometimes felt the pinch worse upon return.

There weren't and still aren't any provisions to protect the interests of college students who may be activated. They are at the mercy of their college or university. Some of my Marines were threatened with failing grades if they went to war. To my this is not occur, but the total lack of coherent school policies left much to be desired.

Another group who sometimes took a hard hit was the self-employed. Anyone who has ever run their own small business can imagine how business would suffer if they had to leave it for six months or more with little or no notice.

Soon after returning, it was apparent to me that I needed a break from the reserves. I had been a captain a while now. Because the Marine Corps reserve establishment is nearly void of lieutenants, captains typically fill the lieutenant billets.

I enjoyed my time on active duty as a lieutenant. I enjoyed my time in the reserves serving in lieutenant billets. Platoon commander was and is a much-loved leadership position, but after seven years and a combat deployment, it was beginning to take its toll.

Friction over a potential speaker for the upcoming Marine Corps Birthday Ball was the last straw. I've always thought choosing the guest speaker was one of the least important issues, but it often becomes the most stressful.

"Captain Caldwell, do you have any ideas?"

"Yes, sir. We could ask Fred Smith, CEO of FedEx. He's a former Marine in the area, or I've heard there's a retired sergeant major of the Marine Corps from somewhere around or living in West Tennessee."

"See if we can get Fred Smith as soon as possible."

"Yes, sir." The next day was Sunday and Captain Meighen called me into his office for an update.

"Did you contact Fred Smith?"

"No, sir. It's the weekend. Even if I had his home phone number, I wouldn't call him at home and expect a positive response."

"I thought I said I wanted this finalized by this afternoon."

"That's just not realistic if you're set on the CEO of FedEx."

His tirade that followed resembled more of a drill instructor addressing a recruit than a captain to a captain about a Marine Corps Ball speaker. Maybe he needed more time to decompress.

Whatever the reason, it was too soon after Desert Storm for me. I decompressed a little on him too. It sounded like two Marines with PTSD. That exchange helped me decide to take a break. I would drop to the Individual Ready reserve (IRR).

The IRR is an inactive reserve status requiring no monthly drills. Presidential recalls are still possible, and a variety of volunteer assignments can be arranged on a case-by-case basis.

I had no idea that I would take two years off, but that probably saved my reserve career in the long run. My motivation level was nil. Some time away from the Marine Corps tedium helped me wind down and recharge my internal batteries.

• • •

Time away from the reserves allowed me certain flexibility that had been missing. There was initially more time for home, family and church.

Lee and I soon completed a trifecta of sorts by participating in Operations Desert Shield, Desert Storm and Desert Stork. It seems the Marines, sailors, airmen, soldiers, and their spouses created a mini baby boom after the return from Southwest Asia.

Franklin Daniel was born in July of 1992, just over a year following my return from the combat zone. Jennifer, JC, and Cannon were excited about our new addition that rounded out our young family.

Our growing family was another reminder that our status quo seemed to be dynamic. The only way for me to significantly improve our family's financial future was to take some risk. A business venture would be more doable without a Marine reserve cloud over my head.

I refocused my attention on serious research and planning to start my own business. It had been in the back of my mind and I had read, attended seminars, and laid the mental and emotional groundwork for years. Greater than my fear of failure was the dreaded possibility of becoming a workaholic. I knew I would have to make a conscious effort to set time aside for family while putting in a time-consuming effort.

• • •

JC had played ball since he was in his crib. It never took any encouragement; he just loved playing any sport with a ball—baseball, especially.

Lee had already taken time to help coach T-ball. Now it was my turn. I loved the thought of it, but I couldn't see myself committing as a head coach. Being an assistant would be enough for now.

Coach Joe and I fielded a great team of boys in a recreational league. The boys were talented and played to win, but this season we all learned a lot more than baseball.

Curt Copeland played the field while wearing a batting helmet. It was the first year that doctors allowed Curt to play any sport. Although he was well behind the others in physical skill, his enthusiasm and determination set the standard for the rest of us. The team bonded in special ways, and the proper balance of fun and competitiveness for a recreational team was refreshing. Curt died a few years later, but his positive impact on the players and the parents still lives.

Another year or so later, Coach Art Walls and I were able to experience the best and some of the worst aspects of little league baseball in one fun-filled year. Recreational leagues require coaches to play every player each game. That's the way we liked it, but a few coaches over the years were known to chase off their lesser athletes so they didn't have to deal with putting them into the games.

Conventional wisdom said that more than one or two on the bench would make it too difficult to substitute every player every game and keep a viable team on the field. We had three to four players on the bench every game that we rotated into the game. Although at first it seemed like a chore, it was also less discouraging for those on the bench not to be sitting there alone and feeling left out. It kept the team atmosphere alive on the bench. Frankly, it allowed all of us to have more fun and made everyone better players.

Three teams were in the running for the championship when the last week of the season rolled around. We finished in first. It was almost a great ending to an awesome summer, but then came all-stars.

As the winning coaches, we had the honor of coaching the all-star team in a mini season of tournaments. It was miserable. Although we knew and liked all the kids and their parents one on one, together they were a nightmare.

Of course all our players were infielders, and they and their parents took it as an insult if they were positioned in the outfield. Most were lead-off batters or clean-up batters on their teams. Now some of them had to bat last. That wasn't well received either, not to mention the ones who had to sit on the bench for several innings.

"Why isn't he starting?"

"You should put him as the lead-off batter."

"He always hits better as the clean-up hitter."

"Right field? He doesn't play right field. He's a natural infielder."

"You need him on first base."

"If he had been at third base, he wouldn't have missed that ball."

"He's too slow."

"He should be pitching."

The bickering and complaining were almost unbearable. I began looking for two quick losses in double elimination tournaments in order to escape and enjoy what was left of my weekend. Even work would be some relief.

There were already enough competing interests on my time. What could compel me to volunteer for something else?

"Hey, John, when are you going to join the fire department?"

"I've been meaning to, but you know... work... family... church..."

"We've got a meeting tomorrow night. I'll come by and pick you up."

"I'll be ready."

If I wanted someone to put a fire out at my house, then shouldn't I be willing to put one out at his or her house? It was and is that simple. Friends from church and around the community were also on the fire department and made me feel at home.

Faded green metal siding covered the building beside the railroad track in "downtown" Nesbit. The building had two, solid, white bay doors in the front and two on the side. A scarcely used office had been constructed above the firehouse kitchen.

Helmets and individual "turnout" gear lined the chipboard walls. Unexplainable junk was stacked under cabinets and in corners and even out in the open. Our volunteers were pack rats by nature. It was partially the Depression-era veterans of the department with a tendency to keep things "just in case," and it was partially necessitated by the fact that the department had been under funded for so long.

Nesbit hadn't been much of a town since its heyday when the cotton gin was in full swing. Now there were only traces of what was the small epicenter of the agricultural community. A few, old, one-room buildings in varying states of disrepair made up the old town. The remains of an old bank building had been boarded up for years. Its cracked and broken red-brick veneer was about the only thing left of the original structure.

Next to it was a dilapidated old building that had been occupied off and on in recent years as a secondhand store. It looked even less safe to occupy than the old bank. The brick had been coated with concrete or stucco, but the coating was chipped and falling off, exposing multiple levels and colors of paint. The shoddy roof leaned and sagged.

Two, small, wood-framed buildings completed the historical line up. One was being used as a temporary church. Another, larger, brick structure across the street housed a weekly auction for a couple of years.

On-the-job training began by assigning a sponsor to help me learn about firefighting. After a six-month probation period, the department voted to accept me as a member. I was honored and challenged. My new name was my number, 712, pronounced "Seven-twelve."

Our equipment was old and nearly worn out, but the continuous efforts of the firemen kept things in working order. The retirees seemed to do the lion's share of the work. Young volunteers like me were busier at work during the day, coaching little league, raising our families, etc. I routinely took night calls. The theory was that the retirees could handle the day, and those of us unavailable during the day would make the night calls. The retirees loved it so much they would often do both.

It was sort of an addiction to some. Once you've helped someone on a scene, you want to help more. Bonds of friendship with fellow firefighters are forged at some horrific scenes and some humorous false alarms.

"Engine-Seven in service."

"Check, Zero-one-twenty-four."

"Hey, Larry, isn't this the same address we've already responded to twice this week about this time?"

"I think so. The last two times she got off work at midnight and set her fire alarm off cooking sausage."

"I thought so. I'm getting a little tired of getting up in the middle of the night for this stuff."

"Me, too, but it's hard not to respond without knowing for sure."

"There's the house and there she is."

"I'm so sorry, guys. I called the sheriff's department and told them it was a false alarm again. Did they not tell you?"

"Lady, if we come out here again and your house isn't on fire, it will be when we leave."

At least she had a sense of humor. Ours was wearing thin, and the chief had just expressed a bit of our frustration. Normally, we truly are glad and thankful when there is no fire or serious accident, but repeated false alarms can get especially annoying.

Fried catfish was the staple and standard fundraiser for us and most local volunteer fire departments. It was probably a better public relations tool than it was a fundraiser.

Although we promoted our fish fries, we never really advertised our true successes. When the house fire is confined to a kitchen, only the homeowner and the firefighters realize that the house would have burned to the ground if the volunteers hadn't made it when they did.

One house was saved after a lightning strike with no one home. Just the laundry room was lost. It was the home of a founding member of the department who had long been retired. That one was especially satisfying.

One building we lost, along with every other department, both paid and volunteer, was the old Hernando School Building. It was historic, and there was debate on whether to renovate or raze it. The fire ended the debate.

Structure fires, grass fires, and even false alarms were expected. The thing I hadn't prepared myself for was the vehicle accidents. In our community the volunteer fire department is called to every wreck. They took up most of our effort and time.

"Nesbit Fire Department, stand by for tone."

"Possible structure fire off Reed Road. Closest cross street is Pine Tree Loop."

We found a homeowner burning leaves near his shed without a permit. Within minutes the fire was out.

"Show fire is out and all Nesbit units clearing the scene and returning to quarters."

"Check, Nineteen-thirty-one."

Engine Seven returned to Station Number Two.

I was in Tanker-7 used for shuttling water. While returning to quarters at Station Number One, we began to hear confusing chatter on the radio without a tone from the dispatcher.

"—MVA, Pleasant Hill Road, east of Station Two—"

"Seven-oh-one with Pleasant Hill command."

"Check, establishing Pleasant Hill command at nineteen thirty-nine."

"Attention, all Nesbit units report to the scene."

"Engine Seven is in the ditch eastbound. The other vehicle westbound is in the road with two injuries and entrapment. We'll need two ambulances on the scene and an ETA on the wing if it's available."

As I turned around and headed to the scene, it was becoming apparent that Engine 7 was not only at the accident but *in* the accident.

Engine 7 was totaled. The car had obviously crossed the yellow line and hit Engine 7 head on. The car's engine was pushed up into the front seat. The make and model of the car was unrecognizable. It's amazing we were able to work a rescue and not just a recovery. I stepped up to lend a hand.

"What about everybody on the truck?"

"Nobody was seriously hurt. Everybody onboard was actually wearing their seatbelts for a change."

Stabilizing the car was important so we could use the Jaws of Life to rescue the occupants trapped inside. One occupant was extracted easily. The second was pinned by the dash and had several compound fractures with bones protruding. He was conscious and was voicing his pain in continuous moans and groans. Fortunately, the Jaws of Life pushed the entire dashboard away in a single mangled mess. As we were about to lift the patient from the debris, our radios went off again. This time it was a tornado warning.

"Attention Nesbit Fire and EMS, a funnel cloud was spotted two miles southwest of Nesbit, heading to the northeast."

It was time to lift him out, not duck for cover. We just had to shrug off the tornado warning and hope for the best. The tornado passed directly over us without touching down. The patients were transported, and the wreckage was removed from the roadside.

Fire calls, church volunteer work and the Marine Corps reserves keep me occupied. My life, my family, my schedule, and my commitments have me about as busy as I think I can be.

• • •

In the meantime, Daddy was being forced out as an independent dealer for British Petroleum. Things had gone downhill in the years since Gulf Oil Company had been bought by BP. Hostile business practices against owner-operated service stations were widespread. BP charged Daddy a wholesale price for gasoline that was higher than BP sold direct to consumers. BP retail operations with the cheaper gas were erected just a couple of miles away in two directions. After 30 years in the same location, still selling around 80,000 gallons of gas per month, they refused to renew his lease.

Financial and emotional strain was coupled with physical tension and recurring chest pains. Daddy reasoned the cause as stress and brushed aside the possibility that nearly 60 years of smoking unfiltered Camel cigarettes had anything to do with it.

"I live on caffeine, nicotine, cholesterol, and calories," he would often boast with a smile.

The station closed unceremoniously in stages. Near the end it was hard for him to hire help, so I agreed to work the night shift for the remaining weeks.

Lee and the children would join me from 10 p.m. to 7 a.m. There was just enough room on the office floor for the kids to sprawl out with their blankets and pillows.

Hard, cold, dull, commercial tile behind Daddy's old wooden desk was the spot where Daddy would catch his naps in the afternoons. As he got older, he started using a collapsible red and blue vinyl kindergarten mat for added comfort. Now his grandchildren used the spot for a mini slumber party.

The station itself was comfort for Daddy. His work was also his play. Plans for the post-station era had not quite been settled, yet his ever-present optimism remained. Total retirement was not in his plans. However, without the seven days a week of work, there should be more time for his antique cars and 4th Marine Division Association activities.

The chest pains continued. Three to five packs per day had taken its toll. Multiple by-pass surgery was scheduled in an almost routine manner. It was not completely unexpected, and the surgery itself was becoming so commonplace that the gravity of the situation didn't sink in.

I stopped by the hospital on the way to work early that morning. They were just about to roll Daddy out of his room and prep him for the operation. Daddy had requested that the by-pass be done as soon as possible. He wanted to begin the recovery so he could attend the annual 4th Marine Division Association meeting in the fall.

None of us were prepared for what happened next.

Initially, the family had begun to gather at the hospital to be there for Momma and to hear the expected good news that all had gone well. First reports were sketchy but positive. Then the post-op period was extended.

"Some people take a little longer to come out from under anesthesia," we were told.

Hours passed. The reports and prognoses got worse as we attempted to dig out information from doctors and nurses.

Finally, the surgeon scheduled a family meeting. Glibly and all too casually, he explained that all had not gone well. How it happened was barely addressed, but he seemed to want to cover his tracks and defend his actions before slipping out of town on his vacation. High percentages of success meant nothing. We would be one of the supposed few families to experience an unsuccessful operation. They did not expect him to live more than a few days.

The heartache was only made bearable by the numbness of deep shock and doubt.

As the days continued to add up, we lost count of the number of doctors and medical professionals who chimed their unwelcome chorus dismissing any hope of a recovery.

My eight siblings and I fluctuated from optimism to despair amid the onslaught of negative news. Momma never wavered. Her resolve was based on her visible faith in God. Physical evidence called on reasonable thinkers to give up.

The initial coma lasted for several weeks straight. Slight movements in one thumb were dismissed by the doctors as insignificant.

"Someone needs to explain to your mother that there's nothing else that can be done."

"She's not giving up."

"He could be like this for some time."

"Don't we have any hope for improvement?"

"You may read about rare occasions in medical journals that are unexplainable, but you shouldn't expect it. It will likely get worse until the end."

More prayers, more heartache, and more medical reports followed. Bed sores, staph infections, and lack of any visible improvement were coupled with an uncooperative Methodist Hospital staff at every level.

Not only did their diagnosis include imminent death at any moment, but they set up ICU visitation in a way that would allow us to see Daddy just once every three days—just two visitors three times a day, and one of those would always be Momma. That was just unacceptable, so the nine of us quietly rotated with each other at each scheduled visit.

"Excuse me, sir. You are not allowed to rotate visitors in ICU."

"I understand the policy, but the doctors have said my father may not live much longer. If we follow your policy to the letter, it would be three days before I could see him again. So you see, we don't really have any other choice."

"Sir, we still cannot allow you in."

"I'm sorry, but I'm going in anyway."

"Sir, I will have to call security."

I stopped dead in my tracks. She may have just been doing her job, but I wasn't in the mood. Narrowing my eyes and lowering my voice, I explained reality in simpler terms.

"You don't have enough security to get me out of here."

As I turned toward Daddy's bed, part of me hoped she would call them. The doctors were making themselves scarce, and I was about ready to release my frustrations on somebody.

Momma still held out for a miracle. All we could do was support her, and we did. As long as she would not give up, neither would we.

Slowly and randomly, Daddy began to move. First, it was a few fingers. Then his eyes opened. The doctors assured us it was only involuntary muscle contractions and that he certainly could not see us. Days passed. He made some noise as if trying to speak. Again, doctors shrugged it off. More days passed.

Hope was renewed, but several more weeks of hospital ups and downs drove a wedge between us and the physicians. At one point an unidentified doctor entered Daddy's room and mumbled a few words at him as he slept. He declared, "No response," wrote something on his chart, and began to leave without addressing any family in the room. I stepped between the doctor and the door as I shut it.

"I don't know who you are, or what kind of doctor you are, but you need to start communicating if you expect to leave this room and get paid for whatever it is you're supposed to be doing."

He did.

I moved away from the door.

None of us questioned the graveness of Daddy's condition or the challenge he presented to doctors. Still, we expected a better level of professional effort and care than we were getting.

As Daddy improved, the nurses began noticing, but the doctors didn't. In fact they seemed to rebuke the nurses for siding with us. Eventually, the doctors couldn't deny it. They conceded some level of recovery was happening but cautioned us that the improvement could stop cold at any moment.

Daddy went on and off the ventilator several more times. Allergic reactions, infections, drug-induced comas and kidney failure were a few of the things that stalled progress and produced seemingly insurmountable setbacks. Momma kept the faith for all of us.

About four months after entering the hospital for Daddy's by-pass surgery, Momma demanded his release. Against the doctor's collective and individual advice, we took him home. During the next two years, Daddy learned to walk again. He could speak clearly and retained remarkable memory. Even kidney function was restored, with no explanation. It was truly a miracle!

My faith was strengthened, but my nerves were about shot. It affected every aspect of life to some degree or another.

Emotional and psychological fatigue oddly paired with a renewed internal restiveness.

• • •

Besides being fed up with the reserves, I was physically tired and just plain restless. My job as an advertising director for a large jewelry supply wholesaler in Memphis was going well but going nowhere. Pay was fair. Working conditions were more than all right. Relationships there were great, but something was missing. The learning curves and challenges were diminishing. I was in a rut.

There was a deeper urge to start my own advertising business, but I had a lot of reservations. Maybe it was the jolt of Daddy's ordeal at the hospital. Was it post-war jitters? I had witnessed the downside of activating my Marine reservists who ran their own businesses. It could cost me dearly. Did I really want to risk it? Plus, Daddy's experience with BP squeezing him out, along with other independent dealers like him, should have been enough discouragement.

Did I selfishly desire the greener grass on the other side of the fence? The urge had come and gone over the years, but this time it was different.

Lee and I discussed it and prayed. We discussed it some more and prayed some more. The timing seemed right in so many ways but wrong in others. Prayers and planning continued.

Finally, we were both at peace with the decision to make the change. I knew my prayers had been answered and that it was the right decision. The clearly right answer, however, did not come with guarantees, and we both knew it.

Friends and family were shocked. They knew life was good for us, and they wondered why we wanted to change it. They rationalized our seemingly illogical choice and frequently commented, "At least you've got your savings—"

Lee and I would always respond with, "Yes, of course," implying some level of financial security.

It kept the ones we loved from worrying about our lack of capital and our sanity. We didn't tell them that our savings amounted to less than a thousand dollars and that this was going to be a gigantic leap of faith.

Frankly, I was so sure of God's will in this decision that I was more scared *not* to try than to risk hitting bottom. There was an unusual amount of clarity for the time being but no prophetic vision of how this venture would end.

We had determined Lee would remain in the critical roles of homemaker and mother, which also limited our financial options. Some of the more predictable income in our business plan evaporated as soon as we had committed ourselves beyond the point of no return. The pressure was immense. There would be no steady income. We were off to an even rockier start than originally anticipated.

It was a difficult time but a spiritually enlightening time. Although there was no paycheck with a boss's signature on a scheduled payday, God provided for our needs. Some of the ways were properly humbling and oddly encouraging.

My business always paid its rent and utilities on time. Somehow, we had enough money or credit to eat and stay in our home.

JC and Jennifer were always well dressed with name-brand hand-me-downs from my nieces and nephews. We tried not to poormouth to them and others about our lack of money, and we felt as if we were putting on a pretty good front.

Then a retired couple in our church family invited us over to their house. It didn't seem unusual at first because we had been there several times over the years. The timing and circumstances were a little haphazard, but we were glad to accept their invitation.

After a brief friendly visit, they gave us a prepared cardboard box of assorted household items. It was an odd assortment by any standard: ketchup, toothpaste, dish detergent, etc. Every item in that box was an item we needed. In fact it looked like they had broken into our house and conducted inventory. Through them our faith was strengthened. It served as a tangible reminder from God that He knows what we need and that He is watching over us.

• • •

Another year: I set aside time to coach little league baseball again. This time it was Daniel's team, and I would be the head coach. I took time off to meet the kids as they got out of school in the afternoon.

Almost the entire team attended Horn Lake Elementary School. It was a typical, single-story grade school with a flat roof and brick veneer. There was a crude but functional backstop of secondhand chain-linked fence nailed to sawed-off telephone posts on the small grass lot beside the school.

Nearly every afternoon, Daniel and his friends burst out of the school at a sprint resembling a stampede. Books would start flying as they dug their gloves and caps out of their backpacks on the run. I know that baseball, exercise, and sunshine were 100% better for them than afternoon television, video games and, yes, even homework. It was also better for me than just about anything in the world.

I loved baseball and I loved children. We had a mix of relatively experienced players and ones being introduced to the game for the first time. Everyone seemed to get along—even the parents.

Our family was living the middle-class version of the American dream. Chores like cutting grass and grading our driveway with a borrowed tractor were part of the accepted routine.

Unresponsive county government interrupted our everyday concerns. My neighbors and I had lived with our road in shambles for months, and then half under construction for several more months, before the slipshod repair was finished.

We also had a neighbor illegally dumping tires and construction trash on property adjacent to our house, and the county government would not respond to our calls. The board secretary even had the audacity to argue with us, claiming that we didn't see what we saw with our own eyes.

It was time to do more than just make a few phone calls. It was time to volunteer to do something about it. I would run for county supervisor in the upcoming election.

I didn't even know my opponent. I think we had met briefly, but we didn't know each other at all. All I knew was that I wanted more from county government than my neighbors and I were getting.

Lee and I prayed about it, but we didn't get a clear answer. She and I kept the thought of our intentions just between us. We knew a lot of our neighbors and friends may also be thinking of running, and we didn't want to discourage any of them. That's why we waited until the last minute of the last day to file. By then we knew we wouldn't be competing against any of our close friends and neighbors.

A quick trip to the old courthouse would change my life. I wasn't even sure where to go in the courthouse to file. The walk from the car to the front door led me beneath towering oaks that partially shaded the dormant grass blanketing the courthouse lawn.

Classic Greek-Revival architecture with massive columns created an impressive entry against the old, red-brick, three-story structure. Upon entering the front doorway one's attention was drawn upward to the larger-than-life murals that told the story of Hernando de Soto's discovery of the Mississippi River. An open rotunda and wrought iron balcony rail on the second floor allowed those on the first floor to see the paintings above as well as the extended height of the domed ceiling and skylights. The circular balcony also allowed for those upstairs to enjoy the view of the decorative terrazzo floor below. Worn and stained hardwood interior doors and trim were scratched with character, adding to the antique feel of the place.

Running for county supervisor was a methodical, calculated decision, and yet I was a little uneasy and awkward walking those hallways. I never imagined how personal politics could really be, but I was quickly introduced to the fact that "All politics is personal."

Off the battlefield I don't think I ever had an "enemy" in my life until that day. Nearly everyone I had ever met, I liked. If the feeling wasn't mutual, at least most folks had been polite about it.

Now, lines were immediately drawn. People who liked the incumbent especially well or those who just didn't like Republicans seemed to naturally set up camp against me, personally and politically. It was a strange feeling that I had never before experienced.

Lee and I were politically green—inexperienced—so I hadn't thought twice about filing as a Republican. That's how I voted, so it was a natural choice. I hadn't thought much about the local political landscape when it came to parties.

For the first few weeks, Lee and I did little but plan and pray. We needed more assurance that this step was within the Lord's will. It wasn't too late to respectably pull out. Then we started getting confirmation that we needed to run, so run we did.

As it turned out, my opponent was not only an incumbent but "a Riley." It was widely believed among local politicos that a Riley couldn't be beaten. Paul Leslie Riley was friendly and likeable, the brother of a previous supervisor and the first cousin of Sheriff Riley, an extremely popular and powerful multi-term county sheriff. The family was well entrenched in local politics, and there seemed to be a Riley working in every government building and every level of government in the county. Maybe we had bitten off more than we could chew, or maybe that could work to our advantage.

"You can't win as a Republican."

"Maybe we can't, but we can work hard and get close. We'll let the good Lord sort out the votes."

"If only you were running in a different district—"

Most people thought we didn't stand a chance, so it was mostly friendly on the campaign trail. We were dismissed by local leadership, but we began to generate some real grassroots support.

I went to a "Nuts and Bolts" training session about running a grass-roots campaign taught by Evelyn McPhail. She was a brilliantly captivating Republican speaker with a "down home" style energized by deep, heartfelt convictions. She was obviously well educated on the exact things I needed to hear. I couldn't take notes fast enough.

It also convinced me that I was overwhelmed and out of my league. Lee and I had great "salt-of-the-earth" support from friends and neighbors in my community, but none of us knew much about political campaigns. We prayed specifically for more political help.

Running for office would absorb our lives for nearly eight months.

It's a good thing there was some personal spiritual renewal prior to this intense period of time. Working from "can to can't" was more than a cliché, it was reality. Lee and I were the only ones who really knew the sweat equity going into the advertising business—before, during and after the campaign.

Advertising and publishing efforts as an entrepreneur squeezed the life out of most days. The precious balance of time was being refocused to a grass roots political campaign for county supervisor.

A few nights of overtime bled into the next day and one episode of more than 48 straight hours at the office without a break was an indicator that something had to give. Two hours of sleep on the carpeted floor started to seem more like the full-time Marine Corps we had left than the new civilian life I thought we had chosen.

Any so-called work routine was long gone. Finding time to coach little league or participate on the volunteer fire department was getting more difficult and approaching impossible. Being at church every time the doors opened was becoming a thing of the past.

Reserves had been a destabilizing element to an otherwise quiet life in the suburbs. Now the Marines had dibs on becoming the closest thing to continuity we would experience ... until one day when the phone rang.

"Major Caldwell, this is Sergeant Jones from Kansas City. Our computers show you are in the graphics arts field as a civilian. Is that correct?"

"Yes, I run my own business."

"Sir, General Punaro is trying to put together a team of Marines with your civilian background for an ADSW—Active Duty Special Work—assignment designing some promotional print materials, if you're interested."

"I've never been able to put my civilian skills to work for the Marine Corps. I am very interested. Tell me more."

"First, it is expected to be a three to four weeks in September."

"That counts me out. I am in the middle of a political campaign, and I can't give that kind of time. If it were another time or if the period were shorter, I'd love to do something like that."

"I understand, sir. Thanks, anyway."

A few days later, he called back.

"Sir, this is Sergeant Jones again. We have assembled a group of Marines with a variety of backgrounds and experiences, but none of them are perfect fits. If you could come for part of the time as a team leader, we can probably go with what we've got. The rest of the team will be here the entire time. You could steer them, then leave and come back. Would you be available for something like that?"

"I never knew the Marine Corps could be that flexible. Let me look at my calendar and get back with you."

The schedule ahead showed no "free" time, but I wanted to make time if I could. After some juggling, I called them.

"I can give you two days a week for four weeks."

"We'll take it. Let me confirm that here, sir, and I'll call you back."

He called back.

"Sir, can you make your dates overlap on the days the general is in town? I have the dates right here—"

"I can do that. We've got a deal."

"Sir, I will cut you orders and fax them to you."

"Great."

This sounded like fun. But I hated that it was going to be so hectic in the middle of the campaign and that I would lose time on the campaign trail.

When I arrived, several team members were already there, but they seemed to be waiting. Apparently, they were waiting for me, so after our brief with the chief of staff, we got rolling.

Everyone seemed to genuinely get along, and we had the necessary expertise to get the job done. As we exchanged the usual pleasantries—"Where are you from?" "What's your MOS?" "What's your civilian job?"—Major Rhinehart, formerly the mayor of Columbus, Ohio, took notice that I was running for county supervisor.

"When we get done here today, we need to go down to the O-club and I'll tell you how to win."

"You've got a deal."

Marines are generally cocky, and officers are the worst, so I was immediately suspect but genuinely interested. We sat down at a small round table near the bar. He drank and talked, and I took notes. His advice was not theoretical. It was almost tangible. Then he challenged me to raise more money.

"Based on what you've told me about the size of your district, you'll need at least another two thousand dollars. Do you think you can raise that in the next few weeks?"

"I doubt it. That's a lot of money for my supporters."

"You can do it. If you do it, I'll throw in a hundred dollars myself. As a matter of fact, I'm so sure you can do it, here's a hundred right now."

"You know, I've prayed for some professional political help. They say, 'The Lord works in mysterious ways.' You may be a strange answer to my prayers."

As I took the generous donation, my motivation level was challenged. More importantly, Lee's and my vision now had some focus. I would make sure we followed his advice to the letter. It was an interesting way and place and time to witness, but it somehow felt right. The major and I met every chance we could during our short period of duty together. Then it was back to the campaign.

Coasting through the Republican primary unopposed seemed almost unfair. The unsuccessful Democrat challenger to the incumbent lobbed countless volleys of malicious attacks in a desperate effort to undermine the sitting supervisor.

Quietly, we knocked on doors. We knocked on nearly every door in the district. We knocked on doors in key areas twice, and some we hit three times.

Yard signs supporting our opponent did not prevent us from knocking. Many times the one answering the door had not committed to vote any particular way. Someone who lived there must have allowed the sign to be placed in their yard, they would say.

"Some neighborhood kids just asked us if we'd mind. You can take it down if you want and put yours up."

"No, thanks, but if you wouldn't mind taking it down, we'd be grateful. But the most important thing is that we need your vote on Election Day."

Very rarely, we would meet an unfriendly response. One such response went like this.

"Good afternoon. My name is John Caldwell and I'm running for County Supervisor—"

"DON'T YOU SEE THAT SIGN IN MY YARD!"

"Yes, sir, but you and I haven't met, so I wanted to stop, introduce myself, and ask for your vote."

"I'M VOTING FOR RILEY!" he yelled in my face.

Not wanting to be intimidated, and trying to have some fun with a guy with apparently no sense of humor, I pressed a little.

"Well then, is there anyone else here old enough to vote that I can talk to besides you?"

"WE'RE ALL VOTING FOR RILEY."

"I'll guess by your response you wouldn't want a yard sign."

He slammed the door.

"Whew. I'm glad they're not all like that one."

When not knocking on doors, we were at barbeques, fish fries, spaghetti suppers, bake sales, car shows, festivals, ballgames, etc.

"Daddy, why are you eating a sandwich? I thought you were going to a fish fry *and* a barbeque?"

"Because I'm not going to eat. I'm going to campaign."

Candidates would glad-hand across the county and even pay fees to speak from a podium. Some event hosts would limit politician's speeches to as few as three minutes. Others would charge by the minute in hopes of either limiting the length or making more money.

Good advice kept me from getting up and reciting my resume. It quickly became apparent that most of that mattered little. Having a college degree meant next to nothing. Years as a local entrepreneur counted some, but only to a small percentage. Being a U.S. Marine Corps officer and combat veteran carried a bit more weight but didn't swing a lot of votes. It seemed the most significant element on my campaign literature was a small reference to Daddy's hog farm in Nesbit. That family history over 40 years before kept Lee and me from campaigning as outsiders.

Some political advice transcends the most stalwart barriers of party, position, and even time. "They don't care how much you know until they know how much you care." Truer advice may have never been uttered to a candidate.

Friends and family can make you proud but disappoint you in politics, as can be the case with family and friends in every aspect of life. If anyone in politics thinks family will naturally jump on board, they need to ask themselves if they and their family help each other weld, or fix cars, or cut grass, or manufacture widgets, or drive a forklift at their warehouse, etc. Career choices can be unique and usually are independent of other family members. In some ways it may seem that politics would be different, but in other ways it is a fair analogy.

The best thing about politics—you find out who your friends are.

The worst thing about politics—you find out who your friends are.

Church family took and takes care of my family when the Marines call me.

Giving back to the community

Annual Training varies from unit to unit, summer to summer.

"Every man's way is right in his own eyes, But the Lord weighs the hearts."

Proverbs 21:2

...8
Conflicts of Continuing

E lection Day arrived without fanfare. We began the day with energy and confidence. Twelve hours later, exhaustion and doubt took over. To embolden the handful of needed supporters, and a few doubters in Riley's backyard, I spent most of Election Day at my opponent's home box. It's plain to see why that idea is not normally advisable. Most of the voters arrived at the precinct with a hug and handshake for him, and most of my would-be supporters hardly made eye contact with me.

A few friends and die-hard supporters lifted my spirits as they entered the polls. Rare displays of affection and support were refreshing. But it didn't take exit-polling to tell that I was getting slaughtered. Although expected, it was entirely different living it.

Bodily and emotionally drained, I chose to burn off the last hints of nervous energy by picking up all the campaign signs as soon as darkness fell and the polls closed. I had no idea how to read the small electorate. We had counted our supporters and thought it would be extremely close. If we were to lose the election, I knew it would be nearly impossible to find the motivation to pull up signs afterward.

On the outskirts of the district, the solitude of a lonely county road was like a sanctuary. Most of my campaign signs had been located and retrieved. My cell phone barely had any reception when Lee called.

"Where are you?"

"I'm out near Arkabutla Lake, pulling up signs."

"Poll results are coming in. You need to get to the courthouse."

"Okay, I'll be there shortly."

Part of my resistance was concerning the signs, but a good part of it was an uneasiness to face the results. It was a difficult day. If I hadn't owed it to my supporters to be there, I might have just gone home and propped my feet up.

Results trickled in. A small early lead vanished when my opponent's large home box reported with over 75% in his favor. His lead was solid with only one ballot box left to count.

The remaining votes were from the Horn Lake East precinct. It was expected to be in our favor, but they had a reputation of not voting. If fact we were cautioned not to waste our time campaigning in Horn Lake. But how could we not? It's where our children went to school, and Lee was the PTO President. It's where I coached and our children played little league. It's where the largest number of our friends lived.

Apparently, an unusually large turnout had the Horn Lake poll's lines backed up. Voters who arrived by 7 p.m. could stay and vote. It was nearly 8 p.m. before the ballot box began its trek to the Desoto County Courthouse.

Every precinct in the county had been counted—except one. All races had been decided—except one. The Horn Lake East vote total and percentage would settle it. Soon, we learned how many ballots had been cast—over 700. That favored us. The margin needed for us to win the district was nearly 200 votes. That favored them. Both sides were cautiously optimistic.

"Horn Lake East reporting with seven hundred and thirty-five ballots cast . . . John Caldwell Sr., five hundred and—"

That's all we needed to hear. I hadn't realized that I was holding my breath. Leaning forward on the courthouse pews, I said a quick prayer and exhaled an intense sigh of relief. It seemed as if a huge weight was being lifted yet not entirely gone. Lee's ear-to-ear smile seemed to indicate her ability to celebrate the victory and the moment better than I could. That moment was as much or more hers, our children's, and our supporters as it was mine. Congratulations poured freely into the pews where Lee had staked out space in the back of the county's main courtroom. There was so much celebration that the reaction of our opposition was unseen.

It didn't take many days before we began to feel some resentment toward us. Friends and supporters of the outgoing incumbent were also county employees I would work with every week for at least the next four years. Most accepted political change as a fact of life, but others, even the board secretary, harbored bitterness for the entire term and beyond.

Elections are set every four years, but the campaigns can seem endless. While some incumbents may have a honeymoon period, or brief period of easing, that luxury was not afforded to us.

Our victory was such an upset that some considered it a fluke. Political opposition from an insiders' network met us at every turn. Our most innocent efforts were undermined.

One simple District 4 reappointment to the county's planning commission was denied by board vote. It was a statement vote: "We control the majority."

Temporary frustration at being so easily marginalized by the other board members was replaced with a deep-seated resolve.

A confrontation at our first meeting symbolized my first term. As the only newly elected supervisor, I had at least one colleague on the board who would ensure this motion would at least get some discussion.

"I would like to make a motion that we tape record all of our meetings."

"I'll second his motion," replied Gene Thach, a seasoned board member.

"The board only speaks through its minutes. What good will a recording do?" replied another.

"For one, it will let the public know we have nothing to hide. Past board minutes are nothing but motions and votes. Errors are hard to identify, and unapproved edits can take place behind closed doors. Discussion is totally left out of the record."

"I like the way we've been done it in the past. I can see a lot of problems with differences between the tape recording and the written record."

"There shouldn't be any material differences. Besides, the cities are already recording their meetings without any backlash."

"Let's vote."

"All in favor?"

Two hands raised.

"All opposed?"

Three hands.

"Three to two. I guess we'll keep doing it the way we've been doing it before you got here."

After that smug comment, I reached below my chair. Quietly but noticeably, I put a tape recorder on the table.

"We voted against tape recorders."

"That's for the county. As an individual, I'm allowed to tape our meetings."

The old heads looked to the board attorney.

"He's right."

They didn't like it. An early political defeat became a small moral victory. I continued to tape board meetings for months until we agreed to document some condensed discussion as well as the vote. Minutes were edited and abbreviated, but they at least captured the essence of any pre-decision dialogue.

Small moral victories were soon coupled with some real accomplishments. Some were very visible. Some were nearly indistinguishable as they happened but made long-term impacts.

At the time of my election, our county ambulance service was as capable as a volunteer service could be. But the population growth meant an enormous increase in calls, and the diminishing numbers of volunteers were being overworked both day and night.

During the first year in office, we began paying for some basic-level EMTs. Within two years the entire service was paid and trained at the intermediate level. Before the end of my first, four-year term, we had a fully operational, paramedic-level ambulance service. We had also purchased several new ambulances. We upgraded older ones and opened new, full-time EMS locations at two volunteer fire stations.

When I arrived, I was appalled to see that basic county asphalt overlay was financed every four years with government bonds. While that had been done repeatedly without a tax increase, we were financing for 15 years something that had to often be redone in less than half that time. In other words, the county had been resurfacing roads for a second and even a third time that hadn't been paid for the first time. The issuance fees and interest nearly doubled the taxpayer's actual expense.

That made no sense to me. Behind the scenes the county administrator and I placed a half million dollars in the annual budget for road overlay contracts. The second year we increased it to one million, and the rest of the board members began buying into the concept. The next year it was 1.5 million, and by the final year of my first term, we were budgeting two million dollars annually. That allowed us to spend five million dollars over the first four years without borrowing a dime. Subsequent terms would reap another eight million dollars of roadwork!

Our issues ranged from the possibility of a new airport runway capable of handling 737s to the spraying of neighborhoods for mosquitoes. Constituents were more concerned about the latter.

The county's efforts to design and construct a $25-million civic center and a $100-million sewer infrastructure did not slow the requests for pothole patching, roadside grass cutting, or burying dead cows.

The business of the fast-growing suburban county was couched in the community expectations of an old-fashioned rural response. Despite a broad and challenging agenda, it wasn't uncommon for constituents to demand to see me on their front porch in the early morning. I always tried to oblige.

"Caldwell, I got a dead cow."

"Now, Mr. Baker, you know we need a veterinarian certificate before we can—"

"I don't need a vet to tell me it's dead; the cow's bloated. It's been dead for days."

"Yes, sir, we'll take care of it."

He wasn't going to listen. He'd had the county supervisor bury his dead cows for 60 or more years. He wouldn't understand why the laws had changed. I called the maintenance department and asked them to handle it. They did. A few years later, the call came again. Maybe I could explain it better if I took another angle.

"Caldwell, I got another dead cow."

"Now, Mr. Baker, the new law says it needs to be a community problem before we can do anything."

"If I leave this dead cow here long enough, it'll be a community problem," he snarled in his age-enhanced, raspy retort.

"Yes, sir, we'll take care of it.

Years later, the call came again. This time I thought I had him. He and I had developed a bond, and I knew he had a great sense of humor behind the gruff facade. His property had recently been annexed by the city. He had been adamantly and publicly opposed. Now his nephew was the mayor of that same city.

"Caldwell, I got another dead cow."

"Mr. Baker, you're a city slicker now. You need to call the mayor."

I could hardly hide my smile through the phone when he barked his reply. "*I already called the mayor! They won't do anything. The city's about worthless!*"

"Yes, sir, we'll take care of it."

In the meantime, we kept our tax rate low and even reduced it just a hair. I always looked for chances to help people, especially, those who might not have received help if I hadn't been elected.

As the deadline approached to file for reelection, the local political establishment, independent forces, and the good ol' boy coalition massed against us. The first campaign had been friendly because so many did not see me as a serious contender until too late. This campaign would be marked by a more hostile, adversarial undertone.

Formerly an elected Democrat, the previous incumbent campaigned to retake his seat by filing as a Republican.

New and equally credible opposition also entered the primary. Tim Ball was a well-liked and well-respected businessman and former high school football coach.

With two stiff competitors in the race, it would be nearly impossible to get the required 50% without a run-off. That's what the opposition was counting on.

Reelection efforts met an extreme array of reactions ranging from friendly overconfidence from some friends to vile and physical threats of people I had never met. Opposing candidates themselves were mostly honorable and respectable, but a handful of their supporters were not.

Misinformation was rampant. The sources were impossible to find, but the intent was obvious. The effort to discredit me was painful to my family and me. After witnessing the good side of politics in our first outing, we would experience a darker side this time.

The Marine inside of me, as well as some of my supporters, wanted to strike back. Surely, no one would fault us if we decided not to "turn the other cheek."

Then I looked into the eight little eyes of my children. They would see how their daddy reacted to ugly politics. The decision was not only clear but easier. Just ignore it. We stayed on our positive message and promoted our successes.

Election Day was a disappointment but not a surprise. We finished in first, but fell just short of the 50% needed to avoid a run-off.

Negative campaigning heated up in the short, tension-filled run-off period.

Other elected officials whose races had been settled weighed in on behalf of my opponent.

Typically, elected officials stay out of other local contests, but the ensuing political frenzy broke that mold. The hostile line-up was nearly unanimous and was unofficially led by the sheriff and the circuit court clerk, not to mention my board attorney and fellow board members. I tried to accept such notable opposition as a badge of honor, but it was adding stress.

The chancery court clerk provided a sympathetic sounding board one afternoon. Standing behind the courthouse as cars passed, Sluggo listened as I vented.

"What I really want to do is get everybody in one room and tell the whole bunch to take their best shot. I don't want them to say later that, 'We should have tried harder or spent more money.'"

"John, do you think you're going to win?"

"Yeah."

"Then do you want to stir that hornet's nest if you've already got the votes to win? It could make things worse."

"You may be right, but I really want this to be over once and for all."

A few days later we talked again.

"Now, John, I'm not telling you what to do, but I gave you some advice the other day that assumed things could get worse. I'm here to tell you, based on the conversations I've had recently, that it can't get any worse. That doesn't mean I'd recommend that you get everyone together and tell them to take their best shot. I just want you to know what you're up against."

"I already know. Thanks for calling. I always appreciate your candor."

If signs could vote, we were sunk. An apparent infusion of money put Riley's name on nearly every corner, or so it seemed. It gave a visual impression of a political surge. Some direct mail and newspaper ads completed the package.

We countered as much as we could. Everyone on both sides knew it wouldn't take much of a pendulum swing with the low turnout in run-off elections.

The small local paper had a large, front-page image of my opponent's campaign sign . . . not exactly unbiased. So I immediately called the editor.

"Hey, Tom. What's up with the front page?"

"What?"

"You've got a close-up of a ten-foot "Vote Big for Riley" campaign sign being held be a twenty-foot giant as the lead photo taking up the majority of the page."

"Your sign's there, too."

"Come on, Tom, it's in the background, too small to read."

"I didn't really pay much attention to the photo, other than we were trying to promote the vote."

"You can't tell me that as owner and editor you hardly knew what was going on your front page on Election Day. I'll just chalk that one up to experience. I don't appreciate it, and I won't forget it."

It was figuratively and literally a sign of things to come. We were informed of several folks in the district who had moved away but were driving in to vote against us. Although they lived out of state, they were still registered and could vote in our race. It was too late to stop it unless I knew them personally and could call them out when they came to vote.

The indicator would be the Eudora precinct. It was Riley's home box and the place that nearly defeated me the first time. There was no way to win there, but we had to minimize its impact.

Arriving at the Eudora Volunteer Fire Department precinct, I noticed my opponent's cousin and four-term sheriff had stationed two cruisers with flashing blue lights and deputies at the entrance to the polls.

"What's up with that, sheriff?"

"That's for traffic control and voter safety."

"Funny how you're not concerned about traffic control and voter safety anywhere else in the county."

Over 30 precincts countywide, including two of my strongest areas with busier highways in front of them, didn't seem to warrant even one deputy.

I set up a video camcorder inside the precinct. There was an immediate buzz of controversy surrounding it. The first to question it was the precinct manager, a friend, supporter, and former Marine, but today, he was working objectively.

"What's with the camera?"

"A judge who gave a poll watcher's class recommended it to me."

"I'm not sure you can have it, and it sure has them stirred up outside. Would you mind taking it down?"

"I really would, but for you I'll cover it with a cloth until we can get some sort of official ruling."

About that time some opposition workers came running in, waving a cell phone in the air.

"Jennette says you can't. Jennette says you can't have a camera."

"Tell Jennette to stay out of it. She's the circuit clerk." *And a Democrat,* I thought but didn't say out loud. "She runs general elections, but this is a party primary. We need the Republican Executive Committee to make the call."

Two members arrived within a few minutes. One had been at the same class I attended and had heard the judge make the recommendation. The other was skeptical and thought we should dig deeper.

We decided to call the Mississippi secretary of state's office and ask their opinion. Before we could dial the phone, my opponent's supporters interrupted.

"We called the Attorney General's office and he said it was illegal."

"You can tell the Attorney General"—*also a Democrat*—"to butt out too. He doesn't run elections."

We quickly called the secretary of state's office—*also Democrat*—for a response.

"You can't do that."

"Could you tell me or fax us the law that doesn't allow it, because I don't want to find out tomorrow that it would have been okay."

"There's no law against it—"

"That's what I understood from the beginning."

"—But there is a U.S. Attorney General's Opinion that says it could be considered voter intimidation."

"That doesn't make sense to me, but I'll abide by it if you can fax it here this morning."

It arrived quickly. The Opinion implied that a video camera could intimidate minority voters. I'm still not sure how an object filming a legal act could intimidate anyone or how that would relate to minorities as opposed to any other group. We took the camera down anyway.

What we didn't capture on video was the unusual "Republicans" coming in to vote. Many had never voted in a Republican primary before.

Two older illiterate minority males entered the door with an escort from my opponent's family. They seemed lost, but their helper who drove them to the polls directed them to the table and gave their names. The poll workers found the brothers' names and showed each where to make their "X".

The two approached a voting booth side by side, with their helper guiding them. They began to vote.

"Wait, they can't vote together."

"John's right. They have to vote one at a time."

At the prodding of his helper, one of them stepped back a half step but didn't want to get far from his twin. The helper began the voting.

"Punch this hole right here."

"Stop. Stop. He can't tell them what hole to punch. If they can't read, then he can read the entire ballot for them, but that's all. He can't tell them what hole to punch."

"John's right again. You can only read the ballot."

The helper—a relative and supporter of my opponent—told me later that each of them punched every hole as he read the names.

Painfully obvious was an opposition grass roots "Get Out the Vote" effort at a level I could have barely imagined. We would have to respond or get beat.

Lee and I decided to pull any sign-waving poll worker off the streets if he or she was willing to make phone calls. We called hundreds of our supporters and located many who were about to skip voting—some because they didn't think we'd need their single vote and some who had forgotten it was Election Day.

"Hello, this is Lee, have ya'll voted yet?"

"John has it made. We were just going to cut hay today."

"We really think it's going to be close, and we really need you."

"Alright, that'll be eleven votes from us that you wouldn't have had."

"Thank you so much."

This was going to be close. Another countywide race for circuit clerk was also being decided in the run-off. Early in the evening's vote tally, that race was settled. Ours was too close to call late into the count.

When the Eudora ballot box was added, the Riley lead grew dramatically. We had split the few precincts evenly, but the actual vote total was nowhere near even.

"Everybody be ready. We could lose this. If we do, try not to show too much emotion. I'll walk over and shake hands and congratulate them. We can cry in the car, but not here."

"Okay, Daddy."

The courtroom was packed. As we pushed through the crowd, we found a door to a corner room not in use. We turned the light on and claimed it as our own. From the door we could see every face in the courtroom.

Some of our opponent's people were high fiving. Their nearly insurmountable lead gave them boldness. Smiles and hugs seemed contagious among them. Their apparent victory was within reach.

Ironically, the same precinct we had waited for in our first election was the last one to be counted again. This time we waited on the precinct chairman to validate her seal of the ballot box. Mrs. Steadham was picked up by deputies at her house and driven to the courthouse to complete the drama.

As we waited, we realized that of the just over 700 votes, about the same number of votes which were cast in that same precinct four years earlier, we needed over 500 of them. It's no wonder the other side was practically claiming victory.

Again, we prepared ourselves and, especially, our children for the possibility we could lose.

"Remember, no crying. I'll go shake his hand and we walk out of here with our heads up."

As if our prayers were answered audibly, we heard the totals.

"The Horn Lake East Precinct cast seven hundred and thirty-five votes. In the District Four Supervisor's race . . . John Caldwell Sr., five hundred and—"

Our room erupted before I could hear the rest. A quick glance into faces in the courtroom showed the other side of a hard-fought campaign.

A short celebration for us then on to the general election.

Door-to-door campaigning continued to be enlightening. I knocked at a certain house on Dean Road. The rural county road had been rough as a cob and riddled with potholes. I had it paved recently with fresh asphalt, improved shoulders and new striping. It was smooth and better than it had ever been. Surely the voters that lived on that stretch would be easy to secure. Not so fast . . .

After brief pleasantries at the front door, we made a connection.

"Oh, I didn't know that was your Mom and Dad. They are such good neighbors of mine. When I saw their car upside down in the ditch that night, I didn't know what to expect. It was such a relief to pull them from the windows shocked, but virtually unhurt! I am so glad now to know you. Can I count on your vote in November?"

"No, I'm a Democrat."

"Have you met my opponent?"

"No, but I'm a Democrat."

"It's a general election. You can cross over and vote for whoever you want."

"I only vote Democrat."

It was a harsh reminder that African American Democrats are first and foremost committed to their party. You can pull their dazed elderly parents from a serious wreck, fix their road, knock on their door, shake their hand, look them in the eye and ask for their support. Just don't expect them to vote for you if you are a Republican.

The rest of the campaign and the victory in the November general election proved to be anticlimactic. The political battle had taken its toll. Physically, we were tired. Emotionally, we were drained. Spiritually, we were exhausted.

•••

We could finally relax. JC was turning 14, and this year's annual birthday bash with his friends could be the last of its kind. From preschool until now, JC and a host of friends would stay up all night in the house, in tents, and in the clubhouse, watching TV, playing basketball on the patio, video games inside, etc. This year it was football under the backyard floodlights. Lee and I had occupied the boys' seats by the crackling campfire in the cool night air. We could see their silhouettes missing the football more than they were catching it.

Next year and beyond it would be different. The boys were getting more interested in girls, who would predictably come between them. But for now, they were all great friends having a great time.

"This is the life."

"They are having so much fun."

"Lee, do you realize that in four years those boys could be fighting a war?"

"Don't say that!"

"Well, it's true."

It wasn't some fireside prophetic vision. It was a simple reflective moment with a basic understanding of world conflicts and the boys' ages. Following Desert Storm, a period of relative world—or at least American—peace followed. History demonstrates that international conflicts will cycle and emerge in a somewhat predictable pattern.

Four years later, the boys would be young men. The likelihood of America being drawn into some unforeseen military clash by then or shortly thereafter was almost certain. In all probability, it would still be voluntary for each of them.

But for now it was time to drop the philosophical thoughts and enjoy the birthday party. Thanksgiving and Christmas would soon follow.

The Wednesday before Thanksgiving meant another campfire, more hotdogs and marshmallows on coat hangers, and a hayride. It had become an instant tradition some years ago and our kids labeled it, "The Caldwell Family Blast."

New Year's Day preceded the swearing-in of newly elected and reelected officials. Only one new member was added to the board of supervisors, but Gerald Clifton quickly aligned himself in such a way for the old 3-2 majority to hold.

Just as they had in the early days of my first term, they reasserted their control and their contempt for dissenting opinion with a bold move to issue bonds and raise taxes. They clung to the often-used political concept of raising taxes early in a new term to give the electorate time to forget. There was little effort to even justify the millions in loosely projected expenses. Moreover, there was zero money intended for construction on needed projects in my district.

The flippant nature of their actions motivated me to promote organized opposition. It only took 1,500 validated signatures to force a referendum on any bond issue. With the help of friends, it was accomplished.

The three board members reluctantly conceded that their solid majority was not omnipotent. Cooperation grew and a cautious level of trust developed with a friendlier tone over the next several months and years.

Life's personal and professional decision points collided now in ways that could not be ignored. What should I do with the business? What about politics in the short term? Long term? Other employment, educational, or political options? Family?

Bills at home and the office were getting paid, but it wasn't pretty. Leveraging against mounting debt with more debt didn't make since, yet, for a very limited period of time, it seemed necessary.

We sought out an investor with enough venture capital to take our small advertising business to another level. A friend led us to a business acquaintance ready to put up $30,000. It would be enough to hire some help and see if we could capitalize quickly.

With money in hand, the push was on. Months of renewed effort weren't enough. Progress was measurable but slower than needed.

The 6-to-12-month projection to take The Artillery Advertising out of its multi-year start-up phase was clearly going to take 18 to 24 more months. Optimism about a quick surge had to give way to reality. Our remaining cash and our regular income would not get us over the hump before the money ran out.

"Lee, we're at another decision point. We could keep going another six months or more, hoping for the best. It could actually work out, or we could very well be out of cash and out of credit. By then we will have spent all of our investor's money too."

"Well, what can we do now if we don't risk it?"

"We could count our losses and let him absorb his, or we could accept all the loss and return the entire thirty thousand. We'll eat about twelve thousand of that to pay him back, but we can keep our good name in the process."

"Oh, well."

"I hate to choke down twelve thousand dollars that we don't have, but it's about all I can do in good conscience. The hardest part is that we're so very close to making this thing a success. If the thirty thousand he invested was part of a larger fortune, it might be worth going for it. But the reality is that he's invested all he has in us and he trusts us."

"Well, I guess that's that. Maybe some reserve duty and pay could help us some."

Reserve Counterpart Training (RCT) was just a term in a laundry list of types of reserve duty. It centered around MOS training alongside your active duty counterparts—thus the name. It made sense, but I had never known anyone who actually participated.

I called the Marines for more information.

"Sir, it takes a written request from an active duty unit. We cut the orders and you spend a maximum of thirteen days with the unit in your MOS."

"That's it?"

"Yes, sir."

I was still in touch with an old battery commander of mine. Lt. Col. Rich Christie was the 2/10 battalion commander. I called the battalion duty office and he took my call. After catching up on family and old friends in and out of the Corps, I got around to business.

"Sir, the reason I called is to see if you had any exercises in the near future. I need to get more artillery experience. I've spent most of my time with the grunts in the reserves. There's a program that will allow me thirteen days' active duty if I am requested by name."

"Who pays for it, John?"

"The Reserve Support Command in Kansas City cuts the orders and foots the bill. The only thing I need is some training as an artillery staff officer. I'll work directly for you and, hopefully, will be able to contribute to your unit's training while I'm there."

"We have an exercise coming up at Fort Bragg called Operation Express Sword that would be great for you and us. We'd be excited to have you. I'm going to hook you up with my XO so he can handle the paperwork."

"Thank you, sir. I look forward to working for you again."

It really was that simple. I faxed them a completed request form, needing only a signature. They in turn signed and faxed it. Orders soon followed.

I was able to work alongside the battalion S-3 and then briefly at the 10th Marines COC (Combat Operations Center). The training was good, and I was contributing in a limited capacity.

One contribution I made was almost an embarrassment. Some foreign officers from Brazil had come to observe the exercise. They needed an officer to pick them up and escort them. That's one way I could contribute. No one wanted that assignment, so I volunteered.

I wasn't familiar with Ft. Bragg yet, but I knew how to read a map, and I had grids to the pick-up and delivery points.

We picked up the officers, who could speak almost no English.

The most direct route to our destination was planned but could not be used; the road was blocked by a tree. We tried the next shortest route. It ran into some backwater that had flooded the road. The third road had to be the charm.

By now we were running late, and I was beginning to sweat. We could not raise anyone on the radio, and I was losing confidence in my navigating ability. I was sure we were close but unsure which road would get us there.

As we increased our speed to make up lost time, we approached a puddle of water on one side of the dirt road. A little mud on the tires didn't concern me in the least. I had crossed much more questionable obstacles but none so deceptive. The puddle was only about 3 or 4 feet wide and about 10 or 12 feet long. The depth didn't occur to me until the muddy water instantly reached my door handle and the driver to my left was above me, hanging on to the steering wheel. It was the closest I've ever come to being flipped in a HMMWV.

The driver maintained his composure and drove through it. I didn't flinch and pretended that was normal. The two Brazilian officers were as shocked as I was or more so, but they didn't want to show it, either, until I turned around and smiled. Then we all had a good laugh. At least the road took us to our destination.

Working in artillery again was just what I needed. It wasn't just a learning experience, it was also a motivational one. Another year finishing my Command and Staff College course, and another RCT (regimental combat team) training evolution, and I would be ready to go back to the drilling reserve status in the SMCR (Selected Marine Corps Reserve).

I scheduled a repeat trip for RCT during Operation Express Sword. By the time I arrived at Camp Lejeune, the training schedule had changed. A number of individuals on the 10th Marines staff were staying behind.

My new mission was to work alongside the 2nd Marine Division fire support coordinator, who was just days away from a PCS (permanent change of station) move. We only saw him for early morning PT and he was off to work on his move.

Major Langford was his assistant. He and I had two tasks. One was an SOP review. The second was real-world fire planning. At the direction of the division commander and the assistant chief of staff G-3, we were to develop an estimate of supportability for a 2ndMarDiv movement-to-contact in the country of Kosovo.

The official word from President Clinton was that there would be no ground invasion. That word had not changed, but it was incumbent on the ground commanders to prepare contingency plans anyway. So we did.

The topographical map told the story of why a ground invasion was not a desired or feasible option. We developed a worst-case, what-if scenario for a division tasking and assessed our organic ability to provide fire support to Marine maneuver units. Our estimate was that the challenge presented to us was nearly unsupportable.

Two weeks later, I returned to the civilian world like nothing had happened and watched Operation Allied Force on TV like everyone else.

ADSW (Active Duty for Special Work) and RCT assignments were typically too short for me to contribute much yet long enough for me to get some refresher training. The real downside was the lack of camaraderie. There wasn't enough time to develop relationships or become a viable member of any unit.

Returning to the SMCR as a drilling reservist and an artillery officer would be an important step to reenergizing me and my reserve career. The tour to follow was one of the most enjoyable tours with some of the finest officers and colorful characters I've served with in the Corps.

Bessemer, Alabama, was the closest and most logical option. Until now I had avoided the long drive to drill. For some of the officers I had met over the years, it was all they knew. Many spend a reserve career with long and expensive trips to drill.

From my house to the drill center was now a hard, five-hour-plus drive on Thursday or Friday afternoons. The drive home on Sunday nights usually ranged from six to seven hours.

Tiring night drives through a nearly endless series of construction zones along U.S. Highway 78 reminded me each month of how good I'd had it in the past. While driving across Northern Mississippi into Alabama, I reminded myself of friends and strangers who still had it worse.

The struggle to stay awake was a lonely and mostly silent one, except for periods of loud music on the radio, or the sound of cold night air rushing into open windows along dark highways. Three naps on the side of the road, coffee refills, and milkshakes sometimes worked better than others. Lee already worried too much about me falling asleep at the wheel. I couldn't tell her about all the close calls that nearly scared me to death.

I was able to serve one year as a liaison officer and two years as the executive officer. There were officers in the headquarters battery from all over. One flew in from Houston each month. One drove in from South Carolina. One flew in from Washington, DC, and another from New York City. I had no room to complain.

Not atypical of reserve billeting contracts, the lowest bid put us in a motel that could almost stay full renting by the hour. Marines had their cars and trucks vandalized, broken into, and stolen. Our alternate motel was even worse. There were closer motels that were better, but the Marine Corps had to save a buck or two.

All the while there was a parallel universe in the reserves that stayed in Hilton hotels and got free meals. I had not yet experienced that dimension, but I had personally spoken to officers who had. It was like hearing a fairy tale that you know is true. One side of me told me to go on a quest for the door to that universe. Another side of me had his boots and mind stuck in the mud. That was not the Marine Corps I know and love. Mine is the "No pain-No Gain" Marine Corps.

"Pain is Just Weakness Leaving the Body."

"Kill `em All and Let God Sort `em Out."

"Nobody Ever Drowned in Sweat."

"Pray for Peace. Prepare for War."

These are my favorite Marine Corps T-Shirt slogans. Why would I want to stay in a Hilton Hotel?

I met kindred spirits in 4/14. The camaraderie that had been missing in recent years was back. The Marine Corps was fun again. Real, lasting friendships were built, and a healthy professional respect was earned and reciprocated up and down the chain of command.

Personally and professionally, things were good. Combining the two, like our St. Barbara's celebration at Fort McClellan, usually generated particularly memorable moments.

Major Eric Merkle was the punch-meister that made the traditional artilleryman's punch. It was a combination of punches from past St. Barbara's Day celebrations. Some were in writing, and others were etched in our memories.

Each one was always unique, and our punch was destined to have its own flavor.

I didn't like the idea of spending a lot of money on liquor, so I went by a liquor store near home and asked for donations. They were very generous, so I bought a small balance of costly ingredients from them. Recipes for an artilleryman's punch vary with the unit and year. We had a bottle of Tennessee sour mash whiskey for out Tennessee Marines, a bottle of Peach Schnapps for our Georgia delegation, a jar of corn liquor (Moonshine) for Alabama leathernecks, a bottle of rum for the devil dogs from Mississippi. Some beer was poured into the concoction representing the Marines that flew in from several other states. A base of black tea poured from a cannon section's swab bucket completed the brew.

The punch-meister added an entertaining personal flare. He sampled and commented on the ingredients as he went, much to the delight of the Marines. Each time he turned a bottle up, the Marines roared with approval. By the time the punch was declared fit to drink, Major Merkle was nearly unfit for much else—too much sampling of the wares.

Those of us who were to receive the St. Barbara's Day Medal drank the finished product first. Following a brief ceremony, Marines dipped their canteen cups into the punch eagerly joining the festivities. It was good to continue the touted custom and enjoyable traditions of St. Barbara's Day. It would be the unofficial beginning-of-the-end of the battalion serving as an artillery unit. It would transition soon afterwards to an anti-terrorism battalion.

Change is inevitable in the Corps and in life. Sometimes, the changes are subtle. Within a few weeks our world was about to change dramatically, and the reserve artillery structure would too.

Campaigning for county supervisor in my Daddy's old Ford.

Serving the county was a great experience, but two terms were enough for me.

*"The horse is prepared against the day of battle:
but safety is of the Lord."*

Proverbs 21:31

...9

Conflicts of Perspective

On the routine drive to a Monday morning board of supervisors meeting, I noticed that I had a little time to spare. Instead of passing the central maintenance facility known as the county barn, I stopped for a quick visit to talk about routine roadwork. It was an uncommon stop at a very uninspiring metal building with several dirty work bays and a few small offices.

By this time county road crews should have been dispersed to job locations across the county's five districts. As I walked into the mechanics' area, an unusually large number of folks were huddled quietly in the far bay.

Pushed against the steel-framed wall with their lesser-used tools and a collection of discarded truck and tractor parts was an old console TV. From the looks of it, the tattered box had been salvaged from the county roadside in times past.

Otherwise mouthy employees were silent. They barely glanced up from their fixation on the screen.

"What's going on?"

"A plane crashed into one of the Twin Towers in New York."

"That's unbelievable. It had to be intentional."

"I hope not."

"It had to be."

"They said the plane may have been hijacked."

"We're waiting for a news conference."

"I'm going to go ahead to the board meeting. It may be a while before we get any details."

On my way to the meeting, the second tower was hit by a second plane. The radio reports were horrific as announcers tried to compute the potential numbers of victims. Now there could be no doubt in anyone's mind that it was intentional. America was under attack. Another plane hit the Pentagon and a fourth crashed somewhere in Pennsylvania.

Was that the end of it? None of us knew. The uncertainty was mixed with fear, disgust, anger, sadness, horror, and resolve.

What was next for us and our attackers? Early logic pointed to radical Muslim extremists as the perpetrators, namely Al Qaeda.

Those of us on the county board of supervisors watched intermittently while trying to resume routine county business. Reports and updates interrupted us several times.

"One of the towers collapsed."

I tried to imagine it but couldn't. The report must have been exaggerated. Collapsed? I'd just have to have a look later and see what that meant.

"The second tower collapsed."

There's that word again.

"Let's take a recess."

It was unbelievable.

Tens of thousands of people worked in those two towers. Loose news estimates of the dead or dying fluctuated wildly above and below 10,000. The nation watched each tower disappear in horrific clouds of dust. No one knew how many were inside.

The painful reality of the once unimaginable invoked an immediate sense of reverence. Some Americans were broken-hearted and in great disbelief and despair. Others maintained hope and quiet resolve. Anger and thoughts of revenge helped many others cope. The emotional roller coaster would affect us all.

President Bush consoled and inspired a country in need of both. The words I appreciated most gave some of his most strident detractors pause.

"You are with us, or you are with the terrorists."

The spontaneous national unity was short-lived. Analysts derided the president's words as being too divisive. In my opinion they were right on the money and should have been repeated often. While emotions and reactions were being sorted individually and collectively, those of us with military obligations knew our lives would be impacted again—dramatically, directly, and soon.

Sunday afternoons back at drill in Bessemer meant officers' call at a less-than-impressive Chinese restaurant. It was a filthy little place with seemingly little business. It was no wonder. Besides being dirty, the food and service were bad. We kept coming back because we didn't have to wait in line, and we could be ourselves without disturbing other customers. There weren't any.

Conversations centered on the prospect of our activation. Officers hypothesized about when and where and how any military response should be carried out. The best we could do was to continue preparing ourselves and our Marines.

"We're going to be one of the first units activated for the war."

"Really? Where are you getting your information?"

"I have a friend at the Pentagon and he's seen *the list*."

If the United States Treasury had a nickel for every similar conversation, this war and others could be financed for years to come with enough change to spare to wipe out poverty and world hunger.

Officers and enlisted alike listened to the rumors and even believed just enough to repeat it—no matter the source. Marines call it *scuttlebutt*.

The commanding officer for my two years as XO was Mark Batchelor. Mark had the keen, analytical mind of an engineer but the down-home mannerisms and colloquial expressions of an Alabama sharecropper. The contrast was fused together with a great sense of humor, and the Marines had an enviable, deep loyalty and affection for him.

Our last AT together was being shaped by events. Originally scheduled as a regimental shoot in Colorado, the advent of Operation Enduring Freedom funneled money from training and travel.

With little notice, my staff was tasked with offering three courses of action (COAs) to conduct an alternate AT to save financial resources for the War on Terror. We presented the regimental commander with three options that involved us shooting a battalion FIREX: Ft Bragg, NC; Lawton, OK; and Camp Shelby, MS. Each option had advantages and disadvantages, but Camp Shelby was nearly a half million dollars cheaper than our original AT and significantly less than the other options.

Our hesitation of going to a nearby Army Reserve/National Guard base melted away when we checked out the facilities and the one-day liberty option in Biloxi.

Training was approached aggressively at Camp Shelby. Frequent tactical moves day and night established a challenging pace. Shooting, moving, and communicating are the most basic combat skills of any artillery unit, and we did a lot of each.

A range control requirement to submit overlays for every battery move seemed extreme. Surely, they didn't mean it how it read. We shortchanged the requirement early in the training cycle but got caught. They called us in and reiterated the importance of following all range rules to the letter.

By threatening to shut us down, their point was made.

The next day our point was made.

"Good morning."

"Good morning, gentlemen. Getting an early start?"

"Just following the rules. You know we have to submit our movement overlays."

"Just hand them to me, and I'll give them to Sergeant Jones."

"Where would you like us to put them?"

"Just hand them to me."

"Okay. We'll bring them in."

Range personnel reminded me of the judge in the classic movie *Miracle on 34th Street* when he asked for the mail to be put on his desk. He really didn't know what he was asking for. The range officer's jaw dropped as we carried in two boxes of overlays.

Other soldiers in the range office tried unsuccessfully to hold back their laughter.

"I've never seen so many overlays since this requirement was put in place. Y'all must be moving a lot these next two weeks."

"These are just for the next three days. We'll be back in tomorrow or Wednesday with some more."

The next day they rescinded the requirement for overlays and let us continue training unimpeded. It was fast and furious from then on. The direct fire shoot culminated two great weeks of live-fire training.

Impacts on junk vehicle targets sent shrapnel whizzing around all of us. The targets were several hundred meters away from the gun line, but the shrapnel still reached us. We rechecked our safety fans and fired again. A few rounds later, more shrapnel landed near us and past us. We adjusted to more distant targets. The shoot ended safely, and an already motivated battalion reached an even higher level of morale.

The only thing left on the schedule was liberty on Mississippi's Gulf Coast. Less than an hour on chartered buses ended with one Marine losing his lunch and the hard liquor he had poured into himself. It would be a sign of things to come as the Marines disembarked in the hotel parking lot.

By nightfall Marines were fully enjoying the restaurants, casinos and other nightlife of Biloxi and Gulfport. That's when a Marine put his fist through the fifth-floor window of our hotel's nightclub.

The sergeant major and I were arriving at the hotel lobby unaware. The duty NCO immediately reported the details to us. The ambulance was on its way.

Then we started corralling the Marines and settling things down. While that was being done, Sergeant Major Howington and I accompanied the Marine to Keesler Air Force Base to get his arm stitched up. They must have used a hundred or more stitches.

Liberty ended without further incident. A predictably resounding call for closer, small-unit leadership was coupled with the reinforcement of individual accountability and personal responsibility.

It's not uncommon or even unexpected for a small number of Marines to ignore, creatively misinterpret, or openly violate a given liberty brief. It is the very reason a command emphasis is placed on liberty plans and that swift, sure, and stern punishment follows any breaches.

That said, there is also a temptation for officer leadership to overreact. It can be the best time to allow and even encourage the senior staff NCOs to apply their craft. It increases their authority and credibility, and frankly, they can usually handle those matters better than officers.

That memorable liberty period ended the prototypical two-year reserve cycle. The battalion had conducted the classic reserve combined arms exercise (CAX) one year earlier. Ideally, units rotated through the CAX training cycle every other year. The odd years allowed for MOS-specific training like the battalion live-firing exercise at Camp Shelby. Those are generally unimpeded by higher artillery headquarters intervention or a supported maneuver commander's requirements.

It would be the end of an era. The CAX was already being reinvented to directly address specific challenges posed in the current world conflict. The 9/11 attack had changed everything.

All the actual perpetrators on September 11th died in the attacks, but their actions unveiled the reality of a bigger, three-dimensional, worldwide threat. Possible conspirators or masterminds of the overall plot became the immediate logical target for some type of response.

• • •

The newly exposed Islamic terrorist threat was associated loosely with sympathetic and even openly supportive foreign governments. However, the world's fastest-growing terrorist organization was operating without respect for established political borders and independently of formal government hierarchy and structure.

Requisite retaliation was the first and basically unchallenged assertion. That response had to extend beyond a handful of individuals. This process of assigning responsibility would include searching out and annihilating any parent terrorist organization, their leadership, and any training sanctuaries, including foreign governments in open support of them.

Finally, a generally accepted but less understood response was a new, pre-emptive element to prevent a repeat of 9/11. Military action against other state supporters of terrorism would be part of the total response package. Those enemies who may have been emboldened by what they witnessed should not be tempted to follow suit. It was a post-9/11 philosophy that, if applied earlier, could arguably have prevented the original 9/11 attack.

That idea was not a total departure from America's past policies, but the first-strike persona had never been so openly and undeniably presented to the world as when President Bush articulated it.

In the Clinton years, an unprovoked America had led almost three months of continuous air strikes on Yugoslavia's national infrastructure. Grossly exaggerated intelligence from the U.S./Clinton administration pushed estimates of ongoing political killings beyond the 100,000 mark. Claims of genocide pushed the perception, and indeed, atrocities of great magnitude were being committed.

However, the U.S. was not under attack then, nor was there a growing threat of attack or any national interest involved. It was a "humanitarian war" to protect the rights, the independence, and the lives of innocent victims.

Ironically, the ones we were protecting were Muslims in Kosovo.

Nevertheless, Islamic extremists worldwide continued plotting against us and against everything America represents. Deadly attacks were planned and extremist Muslim terrorists attacked unsuspecting, innocent civilians as they went about their daily lives. The unprovoked assaults forced us and the free world to rethink how we dealt with such radicalism.

Establishing the proverbial frontline against terror would first involve an invasion of Afghanistan, a known safe haven and chief training ground for Al Qaeda operations. Muslin extremists controlled the Afghani government under the infamous label of the Taliban.

Taliban leaders were directly linked to Al Qaeda, the very organization responsible for the 9/11 attack. As sponsors and supporters of Al Qaeda, the rogue Afghani regime was targeted for change. It would require substantial military force in a rugged, unforgiving environment. Any new regime would be expected to become an immediate and important ally in the War on Terror.

Newly bolstered Islamic extremists, with or without names or notorious reputations like Al Qaeda, were dispersed across the globe. These mobile pockets of potential terror had varying origins and likely resided inside many countries, even those of our allies and our own.

State-sponsored terrorists posed the greatest threat. They had funding, organization, and some level of worldwide legitimacy, which until now had equaled protection or international cover for them. The next logical element of the war would likely involve dealing with Iraq, one of the world's best-known state sponsors of villainous terrorist groups like Hezbollah and Hamas.

Al Qaeda was already a global organization, but the degree to which they were woven into Iraq's populace was questionable. In all likelihood their thread of terror would increase everywhere after the infamous September attacks, no matter what level of response America chose. In fact, without a major military reaction by us, they might have galvanized more solidly and increased in number exponentially.

Iraqi President Saddam Hussein was an avowed enemy of the U.S. During the 10 years following Desert Storm, the Iraqi military committed recurring acts of war against the U.S. and our allies by firing at a number of aircraft patrolling the No-Fly Zones.

Egregious human rights violations and mass political murders marked Iraq's recent past. There was no end in sight.

Furthermore, Iraq was in violation of a host of U.N. mandates which followed the first Gulf War. Deception and open defiance of U.N. weapons inspectors was played out on international television. Discoveries of large missiles that had been hidden for a decade increased the tension and distrust.

All of the above wasn't enough for some Americans. In the U.S., there is largely a natural love for peace and a reluctance to take up arms. Nevertheless, a shaken nation supported an orchestrated military response, and it was basically understood and accepted at the time that Iraq would be the second front.

Even after the attack on our own soil killed nearly 3,000 of us and exposed our vulnerabilities, the case for preemptive war was still not fully sufficient for many. It wasn't until the president and his administration reminded the American people of Iraq's known nuclear ambitions, and its documented use of chemical weapons in war on its own civilians, that broad public support actually began to gel.

Questionable timetables, projections, interpretations, exact details, and pre-war rhetoric aside, all of the most basic and meaningful premises for war remain valid and substantiated to this day.

Although the U.S. didn't start this global conflict, we are duty bound to finish it. It would be more than derelict; it would be a cowardly disgrace to walk away and leave the fight to our children and grandchildren.

● ● ●

Rumors of our battalion's eminent activation for Enduring Freedom turned out to be off the mark. With no mobilization pending for 4/14, my three-year tour came to an unceremonious ending.

Lieutenant colonels like me were being pushed out of the battalion billets, and for me it was about time to make a move anyway. Searching out a new billet led me to 4th Marine Division Headquarters in New Orleans.

The two-lane trek to Bessemer would be replaced with a six-hour interstate drive to and from the Big Easy. Extended time and expense associated with travel was the new routine. Setting the cruise control and leaving it for hours made for easier driving.

Just beyond the pockets of the tourist-friendly downtown, dilapidated narrow roads sank between scores of ramshackle row houses. Parked cars on both sides constricted traffic to a near stall and left insufficient room to dodge potholes.

Lack of road maintenance, coupled with years of shoddy patchwork, seemed to create a tough testing environment for vehicle suspension systems. Even slow speeds could not eliminate the jarring and rattling. Drivers could hardly take their eyes off the road to notice the telltale bars on the windows or the boarded-up churches.

The air was different, too. The smell of stagnant water mixed with a noticeable level of industrial air pollution completed a dubious and unimpressive approach to the riverfront warehouses haphazardly converted to military offices.

Work areas were adequate, but hallways didn't align and, oddly, ended abruptly or led randomly through unkempt storage areas. Passageways, stairwells, and elevators had to be used in unusual combinations in order to get to desired locations in the complex. Dirty concrete steps and heavy, steel, battleship-gray doors coated with countless layers of chipped paint contrasted the nearby polished tile floors leading to varnished wood doorways, etched glass panels, and shiny, new, brass hardware of the entrance to the 4th Marine Division Headquarters section.

Lieutenant Colonel Lou Herrera was walking out as I was walking in. We had met earlier in the Corps.

"Hey, Lou."

"Hi, John. How have you been? I think I have your name on my list."

"That's not much of a 'Welcome Aboard.' Besides, you can't have my name on a list. I haven't even checked in yet."

"Let me see. There you are. I thought so."

"What kind of list is that?"

"It's the names we're submitting to MARFORRES for possible activation."

"You've got to be kidding."

"No, I'm not, and I have to get this list upstairs by oh-nine hundred this morning. If you want to have any say in the matter, I'll sit down with you right now and plug your name into one of the openings. Otherwise, they'll do it upstairs and there's no telling where you'll go."

I was caught a little off guard but not totally surprised. The network news was flooded with Operation Enduring Freedom. We had recently intervened in Afghanistan, and it looked likely the next stop was going to be Iraq. The War on Terror was shaping up to be just the war that President Bush said it would be.

Individuals and units from the National Guard and reserves were already being activated. That's what I bargained for when I first enlisted in 1981, and it was about to catch up with me for a second time.

As a Marine it wouldn't feel right supporting the war for somebody else to fight without going myself.

"Okay, Lou, what have you got?"

"How about MARFORPAC?"

"That'll probably be back filling spots in Hawaii, Okinawa, and or Korea. I think I'll pass. The war is on the other side of the world."

"How about CENTCOM?"

"Hold that thought. At least it's in-theater."

"We've got MARCENT?

"What's that?"

"It's short for Marine Forces Central Command."

"I've never heard of it. It's not the First Marine Division, but at least I'd be with Marines in-theater. What else do you have?'

"That's pretty much it for combat arms, Lieutenant Colonel."

"Put me down for MARCENT. What's the billet?"

"C/JTF-CM. I think CM stands for consequence management."

"What's that?"

"I don't know exactly. Do you want it? I've got to get this list upstairs."

"Okay . . . I guess I better call home. Hey, when would orders likely come?"

"Probably in the next few weeks."

"Ouch. Nothing like a little advance notice."

That's quick no matter how you look at it. Considering that I was already committed to a 33-county political campaign for Mississippi's Northern District Highway Commissioner, it seemed even shorter.

Lee had supported and been a part of my decision to term-limit myself as a county supervisor by not running for re-election. County politics had been good to us. All the good—and bad—of public service was within arm's reach and we had our taste of both. We had mostly enjoyed the two, four-year terms in county government, but it was time to move on. I just couldn't see myself there for the next 20 years.

However, I still felt like I could be of service. So many people . . . so many needs. I looked for a place to serve and thought I had found it. The Northern District Transportation Commissioner's race would be a formidable challenge. There was a 20-year incumbent entrenched in the position, formerly known as Highway Commissioner or, more loosely, as Road Commissioner. It would also be a party race, and all but one of the counties were historically Democrat. I was a Republican.

With odds stacked against us, we committed. I made my announcement. We both were ready for an all-or-nothing campaign over the next 10 months. However, Lee made it perfectly clear that she wanted to campaign solely as the candidate's wife, not the campaign chairman.

The pending activation was going to make it more stressful on her than the campaign chairmanship. She would be the de facto candidate.

In addition to the obvious distraction from what should have been a unified focus of effort, the activation deprived our campaign of its chief fundraiser and lead worker—the candidate.

I was careful not to campaign as a Marine. There are clear, strict guidelines for active-duty Marines, but those guidelines get murky when it comes to reservists. I erred to the side of caution to avoid any appearance of violating any ethical issues.

In the meantime, Lee sweated blood for the family and me. Along with the campaign and her job teaching at the high school, she answered many of my constituents' phone calls and needs while I was away. I was still finishing my second, four-year term as county supervisor. When the Marine Corps called, she picked up my slack.

The activation was almost a sure thing, but we didn't want to cry wolf. We told select friends, family, and political helpers that it was probable. A few weeks later, we got the notice on a Thursday evening.

"Lieutenant Colonel Caldwell?"

"This is he."

"Sir, this call is your official activation notice. If you have a fax number, I will send you a copy of your orders tomorrow."

"What is the reporting date on the orders?'

"Sir, it is Monday morning at oh-eight hundred, but we can get you a hotel room for Sunday night."

"That's only one banking day, and I don't have orders in hand yet. You've got to give me more time than that."

"Sir, they're in a hurry for you to activate. How much time do you need?"

"Give me a week anyway. I can start my regimen of shots, get my family their military IDs, and do some of my paperwork here. The Millington Naval Support Activity is less than an hour away."

"That shouldn't be a problem, sir."

That was easy for him to say. Now that it was official, I had to make some fast decisions. Squeezing in any quality time with my family before pulling out would be impossible. *Just pack your trash and get on the plane.* First, the family had to be told. Jennifer was at work at The Dip. The Dip was the townsfolk's nickname for The Velvet Cream, an old-fashioned dairy bar and hamburger stand in Hernando. You could walk up to the window or use the drive-thru. Although you could order anything from fried pickles to "a Purple Cow," there were no tables or chairs.

"Hey, Daddy."

"Hey, Jennifer. It looks like we're getting Direct TV."

Jennifer burst into tears and ran outside for a hug. It was harder and more emotional for both of us than I had imagined. She was in first grade when I went to Desert Storm. Now she was 18.

She and the boys had been nearly begging for Direct TV for years, but Lee and I didn't want to pay the price. However, we agreed that if I ever got activated again, we would get it. Jennifer didn't need reminding.

It wasn't too late to back out of the political campaign for transportation commissioner, and I sure had a good excuse. I still had time to run for a third-term re-election as a county supervisor, which would have been an easier proposition. We just couldn't. I'd had a good "tour of duty" in county government, but it was time to move on to something else. Lee would continue the campaign as we had planned.

In retrospect we should have made her the candidate. She is a lot prettier, smarter, and nicer than me. I am a little too blunt at times, but I mean well.

In hopes of reducing her stress, we made a hasty decision to hire a political consultant out of Tupelo. It ended up increasing her stress. That was the last thing we needed. She wanted to cut him loose but knew she needed help. That proved even more stressful.

The county supervisor position would remain temporarily vacant while I was away. Lee would handle the day-to-day constituency issues, but she could not participate in board meetings. With the board reduced to four supervisors, it still took three votes for a majority to do anything.

We scheduled a local press conference at the county administration building. I read them my activation orders and took questions. It was good free press for the campaign, and an effective public notice, but it was also a time I needed to be preparing so many things and trying to spend time with my family.

Political support carries an earned reputation of being fickle and unreliable, but we had a core of unmatched support from friends and family who sacrificed their time, energy, and even money to help us through. New friends we met across the state during the campaign were a fresh source of encouragement.

Marine Forces Reserve New Orleans wasn't really set up as a processing center for reservists. If fact, everyone acted as if I was the first one. It was an administrative struggle, to say the least. Within a few days I had orders to Tampa.

There was little processing to do at McDill Air Force Base. That could have been done anywhere, and they required another medical review. I had to wait for my third anthrax vaccine anyway, so I didn't sweat a few days of review. Medically, I was ready to go—I thought.

"You'll need five root canals before you'll be deployable."

"What! How long will that take?"

"We can get you an appointment for your first one in a few weeks."

"That's not going to work. I'm not spending weeks in Tampa, Florida, fooling around with dental work, when the war is just weeks away. Is there anyone else I can talk to?"

"The colonel is down the hall to your left."

"Thanks."

I had to do something. Tampa was nice, but I wasn't planning to spend the war running on the beach and going from one dental appointment to another.

"Good morning, sir. My name is John Caldwell, and the dentist I just spoke with said I need five root canals and it will take weeks for the first appointment. I've got orders to Kuwait, and I need to get on the road if at all possible."

I thought I was up for an argument and a list of excuses. Surprisingly, the Air Force colonel was ready to accommodate.

"Let's see. If we cancel all our other appointments, we can do all five tomorrow. I'll get that done. You be here by oh-eight hundred."

Gulp. The thought of five root canals in one day hurt already. Be careful what you ask for; you might get it. I arrived on time with a sense of purpose. This had to be done in order to deploy. "Grin and bear it" took on a whole new meaning.

"Let's take a look at those x-rays before we get started. Hmmm. We may not have to do all of these after all. I'm going to get a second opinion, but I think these x-rays may have been misread."

He stepped out of the room and went down the hall. I prayed he was right. When he returned to the room, my prayers were answered.

"Just as I thought. It's a very common mistake. We just need to do one root canal, if that's alright with you?"

"Whatever it takes, Doc."

I'm sure my sigh of relief was stronger than the Tampa Bay breeze outside the glass doors of the clinic.

By now I had passed up a chance for duty in Hawaii and Florida for deployment to a war zone in Southwest Asia. My indoctrination over the last 20 years was obviously complete. Some civilians would never understand my choices.

I left McDill AFB for Camp Lejeune, North Carolina, to draw my chemical protective suit and a firearm. Within a few days I was on a bus to catch a plane.

When I disembarked at Kuwait International Airport, I couldn't help but notice the Burger King and Starbucks. The airport was bustling with commerce and was very clean and welcoming. Shops lined the mall-like terminal. It could have been anywhere in the world.

It was hard to imagine that 10 years earlier I had been in the same airport after it had been vandalized and abused by the Iraqi occupiers. Glass had been knocked out and defensive positions built in and around the terminal building. Dirt and debris had filled the airport. Wreckage of destroyed Iraqi military vehicles and a few charred remains of Kuwaiti civilian vehicles had littered the parking lot. Now the place was like any other metropolitan airport. It didn't appear that war was weeks away, but everyone there knew it.

I looked for the Marine who was supposedly scheduled to pick me up. He was not to be found. Now what? I didn't have a phone number to call or, for that matter, know how to operate a Kuwaiti payphone.

A couple of other Marines were arriving on the same plane. Each of us had to clear Customs. A Kuwaiti gentleman was very hospitable and offered us some hot tea, sweetened and served in a little shot glass. Then the Customs official said we would have to leave our weapons until tomorrow. I would have been more concerned, but I saw he had a dozen or so already on the floor behind his desk. We had to sign a form written in Arabic. The only thing legible was our name and weapons serial number. For all I knew I had just signed an anti-U.S. rhetoric paper and given away my pistol.

I was able to hitch a ride with one the of Marines. Arriving at Camp Doha, Kuwait, was a little sobering. On our drive up to the gate, we passed the area where an American had been killed a few weeks earlier.

It was not your standard military gate with the cursory check. These guys were serious. They searched every vehicle with dogs and mirrors and made us exit the vehicle while they searched it.

Being dropped in the wrong area of the base is not a phenomenon reserved for junior enlisted Marines. It was late and I was dead tired. Better quarters were the last thing on my mind. I found the first rack available and crashed. Logically, if no one picked me up, no one was expecting me yet. After sleeping on a top bunk in a smelly, crowded, warehouse-like barracks, I walked all around the makeshift base to get oriented. It more closely resembled a small distribution complex than a military base.

I compared everything to my last trip to Kuwait, when I had lived in a hole in the ground that I dug myself. That was 10 years ago as a captain. Now I was a lieutenant colonel. Just being near maps and computers guaranteed better living conditions.

The large, single-story, concrete warehouse buildings were, surprisingly, air-conditioned. Work areas were adjacent to the living quarters, and a shower trailer was attached. The chow hall and payphones were just a few blocks away.

In the other direction, less than a city block away, was the CFLCC (Combined Forces Land Component Command). CFLCC's daily brief, called a BUA (Battle Update Assessment), was for an Army three-star—Lieutenant General McKiernan, USA. I was there just to get situational awareness for my boss, Brigadier General Cornell Wilson, USMCR, who was the commanding general of C/JTF-CM.

Listening to the daily BUA was enlightening. However, I was a little unimpressed, even disturbed, by the PowerPoint accuracy—or rather, lack of it. The deadline for getting slides into the presentation must have been only hours in advance, because presenters routinely added verbal updates to the slide details. Why would we publish and show a three-star general and the entire staff inaccurate slides? Most Marine generals I knew would have gone ballistic.

I worked in the J-3, our Future Operations section, and as the OIC of the Forward Command Post, if needed.

This was my first joint billet. "Joint" means that a unit is comprised of individuals from the various services: Army, Navy, Air Force, and Marines. Both active duty and reserves from all the components were combined with WMD-response teams from the Czech Republic, Slovakia, Germany, Romania, and the Ukraine. There were some outstanding individuals assigned to the joint task force, but it seemed more disjointed than joint.

Mobilizing a rapid response across the CENTCOM area of operations required training and coordination. Our task force was formed to react to major chemical, biological, radiological, nuclear, or other high-explosive (CBRNE) events which would likely overwhelm the host nation's response capability.

Most of us had daily email access home and somewhat-regular phone calls. During Desert Storm we had treasured our irregular postal deliveries, routinely going several days without any. There was no such thing as email back then and no phone access for nearly three months of the deployment.

Email allowed easier communication with greater numbers of friends and family. Phone calls were still limited in frequency and duration, so they were reserved for Lee and a few for Momma.

"Hey, sir, I'm your cousin Bradley, Dave and Becky's son."

"Yeah, I remember you. I just wasn't expecting to see you here in the chow hall in Kuwait."

I had seen stories of similar chance meetings of family and friends. It was great to be part of one. Other family surprises were also on the horizon.

One was an email from my daughter's boyfriend. He asked me if he could ask Jennifer to marry him. It's a good thing I was on the other side of the world when he asked me that. They were too young, etc. I thought there was a chance he would take no for an answer or at least be put off for the foreseeable future. However, I consented, and at the age of 19, she said yes.

Now Jennifer was engaged and expected her momma to help plan her wedding. JC was completing his junior year in high school and already had senioritis. Cannon and Daniel were playing soccer and still demanded the usual attention. Plus, the 33-county campaign was relentless. It's no wonder Marine wives are revered and held in high esteem by the Corps. Too much is expected, but they somehow deliver.

The war began with the well-advertised "Shock and Awe" campaign. There didn't seem to be nearly enough shock or awe to keep the Iraqis from firing Scud missiles into Kuwait.

Iraqi chemical munitions and capabilities were still wildcards. When any Scud missile was fired from Iraq, we responded by suiting up in MOPP-4 (mission oriented protective posture), which included our full chemical suit, gloves, boots, gas mask, and hood. The first few nights the alarm sounded with aggravating regularity. Then it sounded during the day. Time after time the missiles were launched from Iraq with no effect. We started to get complacent.

Another alarm sounded while we were at work. Most people were down to half-speed or at best three-quarter speed at grabbing their gear and heading to the bunkers. Then . . .

Swoooosh!

Patriot missiles fired from a position near us—no more half speed. Instantly, everyone hit the bunker in full gear. We could hear the Patriot explode, but we weren't sure if it took down the Scud until the few minutes of silence that followed. Even then we didn't know if it had blown a chemical Scud in mid-air that may still have released a chemical agent. Detection units would check things out. Eventually, the "all clear" was sounded over the loudspeaker.

Several more times our Patriot neighbors protected us from incoming Iraqi missiles. We never needed another reminder to go full speed at the first sound of the warning siren.

Missiles came less frequently. Still, our nights were interrupted, but I usually got plenty of sleep between sirens.

KABOOM!

The metal roof on our building shook. That couldn't be good. I lay motionless, hoping it was a bad dream. I knew it wasn't. The eerie silence that followed was broken by others who had been awakened by the intense explosion. The late sirens almost seemed ridiculous after the fact, but was there another missile heading our way?

If I had to guess, I would have said it was within a half mile. It was so loud that some estimated it was just a few hundred yards away. We made our way to the bunkers. When the "all clear" sounded, we went to our work areas, as was our standard operating procedure. It was for accountability but also for action.

This was definitely within our area of responsibility. We immediately sent forward-deployed, chemical detection units into Kuwait City near the site of the blast.

It was suspected to be a Chinese silkworm missile, designed as an anti-ship weapon. It traveled low across the water, and our Patriot batteries had not detected it.

The sound of the impact had traveled over the calm night waters of the Persian Gulf, causing it to sound much closer than the nearly 10 kilometers we plotted on the map.

Loud, but ineffective, the all-clear was sounded soon afterward. It was time to stand down and go back to sleep. The previous sense of security provided by our warning sirens faded away with the night. Now we could be hit with no warning, and no Patriot response. We quickly returned to a routine that kept us from dwelling on that possibility.

Frequency of alarms diminished as our coalition aircraft responded to the launch sites with rockets of our own. A few pesky mobile launch platforms eluded our best technology for weeks.

A Kuwaiti power plant was adjacent to Camp Doha. Its tall, brightly painted smoke stacks could easily be seen for miles and miles. They were nicknamed the "Scud goalposts." It could have provided a tremendous aiming point for Iraqis peering into Kuwait from the border. By splitting the uprights, they could have landed Scud missiles in our laps or the middle of CFLCC's Tactical Operations Center.

As we watched the war progress, we began to sort through the possible scenarios that would require CJTF-CM to react. The likelihood of a CBRNE attack on Kuwait, Saudi Arabia, Jordan, or any other country in the CENTCOM area of operations was greatly diminished. Although an inadvertent chemical release inside Iraq was also becoming less and less likely, it was one of the most likely events that would put us in motion. We planned accordingly.

Pre-attack and early conflict scenarios were focused on augmenting existing emergency response teams from an affected nation. An incident in Iraq would involve a nation with no emergency services in place and a less-than-permissible environment. It would require a different approach.

With no friendly airfields to receive us, our only response would be from the ground. The possibility of a forward command post was considered. A few of us were given the green light to launch into southern Iraq to recon one of the CP sites under consideration on the outskirts of Basra. The site looked okay on the map, but it was instantly dismissed upon arrival.

Stagnant backwater and sewage intermingled. There was little or no drainage in the sandy bogs. Limited security was a must, but there would be no security here for the foreseeable future. The force it would take to secure a forward CP in this populated area would be significant. Our escorts, the British, occupied a better location near the airport outside the city. The list of reasons *not* to emplace a forward CP seemed endless.

In the meantime, the convoy element of CJTF-CMs Czechs had driven up with clean, fresh, drinking water. The locals had formed a line with buckets, bottles, tubs, and jars—just about anything that would hold water. The line quickly stretched about 50 meters. Iraqis came from every direction.

The Iraqi children were especially friendly. One American word they knew was "football," meaning soccer. I showed them Daniel's soccer picture in my wallet, and they went crazy. They loved it. I pulled out a family picture and had to keep two hands on it to keep them from snatching it from me. That picture even intrigued some of the otherwise wary adults enough for them to come closer and take a look.

Noticeably absent were the young women. We weren't sure if it was intentional or not, but there were men and boys of all ages. The women were all middle-aged to old, and it seemed the girls we saw were 10 years old or younger.

I think we were less trusting of them than they were of us.

With any quantifiable threat of WMD or any type of CBRNE gone, our task force was disbanded. The preferred option for me was deactivation and redeployment, but we were hearing rumors of reassignment. Deactivation and redeployment came quickly before a need was identified for reassignment.

Less than a few days at Camp Lejeune and a few more at MacDill Air Force Base and the rushed deactivation was complete.

There was no time to decompress or for a reunion with the family. I hit the ground running. The awaiting political campaign meant that coming home to relax and enjoy some leave and liberty was not an option. The combat zone was fading in the rearview mirror.

Entering Iraq with a special task force enabled me to witness the grateful Iraqis liberated from tyranny.

Warning sirens and trips to the bunker were accented by the sound of nearby Patriot missiles launching to take out SCUD missiles before they could reach us.

"Then said I in my heart, As it happeneth to the
fool, so it happeneth even to me; and why was
I then more wise? Then I said in my heart, that
this also is vanity."

Ecclesiastes 2:15

...10
Conflicts of Choice

Campaign days were painfully long, usually winding down in the far
reaches of the 33-county district after 9 p.m. Three hours on the road
home would come before precious few hours of interrupted sleep.

On the road again by 3 or 4 a.m. to press the flesh at distant, small-town
coffee shops would have been more fun if it weren't required six days a week.
To be on the far side of the district at some popular coffee shop before the
regulars "shuffled in" was sometimes tough to do.

Arriving meant greeting potential voters, the waitresses as well as the
patrons. Heaven forbid someone was slighted. Hours of effort and concern
could be negated with a single, inevitable, political faux pas. A reach across
the booth and the breakfast plates could cost you a vote more easily than it
could get you one. Not reaching across to shake a hand could also cost you a
vote. Even sitting down with a cup of coffee would spawn open critique if you
added sugar or creamer and they drank theirs black.

Court squares gently stirred in the mornings as city and county offices began
to open. Meeting with local officials was nearly required and always friendly. It
had questionable benefit, considering that they and their constituencies were
nearly all Democrats, but there was no way to win without swaying some
portion of them.

We had to break through a tough, party-line vote. In North Mississippi
there was little philosophical difference between a Southern "Yellow Dog"
Democrat and a true-blue Southern Republican—or an independent

populist, for that matter. National party platforms were nearly meaningless, but party affiliation still made a big difference. With rare exceptions, most rural counties expected their local politicians to be Democrats. (Ironically, they voted solidly Republican in national elections). Things would change in the years to come.

Fundraising was high on the priority list, but it seemed as though every potential donor had been squeezed hard by the governor and lieutenant governor candidates. Even very generous and supportive contributors talked candidly about the aggressive, draining and exhaustive, record-setting fundraising in the hotly contested governor's race. With that kind of spending at the top of the ticket, there was little left for "down-ticket races" like state auditor, attorney general, and state commissioners of agriculture, insurance, transportation, public service, etc.

At least Haley Barbour, who was on pace to outspend and unseat the incumbent governor, was very generous with kind words, both on and off the stump. He and his wife, Marsha, shared many miles on the campaign trail with Lee and me once I returned from Iraq.

Despite the fundraising challenges, we raised a respectable and competitive amount, but there was no way to saturate the entire district with the money we raised. So the counties more friendly to Republicans received our focus of effort.

Delta counties were solidly Democratic and, regrettably, didn't warrant a lot of measurable time and expense. I always enjoyed the challenge when there was any chance of picking up a swing vote and, sometimes, when there wasn't.

State Senator Jordan, a staunch, outspoken Democrat, invited me to speak to the Greenwood Voters League. That happened at a chance first meeting in a lobby in Biloxi. He found out later that I was a Republican, but he didn't quite know how to uninvite me. He probably hoped that I would renege.

My friend Mike Hancock traveled with me to the economically and socially depressed Delta town. His family still lived in Greenwood, so we stopped in for some Southern hospitality and a memorable, home-cooked meal. Then we drove into the poorest neighborhood in one of the nation's poorest counties.

Just as we expected, the two of us were the only white people around. That seemed to draw some curious looks on the streets as we parked our car and entered the building.

Some antagonistic comments directed at me and the Republican Party, coupled with an anti-President Bush rant, preceded a cold introduction to the small crowd. Although the opposing candidate let me speak, he stayed standing beside me and acted like he wanted to debate. He finished his tirade in a half dare. I turned to him first.

"I'm not here to run for president, but, for the record, I do support President Bush," I told him before I turned to the crowd.

"Good evening, everyone, and thank you for having me tonight. As we begin, I'd like to get a show of hands of the Republicans in the room."

Pause. Nothing.

"How about anyone who's ever voted Republican—"

Pause. Nothing.

"Even once in your entire life."

Pause. Nothing.

What could I lose? Several dozen attendees sat motionless, almost defying me to stir them.

"That's your problem," I said curtly.

At least now they sat up on the edge of their seats to listen.

"Democrats haven't helped you in Greenwood, Mississippi, and they won't. They don't have to. They have your vote locked up.

"Republicans haven't helped you in Greenwood, Mississippi, because no matter what they promise or do, you haven't and won't vote for even one of them. I'm one of the few who will even spend a little campaign time coming here to ask for your vote.

"The only chance you have in Greenwood and Leflore County is to break that pattern. You ought to start with this race. Do you realize that if Greenwood, Mississippi, voted for a Republican highway commissioner, you'd make national news? No one would believe it. Then you'd have a real chance to see things happen here."

That ignited some genuine, town hall-meeting responses, which allowed me to cover the real transportation issues somewhat before thanking them and bidding them farewell. The crowd and I parted on very friendly terms, but my host and I never closed the political chasm between us. The trip didn't get me any votes, but nobody could say I didn't go ask for them.

While not inclined to vote Republican on a whim, several counties in the hills had shown a past willingness to move to the right when the proper persuasion and an unexplainable mood hit them. Usually, that involved congressional races, presidential election years, or a few statewide races with former Democrats running as Republicans. A rare few lifelong Republicans had captured the support of voters in these counties, but a wholesale change of party affiliation had simply not taken place. Our challenge was daunting but didn't appear to be impossible.

By the time Election Day arrived, we knew we had given it everything we had and then some. Not wanting to hold anything back, I put in more of my own money and credit. To some extent I needed to know there was nothing left. Partly, I felt an obligation to those who had sacrificed financially and given of their time for me and our cause.

Election results started with an encouraging vote from the ones who knew us best in Desoto County. That large lead began to slowly yet steadily evaporate as the other county totals were added. Soon Lee County delivered the decisive blow. With a slim lead, my family, friends, and supporters held out hope, but I knew better. Without Lee County we would not and could not win.

The rest of the night was a formality. I stayed for the inevitable out of respect for the process and the people who supported us, but all I really wanted to do was get some rest. It had been six months since my return from Iraq.

Instead of waking up to a campaign, I'd be waking up to a job hunt.

"John, hi, this is Milton. I hope I didn't call too early."

"Not at all. It's always good to hear from you."

"Well, you and Lee ran a great campaign."

"We gave it all we had, but it just wasn't meant to be. Lee says that by the time the voters got to our name on the ballot, they had voted for about all the Republicans they could stand to vote for. There's probably a lot of truth to that. Now it's time for me to find a job."

"That's what I called about. We have a job opening you may be interested in, and our deadline for applications ends this week. I was really rooting for you to win, but I kept this in the back of my mind because I knew you were in a tough one. This could be a good fit for you. How soon can you get a resume together?"

"Is today quick enough?"

"Great. Why don't you and Lee drop it off . . . I'm sure if she'll be interested in hearing about this too."

Lee had taught for Milton when he was the principal of Horn Lake High School. We had become friends and had helped Milton when he ran for superintendent of education.

At least we had a lead on a job. My county supervisor term did not end for another eight weeks, so I had a little time to breathe. The thought of working for the school district was attractive, but I didn't want to make an emotional commitment. First, a job was not offered. Second, this needed to be fully considered and not be a knee-jerk reaction following a disheartening loss.

Milton sold us quickly on the possibility. The transportation director's position opening had drawn some unwelcome publicity, and he was hoping to end it on a positive note.

"Your logistics experience with the Marines should help on the transportation side, and your experience as a county supervisor will be a great asset to us in dealing with the community."

"It sounds a little too good to be true. Let us pray about it and I'll get back with you."

"Alright, but we've been without a transportation director for too long already. I need to get that position filled soon."

Prayers and discussions continued to affirm our likely decision to accept the job offer. Milton already had plans for an appreciation luncheon for bus drivers and all school transportation personnel. He wanted to announce my hiring there.

Challenges have always motivated me, so I was ready to get started. The 300-or-so transportation employees were less ready. Many were even a little anxious to be getting a Marine at the helm.

Stepping into the shop was eerily comfortable. Maybe it was the familiar smell of grease and exhaust that I knew from my youth at my dad's service station. Or maybe it was the similarities shared between a camouflaged diesel fleet of 5-ton trucks and this fleet of yellow school buses, complete with a mostly predictable and interesting assortment of drivers and mechanics.

"You may not remember me—"

"Wait, you look very familiar, but I—"

"Yvonne."

"Oh, my goodness, yes! We worked together at the warehouse when I was seventeen years old. How have you been?"

"I'm fine. I drive a special-needs bus. Some of us are so happy that you're here. We need some leadership. You and I can talk later."

"Absolutely."

That surprise connection, along with a few other community friends and acquaintances, helped relieve some of the fears of those I hadn't met. I didn't want everyone to have unnecessary worries, but some uncertainties and anxiety could work to my advantage.

Vehicle operations and maintenance would consume lots of time and effort, but this would be a people-centric undertaking. Pupils, principals, parents, professional routers, drivers, and mechanics, even the taxpaying public are bona fide stakeholders. For the next 14 years, I would not need a reminder of that, and I loved it.

Good people I needed made my life and leadership better. Others with challenges and needs made my life and leadership more meaningful. I soon realized that I had the best job in the school district. Ironically, most people thought it was the worst, so no one came looking to take my job.

The normal routine was less than half a day—under 12 hours—from 5:30 a.m. to 5:00 p.m., routinely. My assistant director and a couple of other early birds would come in before 5:00 a.m.

"Hey, Kathy. I don't mind being the first one in and the last one to leave, but if you're determined to be here at four forty-five, you're on your own."

"It helps me to get here when it's quiet. Hopefully, before the phone starts ringing."

"Okay."

Even though the days started early, I enjoyed getting up and going to work. Streets were clear of traffic. Wildlife was especially active on the dark, 12-minute drive along the back roads. I saw foxes, raccoons, opossums, skunks, owls, deer, and occasional bobcats traversing suburban residential areas.

Inside the bus shop, the coffee was always fresh or brewing. Usually, I would enter the locked doors loudly with something random like, "Honey, I'm home!" in order to break the silence of the mostly empty offices.

By the time I arrived, we were already shuffling to cover routes from call-ins. In the big scheme of things, we had very little problem with absences or late drivers, but with over 300 employees, there was always someone or something to cause a little chaos. Then there was the mechanical side with buses not starting, or lights out, or heaters not warming.

And while teachers, coaches, and administrators on 41 campuses, a dozen mechanics, 350 drivers, plus another dozen or so employees, 18,000 student riders, and countless parents, and grandparents were counting on me, the Marine Corps thought I should keep the reserves a priority.

Shifting gears and changing priorities between important civilian responsibilities and military expectations added some stress. So I would just remind myself of the many others who had it worse than I did. The on-again-off-again Marine experiences sometimes provided reflective solace.

It was a sunny Saturday and I had just left an executive session of the lieutenant colonel promotion board in Quantico. We had been considering the list of Marine reserve majors and their official records. Many distinguished combat veterans were among those we considered.

On my time off, a newfound friend from the board and I chose a quick drive to DC and a walk around the National Mall. Although the political divisions and rancor of the nation's capital can be disheartening, I never get tired of visiting and reflecting.

The encouraging sounds of a father walking and talking with his daughter beneath the Jefferson Memorial personalized it all. She couldn't have been more than nine years old, but she was deeply engaged in her one-on-one experience. The father, likely in his late 20s or early 30s, was explaining America's history to her in a refreshingly intimate way as they strolled. He spoke of freedom and democracy with an obvious academic knowledge, but more importantly, he spoke on her level from his heart. Neither public nor private schools could pretend to compete with a parent fully connecting with his own child. It was a breathing portrait of hope.

A few blocks away, in stark contrast to that quiet moment, there was an organized demonstration in opposition to the Global War on Terror, especially, the deployment in Iraq. The group seemed less educated than the father of the young girl. Their message seemed to rely on volume over content. They also directed their efforts to the media and passersby without even relating very well to each other. It was a portrait of ignorance and negativity couched in the lap of liberty.

Free people freely voiced their opinion to abandon a fragile, emerging democracy in the world while they mingled in the shadows of monuments to those who had truly believed in democracy and had pledged their lives and fortunes to it.

Homemade signs and posters voiced personal dissatisfaction with our nation's standing commitment around the world. Around them the silent majority demonstrated their apathy.

I couldn't help but wonder how many of these had supported the war on terrorism when memories of September 11th were fresh in their minds but are now just tired of it.

As the two of us walked through and around protesters, I spied the monuments and memorials I had seen before and a couple I hadn't seen. Even the familiar ones were thought provoking. The marble inscriptions inspired solemn reverence. Over 54,000 dead and over 8,000 missing Americans were memorialized on the Korean War Memorial.

Did the protesters take time to see and read the memorials around them? What about the Vietnam Memorial? The World War II Memorial? What about the revolution for independence itself or the cost to keep it? Robert E. Lee's mansion at Arlington National Cemetery was clearly in view. The protesters enjoyed their freedom. The joggers and walkers and tourists enjoyed their freedom. I enjoyed mine.

Hundreds of thousands have died in America's wars and exponentially more were severely wounded. Some of those who died may have disagreed with the national strategy at the time, a sitting president, a commanding general, or the sergeant's directive on the battlefield. Many were drafted. Many volunteered. Too many never had the opportunity to get married or see their children grow up. Yet without their collective and individual sacrifice, neither would any of us.

For the first time, I visited the FDR Memorial. Would today's protesters have opposed him and the war he entered? The obvious answer is yes.

There were no more-compelling arguments then. There was no greater threat to U.S. mainland or our national security. There were no fewer casualties to count.

People demonstrated greater resolve on a national scale during WWII. Superior national will and individual character shone in the face of adversity. Great moral clarity was also evident as I read Roosevelt's quotes engraved above partially frozen fountains of ice.

The sun began to drop in the afternoon sky and the breeze seemed stronger and colder in an instant. We had skipped lunch to walk and reflect, so we departed for an early dinner.

•••

Meanwhile, wedding plans were coming together for Jennifer and Russell, and the big day was fast approaching. Some questioned his courage, asking me by email the year before while I was deployed on the other side of the globe in Kuwait. Supposedly, his reasoning revolved around a younger brother who could not keep it secret long enough for Russell to wait for me come home. Russell indicated their desire to hold off until finished with college, but that plan quickly evaporated by the time I redeployed and changed jobs.

Soon, an alert notice for Russell's National Guard unit was circulating. The grapevine indicated that his OIF (Operation Iraqi Freedom) activation would not be until late in the summer—after the wedding—if at all.

Our family's history of my two extremely short-notice activations had us all a little more than nervous. The activation buzz became reality just days before the wedding, but thankfully, the report date on his orders would be weeks later.

Russell and the 98th Cavalry were part of the 155th Brigade Combat Team (155-BCT) being provided by the Mississippi National Guard. They would be attached to the Multi-National Force-West (MNF-W), which was the theater name for Second Marine Expeditionary Force (II MEF). In addition to 155-BCT, MNF-W included the 2nd Marine Division (2MARDIV).

It was sad to see our daughter and son-in-law as newlyweds facing such a difficult challenge. Jennifer had seen her daddy activated twice for duty in a combat zone, and now just two months into her marriage, she would be sending her husband to prepare for war.

Lee was diving in headfirst into the community support effort. Not only was our son-in-law going, but other former students of Lee's, our friends, and family members of friends were being called up as well.

We always had great community support when I was activated, but our entire community had never been affected quite like this. The National Guard touched nearly everyone in our county and beyond. Neighbors, relatives, loved ones, and close friends were called to serve. Many more local employers were now affected by the temporary, yet extended loss, of valued employees. The Marine reserve units typically are much more dispersed, and many times were fed from several states, but the 98th Cavalry were all "home folks."

It was hard for me, watching without going. I felt like I had unfinished business in Iraq, and others, even my own son-in-law, were now asked to tie up my loose ends.

Still trying to settle back into my own reserve routine, the results of the FY05 Command Screening Board were pending. It would be my last chance in a highly competitive process for one of the few coveted command billets. When that slate was released, Commanding Officer, 2nd Battalion, 14th Marines had my name on it.

Headquarters Battery was a seven-hour drive to Grand Prairie, Texas. At the time, it was the largest battalion in the Marine Corps, with four firing batteries: Delta Battery in El Paso, Texas; Echo Battery in Jackson, Mississippi; Fox Battery in Oklahoma City, Oklahoma; and Kilo Battery in Huntsville, Alabama.

The first thing I learned about my new battalion was that the unit was likely not to deploy into Iraq as a battalion. We were expected to provide batteries and smaller detachments for assorted provisional missions. It wasn't what I had in mind as an incoming artillery battalion commander.

Both commanding generals scheduled initial meetings with the new commanding officers. I took the opportunity to go on record with my new bosses with the same last name, Major General McCarthy, the 4th Marine Division CG, and Lieutenant General McCarthy, MARFORRES CG.

"General, I've been activated in the past with my unit in Desert Storm and as an individual in OIF-I. I think it's a bad idea to break up the unit integrity of the battalion. My recommendation is that we function and activate as a battalion, preferably, an artillery battalion."

"We've already fought that battle and lost. Your point is valid, but in reality, that's not going to happen."

Even though I wasn't surprised, I was still a little disappointed but glad to be in a position to at least be heard. We discussed it for a few more, brief minutes, out of courtesy, I guess, but that was about it.

"Yes, sir. Have a good day, general."

A few months later, I was back in New Orleans for the division commanding general's change of command. Major General O'Dell was assuming command from Major General McCarthy. This time Lee got orders so she could join me. This was the first time the Marine Corps ever paid for a ticket for her.

At the reception that followed, Lee spent a little time with General O'Dell. After the usual small talk, she worked her way into a more meaningful and enlightening conversation.

"You know, General, John and I are about to build a new home. If he gets orders to Iraq and leaves that for me to do, I'll have to wonder if he asked for those orders."

"Well, Lee, it's not *if* he gets orders, but *when*."

Smiles and the lighthearted atmosphere couldn't take away the sting of that sobering reminder. Lee looked back at me as if I had something to tell her. All I could do was shrug my shoulders.

The Marine Corps reserve artillery was conspicuously absent from the original forces that were activated and deployed to fight in Iraq. There was a lot of speculation as to why and how badly it was or wasn't missed. Whatever the reasoning, an entire artillery battalion was not needed.

Furthermore, my new battalion was in the process of fielding the new, high-mobility artillery rocket system (HIMARS). One battery was already fully involved in field testing the launcher and resupply vehicle. They were non-deployable.

Two truck companies had previously been formed from Headquarters Battery in Grand Prairie. They deployed just before I assumed command.

Within a few months of assuming command, two of my firing batteries would also be activated for provisional missions, and others were on tap to rotate into the fray. This did not feel right. How could I assume command of a battalion, only to see it dispersed to the four winds?

There was still a viable mission for us in the rear; we had to begin the transition from cannons to rockets. Our staff was on the cutting edge of implementing a new weapons system and refining the Marine Corps Force Artillery doctrine. Fox Battery from Oklahoma City and Headquarters Battery in Grand Prairie needed a functioning battalion staff to take their HIMARS training and integration to the next level. It still didn't feel right. My Marines were going forward, and I was in the rear with the gear.

Then my active-duty counterpart and new friend, Lt. Col. Roger Garay, called me. He was the battalion's inspector-instructor (I&I). Within a month of assuming command, I received a call I had hoped never to hear. One of our Marines had paid the ultimate price. He had deployed before I took command, we hadn't met, and he was serving under another commander at the time, yet I still felt a jolt inside as if he were one of mine. He was.

Lance Corporal Louis Qualls was killed by enemy small-arms fire during the Fallujah offensive. He had just cancelled an approved inter-service transfer to the regular U.S. Army. Qualls had been jockeying to get into the fight, and if the Marine reserves had not activated him, he had been determined to go with the Army so he could deploy.

Marines in Grand Prairie rightly determined it would be better if we made the casualty call ourselves. It would be wrong to wait for some faceless Marine assigned at random from Headquarters Marine Corps. They moved extremely fast to ensure there was no unnecessary delay.

The Qualls family was understandably brokenhearted, yet strong and patriotic in the face of tragic news. They knew he died honorably in a worthy cause doing what he wanted to do.

When that first casualty call came, it reminded me of what I already knew. I had to go to the fight. My Marines were over there, and I was secure and safe in the Land of the Free.

During the next drill, we held a memorial service. Although I was a little nervous, I had learned a long time ago that funerals and memorials were not about the speaker but about the one who had passed away. It was a high honor and privilege to address the Marines and LCpl. Quall's family on his behalf. The rifle with bayonet was embedded in a sand-filled ammo can. Dog tags and a helmet were placed on the butt-stock, and desert boots were at the base.

A "roll-call" was taken. LCpl. Louis Quall's name was called out three times with no answer, followed by a report, "Lance Corporal Qualls is missing." Silence. Chills. The sound of taps echoed through the drill hall.

Was this going to be the last, or was it the first of many or a few? None of us knew.

Going to Iraq was not going to be a simple task. Now I was in command and there were still expectations at home. My regimental commander did not like the idea of me leaving, and the division commander had already said no. I made my case for it again and waited for a more opportune time to push.

Delta Battery was then tasked to deploy from El Paso as a military police company destined for the volatile Al Anbar province. The company's platoons would perform missions of base security in Camp Fallujah, convoy escorts out of Al Taqadum (TQ), and serve as prison guards at the Ramadi Detention Facility.

"This is Lieutenant Colonel Caldwell. How's the processing going?"

"Hello, sir. The Battery CO's gone for the evening. Everyone's checked in. We're one hundred percent, except for one Marine who left."

"What do you mean 'one Marine who left?'"

"The Lance Corporal decided he wasn't going."

"I don't understand."

"Sir, he checked in with everyone else and then decided he wasn't going."

"That's what I thought you said. We're not asking his opinion. These are *involuntary* orders. He doesn't get that option."

"Sir, he told us some story about his mom, his work, and some problems he was having with the leadership here."

"Aren't you a Staff NCO in the Marine Corps?"

"Yes, sir."

"You better have someone find him. Strap him to the wings of the plane if you have to, but letting him walk off is *not* an option. Do you understand?"

"Yes, sir."

Although it was getting late in the evening, I hung up the phone and called my battalion headquarters in Grand Prairie. Master Sergeant Orona answered and quickly understood my frustration.

"Sir, let me talk to the Marine. I speak good 'Span-glish.' I'll call you right back."

"Thanks. I'll be up, waiting on your call."

Many of the El Paso Marines and their families were Hispanic Americans, and clear communication was an imperative.

Less than an hour later, Master Sergeant Orona called back.

"Sir, we got him. He was at his civilian job and couldn't be reached. I called his mother and she got in touch with him and had him call me back. He will collect his gear and be back at the battery in the morning."

"Are you sure we don't have to send someone to get him?"

"He'll be there."

"Good job. Now I can get some sleep."

Major Ellis, the battery commander, called too. He wanted to assure me that they would take care of the Marine and his issues in the morning. They did.

Echo Battery out of Jackson, Mississippi, would be split into two truck platoons and support the infantry: 3rd Battalion, 2nd Marines from Camp Lejeune and 3rd Battalion, 25th Marines, a reserve battalion out of Ohio, would each have a truck platoon of ours attached.

"How's the recall going?"

"Good, sir, we're one hundred percent except for one Marine we can't locate."

"What do you mean?"

"None of his phone numbers are good, and we don't have any way to get in touch with him."

"So what are you doing now to remedy that?"

"We've done everything we know to do."

"That's just not acceptable. Pull his serviceman's record book and give me his address, his original enlistment site address, and any other old addresses you have on him."

"Sir, he's from a rural county in Southern Mississippi, but we think he lives and works somewhere in Louisiana now. We've tried everything."

"Just get me the addresses."

This was the second battery that was all too willing to leave a Marine behind. I was beginning to get upset.

A simple Google search and one call to the local county sheriff in the Marine's home county of record yielded results.

"Do you know the family?"

"Sure."

"Can you contact them?"

"I'll send a deputy out to the house. I'm not sure they have a telephone."

The parents were found and quickly contacted their son, who was working on a Gulf Coast offshore oil rig. He responded immediately with a phone call and reported for duty.

With 100% reporting, it was time to readdress the subject of mobilization with the battalion staff. We had the same talk we'd had when I took command a few short months ago.

"Let me reiterate what General McCarthy told the division officers nearly a year ago. Our Marines are going. Marines are paying the ultimate price. Some are on their second activation and deployment. For those of you who haven't been mobilized, you need to get ready to activate, resign, or retire. We can't have our Marines go while our leadership stays home. Any questions, retirements, or resignations?"

There was a confident silence. The battalion officers were well aware of the challenges that lay ahead. Some of them had already served in Iraq in various capacities. Some of their peers were in Iraq as we met. We all knew the chances of all of us being together in Grand Prairie, Texas, six months from this day, were slim and none.

Lists of billet gaps were constantly being circulated from a variety of sources. The Marine Corps was still asking for volunteers for now, but everyone knew there would be increasing pressure for individuals to volunteer. That was the price of our battalion being sourced in a piecemeal fashion.

Then came my turn. Civil Affairs Group (CAG) billets had been floating for three months, hoping for volunteers. Apparently, everyone who was going to volunteer had already done so, and they were still short of officers.

The call reached me on my cell phone just north of Jackson, Mississippi.

"Hey, John. This is Roger. Did I catch you at a bad time?"

"No. Actually, I'm on the way to Echo Battery. Now's a good time. What's up?"

"The CAG deal has come back up again. This time it's a tasker, and Two/Fourteen is supposed to cough up a lieutenant colonel and a captain."

"Well, that kind of narrows the options since I'm the only lieutenant colonel, and Captain Moeller has already expressed an interest if something comes up."

"Technically, it's still a volunteer billet, so if you say no, the boss has already said I could go."

"I know you want to go, Roger, but it's kind of hard to turn down under the circumstances. I'm asking my staff to be ready, so I guess I'm ready. When do you need a final answer?"

"Not until this afternoon. They've got to have these billets filled by us this afternoon."

"Ha, that's typical. I'm going to hang up and call Chris to make sure he's still up for it. When would we leave?"

"The first week of January."

"Wow, that's less than a month. Nothing like plenty of notice."

"I know it's short notice, but you know I'll go in your place if you can't."

"Thanks, Roger, but I'll take it. It's not my preferred billet, but if that's what they need, I'm available. I'll call the boss after I make contact with Chris and tell him to count us in."

A week later, I was meeting with the regimental commander, Colonel Jeffery Fondaw, during our regularly scheduled drill. He explained the story behind the short-fused requirement and expressed his appreciation at our willingness to stand in the gap. I explained that I still hadn't seen any orders or paperwork of any kind and asked if it was a sure thing. He explained that it was 90% sure, about as sure as anything in the Marine Corps before the orders are cut.

When the colonel left, Chris came to my office to ask about the mobilization process.

"Sir, you've been through this before. What do I need to do to get my family and myself ready? It is definite that we're going, isn't it?"

"It's ninety percent sure, according to Colonel Fondaw. I just asked him the same question."

As soon as those words left my mouth, Roger Garay leaned in the door.

"Never mind."

Instantly, the 10% possibility of not going became 100%. Neither Chris nor I wanted to go home and tell everyone that it had changed, especially with the probability it would change back and forth over time. We had begun in earnest to prepare our families, our friends, our employers, and ourselves mentally and emotionally. How could we just turn it off? *Should* we turn it off?

Reasoning that this was the best timeframe for all concerned, and accepting that these requirements would continue popping up until we were finally activated, Chris and I volunteered. Besides, two thirds of my firing batteries and elements of Headquarters Battery would be activated during this same timeframe. If I left now, I should be home for the holidays next year.

To hold my breath and try dodging activation was not a palatable option. Now was the time to find an available billet in Iraq and push a little harder with the boss to get approval. The CG's guidance for me not to go had apparently lost its imperative. I quickly found a contact at Camp Lejeune.

While I was searching for a billet, my Marines were preparing for their own departure. Sergeant Major Crow and I made command visits to the HTCs (home training centers) in El Paso and Jackson.

Marines were ready. You could see it in their eyes. Families were not. You could see it in their eyes.

February was a short month and about to get shorter. Getting the final word on imminent activation orders was unduly difficult. Eventually, orders were cut for Chris and me. The timing coincided with the activation and deployment of the majority of Marines in the battalion. Although we wouldn't go as a command, we would at least be on similar timeframes.

It was the second week of February before I had orders in hand. By the end of the month, I was in Iraq. The sum total of my pre-deployment training consisted of getting my gear issued before my plane departed North Carolina.

We staged at Camp Lejeune at the field house around 1630. White school buses shuttled us to the armory to draw our weapons. The vehicles were a reminder of the yellow school buses, family, and friends I was leaving back home.

For the 2nd Marine Division, this was home. Their families and friends filled the field house to say their goodbyes. Charter buses picked us up to take us to MCAS Cherry Point to catch a government-chartered plane. It was a huge MD-11 with plenty of first class seating for all the officers and the most-senior staff NCOs.

The six and a half hours to Shannon, Ireland, passed quickly. As we approached and dropped below the clouds, the lush green landscape came into view.

Glass panels initially separated us from other civilian passengers in the terminal. As we exited the plane in our desert uniforms, the people in the airport stood and erupted in spontaneous applause. They didn't know if we were going to Iraq or returning, but something tells me it didn't matter to them. That public display of affection and appreciation from total strangers in

Ireland let me know we were really among friends—even family.

Soon, it was back to the plane. We departed to another solemn, standing ovation. It was sad too that some of the Marines they were now applauding would very likely be draped in an American flag for their return trip.

A few hours later, the pilot announced that we were crossing the border into Iraqi airspace, something not possible on my first two trips to the area. After hearing all the negative reports about power grids and outages, I was surprised to see the lights of cities and towns below. The clusters of lights looked a little like an over flight of Arkansas between Memphis and Dallas.

The last time I had flown into Kuwait City we had to fly over the Mediterranean and swap pilots in Crete then enter Kuwaiti airspace from the south. The plane did not stay overnight on the ground. This was because the airport was within range of Saddam Hussein's missiles.

My first trip to Kuwait in 1990 had begun with touch down in Saudi Arabia. When I rolled up to the Kuwait International Airport in a Hummer the first time, the Iraqis had just retreated. The terminal had been ransacked and abandoned. Remnants of Iraqi military vehicles littered the parking lot.

The second time I landed at KIA had been on a scheduled commercial flight. The airport had been bustling with people and commerce. We had been on a collision course with Iraq at a "time of our choosing."

This time I landed on a chartered plane and exited the airport under the cover of darkness. Curtains were drawn on the bus that took us through Kuwait City to a U.S. military airfield to hop a C-130 into Western Iraq.

For the third time in my life I was loading rounds into a magazine that weren't meant for paper targets at the range. It is a sobering reality.

Lighthearted and funny stories were few and far between. Partly, the seriousness came with age. At 43, I had seen enough to know some of what to expect, but even some difficult circumstances would usually offer some comic relief.

We were briefed to stay alert and be prepared to return fire. Oddly, the group in our truck consisted primarily of senior staff NCOs and field grade officers. Instantly, all of us were little more than troops with big paychecks. We would be following our immediate action instructions from the corporal who was our truck commander.

Some senior Marines took exception to junior Marines being in charge of them, but it seemed to make sense to me. We had just arrived from halfway across the world and hardly knew which way was up. I trusted that corporal truck commander more than I would have a jet-lagged O-6 who didn't know the situation, radio frequencies, convoy procedures, etc.

The 1st Marine Division had been in Iraq about a year by the time I arrived. Their staff did well to help me make the turnover a smooth one. My first night in Iraq looked like it would be a sleepless one, so I went straight to work. I knew I had been assigned to the night shift. By morning I began to fine tune my new sleep pattern. Twelve on/twelve off/seven days a week—or 10 p.m. until 10 a.m. every day—for the next six to seven months.

Another level of seriousness is forced upon reserve augments like me. Not having time to develop personal and working relationships in a unit during pre-deployment training necessitates getting down to business and securing professional trust first. Friendships and support from home would help maintain the right outlook for the long haul. In the meantime, a positive outlook had to come from within.

While the 1st Marine Division CG was still on board, things were done his way. Lt. General Natonski was a very tall, powerfully calm man with a deep voice. He looked over the briefing slides in excruciating detail at exactly 0530 every morning.

After the RIP/TOA (Relief in Place/Transfer of Authority) from 1st Marine Division to 2nd Marine Division, I adjusted to Lt. General Huck. His demeanor and physical characteristics were in stark contrast to General Natonski.

General Huck had a short, wiry frame and a more-volatile personality. He was much less punctual and periodically failed to show up for his morning update. He would often wake up early enough to read our already-posted details of the night's significant events before he showed for the brief. Many times, we just reaffirmed what he had read and plotted significant events on the large electronic map for greater clarity. General Huck also wanted to be awakened in the middle of the night for updates on more issues than his predecessor.

Both wanted the overnight casualties first. General Natonski lamented the Iraqi civilian deaths more openly, and General Huck was more aggressive in sharing his desire to kill the enemy. That difference proved to have more to do with the stage of their individual deployments rather than their divergent personalities.

After the morning update, my watch officers and I normally had time to eat before the rest of the staff started rolling in about 0700. On Sundays most of the division staff took the morning off, which made a quiet time for the combat operations center (COC).

Whenever I had the chance to call home, I always chose to omit certain facts. I never understood why others would share the negative. I didn't share that the convoy that picked us up at Al Asad had been late because they had to wait on the road for EOD (explosive ordnance disposal) to clear an IED (improvised explosive device).

I had rationalized earlier how safe it would be at the Division COC. Then I learned that the officer who would have been sitting to my left was killed by a haphazard missile launch a few weeks before I arrived. Sharing those details would only make family and friends worry.

We heard sporadic gunfire and explosions fairly often, and a loudspeaker outside our compound which broadcasted morning, midday, and evening prayers to Allah. The first time I heard them was in Saudi Arabia during the first Gulf War in 1990. It was eerie then and it was eerie now. The chants were in Arabic, and none of us knew what was being said.

Camp Blue Diamond was the dusty remains of Uday's palace compound. The main palace had been nicknamed "J-Dam Palace" in honor of several JDAAM bombs dropped in the middle of it. The building looked more like ancient ruins than a modern-day, livable palace. The steel rebar penetrating from the partially destroyed structure indicated it was not old at all but just built to look like it. Now, Marines occupied those ruins as living quarters.

It was easy to imagine it standing majestically on the banks of the Euphrates River. Around it there were several smaller buildings built with the same sandstone look with an over-abundance of columns and arches.

Scuttlebutt circulated that the smaller buildings had housed guards and concubines, but I wasn't really sure.

The second largest-looking structure had once been a reception hall and had sustained only superficial battle damage. That was now used as the Division Command Operations Center. It had multicolored marble floors, and majestic columns supported rhythmic archways inside and out.

Gaudy, contrasting patterns and designs seemed to have no rhyme or reason. It looked like a hodge-podge approach to a very expensive project reminiscent—some say appropriately—of a third-rate brothel. Large, cheaply-made chandeliers had been torn down, at least partially during the combat or looting phases of the assault. Now, some were rewired in a field-expedient fashion. Wires were exposed, and they didn't hang straight anymore, but they provided light.

Some of the marble was poorly matched and shoddily installed, and there were many cracked and broken places. Decorative woodcarvings in the doorways had apparently been stripped in the first phase of the war when the U.S. Army first arrived.

Remnants of Hussein's heyday were clear enough to easily visualize the pre-war conditions. The complex's interior streets were lined with beautiful palms and flowering trees. A mini fruit orchard stood, seemingly unscathed, yet dated aerial intelligence photos showed that was not the case. Most of the original, larger orchard was simply gone.

Tall, reinforced stone walls and a huge archway with heavy, decorative steel gates continued their security role, only this time we were taking advantage of them to defend ourselves against insurgents. American Marines manned the gate towers and patrolled the perimeter. Trip flares and three-strand concertina wire augmented natural and other manmade defenses.

New arrivals tracked every boom—Where was it? What was it? How far away from us was it?—in everything but feet and inches. Was it short, long, right, or left? I was no different.

Situated on the Euphrates River on the outskirts of the town of Ramadi, explosions were frequent occurrences. Eventually, the sounds of war barely inspired an upward glance. We regressed a little on the real close ones. Sometimes, it was hard to tell the difference between the various proximities and sizes of explosions, and other times it was easy. It became an individual art to distinguish between the myriad booms.

Most harmless to us and the least consistent in characteristics were the ever-recurring controlled detonations. Some unexploded ordnance (UXO) that had been found or some IED would be intentionally blown up by EOD. Sometimes, a warning would precede it; sometimes, not.

Sizes and types of detonations as well as locations varied dramatically. The sound could be hardly noticeable or enough to rattle buildings and shake your very soul. Even the time of day and atmospheric conditions made a difference. Sound travels better at night. Wind or lack of it can also be a contributing factor. IEDs can sound like a controlled detonation but have tragically different results. When conditions were right, even our own outgoing artillery from across the river could give us a jolt.

There was always the period of not knowing if someone was hurt or if it could be the beginning of a coordinated attack with more enemy action to follow. I always played the best scenario out in my mind until hearing otherwise.

Cool February Al Anbar nights with daytime highs in the 80s were accompanied by wind, spitting rain, and thunderstorms. Downpours in dry climates were no longer a surprise. I had experienced desert rains in Southern California's High Desert and in Southwest Asia on multiple occasions.

Multiple roof leaks sent me to my door 32 times. Forecast to end around noon, the showers only seemed to be getting worse. The 1.5-liter bottles that had once held drinking water were now filled with rainwater. My bivvey sack acted like a splash guard for my bed. Two soaking-wet towels also help minimize the spread of water through the carpet. The carpet was a cheap, light brown, indoor/outdoor style with so much sand and dust embedded that the water turned it into mud.

Shower shoes kept my bare feet off the cold, wet floor while I took more water to the door to empty it. Two trips to the head that night caused me to track in more mud. It was pretty poor living conditions compared to home but better than a hole in the ground. I kept thinking that the rain would let up so I could get a little more sleep—no such luck.

Forty-three bottles of rainwater and a constant up-and-down shuttle to the door called for something more. A large trash can reconnoitered from the COC would hopefully allow for more sleep.

When I returned with the trashcan, not only had the water bottle spilled, but another small leak had started in the roof. The trashcan readily accepted the largest steady stream. The carefully aligned plastic bottle stood directly under the new drip. Although there were still two hours until my shift started, I gave up trying to rest and returned to work an hour early.

Rain, thunder, and lightning continued through the night on my watch. By morning even the paved roads of our compound were muddy. Self-pity faded when I walked past several PSD (Personal Security Detachment) Marines who had arrived in armored Humvees with their commanders.

Dried mud covered each windshield. At some point just enough had been smeared off for the drivers to see. The mud over the rest of them had been there just long enough to crust over the top half of the vehicles.

With mud everywhere, the splattered hummers wouldn't have been noticed if not for the contrasting cleanliness of the machine guns in the turrets. The dark metal glistened with a light coat of oil and, from a slight distance, seemed to be immaculate. Marines who manned them were anything but spotless. Not quite as muddy as their rides, the machine-gunners had obviously put their attention on what counted most—their weapons.

These Marines appeared battle hardened. You could see it in their eyes—not showy but serious. They planned on going home soon, and after surviving six months in a combat zone, they weren't going to let their guard down, even within our camp confines.

I returned to my room with a new perspective, but it still hurt a little to open my door and see the damp, clammy condition of the place where I was supposed to get some rest. I saw others with comfort problems like mine, pulling wet belongings from their rooms.

A cold walk in the rain to the shower wasn't great, but the shower was steamy with great water pressure. Then I knew I was spoiled, just a "staff weenie," as we used to call people in my shoes. I was headed back to a rack, not a comfortable one but still a rack. The room would be wet, almost slimy, but I would be comfortable, clean, and mostly dry.

Visiting Daniel's class and other elementary schools and churches was good for me as much as them.

Conflicts of life are more manageable with family

"Better is a poor and a wise child than an old and foolish king, who will no more be admonished."

Ecclesiastes 4:13

...11

Conflicts of Experience

Days and nights at Camp Blue Diamond blurred and blended into a never-ending cycle of recurring events. Tiresome, repetitive reports created a numbing effect to otherwise shocking and emotionally painful stuff.

Duties of the night watch were virtually the same as the day watch but without the mob of primary staff officers looking over our shoulders. We worked the operational links across western Iraq along with the night shifts of senior, subordinate, and adjacent commands. Professionalism, personalities, and the fog of war converged with high tech communications and data links and old-fashioned military phones.

Certain events called for me to wake up the commanding general. We hoped to make it through each shift without that occurring, because meeting the wake-up criteria usually meant bad news, but too often he was awakened by a call from me before morning. We learned quickly not to complain about the boring nights.

Our subordinate commands were under relatively loose reins. Most notably, the routine combat ops were led from the battalion and company levels. Decentralized approaches to most maneuvers were dictated by geography and a depleted, scattered, and unconventional enemy insurgency.

Higher headquarters determined that the highest priority for any close-air support was given to the named operations. Predictably, nearly everything larger than a routine platoon patrol seemed to be submitted as a named operation. Plans for the conduct of operations (ConOps) were sent to us, usually well in advance.

Broad and permissive guidance for the Marine regimental combat teams

(RCTs) and the assigned U.S. Army brigade combat teams (BCTs) allowed them to conduct flexible combat operations and COIN (counter insurgency) ops within their assigned AOs (areas of operation) without interference from us. Still, we prompted them for the necessary information flow that enabled us to do our job. We provided some operational support and protective top cover to them from an onslaught of requests from our own higher headquarters, although they probably didn't notice.

Units would sometimes be unexplainably late, with an incomplete and inaccurate account of events. Administrative friction then escalated quickly, and the vertical lines of communication would get well tested. It wasn't the facet of combat operations I had in mind when I enlisted in the infantry 20 years earlier.

Part of me understood that my operational role as the senior watch officer could and sometimes did impact events on the ground. Another part of me wondered because of the almost-sterile computerized surroundings. The problem with seeking responsibility and emotional credit for some of the division's combat success also meant equivalent accountability for our own casualties. That reality will always remain a sobering one.

Most of the smaller ops were nearly "rubber stamp" items to keep us informed. Yet there were times when supposedly simple operations needed one more set of eyes.

"Have you read the latest ConOps?"

"Not yet."

"It's a basic raid to capture or kill a known insurgent, but it indicates that he's a Mufti. What's a Mufti?"

"I'm not sure."

"I'll ask the G-Two. Hey, Two! What's a Mufti?"

"I'm not sure, but I'll find out, sir. Let's see . . . It looks like a Mufti is like the Sunni version of an Ayatollah."

"Whoa. Let me get them on the hook.

"Hey, your ConOps show a raid on a Mufti."

"Yes, sir, he's a known bad guy."

"Yeah, maybe, but we need to start waking up generals for this one. Military action on any religious leader takes three-star approval. Are you guys sure you want me to wake up the boss and have him wake up his boss on this?"

"Yes, sir. They're set to go tonight."

"Let me speak to your commanding officer."

"He's asleep."

"Well, if you expect me to wake my boss, you better go wake up yours right now."

A few minutes later the phone rang.

"Never mind. We're calling off the raid."

"That's what I figured."

Consequences and casualties . . .

Some nights were a challenge to navigate even a few feet to the head, like stepping off into an abyss.

On one particular night, a late moon and faint ambient light proved of little value to my tired eyes. But before too long, a big, beautiful full moon floated effortlessly in the clear eastern skies of western Iraq. From the building, the dark silhouette of tall reeds along the Euphrates riverbank framed the scene. On the far shore, black outlines of buildings and smokestacks of a glass factory created a panoramic skyline beyond the shimmering water. The drone of an occasional special ops boat from Hurricane Point was reminiscent of fishermen back home heading out to check trot lines. The sounds of a chopper drew near . . . close enough to spray us with remnants of the rotor wash. Scheduled "milk runs," or "bus routes" as we called them, were regularly flown throughout the province on our shift during cover of darkness.

Sometimes, the insurgents seemed to awaken with the Marines on the day shift. Those busy mornings would include back-to-back indirect fire, small-arms fire, and an IED or two and subside in time for me to finish my shift and get some sleep.

One night, four rounds of mortar fire landed just outside our building with no damage or injuries. Two Marines reported wounds from hand grenade fragments in the small-arms engagement, while a random IED missed another group of Marines entirely. The frequent hodgepodge of insignificant close calls didn't seem to interrupt anyone's routine.

Still *it* happens on an evening walk across the relatively safe confines of a base camp. *It* happens while riding routinely in an armored vehicle. *It* happens when standing or sitting alone or in a group. A random bullet or indiscriminate fragment finds its way—and another American falls. A faceless attack with no chance to react seems strangely normal in the wildly hostile Al Anbar province of western Iraq.

There is an unspoken wish that it could have been more glorious—more dramatic, even exciting and heroic. U.S. soldiers and Marines are unusually prepared for the hazards and even the cost of the ultimate sacrifice in an open, violent exchange of gunfire in the defense of freedom and themselves. A loss without that seems worse somehow.

Sobered by yet another casualty report, it is readily apparent that it wouldn't feel any better in a classic battlefield situation. Those happen too. Marines and soldiers bravely face and gallantly fight the enemy with great moral clarity. It is still painful. It still seems just as senseless in ways and yet somehow very meaningful in others.

Regardless of the exact circumstances, there is a bigger picture—a higher and more noble cause. Without our belief systems, Americans would not be Americans.

Nearly as soon as a quiet shift ends, another gets ugly. My first watch with a Marine killed in action (KIA) came within a few days of my arrival. The Marine's AAV hit a mine just one week from his scheduled redeployment home. Two others were wounded (WIA).

Minutes later, we received a call that a Humvee had slid into a canal. One of the U.S. civilian interpreters attached to us drowned, and two Devil Dogs were treated for water inhalation. Over the course of the next 24 hours, 21 U.S. soldiers and Marines were wounded.

Reporting casualties and other negative news was an unwelcome and progressively more-defining aspect of my job. The outbound 1st Marine Division G-3, Colonel Larry Nicholson, pulled me aside one morning about it. In a concerned manner, more like a father and mentor, he passed on some very solid and timely counsel.

"John, you need to pull yourself away from work a little more. If the only time you leave the COC is to break bad news, no one will want to see you coming. You'll be like the grim reaper." He smiled reassuringly.

I knew he was right. It was the seriousness of the job that had absorbed me, not the difficulty or even intensity.

"So pull yourself away whenever you get a chance. Find time to do and talk about something else."

"Yes, sir."

Another morning began with one friendly KIA and one WIA reported. A second report from 155 BCT indicated nine urgent medevacs and six priority medevacs from Kalsu in a truck rollover. That's where my son-in-law, Russell, and other friends and neighbors were stationed. Thankfully, no one I knew personally was injured in the accident.

Uneventful days would quickly create unwarranted optimism. The hope was that those days were the beginning of better times to come. Then a difficult day would follow. Soon, daily up-and-down casualty totals took a backseat to weekly assessments and then monthly comparisons.

Time and stress were taking their toll. The possibility of not returning barely crossed my mind for more than a minute. Still, it was a sobering thought that most if not all Marines must have on occasion. It was also a common thought in the backs of the minds of every wife and child. Still, there wasn't a lot of talk about it; verbalizing it was essentially forbidden.

There was no need to dwell on the negative, so we didn't. It was either acutely practical or it was the advance denial stages of a feared grieving process that became a painful reality for too many.

July was a month of reduced casualties. Just when it seemed things might be improving, things got worse.

On the second day of August, I walked into work to hear reports of more than a dozen U.S. wounded and more than a half dozen U.S. killed. That Marine battalion had already suffered more casualties than any other battalion, even before this tragic day.

We made it through the next night with little else occurring, but morning broke with another mass casualty event from the same battalion. An AAV was flipped and burned by an IED or triple-stacked mine. There were 16 casualties in an instant. Stress rose exponentially. I was sick of "proportional" response and the unemotional, calculated business of war. Revenge, payback, or whatever you want to call it was my desire.

A day later, TV news channels reported the event. I watched the CNN, FOX News, ABC, NBC, and CBS versions. Each was equally difficult to watch. It was like reliving it over and over. The numbers were a little skewed on the low side. A delay in official identification of the charred remains also delayed reporting an accurate total to the media.

I practically bit the G-2 watch officer's head off for disregarding a simple directive the following morning. He probably deserved it to some degree, but I'm sure it had more to do with my stress level than his actions. Worry set in about how I would react at home, especially to Lee and the boys. Would I snap at them, too?

The level of tension now seems to have had little to do with the actual events of that day. It was more of the slow compilation of them all: IDF (indirect fire), IED (improvised explosive device), EOF (escalation of force), SOF (Special Operations Force raids), TIC (troops in contact), many of which involved friendly WIAs and KIAs.

IDF (Indirect Fire) . . .

Impacts echoed just across the river inside Camp Ramadi on an almost-regular basis. They were close enough to make us look up and take notice, but that was about it. They impacted Camp Blue Diamond on a frequent and somewhat diminishing rate. It was simply reported as an IDF event.

Incoming—the kind that gets personal—may seem confusing until the first strike. There's rarely any mistaking it after that. Whether it's the sound of a rocket lobbed aimlessly but close, or a mortar placed in your direction with a little more skill or luck, you start to hear and feel the difference. Subtle differences are now distinct and clear. Random explosions attract less undue attention, but at times it's still hard not to flinch.

I was sound asleep one evening when a first explosion rang out—loud, but not exceptionally loud—probably a small rocket or mortar. It must have been within a few hundred meters.

Then I heard one whistling in. That's close. BOOM. I could feel it. The impact was about 50 meters away. The first one landed out in the Euphrates River. The second one landed between my sleeping quarters and our showers. There were no injuries.

Another time I was sitting up on the edge of the bed when an explosion interrupted an otherwise-quiet day. My bed shook and my rickety metal door rattled. It was awkward to just lie down and go back to sleep under the circumstances, but there wasn't much I could do about it. I just kept my helmet and flak jacket handy.

The sound of yet another rocket sailing over my head in the afternoon woke me. Pulling my Kevlar a little closer to the bed like a security blanket allowed me to dose off again.

Ear plugs helped with everyday noise while trying to sleep. Sometimes, it would just be vehicle motors or Marines talking loudly without thinking about us day sleepers. In addition to the incoming, it was also not unusual to be awakened on occasion by controlled detonations and our own outgoing artillery fire.

Sleeping through it all was the goal. Yet it was a little discomforting to arrive for my shift and hear when an incoming rocket had impacted about 100 meters from me but didn't wake me. One Marine was wounded with shrapnel to his leg.

Somehow, the slow steady beeps from my wristwatch would rouse me following a typical day's sleep. Just five more minutes of rest . . . Sssssssssssssssss schk. Boom! Sssssssssssssssschk. BOOM! The first incoming rocket was close enough to get my attention. The second one was even louder. My bed shook. I listened for shrapnel hitting the walls, but I didn't hear anything. I reached for my flak jacket and helmet and went directly to work. It was time anyway, but it was also a safer structure if the incoming continued.

It was strangely quiet as I stepped out into the dark night. The moon wasn't up yet, and there was just enough light left in the sky to see silhouettes of the close trees and buildings. My usual stop by the shadowy line of portable heads led me to believe it was going to be a routine night. A few steps later, I turned toward the COC. The vehicles out front and the lights told another story.

The COC had taken a direct hit from one of the two rockets I had just heard. As I approached the scene, others walked calmly past me in the opposite direction. I took that as a good sign until I saw a Marine being slowly carried in a stretcher. The slow, careful way he was being carried told me they were in no rush. Either he had been killed or his injury did not require them to hurry. Thankfully, it was the latter.

Chunks of concrete had dislodged from 20 feet above the guard posted at the front door. The Marine's helmet and flak jacket had protected him from falling shrapnel and debris. The Marine told stretcher bearers that he only had his bell rung, but no one was taking any chances. He was treated carefully for a possible back or neck injury.

As I walked through the rubble and into the COC, the dust literally and figuratively was just settling. Everyone was wearing flaks and helmets and talking about where they had been standing and what they were doing when it hit.

Assessments were made of the structural integrity of the impacted roof and ceiling. After that, the night was quiet.

Sounds of a brief sandstorm with howling winds, sand, and debris hitting metal walls woke me a few minutes earlier on another night. The tarps on our roofs meant to reduce the leaks were flapping and slapping the roof. I got up and prepared to walk through it on the way to work.

At least, if the weather's this bad, there won't be any indirect fire, I thought.

About the time that idea crossed my mind, I heard incoming. The explosion was extremely close—probably a 120-mm rocket, but the sound of the impact was somewhat muffled by the wind.

By the time I was dressed at 2135, the wind had stopped and the dust had diminished. But when I walked into the COC, I knew something wasn't right. The numbers of people, their locations, the quiet in the COC, and the body language told me that the impact had caused some sort of casualty or casualties. I quietly inquired.

"What's going on?"

"That last impact you heard hit Blue Diamond. I think we've got one friendly KIA."

"Who was it?"

"Did you know Sergeant Perez?"

"I'm not sure."

I couldn't immediately place his face in my memory at the time. This would be the first Marine killed aboard Camp Blue Diamond since our arrival. Then I saw his picture and recognized him from the dayshift.

Sgt. Perez had been walking in from a training range. The round impacted the roof of the chapel building near him. He died of his wounds while receiving medical attention. A late report of another shrapnel injury and superficial damage to the chapel were the only other casualty and damage.

It was a long-range shot in the dark in high winds. It was practically like getting struck by lightning. How do you plan for that?

The rest of the night was eerily quiet. There was nothing else to do but get back to the routine. But for a while it would be respectfully solemn.

Even a simple walk to the head was a time for reflection. Stepping into the darkness nearly always included a greeting from one of the guards outside the COC.

"Good evening, sir."

"Quiet night?"

"Yes, sir."

"Good."

A quick head call and back to work. By now my eyes had adjusted to the darkness, and it seemed a whole lot lighter walking back. Now I could see the guard as easily as he saw me.

"Oorah, Marine, have a good evening."

"Oorah, sir."

Returning to the routine of the night was small comfort. For those Marines on shift who knew Sergeant Perez best, getting past the death of their friend was exponentially more difficult than for those of us who barely knew him.

A memorial service is proper for paying respects, but it is also part of the grieving and healing. Ironically, Sgt. Perez's would be held in the chapel that took the direct hit from the rocket that killed him.

Temperatures approached 100° F. A steady flow of Marines filled the small chapel. Many stood in the back and even outside the doors of the building. The large crowd was expected, and a second memorial service was already scheduled on the same day for that reason.

Attending immediately after my 12-hour shift, I stood in a daze in the back of the chapel for most of the service. As it came to a close and taps was played, the reality of why we were there sank in. Soon after the conclusion of the service, explosions could be heard in the distance. We had been told to expect multiple, controlled detonations that morning, but the timing made us pause.

Too many well-meaning veterans have reduced their own combat experience to a personal fight for the man to their right or left. Fighting and dying for the man beside you is little more than street gang mentality. Our losses must be different. Our sacrifices must mean more, and they do. Yes, it is still painfully personal, but our cause is great and simple yet complex . . . the inalienable rights of mankind. A privileged people who have been given much now have much required of them. Those who are oppressed deserve a chance to be free and, ultimately, secure their own freedom. We can provide a slim window of opportunity for them, but they must seize their peculiar destiny. Lofty ideas are too soon shelved when the enemy lofts sporadic attacks.

Waking to the sounds of incoming rockets and mortars happened repeatedly. One landed near the enlisted barracks about a hundred yards away. That one was a dud. The second hit the barracks. It didn't hurt anyone but damaged some communications equipment.

It was time to get some sleep. Again, two small incoming rockets went whistling overhead. I was reading my Bible at the time. I hit the floor. It was a couple of seconds before I heard the impacts. They actually continued across the river and impacted near Hurricane Point.

IED/SVBIED (Suicide Vehicle-Born IED) . . .

Ever-present IED reports and attacks demanded the lion's share of our attention. MEDECAV or CASEVAC (medical evacuation or casualty evacuation) requests were commonly our first indication of an IED attack.

"Sir, we've got a request for a CASEVAC."

"Initial chat indicates that it was an IED."

"Three friendly casualties are being evacuated as Urgent Surgical with open head wounds. Another soldier was listed as Priority. A fifth one was transported to BAS as Routine."

Official reports usually follow within a couple of hours with only slight variations with respect to the who, when and where.

Another time I came into my shift with the day already suffering seven seriously wounded. One was from an IED or mine attack on 3/25. I immediately checked to see if it was one of my 2/14 Marines. They assured me it was not, that the Marine was from Ohio.

Then I got an email from Lt. Col. Garay stating that we had one seriously hurt, possibly an amputee. I knew it had to be the same one, so I called back.

"This is a follow-up to my previous call. I'm trying to verify if one of my Marines was injured. He would have been a reservist from Mississippi."

"Sir, the casualties are reservists from Ohio."

"Could I speak with someone from the one-shop?"

"Yes, sir. Wait one."

"Sir, this is Master Sergeant Smith."

"Master Sergeant, can you check on the injured Marines from the most recent IED or mine attack."

"Yes, sir. We've already checked for you, and it was a Marine reservist from Ohio."

"Could you check his Home of Record for me?"

"Yes, sir. It looks like . . . well, Starkville, Mississippi."

"Thanks. That's all I needed."

I sure hated to hear that because I knew it was serious. The Marine was reported to be in ICU in Balad, awaiting further evacuation out of the country. Four more Marines were wounded on my shift that night, one by indirect fire and three by another IED.

A large explosion was heard across the river near Camp Ramadi. It was a SVBIED (suicide-vehicle-borne IED) and it injured one American. Another IED hit the response team, injuring two more. Small-arms fire continued that night at Blue Diamond. We must have awful aim, because the shooting went on for a while.

Three insurgents set off another IED and were chased down, located, and eliminated. Others, firing small arms, RPGs, and rifles, met the wrath of the Marines.

A week or so later, an SVBIED attack killed 6 and wounded 13; oddly 3 and 11, respectively, were female Marines returning from a day of duty at a civilian checkpoint. Most of the dead were burned beyond recognition by an ensuing fire.

One minute we see progress, the next minute we're back to square one, and our own press sadly seems to relish in this conundrum. Then our own U.S. congressmen are seen by all of us on CNN, publicly encouraging the insurgents not to give up and encouraging us and the president to quit.

EOF (Escalation of Force) . . .

We could view CNN and FOX News inside the COC. We watched intently as they reported about a captured Italian journalist shot during her release. One of her bodyguards was killed and another wounded. It happened at a U.S. Army VCP (vehicle check point). The procedure that ended in an infamous international incident was called an EOF, Escalation of Force in military terms.

They are daily occurrences across Iraq with mixed results. Just the other day CG was lamenting the death of an unidentified MAM (military-aged male) due to an EOF. Resulting deaths of innocent civilians are not readily acceptable to anyone, yet we haven't found a way to eliminate it. That is not for lack of effort. EOF procedures are constantly reevaluated and refined.

Innocent Iraqi lives are repeatedly lost, but sometimes, there is no way to know just how innocent some of them were.

A MAM approached one VCP, concealing something in his arms. He was verbally warned to stop. Hand and arm signals were used to make him stop. Warning shots were fired. Still, the man proceeded. With total disregard to the EOF warnings, he was shot and he died immediately.

He was only carrying a sack of grain. Why didn't he stop? Was he deaf and blind or on drugs? We may never know. Was he a decoy paid by insurgents to test the VCP? If he hadn't been shot, then maybe the next day he or another would have walked up as a suicide bomber. If he were shot, maybe they would try to create an international incident against the Americans, as with the Italian journalist.

In another incident, a Marine followed EOF procedures and eventually fired on a vehicle approaching a VCP. The vehicle went up in flames, and the Marines in the area witnessed several secondary explosions. Obviously, it was a SVBIED. The lives of innocent Marines were saved that day by the same, risky, fallible procedures, procedures that require split-second decision-making in a hostile environment.

Two days later, with U.S. and world news still broadcasting the shooting of the Italian journalist and the funeral of her bodyguard, another SVBIED took the lives of two U.S. Army soldiers and two Iraqi commandos. It also injured another soldier and two more Iraqi commandos. The admittedly imperfect EOF procedures were not fully implemented. Could EOF procedures have saved them? We will never know. No news coverage followed. It must not have fit their script.

Air . . .

Methodically unlacing my desert boots, I hesitated. The afternoon was heating up. An air conditioner was providing the only noise. The 12-hour shift and a shower steered me toward a mental shutdown that usually allowed me to fall asleep quickly and rest soundly, while almost instinctively and casually contemplating the possibility of incoming rounds . . . Sssssssssssssscheow!

I almost pulled a muscle ducking for cover. Other personal accounts told of food and trays flying in the chow hall as Marines hit the deck.

Instead of an incoming rocket, it was a commonly requested "show-of-force."

This one involved using British Tornados. I am a big fan of low-altitude fly-overs, and this one must have been below 200 feet. Distant sounds of our jets could be heard on most days, but I hadn't heard anything like that away from a flight line in my life!

The show of force was in support of 2BCT (2nd Brigade Combat Team) in Ramadi. An angry crowd had gathered, and we were making payments and apologies for an accidental death or wrongful detainment of an Iraqi female or something like that. They wanted to stay disgruntled and make more demands while they were enjoying their perceived success.

Just as the U.S. Army commander was explaining to the local Imam that nothing good would come of continued protests, and that only "bad things could happen," the jets screamed overhead. The showy crowd instantly lost its bluster and dispersed. No need for a translator.

TIC (Troops in Contact) . . .

Troops in contact (TIC, pronounced "tick") gets everyone's instant attention up and down the chain of command. While it was getting between difficult and impossible to gain approval for preplanned air strikes, there was an immediate readiness and even eagerness to respond when U.S. Marines and soldiers were taking fire.

Theater-wide, fixed-wing air and Marine rotary-wing close-air support never hesitated. Within minutes and even seconds of ground units reporting a TIC event, pilots would respond. Sometimes, there wasn't a target worthy of an air strike or the enemy would have already been killed or broken contact prior to air arriving on station.

Night shifts were privy to a good share of air activity. From AC-130 gun ships and SOF rotary wing to the instant, joint/coalition response to troops in contact, the airside kept things interesting.

"Sir, two birds just reported setting down on the road due to bad weather. They landed near an army convoy that will provide security until we can get a Quick Reaction Force on the scene."

"I didn't know the weather was that bad? Tell them it will be almost thirty minutes before the QRF arrives."

"Roger, sir, they're also requesting a fuel truck."

"Ha, they're not down for bad weather. They're out of fuel."

Helo pilots sometimes try to stay in the fight too long. Their focus on supporting the Marines on the ground can distract them from the "little things" like fuel.

"That could take a little longer. I'm sure the wing is already working it. Just keep me informed, and I'll have the division ground watch officer notify the QRF that the helicopters ran out of gas and they'll be on site until the fuel truck gets there."

"Yes, sir."

"That squadron commander will have some choice words for those pilots."

"Sir, Dash-One is the squadron commander, and Dash-Two is the squadron safety officer."

"At least they're in a relatively safe area for now. If they're still there at daylight, they'll be in sight and range of insurgent mortars and small arms, which could be a problem."

All ended well that night. Some nights we weren't as fortunate.

"Sir, we just got a report of a flash of light in the sky to the east at fifteen thousand feet."

"Hopefully not a mid-air collision."

While monitoring a roll call of all aircraft in the sky over Iraq, we waited. We speculated. We hoped for the best.

"That was too high for the enemy to have shot anyone down."

"Maybe it was atmospherics or heat lightning."

"It had to be a mid-air collision, but who and how?"

Shortly, it was confirmed that Marine Corps F-18s from the USS *Carl Vinson* were in the process of aerial refueling when the mishap occurred.

"Not much hope of survivors from that altitude."

We began search and recovery ops beneath the crash location.

From tens of thousands of feet to just a few feet off the ground, we reacted in support of friendly air ops on numerous occasions. Downed Predators or other unmanned vehicles were not unusual, yet mishaps involving aircraft were never routine.

One night the ground watch officer sitting to my left quickly interrupted the quiet of the night.

"Sir, One/Nine reported a convoy hitting an IED in Ramadi with five IEDs daisy-chained together."

"Good evening, sir."

"Quiet night?"

"Yes, sir."

"Good."

A quick head call and back to work. By now my eyes had adjusted to the darkness, and it seemed a whole lot lighter walking back. Now I could see the guard as easily as he saw me.

"Oorah, Marine, have a good evening."

"Oorah, sir."

Returning to the routine of the night was small comfort. For those Marines on shift who knew Sergeant Perez best, getting past the death of their friend was exponentially more difficult than for those of us who barely knew him.

A memorial service is proper for paying respects, but it is also part of the grieving and healing. Ironically, Sgt. Perez's would be held in the chapel that took the direct hit from the rocket that killed him.

Temperatures approached 100° F. A steady flow of Marines filled the small chapel. Many stood in the back and even outside the doors of the building. The large crowd was expected, and a second memorial service was already scheduled on the same day for that reason.

Attending immediately after my 12-hour shift, I stood in a daze in the back of the chapel for most of the service. As it came to a close and taps was played, the reality of why we were there sank in. Soon after the conclusion of the service, explosions could be heard in the distance. We had been told to expect multiple, controlled detonations that morning, but the timing made us pause.

Too many well-meaning veterans have reduced their own combat experience to a personal fight for the man to their right or left. Fighting and dying for the man beside you is little more than street gang mentality. Our losses must be different. Our sacrifices must mean more, and they do. Yes, it is still painfully personal, but our cause is great and simple yet complex . . . the inalienable rights of mankind. A privileged people who have been given much now have much required of them. Those who are oppressed deserve a chance to be free and, ultimately, secure their own freedom. We can provide a slim window of opportunity for them, but they must seize their peculiar destiny. Lofty ideas are too soon shelved when the enemy lofts sporadic attacks.

Waking to the sounds of incoming rockets and mortars happened repeatedly. One landed near the enlisted barracks about a hundred yards away. That one was a dud. The second hit the barracks. It didn't hurt anyone but damaged some communications equipment.

It was time to get some sleep. Again, two small incoming rockets went whistling overhead. I was reading my Bible at the time. I hit the floor. It was a couple of seconds before I heard the impacts. They actually continued across the river and impacted near Hurricane Point.

IED/SVBIED (Suicide Vehicle-Born IED) . . .

Ever-present IED reports and attacks demanded the lion's share of our attention. MEDECAV or CASEVAC (medical evacuation or casualty evacuation) requests were commonly our first indication of an IED attack.

"Sir, we've got a request for a CASEVAC."

"Initial chat indicates that it was an IED."

"Three friendly casualties are being evacuated as Urgent Surgical with open head wounds. Another soldier was listed as Priority. A fifth one was transported to BAS as Routine."

Official reports usually follow within a couple of hours with only slight variations with respect to the who, when and where.

Another time I came into my shift with the day already suffering seven seriously wounded. One was from an IED or mine attack on 3/25. I immediately checked to see if it was one of my 2/14 Marines. They assured me it was not, that the Marine was from Ohio.

Then I got an email from Lt. Col. Garay stating that we had one seriously hurt, possibly an amputee. I knew it had to be the same one, so I called back.

"This is a follow-up to my previous call. I'm trying to verify if one of my Marines was injured. He would have been a reservist from Mississippi."

"Sir, the casualties are reservists from Ohio."

"Could I speak with someone from the one-shop?"

"Yes, sir. Wait one."

"Sir, this is Master Sergeant Smith."

"Master Sergeant, can you check on the injured Marines from the most recent IED or mine attack."

"Yes, sir. We've already checked for you, and it was a Marine reservist from Ohio."

"Plot that for me. That's close."

Seconds later, the phone rang. It was General Huck.

"What are those explosions?"

"General, we just had a report of a daisy-chained IED just across the river in Ramadi."

"Oh, okay."

"Good night, General."

As soon as I hung up the phone, the air watch officer to my right reported a helicopter down across the river.

"The helicopter is on fire. It was carrying a load of forty, two-point-seven-five-inch rockets, and they're starting to cook-off."

"I'd better call the general. I just told him he was hearing the One/Nine IED attack, but it may be the helicopter crash."

"Hello?"

"General, you may have been hearing a helicopter crash near Hurricane Point."

"You said it was an IED. I can see the crash site from here."

The tirade that followed probably left a few symbolic scars. General Huck had a reputation for angry rants, especially when it came to his primary staff. I couldn't have reported it any faster or more accurately, but I knew better than to try to defend myself. I wore the experience somewhat as a badge of honor.

In the meantime, more rockets began to cook off as the fire worsened. The ensuing explosions woke up everybody on base. Many thought we were under attack, and it was clear to see how they could have come to that conclusion. Several Marines arrived at the COC ready for battle only to be told otherwise. Only one injury—a broken arm—resulted from the helicopter crash, and no injuries were reported from the previously reported daisy-chained IEDs. It took a while for everyone to calm down. The rest of the night was thankfully quiet.

ISF (Iraqi Security Forces) . . .

One of the items the press likes to harp on is the apparent lack of progress in training Iraqi military. How do you explain progress with the ISF (Iraqi Security Forces)?

First, understand that in March of 2005, 250 may be recruited and hired, and most of them would leave within the first week.

Recruits who were arriving actually showed up with one shoe, and they would run and quit at the first sign of shooting. Sending them home on scheduled leave proved impossible because they wouldn't return.

By June they would arrive with a 250-man unit that would stay even after the shooting started. That's a lot of progress in three or four months. They also do not refuse to operate in Ramadi anymore. Many had been arriving willing to work anywhere but Ramadi. We were beginning to wonder if they knew something we didn't.

Distinct advantages came with using ISF alongside Marines. Mosque entry was much less controversial with an Iraqi escort.

"Sir, we have a patrol entering a mosque. We just want to get clearance."

"You don't need my permission. You just need to meet the list of conditions."

"We think there are insurgents inside."

"You know that's not good enough. If you're in pursuit and see an insurgent enter, you don't need me. If you're taking fire from a mosque, you can always return fire. Heck, if you just identify the enemy in the mosque with weapons that can range you, you can fire and enter. You don't have to call for permission."

"Sir, we just think there might be some bad guys using the mosque."

"Well, you can't go in on a hunch, and we can't get you clearance on a hunch. But if you have any ISF with you, they can usually go in and look around and you can be on their heels."

SOF (Special Operations Force) Raids . . .

Fighting the War on Terror inside Iraq is often portrayed by U.S. media as a constant barrage of enemy attacks, as if we could not or did not take the fight to the enemy. That is flat wrong.

Caring sincerely about and tracking our own casualties was coupled with a reluctance to regress into the Vietnam-era body-count comparison. Therefore, our successes on the battlefield received less attention, and with no enemy body count, it was hard to explain what was happening.

Even when coverage was positive, it would be short lived. Some enormous military successes did not garner even minimal attention from American media. Instead, the mass media simply reported our casualties.

Operation Matador, River Blitz, River Bridge, Spear (Rohme), Dagger (Khanjar), and many unnamed tactical and special operations came and went across the entire Al Anbar province in western Iraq. Notice that the later operations began to have corresponding English and Arabic names. It is another indication of the increased role of the Iraqi military.

Sometimes, our units provided support to special operations forces (SOF), task forces also known as OCF (other coalition forces) operating inside our AO. The first few months of my deployment, we had a great relationship with the task force. They communicated with us as much as possible, and we worked very closely to assist them when we could.

When the task force rotated out, we had much difficulty maintaining the same relations. The new group chose to keep us in the dark most of the time—because they could.

Outside the Wire . . .

A slow night preceded my first trip out of Blue Diamond. I traveled officially as the Division G-3 rep on the CG's flight to Camp Hit and Haditha Dam. Unofficially, I was looking for 2/14 Marines. How were they living? How well were they being treated as attachments?

Helos lifted at 0600. The routine was to leave before daylight to keep from becoming easy targets for insurgents who may carry shoulder-launched missiles or even machine guns or other small-arms fire that could reach the slow and low flyers.

We arrived at Camp Hit (pronounced Heat) around 0700. The camp was more austere than Blue Diamond. There were three, two-story block buildings configured like a cheap motel, but it reminded me more of a Wild West ghost town being occupied by Marines.

The fine desert sand and dust adhered to the buildings, the vehicles, and the Marines. Everything and everybody blended naturally into the stark desert surroundings. A dilapidated mosque and a few buildings housing Iraqis were in plain view several hundred yards away.

While the general was being briefed, he sent the staff out to circulate. That's exactly what I wanted. I met some Marines and checked out the camp. It was easy to find those from Echo Battery by asking for Mississippi Marines.

"Sir, you've got some proud Marines. The walls of the head are covered with stuff about Mississippi."

We all laughed. Although the Marine was joking, I'm sure there was a disturbing measure of truth to what he said.

Most of the Echo Battery Marines were on guard duty on the perimeter of Camp Hit at the time I arrived. Others were part of the night's watch and were day sleepers. I finally ran into one working in the chow hall and two more working in the motor pool. They explained that they had it as well as they had expected and were treated well.

At 0800 we flew to Haditha Dam. The shining lake created by the dam had no vegetation around it; the waterline simply stopped and barren desert began.

Down river was different. Vegetation lined the water's edge. Palm groves were planted in rows and seemed to flourish.

My 2/14 Marines were living relatively well and were well-treated and integrated by their new parent battalion, 3/25. The detachment commander, Captain Chris Moeller, gave me a tour of their living and work areas.

The Marines were motivated, and that motivated me. I felt more at ease out with the Marines than I had since arriving in Iraq. Better to be with a Marine and an MRE than to be with a map and a computer, but I had to return.

Weeks passed before I found my way out of Camp Blue Diamond again. This time it was a short convoy ride across the Euphrates River to Camp Ramadi. Some of my 2/14 Marines out of Delta Battery were there, operating the Ramadi Detention Facility.

The facility was inconspicuous. Like most buildings on camp, HESCO barriers surrounded it for protection. HESCO barriers were the force protection item of choice. They came in various sizes, the most common being about 4' x 4' at their base and maybe 4-5 feet tall. The barriers are made of a gray, synthetic material surrounded by a heavy wire mesh to hold the barrier's basic, building-block shape.

Only a few marked vehicles out front and the handful of warning signs about deadly force being authorized gave it away.

"Good morning, sir."

"Good morning, Marine. Is Major Ellis around?"

"Yes, sir. Wait one."

"Hey, Chuck. How's it going?"

"Great, sir. Come in. The Marines will be glad to see you."

Major Ellis and I had a quick visit, and he gave me a tour of the detention facility. As we went into the crowded medical area, they were processing some new detainees. A quick but thorough medical check-up and the immediate issue of the bright orange prisoner wardrobe preceded putting them in a cell.

The facility was crowded, and while conditions seemed tolerable, the civilian press would have a heyday. Although made of cement blocks, the layout reminded me of old western frontier forts. The cells formed four walls, with the doors opening inward to a courtyard of sorts. There was a chain-link, gated gap in the front center. A catwalk ran around the inside perimeter above it all for the guards. There were also simple guard towers at the corners. The courtyard was nearly filled with some makeshift cells with fencing that resembled dog kennels. The fenced cells had general-purpose tents for cover with simple, pallet-like floors to elevate detainees slightly above the sand.

About 45 of the detainees were in the pens. Typically, the Ramadi Detention Facility was a holding area that did not hold detainees more than two weeks. But the transfer of those 45 detainees to more-permanent quarters at Abu Ghraib had been canceled due to weather.

From the COC, we had reports of detainees being picked up for suspicious activity, breaking curfew, digging and emplacing IEDs, SAF and IDF attacks, and being caught with unauthorized weapons, fake IDs, or anti-coalition propaganda. We even brought in some for laughing when they were searched, having suspicious tattoos—indicating they were possible criminals or hostile—or simply because their stories didn't match when they were questioned by a patrol or at a VCP (vehicle check point).

From our vantage point at the COC, we called it the "catch-and-release" program. Just like the catch-and-release program keeps our lakes stocked with fish, we seemed to keep putting the insurgents back in circulation shortly after they were detained. The pat answer we got was that they were of no intelligence value. Maybe not, but to us it seemed better to have them off the street than on the street.

Before I knew it, the visit was over and it was back to the maps and computers.

The temperature started to rise. Afternoon temps had everyone taking appropriate cover. Surges just over 100° F hardly got our attention, but sustained temps of 110, along with particularly humid, hot nights, made all of us take notice.

Very little outdoor activity during the day resulted in a near-deserted camp heavily accented with HESCO barriers. The empty shells were easy to set up. Once in place, they were quickly filled with plentiful sand or dirt, using a front-end loader. Smaller HESCOs and/or prefabricated concrete barriers were sometimes stacked on top of each other and layered to reach a greater height.

Placed between roads, key buildings, and around billeting areas, they offered substantial protection from direct fire or shrapnel from a blast on the opposite side. No overhead cover or protection meant that indirect fire could still land just about anywhere, including inside our flimsy trailers and showers. One actually did land directly on a shower facility in Camp Ramadi. Fortunately, the round didn't detonate and no one was hurt.

Camp Fallujah was another destination that briefly allowed me outside the wire. Any road trip came with additional risk. Camp Fallujah housed more of my Marines, also from my battery in El Paso. Their primary role was camp security. In addition to basic guard duty, they familiarized themselves with the 60-mm mortars and fired hundreds of rounds, mostly illumination. As artillerymen, they were firing 155-mm cannons a few weeks before the deployment, now mortars, and weeks after their return, they would manning new HIMARS rocket artillery.

• • •

"This has got to be my last Easter with the Marines. Two in desert training in Southern California and three in Southwest Asia in combat zones is enough."

Even so, there is something special about being with Marines on Easter. Mostly male Marine voices singing Easter hymns have a distinct sound. This year it was inside of one of the outer buildings of Hussein's palace complexes.

The Sunday after Easter is also interesting. It's normal to see attendance numbers fall off, but the drop is not as dramatic here as in churches back home in the States.

Today in our staff meeting, Col. Chase was echoing the general's concern that we're not killing enough bad guys. Some snipers missed their targets and reported shooting the tires out of an insurgent vehicle.

"We are supposed to shoot and kill the enemy, not their tires. I might expect it out of Three/Twenty-five, but these are our own guys."

Col. Chase didn't mean anything by it. He probably forgot it as fast as he said it, but the comment reflected a prevailing undertone that, while much improved, had not totally vanished from the regular establishment.

His reaction implied that 3/25 was *not* "our own," which is more disheartening than any concern for reserve Marines' technical skill levels.

Halfway through my seven-month deployment, the division chief of staff threw a tantrum in view of a small host of staff officers. It revolved around the deployment schedule, and it focused on reservists.

"Everyone's staying for the full twelve months. That includes reservists!"

That would have carried a lot more meaning if even half the regular Marine officers were going to complete their own 12-month deployments. Many were leaving for school assignments, command selections, PCS (permanent change of station) moves, etc.

The controversy centered on the division's designated IMA (Individual Mobilization Augmentation), a detachment of reservists habitually assigned to Camp Lejeune. My situation was a little different coming as a battalion commander with my Marines, but I was still a reservist."

In an unrelated meeting, Col. Chase made reference to a Marine officer at MEF (Marine Expeditionary Force) he didn't particularly like.

"He's got three problems: One, he's a reservist, Two—"

At that point I lost him. The other two reasons were not even heard. Then he realized what he said, so he tried to recover. "I guess I just offended about a third of the room." We all laughed and moved on, but it did reflect some of the lingering undercurrents between "us" and "them."

Colonel Fondaw, the 14th Marines' CO, came to the rescue with a strong and clear email explaining my situation as a battalion commander with specific commanding general approval to deploy during the same timeframe as the bulk of the battalion. That nearly ended the debate on my departure.

Then a week later, the chief, the OpsO, a few others, and I were around the coffee pot. I had just walked up. The chief and the OpsO were in the middle of a conversation about the personnel turnover in August and September.

"Who's leaving, sir?"

"All of the reservists," he angrily shouted. "Lieutenant Colonel Caldwell, for one."

I bit my tongue with a half-smile. It wasn't the right time to respond. The

OpsO, a regular officer, was scheduled to leave before me, yet nothing was said about him. Three other regular Marine officers out of the same operations section would be gone before me, but he harped on reservists with unjustified prejudice.

A growing list of the regulars who were deploying for less than a full year resided in my left front pocket. I had prepared the list for my own defense at a more opportune time. I already had over 20 names of regular Marines from within the COC with short tours—many were well under six months and some were a little over—and I wasn't through yet. If I counted their replacements coming in late for less than the full tour, the count quickly jumped to over 40.

Hastily, I retrieved my coffee and exited so as not to be drawn into the fray. It amazed me that 2nd Marine Division was counting on reservists to provide stability for the division staff, while they rotated a plurality of their own.

A shorter tour meant an earlier arrival to the much-anticipated halfway point, a milestone on any deployment, but especially in Iraq. I was nearing mine.

In the big scheme of things, the level of acceptance of reserve Marines by regular Marines has grown dramatically in the last decade or so. Like most prejudices, those past biases and misconceptions were based on ignorance.

Today, the integration of reservists is so commonplace that most false impressions have faded. One overweight or unprepared reserve Marine no longer discredits the entire reserve establishment any more than one over-weight, unprepared regular Marine will discredit the entire Corps. There are still inherent differences, but there is a greater effort to capitalize on those differences rather than harp on them as weaknesses.

Misunderstandings were not limited to those between regular and reserve Marines. Disconnects between an optimistic defense department and the pessimistic view from our American media left no shortages of opinion, educated or otherwise.

Iraqis also demonstrated conflicting perspectives and agendas from the local political, and religious leadership from families just trying to survive, to foreign fighters now commingling within their neighborhoods. Our acknowledgement of unavoidable cultural differences as well as some less-admitted similarities had prompted a new round of cautiously optimistic negotiation.

A high-ranking coalition military/government delegation and the local Sunni leadership in Ramadi met for a rare dialogue at Camp Blue Diamond.

We hoped we would soon be able to measure how closely the Sunni leadership was tied to the insurgency, especially the foreign fighters and organized terrorist groups. It is sometimes difficult for some of us to separate them, so it was imperative to make certain the meeting would not be considered "negotiation with terrorists." Security was heightened and everyone was briefed accordingly. Attendance was strictly limited to essential personnel, which did not include me.

It was a tense period with very much doubt whether the meeting would do any good. Our "inside information" may not have been much more than high level scuttlebutt, but we soaked up any feedback from the talks that we could get.

"I heard the CG told them their only option was to lay down their arms and join the political process."

"I heard the Sunnis said they would be glad to as soon as we gave them a date when we would leave."

There was no trust between the two sides, but the talks set the stage for a demonstration effort by the Sunni leaders to prove they had some direct or indirect influence on the insurgency.

We were tasked with monitoring a very dangerous area in the town of Ramadi where insurgents placed roadside bombs almost daily. Small-arms fire and mortar attacks were also routine occurrences in the area. During the designated period, the numbers of attacks were reduced significantly but not totally eliminated. It was quantifiable proof of real yet limited influence.

In the first four months that I was in Iraq, there were nearly 4,000 significant combat-related events in our AO. That's about 30 to 35 per day. The events ranged from a one-round, "small-arms fire" attack that missed, to a coordinated ambush combining a deadly roadside bomb with effective small-arms and indirect fire. Many of the events were wildly sporadic—indirect fire from rockets and mortars or randomly ineffective IEDs.

There were countless other combat-vehicle and dismounted patrols that didn't report anything significant. At one point we seemed to be making chartable progress; the next minute events on the ground had us second guessing our optimism.

Specifically, we seemed to turn a corner in July of 2005: only nine FKIA that month. That was a major reduction from the previous month and the same month the previous year, but nobody published it. Then the first week in August was horrific, losing over 20 the first week. No trouble getting that reported.

At the same time, U.S. congressmen were being quoted and shown on TV saying, "We are losing ..." (Translation to the terrorists: "You are winning. Keep up the assaults. Kill more Americans and you will eventually prevail.") It is no wonder that similar attacks in Afghanistan increased after that announcement from our congressmen, promulgated by our own press.

The press had been extremely negative since they pulled out the embedded reporters. The embedded reporters could see and experience the truth on the ground. The problem for our side was that our own news coverage was not concerned with the truth. It was more concerned with making money and promoting its own agenda.

In subsequent years, the truth was hidden by blind rhetoric. Egotistical anti-Bush anchormen, newscasters, and other talking heads enjoy the peace, safety, and ridiculously high pay of their positions. They are not asked to fight; somebody else is willing to do that for them. Yet they continually undermine the efforts of those of us in the combat zone.

Members of the media hide behind the cloak of freedom of speech and of the press that is bought and paid for with the ultimate sacrifice of others. Courageous writers in the 1770s risked their lives and fortunes on the side of our nation's liberation and squarely on the side of democratic principles of self-governance because they believed in it. In the new millennium, the press is on the side of protecting their personal lives, affluence, and influence, even at the detriment of our own freedom as a nation. Freedom of the press seems to be the only constitutionally protected freedom that matters to them now.

I have always said, "The only thing worse than a free press is a government-controlled press."

Camp Blue Diamond, Al Ramadi, Iraq

"Rejoice with those who rejoice, and weep with those who weep."

Romans 12:15

...12
Conflicts of Emotion

No huge reception—we traveled alone on individual orders or in very small groups, but collectively, we filled the plane. Some of us were "mission complete" overseas but not necessarily home upon our arrival at Camp Lejeune. Others were going home to the Marine Corps base in North Carolina but only for a few weeks before returning to combat. No huge reception at the airfield, but touching U.S. soil still felt great.

Charter buses took us from the airfield. Everyone gravitated to their own personal homecomings as we exited the bus at Camp Lejeune. Each return involved excitement and uncertainty.

Family situations vary. It is different for the single or married—happily or otherwise—or the divorced and those with or without children . . . or parents or brothers or sisters or friends.

I watched earnestly as a spectator. Most of the Marines were greeted with emotional hugs, cheers, and tears by their family and friends. A few others, like me, were now ready for the next leg in their trip home. Timing, geography, circumstances, and emotions influenced the vast array of returns—some good, some not so much.

Ongoing political campaign commitments and stress had dampened my last return from the combat zone. This time we would not let anything get in our way. Lee flew into Jacksonville, North Carolina, and met me the next day. A little quality time with just the two of us proved much less stressful than a formal homecoming event.

Lee headed for home a few days later while I wrapped things up in North Carolina. Out-processing at Camp Lejeune was completed quickly. I was able to arrange an overnight layover in Memphis on my way to final deactivation at the reserve center in Grand Prairie, Texas.

Upon arrival at Memphis International Airport, I was greeted at the gate by an intimate family reception, thanks to some thoughtful airport security personnel. More family and friends from church and work met us just beyond the security checkpoint. It couldn't have been better.

The short ride home would be uniquely different this time. Before leaving for Iraq, we had barely broken ground on a new home. Since then Lee had completed construction, made the move, and sold our home of 19 years. I had seen some pictures as the new home was being built but had never been privy to a complete photo gallery of the finished house.

Glimpses through the final tree line sparked a new level of excitement and anticipation as we approached. Standing near the small stock pond on what had been a cow pasture months earlier, the two-story white home with an architectural, green shingled roof was striking. Leaving the pavement and pulling onto the limestone gravel drive revealed a full view of the country home and wraparound porch. The long drive circled a flagpole just like we had always wanted. The family, even the dogs—one old and one new that I had just met—excitedly escorted me to and through our new house.

Everything was in place. A beautiful tile entryway was complemented by handsome hardwood stairs. Pictures were hung. Decorative accents were in place. No number of photos of the house—under construction or finished— could quite tell the story like seeing the real thing.

It was amazingly familiar as we walked the floor plan. The 2,700 square feet doubled the size of our old place, and the details were a cut above. The furniture was nearly all the same and somehow fit perfectly. The tree-lined estate and freshly cut grass could be seen on all sides through floor-to-ceiling windows and French doors.

The first day in the new house was followed by the first night. I was home. Sleep was good.

The black Timex Ironman sounded the early alarm tones. Steady beeps from the Velcro-banded wristwatch unveiled a pitch-dark house. An overnight storm had knocked out power. It was astonishing that the edge of a Gulf Coast hurricane had so quickly reached us with enough punch to affect us. We lived hundreds of miles from the center of the storm named Katrina, yet we were still on the fringe of its massive reach.

Within minutes Lee and I were dressed and driving to the airport for my morning flight to Dallas. Deactivation was almost complete. Only a few routine administrative items remained to finish my activation orders at the drill center in Grand Prairie.

The sun hadn't risen yet, but some ambient light and the Explorer's high beams allowed us to see enough. A few of our neighbors' trees were downed by strong winds, and smaller limbs and leaves littered the county roads.

Radio newscasts reaffirmed that the worst of Hurricane Katrina had missed New Orleans. Cautious optimism sounded from the dashboard as we scanned the FM and AM stations. Everyone knew that the less-populated Mississippi coast was being slammed; however, it was hardly mentioned. The Big Easy was apparently spared and that's all that seemed to matter to the media hierarchy. The apparent blow to Biloxi and Gulfport was being mentioned as an afterthought, even though the eye of the great storm had reached land near the small town of Waveland, Mississippi.

By the time I landed at DFW (Dallas-Fort Worth International Airport), the reporters had changed their tune. Everyone eagerly sought an objective look following the dawn, but the winds were still wreaking havoc. Storm surge estimates ranged from 20 to 30 feet. Rumors quickly surfaced of a levee or levees being breeched in and around New Orleans. Spotty reports began painting a precarious and grimly shifting assessment.

From the airport TV news to the rental car radio accounts, an uglier picture was unfolding as the hours passed. We tracked events from the drill center and began planning to assist if needed.

Although Marine reserves were typically not called to respond like National Guardsmen, it seemed like the right thing to do. The first thing that came to mind was the fact that we didn't have the legal authority to do anything. We also knew that we didn't have the money or mechanism to write orders to pay Marines or purchase fuel for any convoys we hoped to send.

I was still on active duty orders in support of Operation Iraqi Freedom, so I volunteered to assist in the relief effort. The Marine Corps and the ad hoc support staff seemed unable to deal with any more variables, namely me. Back from the war only a few days, tired and not fully decompressed, I was almost glad they didn't accept my offer to help.

Procedures were not yet developed for active duty or Marine reservists to respond to natural disasters. That duty was almost solely in the hands of the civilians and National Guard, but Katrina was already forcing a rewrite of the rule book as we waited.

By the time I arrived at the drill center, I had had several cell phone conversations with my own staff, who were determining the vehicles and manpower available for a potential mission. They were also providing a facilities assessment to provide space for 4th Marine Division staff, which had been displaced from their headquarters in New Orleans.

I drove from Grand Prairie to regimental headquarters in Fort Worth to speak with the staff there. Marine Forces Reserve Headquarters staff from New Orleans was already setting up shop in the regimental offices. Most of my battalion staff officers and the regimental staff were in Korea, participating in a training exercise at the time, but the I&I, Lieutenant Colonel Wayne Harrison, was waiting on a call from Korea to update our boss, Colonel O'Leary.

Eventually, about four dozen enlisted volunteers from my battalion were given active duty orders. They drove a convoy south to help with recovery in Slidell, Louisiana. My orders expired and I returned home.

It would be a couple of weeks before Lee and I would be able to contribute directly to the hurricane relief effort. A small, three-vehicle caravan of supplies was collected from multiple churches in our county. We accompanied our friends Mark and Elaine, who had already experienced the life-changing post-Katrina journey to South Mississippi.

Years as a volunteer fireman and three combat deployments, including the last six months in Iraq, spawned no nightmares or bad dreams. A few daylight hours on the Mississippi Gulf Coast, witnessing the aftermath of Hurricane Katrina, and I dreamed about it for weeks! It was as if my brain couldn't absorb what my eyes had seen.

Our first observation had been the slight wind damage starting at home about two weeks earlier. The progressively worsening effects halted our little caravan just south of Jackson as a likely last chance for gasoline.

Hattiesburg was just getting electricity back in a few spots along the highway as we drove through. Power lines and trees were still down in every direction as far as the eye could see. The town allowed us a welcome and final pit stop still 45 miles north of our destinations in Waveland and Bay St.

Louis.

It was now two weeks after the storm hit, but telephone lines and debris still lay on the ground across the divided highway. Side roads were barely passable, from the looks of things as we drove.

We brought groceries to some of Mark and Elaine's friends in the small town of Wiggins. Neighborhoods looked as if an F1 or F2 tornado had traveled each and every street in town plus every country road. Blue tarps covered all or part of every roof in sight. Large trees were down everywhere; only the ones creating immediate hazards had been touched.

Traffic was bumper to bumper as we neared Gulfport. Trucks and vans of all sizes were filled with volunteers converging and merging with local residents trying to cope. Everyone could feel the solemn unity of purpose in the air.

As we turned west on I-10, we could see billboard skeletons stripped of their messages. Some only had the main pole left standing. Forests were already brown from effects of the storm. We arranged to meet a local pastor at a service station beside the Waveland off-ramp.

"Well, the parking lot was definitely underwater. There's silt and mud all over it, but I don't see a waterline."

"We're maybe a mile or more from the shoreline. It was probably still pretty deep. It may have covered the building, but it's hard to tell."

"Wow! There's the waterline, up near the interstate."

"They said 'thirty foot' storm surge, but I wouldn't have thought it would be that high this far inland."

"We would have had about twenty feet of water over our heads!"

Our escort arrived to lead us in.

"Look at all the cars and boats."

"They're scattered along the road like litter."

"How did they get here?"

"Were they abandoned here?"

"No way. They had to be washed in with the storm surge. The road between the pines was the path of least resistance. The water and everything with it must have run like a river. As the water subsided, the cars and debris were left up and down the road. Some were likely pushed off the pavement by the earliest-arriving emergency response teams."

"Look at that house!"

"Look over here."

"Look at that."

"Did you see—"

"Man, it seems so much worse in person."

"Oh my God—"

"The people are camped out over in the K-Mart parking lot like refugees in a third-world country."

"Where do they use the bathroom?"

"I can't imagine the depth of water here. Everything in sight would have been underwater."

A short drive to the nearest public school included a maneuver around a large house that had floated off its foundation and into the street. The school location provided an easily identifiable spot, ideal for residents in need of help, although the buildings weren't usable.

Classrooms were lit by the sun shining through drop-ceiling grids. Some ceiling panels were some of the few things left in place. The roof was gone. Ocean water pooled inside the school's outdoor light fixtures. A brown water-line bisected the emergency exit signs above the interior gym doors. Shiny black sludge completely covered what would have been the basketball court. Snakes, frogs, and other animals left tracks in the wet and otherwise-smooth mud. The smell of mildew was strong and already visible on the walls.

People filtered in with some regularity to survey the donations and pick up necessities. Before we could unload our vehicles, a mother with a young child came looking for a mattress. They were sleeping on the floor at their nearly unlivable home. We transferred one immediately from our vehicle to hers. It seemed like it was such a small contribution among such vast need, yet it brought the grateful mother to tears.

We tried to donate our own pop-up camper at another relief sight, but they could not take it without a title, and we hadn't thought to bring it. Almost instantly, we found a family in need and gave it directly to them. It's hard to imagine we nearly left it behind because it was not in great shape. Compared to what we were seeing, it would have been a huge improvement for most.

Shocking, unexplainable, unbelievable scenes could be seen in every direction. Humorous sights, like a boat that was randomly dry-docked in the

Burger King drive- thru window, were few and far between. It was 360 degrees of pain and suffering as far as the eye could see.

Even my experience with several tornados and their aftermath had not prepared me for this. Tornados nearly always have an untouched area, sometimes, odd and inexplicable. Visual and emotional relief is often nearby. This hurricane seemed to have no respite.

Irony becomes the closest thing to a breather. A memorial to Hurricane Camille stood in Bay St. Louis. An unusual flagpole corkscrewed by the 1969 storm lay beside a newly bent and equally unique flagpole twisted by Hurricane Katrina.

Historic steeples were broken from the church tops and strewn on the sidewalks as if intentionally removed and discarded by some unforgiving mechanical monster. Some church folks were already in full swing with relief operations in their heavily damaged structures. At this point our work was done. We had delivered the goods. Now we were little more than compassionate tourists who didn't need to be there, so we headed for home.

The return trip meant another six hours on the road. It was a relatively quiet ride home. First, we were exhausted. Second, it was a time for reflection on what we had experienced. Lastly, there were simply no words to explain our feelings.

I couldn't help but think of my Marines. Echo Battery was still overseas with only days remaining on their deployment. In the meantime, much of their family and friends in South Mississippi had been pounded by one of the most devastating hurricanes to come ashore in modern history.

Soon the Mississippi detachment arrived at Camp Lejeune for initial redeployment processing. I had arrived to be there with them and for them and, hopefully, ensure their stop-over in the Tar Heel State would be a quick one. Their adopted battalion, 3/25, had fittingly scheduled a memorial service for those who did not return.

My plane reached Jacksonville with no time to spare. Post flight hunger and thirst would be set aside for a rental car sprint to the Marine Corps base. The guard at the front gate pointed me in the right direction.

Parking in the small, designated lot aboard Camp Lejeune wasn't difficult. In fact, there were plenty of places to park in any direction. There were no indicators of any significant activity in the area. There were two Marines, conspicuously standing by. Apparently, they were stationed there for anyone like me.

"Excuse me, Marines. Can you direct me to the FSSG amphitheater?"

"Yes, sir. It's just behind this building."

"Thanks."

I had made it to the Force Service Support Group with about four minutes to spare. The solemn reverence of onlookers and hundreds of Marines in formation overtook me as I walked up behind the silent battalion standing at parade rest. The symmetrical unit, all in desert camouflage, stood nearly shadowless in the midday sun, facing the curved, green contour of the river. The centerpiece was a semicircle of 48 rifles perfectly inserted into the earth with mounted bayonets. Empty desert suede combat boots softly rested symbolically in the neatly cut lawn. A Kevlar helmet capped the butt stock of each rifle as a Marine stood guard at each of the temporary memorials.

A CH-46 Sea Knight flying over the natural backdrop of New River provided appropriate background noise to penetrate the silence. Peaceful yellow butterflies took turns surveying the spectacle. They fluttered effortlessly in and out and over the formation as the Marine Corps helicopter and its familiar sound faded into the distance.

"Ladies and Gentlemen, the memorial service is about to begin. Please take your seats."

Families of the memorialized Marines and sailors mingled with VIPs and invited guests under a red-and-white canopy. A few prayers, a few words, a few songs, and a 21-gun salute were the right things at the right time for these leathernecks of 3rd Battalion 25th Marines. Forty-eight Marines and sailors of this reserve battalion had paid the ultimate price in Iraq. It was the most suffered by any battalion in the division.

Marines from Echo Battery had been attached to the Ohio battalion for the entire activation and deployment. I stood respectfully behind their part of the formation during the service.

Taps echoed across the amphitheater, the river, and Camp Lejeune. The all-too-familiar sound pierced the heart as usual. Pain and loss can weigh heavily on mind, body, and soul as those who gave their all are memorialized.

There's one thing much worse than the acute pain of remembering—that's forgetting. A twinge of "survivor guilt" naturally surfaced. I replaced it with a personal challenge to myself to honor their sacrifice at every opportunity.

As the service concluded and the formation was dismissed, Marines paid their last respects down the arched line of memorials.

My Marines who had been attached as a truck platoon to the battalion for their pre-deployment training and the entire time in Iraq were also emotionally attached. They had melded into a cohesive task force.

As E/2/14 Marines dispersed from their position on the rear left flank of the formation, they were stepping away from 3/25 for the last time. I was able to address them briefly to let them know that I was proud of them. I also told what I knew of Hurricane Katrina, sharing a little from my brief experience as a church volunteer there. Most of them were extremely interested, and some had still not heard from some family and friends in South Mississippi.

Soon the discovery of a quirky plan to fly them home became a call to action. At least seven different flights were separated by a 13-hour window. Several Marines would not make it home until 11 o'clock that evening, while others arrived in the morning. That would be a haphazard, all-day-shuttle homecoming at best. We were told that's the best they could get.

Within three hours, and after some unpleasant effort, my staff and I had whittled it down to four flights within a four-hour window. That was still not good, but it looked like the lesser of the evils.

"Sir, we just got a call that General Bergman is getting a C-130 Transport out of Fort Worth."

"Where did that come from?"

"Apparently, after the memorial service, he took a walk through the barracks to speak with Marines. The Marines told him what was going on, and he said he would fix it. We'd already looked into that possibility and there were no C-130's available."

"He owns 'em. If he wants it he'll get it. That would be a great solution! I just wish we'd known this before we jumped through all these flaming hoops and made the travel office so mad at us."

The general did make it happen. Problem solved.

Marine Corps issues and a military mindset had to begin to shift back into the background. Focus of effort and professional attention had to return to my civilian career. Not only did I have to adjust, but everyone else had to adjust to my return.

• • •

After six months away I immediately noticed changes at the school district transportation department. Some employees had been fired or had quit while I was away. Changes—good and bad, obvious and obscure—would be revealed in random sequence.

Returning things to normal would not be easy, but it would be friendly. The patience and understanding from everyone at work helped immensely.

While Lee and I were catching up on some weekend shopping with friends, the cell phone in my pocket rang. I recognized the number as my regimental commander.

"Hello, sir."

"Hey, John. This is Colonel O'Leary. I need to know if you would rather your bronze star be presented to you at the Commander's Conference next week or in front of your battalion."

"Sir, you've caught me a little off guard. I don't really know what you're talking about."

"Oh. (Pause) Well, congratulations. I thought you would have already known that you were written up."

"Actually, I thought a commanding general's coin and a plaque I received was it for me. I'm completely surprised. The conference will be fine with me."

"Apparently, you impressed somebody while you were in Iraq."

"I just did my job the best way I knew how."

"Is Lee coming with you?"

"Yes, sir."

"Great. I'll let General O'Dell know so they can be prepared to present it to you there. Again, congratulations. I'll see you in San Francisco."

"Thank you, sir."

It was almost embarrassing turning to Lee and our friends to share the good news. We were all excited.

The phone rang again.

"Hello?"

"Hey, John, this is Reid. They're rushing Linda to the hospital."

Linda was the matriarch of our transportation department. Her years of experience were invaluable. Our unusual friendship was surpassed by a unique professional partnership which naturally balanced our individual strengths and weaknesses.

Bus drivers who had difficulty with my leadership style gravitated to her for counsel or remedy. Those who had more trouble with her and her ways would turn to me. It was easy to capitalize on that. The phone call would have an immediate personal and professional impact. Our family of co-workers was already spreading the news.

"What happened?"

"Kim called and said she collapsed at the casino."

"Kim's calling now. Let me take her call. Thanks."

"Hey, I just got off the phone with Reid."

"John, it's really bad. You need to pray."

"Where are they taking her?"

"Baptist Desoto."

"I'll meet you there."

We beat the ambulance to the hospital. Waiting at the entrance to the emergency doors, my cell phone rang again. Colonel O'Leary's number appeared.

"Yes, sir?"

"Today must be your lucky day. The colonel's list is out and you're on it. Congratulations again."

"Thank you, sir. That's great news, but I can't celebrate that right now. I'm standing at the emergency room doors, awaiting the arrival of an ambulance. My friend and co-worker apparently had a heart attack, and it doesn't sound good."

"I'm sorry to hear that. I'll let you go. I hope it turns out alright."

"Thank you, sir."

The EMTs were still performing CPR as they arrived, but it looked as if they were just going through the motions as they moved Linda from the ambulance.

No chance of slowly settling into a normal routine. Emotional intensity and everyday stress seemed to crank up to new and unusual levels. Before we could begin healing and working things more into the direction of normalcy, I was asked by Linda's family to share a few words at her funeral.

It was not dissimilar to speaking at a memorial service for one of my Marines. Bus drivers lined the miles between the church and cemetery with dozens of yellow school buses adorned with black bows. As the hearse rolled, drivers stood reverently in front of their buses with their hands on their hearts. It was a fitting tribute and a visible reminder that relationships with God and man need to be well tended.

Back to work in the civilian world also meant back to work in the reserve life. Only on active duty can a reservist enjoy the luxury of a single professional focus. I'm not sure which was the most difficult adjustment—the full-time civilian world of home and work or the now part-time Marine Corps.

A near-constant barrage of requests for Marine personnel had already taken its toll on us. The pressure to fill the quasi-volunteer officer billets ratcheted up as the pool of officers diminished. Most had already had a trip or two to Iraq or Afghanistan. It was more apparent that the remaining individuals would not volunteer without some pressure being applied.

Major McCulley had already turned down an opportunity to command Marines in combat after transferring from a unit in a self-professed search of command opportunities. He left just weeks before they were activated for Iraq in a provisional role.

Next, he turned down another Iraq-bound billet that was tasked to us to fill. Technically, the billets were still considered voluntary for non-obligated officers and staff NCOs, and nearly all were out of our professional expertise.

"Sir, although that billet is assigned to our battalion to fill, it is not in artillery. If I'm not mistaken, they're all still voluntary."

"Yes, Major, they are technically voluntary for us, but we're leaders and we're sending our Marines without that luxury. That's why the general passed the guidance and I reiterated that we need to get ready to go, resign, or retire. I came to the battalion to be on the cutting edge of HIMARS, not to be a truck platoon commander. Any lieutenant or staff NCO could fill that billet."

He was right about that. But there are no lieutenants in the reserves, and we were not sending Marines without officer leadership. His stance was disappointing to say the least.

Shortly thereafter, a rare artillery command assignment was presented to us—a short-fused artillery mission for a HIMARS unit to Afghanistan as part of Operation Enduring Freedom.

"Can we fill it?"

"How much time do we have?"

"Maybe a month."

"We can do it. Let me make a few phone calls."

"Major McCulley, this is Colonel Caldwell. We have a tasker to send a rocket platoon in support of OEF. They will need someone with your knowledge and abilities in command."

"Sir, this is a real bad time with everything at home and the job. I won't be able to volunteer for it at this time."

It was beyond comprehension that any Marine artillery officer would turn down an offer like that. To make matters worse, it was one of my officers.

Within minutes I had other officers and staff volunteering for the key billets. Then the requirement went away almost as fast as it came, but the recent response from Major McCulley haunted me. Here was the first and only Marine officer I would be forced to drop from my unit to the IRR because of an unwillingness to deploy.

Officers must have the moral courage to stand up and be counted. We are sending Marines into harm's way. They need and deserve our leadership, and we are to lead by our example.

Junior enlisted Marines are under contract. Most reserve officers and staff NCOs are not. That means the officers and staff could actually avoid activation by dropping into the Individual Ready Reserve just prior to an expected activation.

As was said and reiterated on several occasions, "If you haven't seen Southwest Asia yet, get ready to go or get out."

The awkward part was drawing a hard line like that in the reserves while knowing many of our active-duty counterparts had yet to be held to the same standard. Some Marines, enlisted and officers alike, wanted, even begged for, orders but could not get them. Other individuals quietly avoided orders on their way to a comfortable retirement. Neither scenario made sense to me.

When my friend Roger Garay, my active-duty counterpart and battalion I&I returned, it took him a little while to decompress. Roger had been imbedded with an ill-fated Iraqi battalion in the violent insurgent hotbed of Ramadi, and he had apparently had a difficult deployment with much enemy insurgent contact. He reported that the Iraqi unit he was alongside in Ramadi suffered the highest percentage of casualties in all of Iraq. On the surface he quickly returned to his usual self and was positively focused on the details of tomorrow's challenges.

"That was nothing like what you guys said it'd be. Hell, we lost seventy-one percent of our Iraqi battalion."

Another Marine officer we knew had a fairly uneventful deployment at the same job in another part of Iraq. His personal accounts had Roger expecting something much different than his eventual reality.

Deployments of provisional truck platoons, security detachments, and military police companies were soon behind us. Considerable effort by the battalion staff enabled us to begin reconstituting ourselves as a functional artillery unit for annual training. Practically the only Marine battalion shooting artillery anywhere, we proudly prepared to train as a unique, mixed battalion of cannon and rockets.

The battalion-sized firing exercise was planned for Fort Bliss near El Paso, Texas. Hot desert training was a welcome reprieve from the real world of IEDs and KIAs.

As we convoyed from Fort Bliss to the training area, we passed a typical Texas-style ranch gate with the words "Jackass Flats" above the drive. We fondly adopted that term for our temporary home in the desert training grounds.

Not only was getting back into an artillery mindset therapeutic, I expected this would be one of my last hurrahs. I was doing what I loved and loving what I was doing. It seemed like I was a fish being thrown back into the water. Marines were motivated with just enough complaining to know they loved it too. It's been said many times that Marines aren't happy unless they are complaining.

After a PX run in the otherwise desolate area, I heard a Marine return and let the others know he had seen an attractive young woman there.

"Wow, she was hot!"

"Well, was she 'Jackass Flats' hot' or 'Dallas hot'?"

"Oh, she was Dallas hot."

You would think their two weeks of training had taken them around the world for a year without seeing females. It's amazing how quickly that mindset overtakes them (us). Still, we were able to focus enough on artillery to conduct an aggressive and hugely successful annual training event. Rockets and cannon artillery rocked the South Texas desert impact area.

Marines coming together for two weeks, eating, living, and working together for a common training mission, was like a vacation compared to recent combat deployments for most of us there.

When our work was done, a simple day of liberty was more than welcome; it was expected. There is always great debate on the value of liberty following two weeks' annual training. On one side is the Inspector/Instructor staff that thinks it is an unnecessary risk of something going terribly wrong. On the other side are the reservists, who are certain their day of liberty has been earned. Additionally, it is great to build some esprit de corps and better memories.

The debate was not a small one, but it was a perpetual one. It usually came with emotional arguments from strong-willed individuals on both sides. The debate would begin a year in advance, during planning, and would resurface from month to month. I've seen liberty denied, cancelled, and developed into a royal Charlie Foxtrot complete with regrets and more than one "I told you so." As an outgoing battalion commander, I was determined to protect liberty for my Marines even though my regular Marine counterpart advised strongly against it.

"John, you really need to cancel liberty. It's not worth it."

"Roger, we're not cancelling liberty."

"Nothing good can come of this. We're just a few miles from Juarez, Mexico."

"—and that's off limits."

"—and you know Marines."

"Yes, I do. If Marines are determined to go to Juarez, we would just cancel liberty for everyone except the ones who don't follow orders. They'll find trouble anyway."

"Just mark it down that I'm totally against it."

"So noted, and thanks for the unvarnished assessment. Let's hope the Marines don't prove you right."

No liberty incidents were reported, and everyone made it back on time. Hopefully, they enjoyed it. I was a little nervous for the duration. After all, the regimental commander, Colonel O'Leary, was coming down for my change of command to close out our annual training.

I had chosen for the ceremony to take place in front of the battalion formation. Otherwise, it would be at a much smaller, headquarters battery event.

Holding it in Grand Prairie would have provided a better opportunity for guests and celebration, but this seemed much more appropriate. I loved the Marines in the field. It was where I have always been most at ease. I've worn out my share of boots and utilities, while all my dress uniforms are still as good as new.

The Texas sun shone brightly for the traditional passing of the colors. The dry heat was perfectly bearable. A warm yet comfortable breeze brought life to the flags and the formalities. The customary commands resonated across the parade deck. Normally, these ceremonies seemed to drag, but this being my last hoorah of sorts, now they seemed to pass in an instant.

It was strange leaving such a desired billet with no assurance I'd ever command Marines again. A huge feeling of pride and accomplishment was coupled with sadness. It was sad to leave the Marines and the esprit de corps. It was sad to think of things left undone. It was sad to see an end of a career on the horizon, namely mine.

• • •

Promotion to colonel was a high honor, but it was going to be a real challenge to find a meaningful billet. In the Marine Corps there are few colonels. In the reserves there are even fewer, and we are scattered across the 50 states and the world. Most staff positions for colonels in the reserves were just boring. I began the search for something more.

"John, you ought to join us in New Orleans."

"What could I do in the air wing?"

"Don't you artillery guys do targeting?"

"Sure."

"We have an opening for a targeting officer in the MCCLAT."

"The what?"

"It's just an acronym for our liaison team that works in the CAOC."

"The what?"

"You may know it as the JAOC—Joint Air Operations Center. The JFACC and the CFACC—the Combined Forces Air Component Command—are the same, except one theatre of operations uses J for Joint and the other uses the C for Combined."

"Okay. Targeting and liaison work I know. I'll obviously need to learn a new set of acronyms. Where do I sign up?"

The learning curve did not disappoint, and the wing was definitely a different animal than the division. It's been said, "If you can't swing with the wing, then party with arty!" I was about to learn the truths behind that.

One of the first events when I arrived was an already scheduled PFT. I was in good enough shape for the Marine Corps physical fitness test, so I wasn't concerned. Interestingly enough, they had the three-mile course laid out at Chalmette Battlefield/Jean Lafitte National Historical Park. The Battle of New Orleans site was a better option than simply running the streets of the city.

The quick description of the course left me with questions. All of the other 4th MAW officers had run it before, but I didn't want to make a wrong turn.

"Could you go over that again?"

"Just follow somebody."

"I plan on being in the front."

They all laughed and thought the new guy was joking. Thankfully, I was able to back that up and beat them all handily. I was just too competitive to follow along the course behind someone.

Our training focus supported large evolutions exercising air operations centers around the globe. We also provided individual augmentation to joint and wing billets for the war effort in Southwest Asia. I had some familiarity and a little experience in joint and combined multinational target planning, but this put my training and my adaptability to the test. My peers helped me get up to speed.

Notably, these Marines were exceptional goof-offs. When work was done, or the schedule was light, they didn't even pretend to earn their money. When I arrived that's the first thing I noticed.

Then I saw them work. Whether interacting with general officers, junior enlisted, or our allies, they proved to be some of the most knowledgeable, competent professionals in uniform. Work hard; play hard.

Now that I was swinging with the wing, it was decided that I needed a call sign. All the pilots had them. Another artillery officer on our team with the last name Cannon was given the call sign "Loose." For me they took note of my civilian career in pupil transportation and named me "Otto" or "Otto Mann," after the bus driver on the animated series, *The Simpsons.*

Soon I was honing my targeting skills in South Korea, then Tucson, Arizona. We still had to get all the annual "check-in-the-box" training that the Corps required of every Marine. For that we chose other interesting locations such as Annapolis, Maryland, and Pensacola, Florida, for professional development and meeting classroom requirements.

At the National Naval Aviation Museum, my cohorts were like kids at a candy store.

"That was my first aircraft."

"I flew one of those."

"I think that very plane was in my squadron."

"Look, you guys, if your planes have already made it to the museum, it may be time for you to retire."

We stopped at the officer's club only for them to get another reminder of their seniority. We saw some of the students from flight school.

"Look at these youngsters."

"Did we look that young as lieutenants?"

"Probably, but it's hard to imagine."

"What's hard to imagine is that we let those kids fly planes!"

"They barely look old enough to drive a car."

"Come on. Let's get out of here."

It was determined that the bulk of our training should be in support of large exercises and not drill in New Orleans if we could help it. That made perfect sense. A top-heavy organization like ours, loaded with colonels, didn't need a weekend in garrison, drinking coffee.

Annual training opportunities from Korea to Germany and across the country were listed on a whiteboard with ad hoc teams assigned for support. I had been to the Korean peninsula a few times with the ground side, so getting there with the wing was nothing new. However, a unique chance to train and get some liberty in Europe seemed more like a reward than work.

Arriving in Germany with some remaining daylight created an opportunity for an excursion from the airport to the base. At least one or two of the pilots flew international routes regularly with their civilian jobs. Several of us were there for the first time and were wide eyed. We made some random stops in our rental van and set a pattern for the days ahead. Our approach to future outings steered away from typical tourist spots. If a town had more than one or two *bier gartens*, we would declare the town was too big for us to stop.

With one full day of liberty after our training concluded, we set our sights on Belleau Wood. In the mind of Marines, that storied World War I battlefield in France is second in significance only to the small Pacific island of Iwo Jima from World War II.

It was near where U.S. Marine Captain Lloyd W. Williams famously responded to the "retreat" order of the French commander, "Retreat Hell, we just got here!" The German advance was halted, and it marked a turning point in the war. It was also the location where Marines were first called *Teufels hunde* or devil's dogs to describe the fierceness of their fighting.

Today, the battlefields are blissfully silent. Impressive monuments let us know that we have arrived somewhere special. Beneath the memorials, rows upon rows of white crosses stand erect in manicured grass.

We had followed the GPS and small "American Cemetery" markers along rural roads of the French countryside. Brilliant yellow flowers blanketed the rolling rapeseed fields of Eastern France. Yet, scattered within the lush agricultural area were special reminders of battles fought and lives lost across the same acreage.

Barbed wire and visible remnants of trench lines and shell craters marked the hallowed grounds kept in memoriam. It was especially sobering to see such stark and stoic scars still visible from a war fought nearly 100 years before.

A cozy lunch at a rural French café was our first choice and only option. No one there spoke English like many do in the cities, and none of us spoke French. But we could make out enough on the menu to point and smile and pay. So friendly . . . Our journey continued.

The Aisne-Marne American Cemetery—including Belleau Wood—Saint Mihiel American Cemetery, and the Meusse-Argonne American Cemetery were some of our stops. The French Cemetery memorializing the fallen at the Battle of Verdun, and even a quick stop at small German Cemetery, added perspective to our journey.

It was getting late and we ended our rich experience at the final resting place for nearly 15,000 Americans. Meuse-Argonne is the largest American battlefield cemetery in the world, but the sheer magnitude was overshadowed by the silence. We could almost hear the sun setting. All of us were speechless.

Maybe we were a little tired. Maybe the size was overwhelming, especially when added to the numbers of individual markers we had seen within this casual day's drive.

Beyond our imagination and the tens of thousands of personal markers that we respected were over 10 million civilians and nearly 10 million military personnel lost in The Great War. The "war to end all wars" ended with the armistice signed November 11, 1919. Sadly, just under 20 years later, World War II began with Nazi Germany invading Poland on September 1, 1939. More reflections on history would have to wait. We wanted to be out of France and back into the peaceful, unified Germany, and at a new bier garten by dinnertime.

Not long after the exercise ended, so did my time with the wing. The Command Selection list was released, and I was assigned as the first deputy commander of 14th Marine Regiment, headquartered in Fort Worth, Texas. It was the largest regiment in the Marine Corps, with five battalions of artillery scattered across the country. Some units were going away or transitioning to anti-terrorism units. The battalions that remained were preparing for assignments in and out of their MOS, depending on the needs of the Marine Corps.

Drill would require a seven- to eight-hour drive. The drive was somewhat familiar, since I had served some years in Fort Worth as a major and then in Grand Prairie as a lieutenant colonel. It was technically a command assignment as the senior reservist, but the active-duty regimental commander was the boss. Colonel Al Orr quickly became a dear friend and valued professional mentor. Everything seemed to be going right. I was even able to get into the field with Marines firing artillery.

• • •

One of the hottest summers on record seemed to also be one of the longest. It was late September 2010, and temperatures in the shade were still flirting with 100° F in Mississippi. Our schools had been in session since August 5th, so our summer had unofficially been over for eight weeks. Professional baseball was in the home stretch for playoff runs. High school, collegiate, and professional football seasons were in full swing.

Congressional politics filled any gridiron gaps. Newscasts focused on the growing national debt and deficit. The economy was in the tank. Unemployment was hovering near 10%, and predictions of a political turnover in the U.S. House of Representatives were widespread. The Global War on Terror had already been stripped of that title and was not a major topic for any of the networks. Operation Iraqi Freedom was over. Operation Enduring Freedom and the military surge in Afghanistan were hardly mentioned except in the context of their contribution to the mounting deficit and the arbitrary and distant withdrawal deadline set by President Obama. Words like *war, victory, freedom, human rights,* and *democracy* languished.

Only public outrage to a proposed mosque at Ground Zero in New York momentarily aroused our war-weary nation. Otherwise, the war, which was ushered into America's living rooms on 9/11, was headed out of sight, out of mind. Our country, once diverse yet unified, was now merely divisive.

Amid the congressional campaign season, a local school board race had grabbed our attention. Lee had become the de facto campaign chairman for a friend, Mr. Theron Long. One routine night Lee was making some calls to schedule a rally for Mr. Long.

"Hello, Miss Cheryl. I was calling on behalf of Mr. Long's campaign—"

Lee, as usual, walked inside and out of the house while talking on the phone. I continued my piddling. Usual pleasantries faded through her brief conversation. Miss Cheryl shared some unrelated bad news with Lee shortly into their conversation.

"Thank you for letting me know. And please, let me know if you hear anything else or if there's anything we can do. Goodbye."

Soberly, Lee walked in and turned to me. "John, Ross and Sissy Ose's son Josh was killed in Afghanistan."

Thoughts, feelings, questions, compassion, anger, sadness, even guilt swelled inside. Now what? Call? Visit? Wait? How and when? There's no imagining the grief of parents who have just been notified that their 19-year old would not be coming home.

The proud family was less than a month removed from a final visit and emotional send-off at Camp Lejeune. Josh was two weeks in country and several weeks from his 20th birthday when hostile fire found a gap in his body armor. Only denial helped me get a little sleep that night.

The next morning began like any other for us, except that Josh and Ross and Sissy were my first thoughts. Mutual friends began calling and asking if I had heard the news. Lee called me a few hours into the day. Her voice was soft and low.

"Hey, I spoke with Sissy.

"How are they holding up?"

"About like you'd expect . . . still in shock. I told her how sorry we were and offered any help. She said they were looking for a Marine escort."

"You know I'll do it."

"I already told her you would. She was very grateful."

It must have confused the CACO (casualty assistance calls officer) when the request was made for a colonel to escort a junior enlisted Marine. The CACO's first call did sound somewhat hesitant.

"Sir, this is First Sergeant Mauro. Are you aware that you were requested by the family to escort PFC Ose?"

"Yes, I'm a friend of the family and will do whatever they need. Can you let me know what will be required of me as an escort? I've never done this before."

"Sir, will you be the official escort?"

"I didn't know there was any other type. Whatever the family wants is fine with me."

The week ahead seemed to drag. An unexpected stress vacuum seemed to paralyze me. Basic tasks at work, school, and home were not getting accomplished during the days following Josh's death.

Anxiety grew. The feeling of loss was accompanied by new and unfamiliar personal and professional expectations. Even fret over uniform readiness or un-readiness disturbed normal sleep that week. This would be one of the most important tasks I had ever been unprepared to do. It may have been less stressful if they had asked me to lead a thousand Marines into combat.

At least the obligatory wait was long enough for the Marine Corps to verify Josh's promotion to lance corporal. It was earned through the recruiter's assistance but had not yet caught up with him. The family had asked if that could be fixed and they were counting on it.

An official escort, Lance Corporal Martin, was assigned by the Marine Corps from Quantico. I was flown to Dover as a special escort representing the family.

The high honor came with unpleasant reality and pain. As a young boy, Josh had brought visible joy to his parents. At social events or bumping into the Oses in the grocery store isle, they had readily shared their pride in his choice to become a Marine. I have known other Marines who have paid the ultimate price, but I've never known the surviving family in this way. It is painfully different.

Lance Corporal Ose arrived home in a flag-draped casket to a heartsick throng of family and friends. Too soon. Too young.

As our Falcon 20 charter taxied toward the hangar, I could see the pilot and co-pilot hesitate at the directions they were receiving on their headsets. Cars had made a parking lot out of the taxiway, and they were being told to pull between the cars and toward a waiting throng. I leaned forward and assured them that was the expectation. As they inched closer, they spotted a staff sergeant in dress blues providing the familiar hand and arm signals bringing them in to park.

Wow! After trying to prepare Lance Corporal Martin for a couple of hundred family and friends, I realized that no one had prepared *me* for what I was seeing. Dozens of airport ground crews in safety vests stood erect and online. Tennessee Air National Guard and Memphis police and fire department vehicles and personnel positioned themselves alongside dozens of uniformed officers from Josh's home county. Dozens of motorcycles from the Freedom Guard organization were inconspicuously parked at the side of the hangar as we arrived. The semi-private arrival had become very public, and my guess of a couple hundred had been exceeded by many hundreds.

Following brief planeside honors, the motorcade began. Police escorts proceeded slowly. From the front seat of the hearse, I watched things unfold. At first, traffic stopped in simple reverence if not from the forced inconvenience placed upon them by the huge escort of blue lights.

Beyond the airport reception, we had expected some roadside respects but were honestly surprised to see it begin before we reached the Mississippi state line.

Proud folks stood alone with a flag or in groups with friends and strangers. Caring families stood together with children of all ages. Business owners along the route emptied strip centers of their customers and employees to pay respects. Some wept openly. Others held onto each other for support. Veterans were easiest to spot with their proud and personal salutes. Shirts and ball caps displaying service affiliations, veteran organizations, and the like adorned the roadside.

Precious preschool faces pressed curiously against one daycare's chain link fence. As the procession passed, short, innocent fingers gripped the fence wire along with their miniature American flags. Salutes from two-, three-, and four-year-olds dotted the playground, and hands over tiny hearts were scattered among the few children who could not get a spot at the fence. Their teacher had ensured they were not just watching—they were participating.

Some of the drivers who were inadvertently caught in the traffic mayhem got out of their cars and stood reverently with their hands over their hearts. The vehicle procession from the airport to the church stretched for more than two and a half miles, and the crowds grew progressively larger and denser.

On multiple occasions I was moved to tears. Eventually, we reached Josh's former schoolmates at Hernando High School, who were standing and mourning en masse along the last half mile of the 20-mile journey. The show of support for one fallen Marine, a friend and native son, could not have been more spectacular or heartening.

Personally, I was still balancing the Marine side with the family/friend side . . . maybe not as well as I thought or hoped I would.

A former minister had once told of the time he preached his first funeral. He was worried how he would do, what he would say, even how he would say it and how he would be perceived. As the pressure mounted, it suddenly dawned on him, "It's not about me." He told how that revelation reassured him through his first funeral as a minister. The same self-doubts plagued me; that same reality steadied me as personal and professional emotions collided. This was about Josh.

The days blurred. The emotional drain was real, but mine could not have compared to that of Josh's family. I longed for the daily grind and time to separate me from the intensity of emotions I felt in those days and weeks.

Presenting the 2nd Battalion, 14th Marines to the Regimental Commander at my own change of command following a successful artillery rocket and cannon live-firing exercise at Fort Bliss, Texas.

*"Not that I speak from want, for I have learned
to be content in whatever circumstances I am."*

Philippians 4:11

...13
Conflicts of Circumstance

S ummer heat faded away and was well in the rearview mirror. Fall was a welcome relief in many ways. Work, school, family, reserve duty, and life settled into a more predictable yet busy routine.

Gloomy weather greeted me at a national pupil transportation conference in Portland. Instead of breathtaking Oregon panoramas, low-lying clouds with short spells of cold, light rain lingered from day to day.

The conference getaway muddled along. As sometimes happens, a couple of back-to-back morning phone calls changed things.

"Hello."

"Hey, John. Have you heard about Bill Minor?"

"No."

Commissioner Bill Minor had beaten me in the general election seven years earlier. Now he had died suddenly of a massive heart attack, and it was expected there would be a short-fused special election to fill the vacancy.

"Thanks, but this is too soon to start talking about it."

"I understand, but things are about to happen quickly."

First one call then another. It was starting a buzz.

"Hey, John. This is Kevin. Have you heard about Bill?"

"I just did."

"We're all wondering if you're going to run."

"Wow. Don't you think this is a little early to be talking about it? We should let him be buried at least. In the meantime, I'll give it some thought."

I had made a new friend, also a former Marine and transportation director from a school district in Louisiana. As we ate dinner that night, I told him of the turn of events. Then he asked me a question.

"Do you know how to make God laugh?"

"No. How?"

"Tell him what *your* plans are."

That was my first real nudge in the direction of running. It certainly wasn't in my own plans, but I knew to be open to God's plan. As recently as a few days earlier, I had answered curious friends about my political aspirations.

"So, are you planning on getting back into politics?"

"Not as a candidate. First, I need to help ensure my boss is re-elected, preferably unopposed, for Superintendent of Education. Then I have a friend running for County Supervisor in District Two. After that I'll likely try to help a few more state candidates I know and like."

"What about you?"

"I'll tell you like I've told others before you. I'm not burned out on politics, but I don't have the fire in the belly it takes to run a campaign."

So, had Commissioner Minor's death changed that? Only time could tell, and there wouldn't be much time to deliberate. There would be a few days to pray and talk and sort it out with Lee, but the decision whether or not to run had to be made soon.

Catchy phrases from sermons and some select Bible verses come to mind from time to time. Great and small words of wisdom can be reassuring, challenging, and thought provoking. Few words reoccur as often as these from some teacher or pastor. I cannot recall their name but their truths are no less significant: "In order to find God's will, you must first do God's will." At first blush, it seems a bit of a "chicken or egg" quandary, but with more introspection it becomes clearer.

Doing what little right we know proves more difficult when we are focused on all we know that is wrong—whether within our own lives or around us. In other words, "First, do God's will." Finding God's greater purpose is much more imaginable in the shadow of simple submission.

Okay, so no easy way out; I would just have to push forward. Everything doesn't have to be a leap of faith. Are life, family, work and church in order? Yes and no, as usual.

Keeping an open heart and an open mind was difficult. Initially, I told myself to forget about it. After all, I had lost the election for the same position about seven years earlier to Bill. Sure, it had been a fairly good run against a very seasoned state senator, but after that defeat I completely turned away from political aspirations. I wasn't bitter, just happily done—or so I thought.

Encouragement to run came from many directions. Friends I had met along the campaign trail seven years earlier were surprisingly ready for another round. Some former political adversaries even joined the list of recruiters. This time would be different. In a special election to fill an unexpired term, there would be no party labels on the ballot. That could prove good or bad.

Days passed and the discussions ping-ponged from the ranks of political pundits in local coffee shops to the state capital. Again, if I ran I would be the underdog. A longtime state representative was likely to enter as the early favorite with widespread support from the road-building lobby, not to mention some of North Mississippi's largest contractors. Hadn't I once committed silently to myself that I wouldn't run for that position again? Another political veteran and county supervisor who entered the race was a statewide officer in the Mississippi Association of Supervisors. Both would have more name recognition, along with organizational and fundraising advantages.

The regiment's Marine Corps ball was in a few days. As Lee and I drove to Fort Worth, we bantered about the pros and cons—personally, professionally, and politically. Ultimately, we needed to know if running would be the right decision for the right reasons.

"Our children are grown, so it's a good time."

"We want to spend time with our grandchildren, so it's a bad time."

"It's happening during Christmas, so it's a bad time."

"We'll both have time off, so it's a good time."

"Cannon and Daniel will be out of school, so it's a good time."

"Jennifer and Kylee will be here visiting, so it's a bad time."

"Laura Ashlynn is a newborn, so it's a bad time."

As we drove and shared and collected our thoughts, we flip-flopped our decision frequently on the eight-hour trek. At the end of the trip, we both were ready.

"Let's do it."

"Okay."

"If we sleep on it and wake up with the same decision, we'll do it."

We did. As soon as the decision was made, the calls and available help from volunteers and encouragers diminished and practically vanished. Of course, it was almost Thanksgiving, and Christmas was around the corner. Most folks normally interested in politics were not. An off-cycle holiday campaign for a down-ticket position didn't appeal to anyone. Still, we had to proceed. Stress rose as interest dropped.

• • •

Deciding to run was further complicated by my new military assignment as Commanding Officer of Task Force African Lion. Debate had surfaced a month earlier between some general officers on whether a reserve or regular Marine colonel should be assigned. Brigadier General Lariviere argued on my behalf with his boss, Lieutenant General Kelly.

"John, it's official. You have command. Don't (mess) it up."

"Thank you, General."

Containing my excitement wasn't easy, but I wanted to act like it was "all in a day's work." It would be an honor and a challenge, even without a concurrent political campaign.

As the commanding officer of Task Force African Lion, I would have responsibility for the success or failure of the single largest combined-arms exercise on the continent of Africa by U.S. forces. The joint-bilateral Theatre Security Cooperation (TSC) live-fire exercise consisted of U.S. Marines, Navy, Army, and National Guard units from several states. We would be working and training side by side with Moroccan allies over several weeks.

Combat arms and combat support Marines would be in the Moroccan desert shooting, moving, and communicating with the usual tanks, engineers, artillery, and infantry. More Marines would be training with Moroccans to practice peacekeeping operations.

National Guard units augmented us with heavy transport in the field. Other Guard units from Utah provided doctors, nurses. and veterinarians for multiple medical missions across Morocco.

Fourth Marine Air Wing provided two C-130s and their crews to conduct aerial refueling operations with the Moroccan Air Force. They would also provide us with some cargo and personnel transport.

To get our personnel and equipment there and back, we exercised the Navy's JLOTS (Joint Logistics Over the Sea) concepts, the Air Force Military Airlift

Command, and numerous military and civilian logistics agencies across the globe. This was big time. Besides the usual visibility of such a large, bilateral training operation, the secretary of the Navy had apparently had a personal conversation with the Commandant of the Marine Corps about the importance of this exercise.

My staff was an ad hoc group of regular and reserve Marines scattered from state to state. We relied on the regular I&I staff of the regiment and the 3rd Battalion staff to keep us on task. In fact, our regular staff did the lion's share of the work, and reservists like me would plug into our roles as our civilian situations and initiatives would allow.

Still, the political opportunity was calling. The groundwork was now being laid for me to be able to do both, plus work at my "day job," as if I could forget about supervising over 350 employees and transporting over 18,000 students to and from 41 campuses each day.

Multi-tasking was nothing new, but this was pushing my limits. Of course, the family was drawn into these sorts of political decisions whether they liked it or not. With a growing family and Christmas drawing near, it was going to be a strain on our entire clan.

Then, without warning, while on a short, three-hour solo trip up Interstate-55 from Jackson, I received an unexpected call from my mentor and friend, Colonel Alan Orr. Suddenly, the already higher stress levels went ballistic.

"Hey, John. We just got a call from division, and they're tasking us to provide a staff section, including an O-Six, to activate on short notice to Bahrain."

"You're kidding."

"Nope, we were just notified."

"Well, I guess that's me since I'm your only O-Six on the staff."

"Yep."

"How soon?"

"Activation will be almost immediate, and deployment overseas will follow in a few months."

"What about Morocco?"

"I'm not sure what they were thinking on this. I'll be calling them back in a few minutes to get more details, and I'll ask them if they've thought about that."

"Whew. This is a shocker. Call me when you hear more, especially activation dates and deployment timeframes."

"I will."

There was no way I could call and tell Lee. The last time I ran for commissioner, she ran my campaign for six months while I was in Iraq. I couldn't even imagine this again. We'd probably have to drop out of the race. How and when to tell her would have to be decided later; on the phone as I drove up the interstate was not an option. I decided to call my old friend Clovis for some moral support.

"Hooty-hoo."

He answered his cell phone, as he had on many other occasions, with an inside joke of ours.

"Clovis, you can't tell anyone what I am about to tell you. (Pause) I just got a phone call. (Another pause and deep breath) I'm being activated by the Marines."

"That's not funny."

"I'm not joking. This is for real. I just got off the phone, but I can't call and tell Lee yet. Heck, it's a wonder I didn't wreck the car. I can't imagine telling Lee, but it can't be a secret long. It wouldn't be fair to do this to her again."

"Let's think about this. Can you get out of it or at least put it off?"

"No way. I just finished reminding the regimental staff that they were paid to be ready, and if they weren't, they should resign or retire. Plus, one of my bosses, a three-star general, recently lost his son in Afghanistan. I can't just waltz up and tell him, "Hey General, this is a real inconvenient time for me to go to Bahrain."

"Yeah, I see what you mean. Don't tell anyone else until we've had time to think about it."

"No kidding. That's why I called you."

For some nebulous amount of time, we talked through the implications of the news, and then I drove in silence under near paralyzing stress. Abruptly, I jerked the steering wheel and whipped right off the interstate, nearly missing my exit ramp. A couple more miles, minutes, and turns to go. With the lights of the house in sight, the phone rang again. It was Colonel Orr.

"Hey. They changed their mind. When I asked them about activating their newly assigned commanding officer of African Lion, they determined they weren't going to activate you."

"I'll do whatever, but I need to know for sure."

"You're not going."

"Are you sure? Because I'm about to pull into my driveway and tell Lee."

"I'm sure. Don't sweat it."

"Thanks, Al. I'll talk to you later."

The high stress level did not immediately subside. Within a few minutes I collapsed on my bed and stared at the ceiling. The interstate drive had been tense and full of extreme thoughts and emotions. My mind had been racing through what I needed to do concerning my family, my job, the campaign, the assignment in Morocco, etc.

Lee observed my flop and knew it must have been a long day.

"I know you're tired."

"You have no idea. I was going to keep it from you until a better time, but I don't have the strength to hold it in. I was activated by the Marines on the way home, and just before I pulled into the driveway, they called back and said, 'Never mind.'"

"Are you sure they won't call back tomorrow?"

"No, but Al said they wouldn't because of my assignment in Morocco. I couldn't imagine dumping another campaign on you."

"I don't think I could do it."

"You could do it, but I don't know if we'd want to or should."

The short fuse and stress of a special election was now exacerbated by the always lingering possibility of activation. Also, pledges of early campaign contributions were not being backed up by actual donations. Low funds raised doubts about our decision to run.

"John, can you and Lee be in Jackson for a fundraiser this week?"

"Absolutely."

"We have about forty thousand in commitments."

"Wow! If we come out with half of that, I'll be excited."

"These guys are for real. We should get pretty close."

"Great. We need it."

We parked near the front door of a quaint, inconspicuous restaurant. The open parking was the first clue something was amiss. Even the small private room seemed huge in the absence of contributors. A few recognizable faces and a handful of checks from friends were the only encouraging aspects of the event. We couldn't get out of there fast enough. It was a bust. We just didn't know how bad it was yet. Then it went from bad to worse.

"Hey, John, here's the bill from the restaurant."

I thought this was a sponsored fundraiser. Lee and I tried to hide our shock and maintain an appreciative attitude. It was even harder when the $40,000 in commitments translated into a humbling $4,000 or so with additional verbal reassurances that more was still coming. It was a long ride home.

Family and friends were making ready for a busy holiday season, and no one was looking forward to a campaign, except maybe some of our opposition, who were naïve and might not have known any better.

The field of candidates had swelled so that no one expected to reach a required 50%+1 victory. The top two would have to face each other in a run-off election. The odds makers placed a senior state representative, Warner McBride, in the front-runner position. A senior county supervisor from Tippah County and I seemed to be wrestling for the number two spot, although there was a fourth contender. A credible newcomer, Mike Taggert, was in with a high level of political energy that comes with naiveté and the financial energy of a more affluent family.

Election Day was set for January. That day, an unusual snowstorm blanketed one of my opposition's strongest regions, keeping hundreds if not thousands of his votes at home. A military planning conference in Morocco kept me from experiencing our snowy success at the polls. While my family and support-ers were rounding up votes in the freezing temperatures and blowing white stuff, I was in Agadir, Morocco, running five miles on the beach. I did work more than 12 hours a day in the planning conference, but I had learned as a child that was only half a day. Our planning team even enjoyed some hours of liberty in the friendly resort city.

• • •

We finished the special election in first place but without the required 50%. Just a few hundred votes separated the top four contenders. My work in Morocco diverted my time and attention when I really needed to be capitaliz-ing on the good news of a top finish.

Surprisingly, the two other expected contenders of the conventional, political know-it-alls did not make the cut. It would be Caldwell and Taggert in the run-off.

It shifted the dynamics of the race from a conventional Democrat-Republican affair to a contest between two similarly conservative Republicans. It was hard to separate ourselves ideologically or practically, and it was a very friendly campaign.

The main division came from the world of Jackson, Mississippi, politics. Most of our would-be constituents didn't even know who the executive director for MDOT was. Yet the pundits in the capital city were abuzz with one question, "What are you going to do with Butch?"

The Department of Transportation's executive director, Butch Brown had been accused of being drunk and disorderly and resisting arrest. It was not the first time he had embarrassed the department or himself. It was not my issue or my reason for running, yet his job hung in the balance. A newly elected commissioner would be the swing vote whether to keep him or not.

I knew that I would fire any school bus driver working for me with the same issue. So my honest and unequivocal answer was a blunt one. "I'll fire him." It wasn't a very politically savvy answer; it was simply the truth.

Few like hearing direct truth in political circles, especially his friends. Now the push was on by some key roadbuilders to support my opponent, who had remained noncommittal. A growing number of road contractors wanted to keep the status quo and lined up with Taggert in hopes of keeping their embattled executive director.

As the run-off approached, some of the friendly opposition had turned less friendly. Some African American friends let me know they were hearing from their preachers that my candidacy was going to return them to slavery. I am not sure of the original source of that, but it was probably some less-than-friendly push-polling that had already been used against us. That sort of overtly suggestive polling is illegal in some states. The rumor was especially prevalent in black churches. It was apparently the opposition's way of differentiating us in a way that would swing some votes. It did.

Just a few days from the run-off, we contacted some minority supporters in Coahoma County. They had agreed to find us ten workers at $10 per hour on Election Day in the predominantly Democratic area.

John M. M. Caldwell, Sr.

"Find out how we're supposed to pay the workers. Do we write one check, or more, or do we pay cash? Do we distribute it, or do they do that?"

Shortly after I tried to close that loop, I realized we may be in more trouble than I thought.

"They said the price went up."

"What?"

"They said the price is now thirty-five dollars *per vote.*"

"Tell them we don't pay thirty-five *cents* per vote. That's against the law."

"After you tell them, don't call them back."

I wasn't even sure how that was supposedly done, but I didn't want to even ask for fear of association. If I had had time, I would have called the FBI and tried to get a conversation like that recorded.

Since that exchange, I've heard first- and second-hand accounts of how Election Day antics crossed ethical and legal lines. Tales of money and whiskey, even guns from actual witnesses . . . tales from the driver of truck-loads of registered voters hauled to the polls and told or shown how to vote . . . actual- and pretend-illiterate voters guided by hand to certain names on the ballot by the one who "helped them read . . ."

The most unusual was a tale of two men bidding for votes in Alcorn County. This secondhand account was extremely detailed. The two men, each in his best Election Day attire, stood together under an oak tree. One man held red pencils. One held blue pencils. In one direction there was an old country store. In the other direction was the polling place. Truckloads of farmhands would arrive to vote, and the two men bid with each other as if bidding for hogs at a sale barn. The highest bidder—a low, seemingly token amount—would pass out pencils to the workers going in to vote. After voting, the same men would enter the store, grab a drink, maybe a candy bar, and a boloney sandwich and hoop cheese. He would pay the store clerk with a single pencil. At the end of the day, each of the two men from under the oak tree would buy back the pencils to settle their accounts.

We just had to go with what we had and hope that sort of shenanigan—and others unknown—didn't hurt us too badly. I was also curious who was paying. I did not suspect my actual opponent, but it could have been any number of his supporters. I had a few in mind.

Thunderstorms moved in on the eve of the election. Relentless high winds and driving rains pummeled any voter who dared brave the conditions in our home county. It lasted all day. Meanwhile, good weather prevailed in our opposition's back yard. The ominous weather assured a poor voter turnout for us. We won where we needed to win, but not by enough. We lost the race by a respectably close margin. Close was and is not good enough.

As the votes were called into us at the courthouse, there was a lot of optimism among friends around us who hadn't tracked our full path to victory. I saw the writing on the wall early when solidly Democrat counties were voting strongly in our opposition's favor. We needed those to be more of a wash.

Because the loss was in large part due to Democrats being somehow motivated in this special election, some could see a real chance to win a few months later in the regularly scheduled primary process. In addition to the rumor of votes being bought, we saw that one Democrat precinct voted 100% for my opponent. That's not normal, even in the smallest of precincts. I wasn't ready to think about it, and I had already stated publicly that I would not run if I lost in this special election.

Then the new commissioner blindsided some of his biggest supporters. He fired the department's executive director the first day on the job. Ironically, those roadbuilders had turned against me because I openly stated that the executive director needed to go.

"Hey, John, did you hear what Mike did to Butch?"

"Oh, yeah, I heard."

"The roadbuilders are hot. They thought they had an understanding that he would keep him. We could raise you two million dollars for your campaign this week if you're willing to run."

"No, thanks. I'm done. I wish I could say that I appreciate the call, but that's the kind of politics I can't stand."

As weeks passed and I got some rest, the competitive side of me was being rejuvenated. Maybe I should run. Looking at the numbers, I thought I would have a realistic chance, even if the big money and roadbuilders didn't get on board. At least I should file to run to keep my options open.

When I did, an immediate question came from a political reporter at a prominent regional newspaper.

"You said during the special election that you wouldn't run in the general election. How can you justify running now?"

"Great question. I certainly meant it when I said it. Think about it this way. Many women in labor and delivery have said openly that they would never have another child. As the labor pains subside and time passes, the answer sometimes changes. It doesn't make them a liar."

Still, filing had to be done to beat the deadline and keep my options open. I was still not fully committed; it was still a matter of prayer. Eventually, I opted out. I wasn't really ready for another political campaign, and my boss wasn't either. He encouraged me to stay with him, and I did.

• • •

Then a new political twist . . . As we sat in Mi Pueblo having lunch, our county supervisor announced across town that he would not seek reelection. My phone started to ring.

"Alan's out. Are you running again?"

"No, but I know someone who might." I looked across the table. "Lee, you've mentioned this over the years."

"I'm ready. I'll call Alan first to make sure he means it. He's our friend, and I won't run against him."

It would likely be a full field for an open seat, and Desoto County had never elected a woman supervisor. In many ways it was still considered a man's job. Less than a dozen of the 410 supervisors throughout the state were women. Frequently, those exceptions were wives of supervisors who had died in office and were appointed to fill the vacancy.

Some of her critics questioned her independence.

"She'll just do whatever John tells her to do."

"John would be pulling the strings."

They obviously didn't know her very well. Heck, if that—doing what I tell her— were true, I'd have encouraged her run for office soon after we were married. Thankfully, we both share many ideals and foundational principles in life, religion, government, and politics. But she is strong-willed and independent-minded.

Five others lined up for the open seat: four Republicans and a Democrat. Conventional wisdom said we should prepare for a run-off. We'd had that experience recently in my commissioner's race and again in the primary for my second term as supervisor. Lee set her sights on winning the primary in the first round.

• • •

My sights were set on leading the transportation department for the largest school district in the state and simultaneously preparing for my command of Task Force African Lion in Morocco. The command would be over and school would be out before the full force of Lee's campaign hit us. The adage "No rest for the weary" comes to mind.

Early planning trips to Morocco proved especially valuable. Seeing training areas provided predictable benefits for determining space allocations, safe shooting, moving, communicating, etc. A brief stop in the capital city of Rabat to meet with the U.S. ambassador and his staff proved especially useful. The ambassador seemed underwhelmed with the previous year's exercise and asked if it would be the same this year.

"So, we'll arrive and see some puffs of smoke in the distance—"

"Sir, I can't speak for last year, but I can assure you, it will be much more than that."

The chief of station also informed me that the ambassador's wife was very much a "player" in the world of politics.

"If it weren't for the fact that this is a Muslim country, she could have just as easily been selected as the ambassador."

With a strong and capable wife in politics myself, I understood completely. Putting faces with names and gathering those nuanced tidbits of information were well worth the trip to Rabat.

I had already made a familiarization trip to Agadir with the division commander during the previous African Lion exercise. The command post was a shambles and the living areas looked like a second-rate frat house. Beer bottles filled poolside tables with no room for one more bottle. There were bottles at the bottom of the pool, and garbage cans were overflowing. We had seen young soldiers in the pool a day earlier. It resembled a co-ed college hangout. However, the mission purpose—our interaction and training off-site with our Moroccan allies—seemed to be going fairly well.

At some point during a lull in the training, the secretary of the Navy made an impromptu stop to see what African Lion was all about. He must have seen what I did, because he admonished those under his purview to make better use of our opportunities there. The next year we did.

The first advantage I had was Sergeant Major Davis. His leadership ensured this would look and feel like a military operation rather than a party. Liberty and some good times would also be preserved, but his watchfulness over the enlisted ranks was invaluable.

A year earlier the command element had been much, much lighter, and, subsequently, less capable. Having a regimental staff supplemented by a dedicated battalion staff paid huge dividends. The command post operations and capabilities would be equipped and staffed at a level befitting a joint/bilateral combined arms task force. Exercising the highest levels of C4 (command, control, communications, computers) became an integral part of African Lion training while enabling us to function as a true task force command.

Concurrently, we conducted independent exercises literally across the country. All of it involved the primary mission of enhancing bilateral cooperation with our Moroccan friends. As reservists it was also our annual active duty training, so we needed to make the most of it.

Aerial refueling was done with Marine Corps Reserve C-130 refuelers. The Moroccan Air Force linked up using their American-made F-16 Falcons. The airfield for their training was in the northern region, but the crews could easily meet us in Agadir to shuttle down to the training area on the southern coast.

Moroccan military planners joined us in a typical command post exercise (CPX). A fictitious scenario played out on a map in a more academic setting. This enabling interaction between partnering military staffs was not very flashy, but it was an important piece of our puzzle.

Peacekeeping operations (PKO) training was done in a more remote outpost. Here the Marines would eat and live alongside their Moroccan counterparts. Non-lethal training included some Marine Corps martial arts training, the use of riot gear, and Taser training that included getting tased and shooting Tasers.

A medical detachment of Utah National Guardsmen brought doctors of all sorts. Planned stops in some medically underserved areas brought long lines of Moroccans seeking help. Some needed a simple exam and not much in the way of treatment. Others sought preventive care and meds. Each day a different town and another line of Moroccans waited to be helped.

Veterinarians also came from Utah's National Guard and we went to the rural areas. Goats, sheep, donkeys, and horses were the primary customers. Vaccinations by the hundreds and examinations of various abnormalities seemed very much appreciated by the Moroccan herdsmen.

These medical and veterinary missions placed us out across the countryside. Daily diligence of our doctors reflected well on their professionalism and contribution to our mission.

On a command visit to experience their efforts firsthand, I witnessed Moroccan tree goats. When I first saw photos and souvenirs depicting the goats standing in trees, I thought it was like the mythical "jackalope" in the American Southwest—just a catchy, touristy fascination created by someone to get attention. Then I saw goats standing on branches in the indigenous Argan trees with my own eyes.

Desert combat training was the largest conventional component of African Lion. That training culminated with a desert live-fire demonstration with machine guns, tanks, and artillery. The units put on a show worthy of the high-ranking military and civilian dignitaries in attendance.

Hundreds of 155-mm artillery rounds began hitting targets, and machine guns and tank main guns fired into 50-gallon drums filled with diesel fuel. Smoke and fire preceded the rolling, mechanized formations while explosions rocked the earth. VIPs were noticeably impressed. The ground shook again and again. The concussion effects from the not-too-distant impacts could be felt in our chests. The U.S. ambassador turned from his front row seat to find me in the seat behind him. A huge smile and a thumbs-up were reassuring that this was much more than his experience from the previous year that he had described as "a few puffs of smoke."

The live-fire demonstration was followed by a celebratory reception with plenty of food and drink. Moroccan generals lined up to meet the commanding general of Marine Forces AFRICOM, General John Paxton Jr., and the accolades piled high. One after another of the Moroccan generals was heard bragging about the day's events and our longstanding relationship. It let me know that our mission had been accomplished. Several sought reassurances from the general that he would send me back the next year to command again. It was a high compliment, but commands like this are fleeting opportunities.

Upon my return to my billet as deputy regimental commander, it was apparent that the command for next year's African Lion would pass to the new, incoming regimental commander. I took that as a signal to move on. It was about time to hang up my boots for good. I announced to my boss that I would be transferring to New Orleans to serve on the commanding general's inspection (CGI) team. From this CGI billet, there would also be continued opportunities to fill vacancies on important and impactful promotion and command selection boards. These multi-week duty assignments in Quantico helped set the leadership slates for years to come.

Retirement was getting close, but I wanted to hang on long enough to get someone, anyone, to sign my retirement papers other than the current occupant of the White House, President Obama. As our Commander-in-Chief, he never seemed to fully support us. Regrettably, he was reelected, and I was reaching my commissioned service limit. So his signature was the one on my eventual retirement letter.

• • •

Marine reserve duties of all kinds absorbed a lot of my personal and professional energy. Still, I had to get home to my primary job and full-time income as the transportation director for our county school system.

Fourteen million-dollar budgets annually, 18,000 student riders twice a day, nearly 400 employees and 41 campuses required a big-picture approach. Details and the sensitivity of dealing with people—whether parents and children, principals, or bus drivers, among others—required more up-close-and-personal leadership.

"Good morning, all y'all! This is Bus Eighty-six, eastbound to Bridgetown where all the rich white folk live."

I just bit my tongue. We didn't allow freelancing and loose communications like that on our radios, but Mr. Payne, an 80-year-old African American driver, was a little bit of an exception. Everyone recognized the voice and knew they wouldn't get away with the same.

Once, at a transportation director's conference, the subject of old bus drivers came up.

"Hey, who has the oldest bus driver?"

"You do, 'cause you asked. What you got?"

"I've got one who's ninety-two, kin to a school board member. If that one leaves, I've got another one who's eighty-eight."

"I'm not sure congratulations are in order, but that's impressive."

Eventually, all three of my over-80 drivers called it quits. While it was a relief, it was also more than a little sad. They were great examples of dedication and loyalty. It seemed to be ending an era.

Bus drivers—*my* bus drivers—were some of the best employees in the world. They loved children. They loved their job. They saw it as more than a job—and it was. They showed up on time, and they showed up every day. You could set your watch by many of their routines. Of course, there were disappointing exceptions but amazingly few in a group of nearly 400 employees.

The first time I had to drive one of my buses was a busy Friday afternoon. Many of our coach drivers were driving their ball teams, so we were short subs.

"Put me on an easy one."

"We have a short elementary route that has just two apartment stops."

"Perfect."

Nerves still got my heart rate up. This busload was going to be counting on me and no one else. Other drivers would be watching me, and I didn't want to foul it up.

First, I got hugs from several children as they were dropped off. It was a pleasant surprise. That set the tone for my entire career and reminded me of the precious cargo we transported. Then a little girl screamed, "He got my umbrella!"

The boy shot past me in a flash, but I grabbed his backpack just before he was out of reach. As I lifted him up from the stairwell to my level, I realized I probably shouldn't manhandle the children, but it was too late, and he didn't mind. He had a mischievous smile.

"But that's my cousin."

"It doesn't matter if she's your cousin. Give it back."

She smiled like a younger sibling getting one up on an older one. Everyone left happy, and my first bus-driving experience came to a quick, successful end.

One morning several weeks later, I received a disturbing and almost unbelievable call from a parent.

"I'm coming up there. Your driver is not going to cuss me and get away with it."

"Ma'am, I'm sure there has been a misunderstanding. She's been driving for years and nothing like that has ever happened."

"I was just trying to talk with her, and she cussed me and slammed the bus door in my face."

I was confident there must have been a misunderstanding. Miss Linnie was always smiling and quick with a big bear hug and kind words for everyone but her husband. She had her own little comedy routine roasting him which kept us all laughing. Miss Linnie was a big woman, elderly, experienced, and especially lovable.

The parent was an unknown. How mad was she? She sounded unstable. Would she be violent? Would she bring a gun? A quick phone call to get some details before the parent arrived might help.

"Miss Linnie, this is S-Six. We just got a call from a parent who says you cussed her at the bus stop."

"I might have. She said she was going to kick my fat, black ass. So then I might have told her I'd kick her skinny little white ass."

"Okay, I get the picture. I'll talk to the parent first. You and I can talk later."

The issue was resolved to everyone's satisfaction. Not all are. Few that rise to that level of tension are settled so quickly and completely.

Morning routes usually had less disciplinary issues than afternoon routes, although it was not unusual to be called out to a morning bus wreck or other incident. Usually, it was little more than a bumped mailbox. Other times it was much more.

A typical start to a Friday included fresh coffee and the slow trickle of employees arriving at the bus shop between 5:30 a.m. and 6:00 a.m. Bus radio chatter was low and the shortened fall days started with the familiar and lingering darkness from the night before. Driver routines were in full swing. Students were beginning to board the first few dozen or so buses, while hundreds of other bus drivers were preparing to leave their bus lots. The usual predawn quiet was interrupted by an urgent, trembling call from a driver in distress.

"Bus Three Eighty-six to shop. One of my students was just hit by a truck while crossing the road."

As I made a break for my truck, I could hear the dispatcher behind me getting additional details.

"He seems to be unresponsive on the side of the road."

That transmission made all our hearts sink.

Within a few minutes, I arrived at a scene with a small crowd building in the darkness and numerous vehicles of passersby parked on the shoulder with their flashers blinking. Stepping out of my truck, all my fears were realized. The shrill scream in my ears reminded me of the same scream I have heard repeated on local news broadcasts when a mother realizes she's lost a child.

A few more steps and I was relieved to find it was not the mother but the sound of the young student writhing in pain. The adults leaning over him were trying to keep him still and calm. The screaming, strong breathing, and only a little bleeding were very encouraging signs. But fears of internal wounds, head trauma, and spinal injury allowed only cautious optimism as we longed for the paramedics to arrive.

There was no need for me to stand over them, and more folks were arriving, so I went to the bus. The driver was visibly shaken, and most of about a dozen middle school and high school students onboard were crying. I tried to reassure them that their friend was conscious and getting the help he needed. Most had already called their parents, who were on their way to the scene as the sun began to rise.

The bus driver, students, and witnesses in other vehicles explained that the driver of the truck ran the bus stop sign. It was also reported that another vehicle also ran the stop sign immediately before the one that hit the student. It is the most dangerous time on any bus route and something that bus drivers across the country experience all too often.

I provided a very brief update on the bus radio channel that the student was conscious and would be transported soon. Drivers and students across the county had been quietly and earnestly listening for that bit of good news. We watched prayerfully as emergency responders prepped our student for the Life Flight helicopter.

Stress and relief expanded and contracted like an accordion that day. Continued good news followed: broken bones but no major internal injuries. Full recovery expected. Charges filed against the driver of the truck. Back to work.

We try to maintain an uneventful routine. Funny stories, minor discipline issues, changing weather, and a few old memories keep us from getting too tense or too complacent.

There is an unspoken awareness that it could only take a second for a school bus driver to be back in a life-or-death scenario. Maybe that's why some of the lesser craziness and even complaints that break our routine are appreciated for their entertainment value.

One parent called to request that we adjust a certain bus route and stop time to match the first commercial break of the Pokemon cartoon.

"You see," she explained. "Johnny begins to eat his cereal and watch Pokemon every morning. At the first commercial break, he'll get up to brush his teeth. Then, while he's not looking, I turn the TV off. Then Johnny isn't distracted by the Pokemons, and he'll walk to the bus stop without incident. If the driver comes any earlier or later, it disrupts that routine."

"I'm sorry, ma'am. We simply can't run our bus schedule around *The Pokemon Show*."

Another morning I rode with some disruptive students. I sat beside the student giving the driver the most lip. Seats were already limited, but I made sure to not allow the student any extra room to move. He pushed and shoved a little, but I pretended not to notice. The he stood up and threatened to hit me. I barely reacted and suggested that he sit down. He reluctantly did but continued to mouth and threaten me under his breath for the next 20 minutes. When we arrived at the school, I released him to his principal. Student witnesses told the principal that others had also threatened to use their baseball bats on me if a fight had broken out.

Radio calls to assist drivers were all too frequent. Student behavior—like that of the rest of society—was degenerating. Even "good kids" were less respectful—like the times they would see my name on my shirt. I never liked children calling adults by their first name without at least a respectful prefix such as "Mr. John."

Combine that personal quirk with a twisted Marine Corps sense of humor and I almost got myself into trouble with a fifth-grade boy in the afternoon lineup.

"Hey, John."

"How do you know I didn't kill John and take his shirt?"

Oops! Thankfully, the kids on that bus could take a joke. I did call the shop out of an abundance of caution to have them be ready for a possible parent phone call. None followed.

Another time the Marine in me came out in an afternoon lineup at another elementary school. As I boarded the bus, several students began to squirm and squeal. A spider was crawling on the ceiling. I calmly walked over and smashed it loudly on the metal roof with my hand. As everyone jumped, I felt the remains of the spider fall invisibly down my arm. So instinctively, I pulled my hand from the ceiling and acted like I ate the spider, then showed them my empty hand.

"Mmmm, tasty."

"Eww!"

"That man ate that spider!"

"Hey, did you really eat that spider?"

"Gross."

"Eww!"

"Okay, y'all calm down. There's no more spider."

Elementary buses were my favorite. If we had to wait for some reason, I would sometimes have them all get off the bus and do push-ups together for fun. The only problem was that each time I would return to one of those buses, they would remember that experience and want to do it again.

High school buses were much different, and sometimes, serious issues arose. For a time we could count on police to help. Once, while responding to a request for help, I arrived to find a very loud, disruptive, and insubordinate group of students. The driver simply stood at the door, hoping for some assistance. As I boarded the bus, it was immediately obvious they didn't care I was there. They simply did not respect any authority.

"Everyone back in their seats. Be quiet and listen. Put your phones away."

A young sophomore student within reach kept texting in defiance. I snatched the phone and put it in my pocket. He immediately jumped to his feet and got in my face, his arms cocked as if he was going to assault me.

"You don't know who you messin' with, fool!"

"No, I don't think you know who *you're* messing with, and you better find your seat."

His older brother came running to his side, also a little belligerent although somewhat less threatening. After he and I made meaningful eye contact, he began to hold the younger brother and try to help de-escalate the situation. It didn't happen quickly, and others were still trying to stir things up. In moments such as this, I felt a special calm, as if I enjoyed it a little too much.

"You won't be finishing your ride on my bus. Bus shop, do we have the police in route?"

"Yes, we do."

"Ten-Four." Turning to the student, I said, "You'll be getting another ride home today when the police get here."

Court rulings had already limited our disciplinary authority, and subsequent rulings limited our ability to get future help from law enforcement. The new interpretation from our youth court judges nearly required someone to be bleeding or personally threaten an arriving police officer for students to be taken into custody. We had to get more creative as the students saw and felt our authority shrink.

Special-needs transportation brought more challenges. Sixty special-needs buses dealt with a range of situations from transporting a 12-pound three-year-old to a 90-pound four-year-old in the same year. People often envisioned us simply taking mildly autistic students on field trips to the zoo. We did that, too. But we transported gifted students in wheelchairs along with emotionally disturbed students prone to violent outbursts. Each had an Individual Education Plan (IEP). Those IEPs were often incomplete and didn't necessarily mesh with the other individuals on the bus. One student may need quiet and soft-spoken discipline, while another on the same bus may require louder, more forceful direction to get or expect compliance. Combinations were endless. One may calm down with a soft touch, like a hand resting on their shoulder, while others would go ballistic if you touched them in any way.

One afternoon I arrived at a bus where a 12-year-old special-needs girl was having an emotional meltdown. The driver had pulled over and a police officer had stopped to offer help. Nothing on the usual list of "things that work" with her was doing any good.

"So how far away is her home?"

"Just a few miles."

"I'll leave my truck here and ride with you. You can bring me back after we get her home."

"How are you going to get her under control?"

"I'll ride in the seat with her so the bus aide can deal with the rest of the students. You just focus on getting us there. It's only a few miles."

"Good luck."

It was a physical effort to keep her from hurting herself and others. I tried to remember all the acceptable ways to hold her and protect her and protect myself. Eventually, she contorted herself to get enough leverage to kick me onto the floor of the bus. As I recovered I made eye contact with the driver in her mirror and motioned her to keep driving. We eventually made it.

Video of that would have garnered a lot of laughs back at the bus shop. Cameras on buses have given us all some laughs, cost some drivers their jobs, and saved some drivers their jobs. Videos have proven students were telling the truth and, sometimes, showed students were lying. Other times, some knucklehead standing in front of the camera would block any hope of getting events properly recorded. Too often, technology would let us down and no recording was available. When that happened, you can bet parents were screaming that we were intentionally hiding something. To my knowledge we never did. Some days were crazier than others—with and without video.

"Bus Shop, this is bus number one eighty-seven. I've been hit by a parent vehicle that was trying to flag me down."

"Ten-Four. Is anyone hurt?"

"No injuries on the bus or in the car, but there is damage to both vehicles."

"We have some help on the way."

"Bus Shop, this bus number three sixty-three. I'm turning this bus around and going back to the school."

"Wait, Bus Three Sixty-three. Can you just get them home and write them up?"

"No. I'm heading to the school."

"If you can't drive them home safely, how can you drive back to the school safely?"

"Never mind. The parents have surrounded the bus. I can't move. Can you call the police?"

"Ten-Four. We have some help on the way."

"Mr. Caldwell, we have a parent on the line, claiming that her son and a couple of other boys were sexually assaulted on Bus Forty-nine."

"I better take that call." (Pause.) "Yes, ma'am. We'll get right on it." (Pause.) "Shop to Bus Forty-nine. Did you have anything happen on your bus this afternoon?"

"No."

"We'll need you to call the shop when you get parked. I'll get a fleet manager to pull the video on the bus."

"Ten-Four."

The bus wreck was resolved simply. The police call to help with irate parents also resolved itself quickly and without incident. We had to wait on the video and the driver to investigate the sexual assault allegations. The video was retrieved as the crazy afternoon came to a close.

Early the next morning, the mothers of the three boys claiming they were assaulted were at the bus shop, demanding answers. We had been focused on the morning routes, so we didn't have any answers yet.

They were invited into my office to share their concerns, but I did not expect the ugliness of their demeanor. All three leaned forward and practically beat on my desk.

"We are here to see that video."

"There are other students involved and privacy issues, so that may or may not happen, but first, I'll watch it. I haven't had a chance yet."

"You would be more concerned if this was three girls being sexually assaulted by boys."

"I can assure you that we're taking this just as seriously. Yesterday, we had multiple events happening at the same time, and your children's driver wasn't aware of anything out of the ordinary and no one told of anything like what you are accusing."

"Well, our boys couldn't just walk up and tell her in front of the other students."

"Hopefully, we'll get a good video that we can share with you."

"We'll just get a lawyer—"

"That should do it here."

"We're not done."

"Yes, we are. If you're getting a lawyer, just have yours call ours."

I showed them the door and quickly got ready to view the video. It easily showed that the boys were not telling the truth. I've never been more ready to let parents see a video. I called the principal and told him the video was heading his way to show the parents.

Surprisingly, one of the moms marched her son into my office that week with a verbal and written apology and an apology of her own for her comments and actions. The other two parents did not.

Another parent similarly saw that her daughter had lied about an incident. She was in tears and very distraught. "I can't believe she lied to me!"

"I'm not trying to excuse her, but she is a teenager. It likely won't be the last time that she's less than completely truthful with you."

Lastly, we had parents in denial. Once, a father saw the video then held up his hand to block what he was seeing and stated his denial out loud. "I choose to believe my daughter."

"Well, then, we're wasting my time and yours. Have a nice day."

The bus stories are never-ending. Parents, students, bus drivers, and more kept us from getting bored. Just when I thought I had an extreme tale to tell when I got home, Lee would trump my story with one of her own from the high school where she worked. After she changed to a job at the district office, sometimes, I could win our in-home storytelling competition.

•••

With Operation African Lion and another school year in our rearview mirror, it was time to shift our focus to Lee's campaign. We knew the district well, politically and personally. Winning without a run-off would be a high bar to reach, but with the right strategy we could do it. All her opponents campaigned for a second-place finish in hopes of overtaking her in a low-turn-out run-off scenario. Sixteen years earlier, people were shocked when I won as a Republican. Now, Democrats seemed to have no chance. Lee campaigned for the win: 50%+1 vote. She and we continued the push until the last vote was cast in November, and our strategy and determination paid off.

As we gathered at the courthouse for the official votes, we were already adding up the tallies posted at each precinct. Her victory was our victory. Family, friends, and supporters celebrated. We prepared for the general election, which was expected to be a slam dunk.

It somehow seemed much nicer to have her in office instead of me. I knew the challenges and headaches that came with the modest salary. It seemed to signal an end to my own political career, and that was fine with me.

14 years on the civilian side of things was loving and leading school transportation

*"Be warned, my son, of anything in addition to
them. Of making many books there is no end,
and much study wearies the body. Let us hear the
conclusion of the whole matter: Fear God and
keep his commandments: for this is the whole
duty of man."*

Ecclesiastes 12:12-13

...14
Conflicts of Conclusion

S aying goodbye to the Marine Corps was more difficult than I thought
it would be. More weekends would be free to enjoy rather than work.
Summers could include a real vacation instead of weeks of active duty. No
expectations of a presidential recall for a fourth time. Working just one job for
the first time in more than three decades ...

The decision to leave had been made years earlier when I opted for an
MBA degree instead of completing the War College requirement. An already
unlikely promotion to brigadier general would not be possible without it.

Awkward departures for retiring reservists were the norm. Unlike active
duty retirements, full of pomp and circumstance, reservists tended to fade
away inconspicuously.

"Where's Bob?"

"He had to work his civilian job this weekend."

"But I thought this was his last drill, and we were at least taking him out on
the town to celebrate."

"That's a pretty pitiful way to end a career. We need to do better."

It happened often.

Lee and I planned our retirement celebration at home with family and the
friends who had supported me for my entire life. It was a nice ceremony with
Marine Corps JROTC youth in dress blues and old friends from the Marine

Corps League in their uniforms with scarlet and gold covers adding just the right atmosphere in our church gymnasium.

When it came time to make my prepared retirement remarks, emotions took over. Public speaking was not usually difficult, although sometimes, it was more awkward than other times.

This one was different. Was it the keen awareness of the gravity of the day? Was it survivor's guilt? Maybe it was family present or family gone like Daddy. I'll never know exactly, but the emotions I seemed to have been holding back were destined for release. I basically cried through it as I uttered these words with the utmost sincerity:

"I am wrestling with pride and humility as well as joy and sorrow, even a bit of anxiety and peace as I try to close this occasion with some personal reflection. The cake says my journey began in 1981 when I enlisted. Actually, it began growing up the son of a Marine. Even before I considered putting on the uniform, I had heard of places like Boot Camp, San Diego, Camp Pendleton, Iwo Jima, Saipan, and Tinian from my daddy's own time in the Corps. I also witnessed core values of honor, courage, and commitment before they were ever printed on any recruiting poster. When the time came for me to enlist, there were no other service options to cross my mind. I would be a Marine.

"There are hosts of others I need to thank personally and on behalf of Marines and Marine families everywhere:

"To my employers:

"Outside of about five years of self-employment and my four years of active duty, just two employers have shared this experience with me. They are both here today. During the first activation of U.S. Marine reservists in fifty years, I was working for James Delgadillo. He and his wife, Miller, took me in as much as family as an employee. We had several good years, and I will always remember our time together with a smile. I was self-employed and a county supervisor during my second activation.

"During my last activation, I was working for Milton Kuykendall, again a great relationship and awesome support. There are those, including friends of mine, who didn't enjoy employer support and even lost their jobs, despite laws meant to protect them. I am forever grateful and happily indebted to the two of you.

"To the Marines:

"Marines beside me of all ranks propped me up and carried me through good times and bad. They did what this country asks of them and more, and they did it with a twisted sense of humor sometimes only a fellow Marine can understand.

"To all fellow veterans:

"It is with great pride that I join the ranks of those who once served but now may only wear a uniform on special occasions. Whether it was in the Army, Navy, Air Force, Marines, or Coast Guard, during war or peace, a few years, ten, twenty, or thirty, your service paved the way for better times and a better road ahead for those like me.

"To family and friends:

"Thanks for your support and understanding for the missed weddings and funerals, baptisms and birthdays. Thanks for your support of me and my Marines, even when you didn't understand or agree with us.

"Your care packages arrived at all the right times with all the right things—even when a birthday cake arrived carefully wrapped but sufficiently moldy, it served its true purpose. I'll never be able to thank everyone enough.

"To my momma:

"Thanks for supporting me even after first openly opposing my decision to become a Marine.

"To our children:

"Your mom and I and your country have asked the most of you and you delivered—not just the three deployments of your dad in a combat zone with your mom stressing on you at home, but your entire lives spent asking, 'Where's Daddy?'

"Let me publicly apologize here for missing recitals, ball games, inductions, awards nights, and seeing your own achievements take a back seat to Marines you never met. Let me apologize also for flying across the country or even across the globe and forgetting to tell you that I was leaving town again for a few days or a few weeks. I really did think of you more often than I told you, and your attempts to make me feel guilty were more than successful, although I tried not to show it.

"*Yet* . . . There are things I won't apologize for:

"I won't apologize for your life as a child that prepared you to be the responsible adult you have become—a life that gave you a global perspective but not a PC 'world view' or the life that developed the heart and social conscience, inner strength, and ability in you to change this world for the better. Lord knows it needs you now more than ever.

"I won't apologize for the pride in my heart when my son or daughter shakes the hand of another adult, looks them in the eye, and calls them 'Sir' or 'Ma'am.' Your mom and I are proud of you. You have served your country well, and I am looking forward to serving alongside you in years to come.

"To my wife:

"I know. I know. I've said it too many times to too many people—'Sorry doesn't cut it.' But I am sorry.

"I have always been sorry when I dumped all the home front responsibilities on you without seeming to look back. Trust me, I did look back, and what I saw can't be explained to the casual observer.

"You watched the dog die in your arms while I was playing Marine.

"Lawn mowers, cars, washing machines, and just about anything mechanical broke while I was playing Marine.

"You were the family veterinarian force feeding, medicating, bathing, vaccinating, grooming, and comforting family pets of all sorts while I was playing Marine.

"You were the lone family physician when fevers rose, and Band-Aids, splints, and wraps were needed while I was playing Marine.

"You were alone when the kids spent the night with friends and too many times the lone parent dealing with nurses, doctors, pharmacists, insurance companies, banks, loans, checkbooks, debts, homework, and more—all while I was playing Marine.

"Other military wives were watching you and were trying to capture just a small portion of the grace and class and strength that you show as effortless and beautiful in times of crisis and challenge. They knew you were there for them, so they called. They called early. They called late and they called often. You comforted them. Some may never call again, but they'll never forget they had a friend when they needed one.

"Especially during Desert Storm, when there was no email to keep us connected, no phone access for months, and the relentless CNN reports bombarding our families, you kept it together. Through all the scuttlebutt, bad news, good news, phone trees, and pressure, you were true to yourself and to others. I saw you from across the room and across the globe. You didn't require medals and you didn't get them. You simply embodied the Marine Corps motto, 'Always Faithful.' I was and I am still amazed by you. Your belief in me shaped any success I've enjoyed the last three decades. If in fact love is a decision, then you, Lee, are the best decision I've ever made.

"I'm humbled by the opportunity to wear the uniform of our country for thirty-two years. And the Marine Corps owes me nothing, while I owe the Marine Corps very much. I will never be able to repay it, nor will I ever be able to repay those of you who have made my military career possible and shared it with me in so many ways.

"I am a better husband, a better father, a better brother, a better son, a better friend, a better neighbor, a better American for having become a United States Marine. I'm excited about the next chapter of our lives—although, if you don't mind, the next thirty-two don't need to be quite as action packed as the last thirty-two."

Hopefully, my words and maybe even some borrowed phraseology were heard with the genuine gratitude I felt. It was a better way to end a career than quietly being deleted from a reserve unit roster.

Viewing the world through such a unique prism didn't change just because retirement paperwork arrived in the mail. Thankfully, the lifelong friendships and connections with veterans I meet along life's highway tend to be a mental and emotional support group for me. That's especially important in a world, country, and community that become further estranged from our way of thinking.

• • •

Nearly four years after retiring from the Marines, the thoughts of retiring from school transportation began to surface. The state minimum 25-year retirement threshold was met with nearly 14 at the schools added to 8 as a county supervisor and 4 years' military credit. Restlessness set in like an infection. Retirement was in greater focus than the next school year.

Calculating advantages and disadvantages of a 26-year retirement verses 28 years or more was on my mind more often. As my internal motivation shifted from countless inspirational challenges in the bus world to something as mundane as financial incentives, I knew it was about time to leave. I had never been motivated by money, and our bank accounts showed it.

Maybe I just needed to recharge. I didn't have the Marine Corps anymore to provide a mental and physical separation from the daily grind of school transportation operations. There was a NAPT (National Association of Pupil Transportation) conference in Dallas. That should be just enough of a break to get me refocused . . . or maybe not.

That didn't seem to do any good, but spring break was soon to follow. A week off should get me motivated to wrap up another great school year and gear up for the next. It didn't and I wasn't. It's been said, "When it is time to go, you'll know." I knew.

I sought advice from several life mentors, family, and friends about retiring. The advice was wide ranging but helpful in formulating my thoughts and solidifying such a difficult decision. After all, I was in a job that I enjoyed with a work family I loved. If I were the sort of person who could just go through the motions and draw a paycheck, I would have stayed. My sense of purpose and level of motivation was simply not acceptable for the responsibilities of the position. Regrettably, it didn't appear to be coming back. Few if anybody would have noticed, except the one that mattered—*me*.

Fourteen years may not seem like a long time for some, but it was the longest stretch in one position that I had ever had, and it was a doozy. Even 32 years with the Marines involved several promotions and shifting from billet to billet. Maybe that "up or out" Marine Corps mindset was leading me to make a move. Whatever it was, it won the day, and I informed my boss. Walking away meant stepping out of my comfort zone—again.

This retirement reminded me of moving away from family and friends. Unlike the Marine reserves that almost weened me from the reserve routine prior to retirement, this would be a hard break. Practically what was a 12-hour-per-day routine would end abruptly, and I would not have a job and would not be looking for one. It was a great and awkward feeling!

Six Saturdays and a Sunday comprised my new weekly schedule. I slept late—until about 7 a.m.—in my new routine. Tan lines were gone where I once wore a watch. Some "Honey-Dos" were getting done but not as many as expected. Thankfully, I was no longer pressed for time.

Expecting some emotional withdrawals and even some unwanted phone calls when school started in August, Lee and I made plans to be out of touch on an eight-day excursion to the Black Hills of South Dakota when school buses began to roll. Looking back, it was our first full week on a vacation trip in 20 years. We also recalled one four-day trip 10 years earlier. That's not saying we didn't have days off, working vacations, or long weekends along the way. We did. Formal vacation trips just never seemed to materialize. We had chosen to spend potential vacation money on our "stay-cations" at home with horses, bikes, a pool, and a hot tub.

Feeling like college students on a road trip, the retirement trip took us to visit friends in Iowa and Nebraska on our way to the Badlands, Crazy Horse, Mount Rushmore, and other typical tourist stops. We saw more friends in Colorado, along with a trip to Pike's Peak. Then we travelled to Indian pueblos, and the Rio Grande Gorge in New Mexico. Those were followed by the Cadillac Ranch in Texas, Cherokee Nation Museum in Oklahoma, and more friends in Arkansas. The eight-day whirlwind couldn't have been better, but vacationing for the rest of my life was never the plan. With no work conflicts, I was free for breakfast, lunch, dinner, and everything in between.

Breakfast at a local monthly gathering provided for plenty of home-grown, state and national political discussions. Prayer was at 7 a.m. and food sponsored at the offices and kitchen of B&P Enterprises was always ready. Scrambled eggs, grits, hot biscuits and gravy, the best bacon, sausage patties, smoked sausage, and on occasion, salmon patties were served with coffee and orange juice and plenty of conversation. Usually, a couple dozen men and a lady or two or three would attend. During election cycles, the crowd would double.

Four months into retirement and a half-hearted job search, Josh Prewett, who ran day-to-day operations, was joining our conversation at his father's breakfast table.

"So, you're retired?"

"Yes, I've been retired a few months?"

"Are you ready to go back to work?"

"I'm looking, but not very hard at the moment."

"We're needing help with our fleet if you're interested."

"Sure. I'm definitely interested."

"Great. Call me later today, and we'll talk more about it."

After some of the usual interview questions and employment discussions, we thought this would work well for all of us.

It was Monday through Saturday to start, as well as some Sundays, starting before sunrise again. I knew my learning curve would require some extra effort, so I didn't balk at the hours. Adjusting to the world of heavy trucks and heavy equipment maintenance was the easy part but still different than school buses or tactical military vehicles and equipment with which I was most familiar.

This fleet was in support of railroad operations and, more specifically, train derailment response and emergency track repairs. The railroad world was especially unique and fed my desire to broaden my horizons and learn new things.

Constant cursing and rough, politically incorrect conversations were much different than working around schools and school-aged children with all the rules and sensitivities. This new world was much more reminiscent of my days in the Marine Corps, except that Marines had a more prevalent moral compass.

Train derailments were more common than I ever dreamed. Reaction to a derailment call was swift and furious. Neither time of day, weather, location, circumstances, conflicts, challenges nor any other excuses mattered. It was the business. Any call warranted a full response and mobilization comparable to a complex military operation. My participation in the derailments was limited but eye-opening.

Between derailments the company serviced any and all calls from railroad companies: requests for rail maintenance, clean up, water, snow blowers, equipment shuttles, rail yard shuttles, storage, special deliveries, etc. There was simply no request too large or too small.

Formulating a detailed plan to support such an effort was necessary for making some short- and long-term maintenance improvements. Daily effort was required to put the right pieces in place.

Good things were happening and progress was being made. Plenty of light was at the end of my new tunnel. All aspects of life and work were good. Then things changed dramatically.

In short, it was a family business with extreme family frictions. I knew them well and thought I could navigate it. Then the day came when the father placed another one of his son's to oversee one of my critical functions.

"Okay, Bruce, so who do I work for now? Josh or Kendall?"

"Both."

"Yes, sir."

Working for two brothers who can't stay in the same room with each other seemed more than precarious. Realizing that position was completely untenable was the simple part. What to do about it was more complicated. I didn't want to just walk away.

Lunch that day was already scheduled with three brothers who did work well together in a different family business in South Mississippi. I knew them from my years in school transportation. The timing was impeccable.

"Hey, John, we're going to expand our statewide operations from our place in Laurel and open a facility in North Mississippi."

"That sounds exciting. I know you've been looking into that for a long time."

"Yes, we have. More importantly, we need someone to manage it, and we think you would be perfect."

"Funny that we're meeting today. If you had been here last week, I'd have turned you down. Today, things changed, so I'll definitely think about it."

A few more phone calls . . . a few more meetings . . . a few more incidents at work reassured me that a move was in order. The opportunity at Burroughs Diesel would be akin to opening a new business. Parts and service and vehicle sales in a huge territory would require a massive commitment from the company and from me.

Competition in North Mississippi is already fierce, and rivals would not sit idly by to let us horn in on their business.

Six months of groundwork began making a difference. The customers and potential customers were excited, but they wanted to see our level of commitment. Our company leadership could not or would not settle on a location from which to operate.

Delays followed more delays and indecision. Promises, locations, and dates came and went to the point of absurdity. It began to erode our credibility with customers, suppliers, and potential employees. Everyone was expecting our home office to punt and told us as much.

Meanwhile, my father-in-law was scheduled for multiple heart bypasses while daily work routines continued. Surgery was scheduled at a hospital in the Ozarks, so I stepped away from work for a couple of days. I kept my boss informed, as would be expected. Surprisingly, I got a call on the day of the surgery. It was not a call of concern.

"Hello, John. I need you to be here for a meeting tomorrow."

"My father-in-law isn't out of surgery yet. It'll be difficult, but if all stays well here, I should be able to make it."

"We really need for you and Rodger to be here in the morning."

"Okay, I'll call him."

It would be hours before Pappy would clear recovery with good news. Anxiety was high because my own father's heart bypass surgery had been followed by four months of intensive care and permanent issues that changed our lives forever. We remained optimistic and everything went well, with only four rather than the expected five bypasses. Other serious complications arose but were handled skillfully during surgery.

I made a five-hour solo drive home that evening. I was counting on Rodger driving the next morning for our seven-hour round trip to our meeting in Laurel. Then I'd have to drive another five hours back to family and the hospital.

I knew this would be a serious meeting. Either we'd receive an ultimatum with a hard timeline or a termination. I called the boss as Rodger and I drove to our meeting.

"Good morning, Michael. So what's this meeting all about?"

"We'll discuss it when you get here."

"It would help if you could just tell us."

"Is Rodger with you?"

"Yes. He's driving."

"I need you to turn around and bring both vehicles."

"Now I really think you need to tell us what's up."

"I'm not going to talk to you about it over the phone. I need to take my child to school. We can talk when you get here."

As that phone conversation ended, my conversation with Rodger was more direct.

"Well, that adds another hour. I don't plan on driving eight hours to get fired. I'm going back to my wife and Pappy. You can drive down there if you want."

"Did he say we were fired?"

"No. He didn't have to."

"You can drive down and be paid for another day's work if you want. I'm not sure if they'll drive us back, fly us, or tell us to get our own ride."

"I'm not going if you're not going."

"Look, I could be wrong."

"No, you're right."

"Well, you do what you want. I'm calling Greg."

We turned the truck around.

"Hello?"

"Greg, do you want to tell us what's going on?"

"What are you talking about?"

"Michael called yesterday about an important meeting happening today. I called him this morning to see what it was all about, and he told us to bring both trucks. It doesn't take a rocket scientist to figure this out. I wish he would just shoot straight."

"Let me call and find out. I honestly have no idea what you're talking about."

"Thanks, Greg."

It was obvious. It was the last day of the pay period. I had fired or laid off lots of people and I know the drill. I also know that it can come at inconvenient times. I probably fired people on their anniversary or child's birthday, and I know I've had to fire them when their own surgeries were pending. It's ugly, but I always tried to be straight forward and honest with them. In a case like this, I would have at least sent someone to pick up our trucks rather than put me on an 18-hour ordeal while my father-in-law was in recovery and my wife was still sleeping in the critical care waiting room.

"Hey, John, this is Greg. You're right. We're going to shut down our expansion efforts in North Mississippi. Our Western Star dealership application was denied. I had no idea this decision was made."

"Look, I get it. We could see the writing on the wall. Michael should have just told me, but I'm not driving all day with my father-in-law fresh out of heart surgery just to get fired. Someone will have to come get these trucks."

"I hate that it had to happen this way."

"Okay, Greg, I appreciate your candor. I'll tell Rodger. Thanks for the opportunity. I hate that it didn't work out for everyone. I'm heading back to

Arkansas. We can talk later. 'Bye."

"Well, Rodger, I guess that's that."

"I'll only be taking family calls for the rest of the day. If anyone calls from Burroughs or one of their customers, you can pass that along."

Returning to the ranks of the retired would suit me fine. Our bills were being paid. Pappy came home with us for his recovery, and I had more time to enjoy with him. While recovering from heart surgery, he fell at our house and broke his wrist and kneecap. Recovery took a little longer.

Thanksgiving and Christmas were around the corner. The job search was put on hold indefinitely, at least beyond New Year's.

A year and a half and two jobs after my initial retirement, I was facing a year of uncertainty. Was I really going to chill or not?

• • •

January meant that Lee would file for re-election. Our hope for her, as with any incumbent facing an election year, was to arrive at the filing deadline unopposed. She and we would not be so fortunate this time.

Not only did she get opposition, but it was also someone we knew well from a former family of supporters. It was one of the brothers in the family I had worked for briefly in the derailment-response business. Thankfully, his record in life was mostly a train wreck. Regrettably and predictably, he adopted a campaign strategy to match.

We knew he could and would spend lots of money—his daddy's money. We also knew him well enough to expect the darker side of politics. Our confidence that Lee would win anyway was high, but we dreaded the inevitable ugliness ahead. Family friendships would be strained.

Lee's support was already strong, but it was galvanized early when the opposition's name surfaced. Many who knew him were lining up to help Lee beat him. His reputation preceded him, and it wasn't good.

Another shift on the political landscape occurred when the Northern District transportation commissioner announced that he would not seek re-election. At the time, the announcement was a simple surprise yet insignificant. Several friends called to see if I was interested in another shot at it.

"John, Mike announced that he's not running for re-election. You'd have a good chance if you're up for it."

"No, thanks. Lee has opposition already and we'll be focused on her campaign."

"Let me know for sure. I'll support you if you're running, but if you're not I'm committing to someone else."

"Thanks, but no. I can't even think about two campaigns in one house."

Weeks passed and more calls came and went with nearly the same exchange. Now it was late in the filing process and the field was filling up with candidates. Potential supporters were committing to the others.

"John, several of us are not comfortable with our options for commissioner and want to know if you're interested?"

"No. I've been pretty clear."

"Well, could you at least quit saying no for now and give it some more thought?"

"Okay. I do appreciate the interest and the encouragement. Out of respect for those of you who have called, I'll stop saying no and I'll think about it."

"That's fair enough. Thank you."

More weeks passed. We held a fundraiser for Lee and raised nearly enough in one night to fully fund her campaign, based on our plan for her.

Others began hearing that I was considering a run. Calls continued, but I was still very reluctant. Most of the encouragement from others was very localized. The district encompassed 33 counties, and I wasn't reaching out at all. The field was full—already, there were three other credible candidates. A fourth and fifth would virtually clinch that nobody would reach the 50% threshold required in the primary to avoid a run-off.

I've been here before when I ran in the 2011 special election with a large field. Getting to the run-off is good, but losing in a run-off hurts. I've always believed if you're going to compete, you better be able to take a loss like a man. I was not sure I could do that this time.

"Hey, John, the roadbuilders could be with you. A growing number of them don't like their options."

"Well, lots of them will support the process over a single political candidate and will put money on more than one of us. That's not what I call support. They'll need to put serious money down for me to get in the race."

"Without you filing to run, it's hard for *them* to commit."

"Well, without money it's hard for *me* to commit. I guess we're in a Mexican standoff, so I'm probably out."

"Don't decide yet."

"Okay, but it's looking less likely every day."

Lee and I took a quick trip to Florida to visit grandchildren—and their parents. This would be a relaxing and energizing trip to get us prepared for a long summer of campaigning for Lee. If I also ran, it would be the two of us full tilt until August and beyond.

With one Republican challenger and no Democrats or Independents, Lee's race would be over the first Tuesday in August. I, on the other hand, would likely go to a primary run-off three weeks later. If I secured the Republican nomination, we would campaign several more months, through the general election in November. That's a heavy commitment.

Every time I ran that logic train through my head, I decided not to do it. Then I asked myself if I wanted to make a difference or not. I asked myself if I could fully enjoy retirement if Lee was still working.

Running for office returned as an option. Then the actual challenge of getting into the race late, competing, and being able to win entered the equation. Maybe it was a little too late. Maybe it would simply be too much for too little.

I looked at the pay scale to decide on whether I could stay in the retirement system and draw partial pay or I had to get out and draw the statutory salary. I didn't get the calculator out, but I knew that with either option I would net little or nothing, with a paycheck of some lesser amount replacing the larger retirement check. It would be a real act of public service rather than personal financial gain. But first, I'd have to win, and I hadn't yet decided to run.

While driving Lee to Jackson for county business, the discussion of the commissioner's race heated up. Our county administrator, Vanessa Lynchard, and Lee were unapologetically pushing me to file to run for commissioner. I had arranged to meet the executive director of the Mississippi Road Builders Association, Mike Pepper, at the Waffle House near the capitol. Lee and Vanessa had business there.

When Mike and I met, he shed some light on the industry but little on the political landscape. As we discussed roadbuilding successes and challenges across the state, I could see the need for change, but I was unsure how I would fit into that scenario. Breakfast ended with the usual cordiality.

"Thanks for the breakfast. I enjoyed it, but I think you can count me out."

"Thank you. I enjoyed it as well."

A few minutes later, I picked up Lee and Vanessa near the south entrance of the capitol. For some reason their final push resonated. It prompted an old thought that rattles around in my head and rises at some of the strangest times: "No one will remember the round left in the chamber. Take aim and take your best shot."

We went straight to the bank and withdrew the $500 filing fee. Then we dropped by the Republican headquarters, only to find that the fee was $1,000. Back to the bank.

The Mexican standoff was over, and I lost. I would file with zero campaign money in hand and, now, $1,000 in the hole. I called Mike Pepper to correct what I had told him two hours earlier.

"Do you remember what I told you about not filing?"

"Yeah."

"Scratch that. I just filed to run. I'm all in."

"Well, okay. Best of luck."

"I'll need it."

Lee and Vanessa were super excited. We began the task of campaign planning on the drive home. I had to call the family. A decision of this sort involves them directly. None of our four children acted completely surprised, but there was a higher pitch in their voices as they wished me well. They knew what was coming. They had been there with us as young children, youths, and young adults. Now both of their parents were in simultaneous campaigns! It was not what they had in mind for their summer ahead.

Money did not come pouring into the coffers—and, frankly, wasn't expected. Support seemed a bit tepid, with a few notable exceptions in the asphalt-and-roadbuilding industry. Three of my competitors had a month or two head start in organization and fund raising, and another last-minute candidate entered after me. That made a total of five Republicans and one Democrat.

To say that I was the underdog was an understatement. There was no tactical advantage to entering the race late. I had previously passed on much-needed support in the early days. Many with an interest in the race had already committed to my opponents. Others saw the challenges I had ahead and counted me out in their minds. At least three of my opponents had raised more money and already had professional help and a plan. I had none of the above.

Political powerbrokers in and around the state capital were already choosing sides, and they weren't choosing mine. Some solace came in reminding myself that the politicos from the state capital were not located in or voting in the Northern District. Still, it's always better having someone for you than against you.

At least my home county was the largest Republican voting block of them all. Even within it, I contended with naysayers who supported the others for a myriad of reasons. The rest of the district was politically diverse and responded differently to politics and politicians. One consistency was that everyone thought their roads were the most important roads in the district.

Trying to size up the competition wasn't difficult. There was a geographic spread, an age spread, a measurable difference in finances, and a variety of political experience, including the campaign professionals involved. The top three others had hired campaign advisors I knew and would have gladly hired if I had entered the race early enough. I didn't raise enough early money to hire consultants anyway, but having experience with them and knowledge of their reputations, strengths, and weaknesses was helpful in formulating my own plan.

Retail politics would be my strength and is my favorite part of the process. It's getting on the road and meeting all sorts of people, making new friends, and seeing old ones. Fish fries and barbeques from local party events to volunteer fire department fundraisers and political speaking engagements were scattered across the 33 counties. Retail politics alone was not enough.

With all the campaigns for all the statewide, regional, and county races focused on the August primaries, there was plenty of places to go and many people to meet. Crossing paths with opposition and so many other candidates would sometimes make it hard to sort out the actual voters in a crowd. People of all shapes and sizes and crowds large and small . . . still, it was a somewhat lonely road.

A handful of key friends and supporters would drive for me to some of the events so I could text and make phone calls. A few made many trips. Several other friends made one or two trips just when I needed them most. I physically, mentally, and emotionally could not have done it without those friends driving and encouraging me. There were enough solo trips too. Sometimes, I left too early and returned too late to dare ask anyone else to drive.

One muggy Mississippi Saturday I crisscrossed the district with the usual sorts of events. The big one for the day was a quintessential, old-fashioned political event at the community of Black Hawk. A bluegrass band with a popular rendition of the locally inspired Carroll County Blues preceded the lineup of politicians. The high steeple reached to the sun on Black Hawk's historic white church just across the country road. The equally renowned and historic schoolhouse building was opened to serve food and provide some shady relief to those who were hungry or unable to bear the oppressive heat outside. The bulk of the crowd was outside, listening to the band and the banter of the politicians.

Sweating with several hundred locals is just part of the process. They appreciate the one-on-one interaction, especially judging the grip of a simple handshake and looking into the eyes of those of us asking for their vote. It was becoming painfully aware that I wasn't picking up any votes for the Republican primary. Nearly everyone was voting in the Democrat primary, which would determine all their county officeholders. Then it was time to speak.

"Hello, Carroll County! My name is John Caldwell, and I'm running for Northern District transportation commissioner. So how many of you are Republican?"

Only about six hands rose out of the hundreds in the crowd. I knew what the response would be before I asked, but I also knew the next answer.

"Well, how many of you support Donald Trump?"

They all smiled and cheered. It was just the response I was looking for, and it led to a friendly reminder and quick finish.

"Great, I get it. Most of you can't help me in the primary in August, but I'd sure appreciate your vote in November if I make it that far."

I bought a glass of iced tea and was back on the road, racking up miles on my suburban. Ultimately, I amassed 60,646 campaign miles over ten months. All the while, Lee was racking up her own miles.

BAM! The heavy tool truck hit squarely across the front left quarter panel of Lee's Explorer at about 45 miles per hour, spinning them around but unharmed. Lee had a friend driving her on an afternoon of campaigning so she could multitask in the passenger seat. The friend was unfamiliar with a two-way stop intersection and treated it like a four-way. Just another unplanned event to keep life interesting.

We were already trying to recover from water damage from a washing machine that had flooded our house as our campaigns were getting started. Water soaked into wood floors, cabinets, and walls in several rooms. The campaigns didn't allow us time to fully deal with it for months. Maybe the anxiety of two campaigns was a contributing factor.

Then we had a hailstorm hit us, and we had to get repairs done for that. Three insurance claims combined with two political campaigns compounded our stress. Maybe we should have had the roofer cut us an extra vent to release the stress from our house. We tried to keep our sense of humor through it all.

Eventually, just as we figured he would, Lee's political opponent went on the attack. The misleading and inaccurate mailers did not warrant much response. However, it was about to get uglier.

It took several strange phone calls and a few weird conversations to understand what we were being told. Arrests, accusations of wrongdoing, and claims of recordings came from people we had never met. Was it real? Were our phone calls being recorded? Who were they? What even happened? Information was choppy and out of sequence. The tawdry nature of the events left us uneasy.

Apparently, the unknown caller was arrested for taking down one of Lee's opponent's signs. There was some personal bad blood between the two men. Lee's opponent was believed to be sleeping with the ex-wife of the caller's friend. Already, too much drama for me. False claims of a witness seeing the caller steal a campaign sign from the roadside was somehow enough for the sheriff to make an arrest. A local judge set a suspiciously high bail of $5,000 for the caller, who admitting to pulling down the $30 sign. This was not sounding real, and why were we getting a call from this stranger?

It might have ended there, except the ex-wife contacted the caller with threats of additional legal action, other false charges—even felony charges—in courts with ostensibly bought-and-paid-for judges. These threats came with a demand. If the caller would just implicate Lee in his crime with false statements, they'd drop his charges and the pending litigation. Thankfully, there was a follow-up call, and the extortions were repeated. This time the call was recorded by the one being threatened. That ended their dream of having Lee wrongly arrested.

Not only was the caller honorable, but he was also motivated to publicize the entire fiasco and more on social media. It attracted immediate attention. Others who felt personally and professionally mistreated by Lee's opposition over the years used the caller's social media site to bash him. They posted excerpts of old arrests, ugly court records, and ongoing legal proceedings alleging multiple egregious civil rights violations against Lee's opponent. That Facebook firestorm spread to local television, too.

We watched curiously as numerous others joined the chorus of critics bashing Lee's opponent. If he had any delusions of winning, surely this would end them. No such luck. He arrogantly pushed ahead as if he were in a much different position. He continued attacking Lee on the radio, on social media, and with direct mail pieces week after week.

Thankfully, while her race was getting ugly, the commissioner's race was clean. It was also much more competitive. While any casual observer could see that Lee was well on her way to a likely victory, my race was hard to call.

The top four candidates had significantly different geographic bases of support. One had raised the most money and boasted of polling data putting him in first place. The rest of us didn't have enough campaign cash to conduct valid polling, so we were flying blind.

Our race was especially friendly, with only a few choice instances of one of us talking badly about another. In the world of politics, we could all be thankful. That neighborly competition allowed each of us to put our best foot forward.

The campaign trail was long and stressful. Early mornings alone or with a friend driving were combined with tiring, late finishes. Some days would appear to have been wasted. Others were more productive. Most were combinations of reassurance and discouragement.

I'd arrive home, thinking my day was done, only to hear of campaign issues from Lee's campaign that needed to be addressed before I got any shuteye. Conversely, she would hear of mine. We were burning the political and emotional candles at both ends.

Election night "round one" finally arrived. In DeSoto County the counts were done at the polling places and fed directly into the computer, providing quick results. Lee dispatched her opposition with an 80-20 rout.

I also did well in our home county, but votes were peeled away in four other candidate directions. Plus, the district included another 30-plus counties, many, like our opposition's home counties, in which we had no chance of winning. It would be much later before results could be tallied for me.

Friends from around the district were calling in results. Some good. Some not so good. The second-largest voting block went solidly for our opposition. The four-way split helped soften the blow.

We had tried to manage expectations in my race. I only needed to finish in the top two, and we emphasized that as election day approached. First or second meant a fresh start and a three-week hard sprint in a primary run-off.

Our lead opponent did not manage expectations. He had boasted that he would come in first and, possibly, win outright. Our strong first place finish surprised those who had bought into his claims. Whether those claims were just political posturing or misguided belief, his second-place finish hurt his momentum and helped ours.

We scrambled to raise enough money to finish and win. The first order of business was to tactfully approach the third- and fourth-place finishers for their support.

One had been a longtime friend and promised his support, but he was returning to a job that prohibited a formal endorsement. His assistance was still valuable and appreciated.

The other did not take or return my calls. He soon openly endorsed my opponent. It was somewhat of a surprise but not overly so. I had been around long enough to not take things like that for granted.

My fears were a repeat of my last run-off nine years earlier. In that race we finished in first, originally without a majority in the special election, but lost the run-off. That experience propelled me to work smarter this time. With Lee's race over, she and her team provided a much-needed boost of energy.

Our busy family had weighed-in off and on throughout our campaigns when they could. In the home stretch they all found more time to help us close the deal. That extra effort energized the campaign with real practical assistance. More importantly it gave me an emotional lift I needed!

Money to finish was trickling in, and I pushed to increase the flow. Some recommended taking out a campaign loan and work at paying it off later. I wasn't a fan of that approach, so we financed our effort as the contributions allowed. There's an old saying, "If you can't raise enough money to win, you probably won't." We raised what we could and took our best shot, finishing on election day with no debt.

As the primary run-off results rolled in, I knew quickly that our path to victory was solid. The right counties came in with the right margins. We won the most counties, although the popular vote was all that mattered. Both of us won our home counties handily, and if both of our home counties were taken out of the equation, we still had the most votes. Personally, for me that was an important distinction. It was an unequivocal win that set us up for a slam dunk general election.

The rest of the campaign was much more fun, with Lee joining me even more. We enjoyed our newfound time together, like the Trump rally in Tupelo, dinners with Republican Women's groups, and community events like the annual Sweet Potato Festival in Vardeman. We didn't want to get caught sleeping or overconfident, so we outworked our Democrat opposition.

We were at least confident enough to schedule an election night party at The Gin in Nesbit to watch the results come in. It was the same place we began the campaign in earnest with a political kick-off rally in April. That party included barbeque and a band, along with a couple hundred supporters. The election night party was a smaller crowd, this time with an assortment of pizzas. Results arrived by phone and computer and were announced to the crowd for every local, regional, and state race.

After being the Republican nominee in 2003, losing in the general election, then taking first place in a 2011 special election and losing in the run-off, this 2019 victory was, if nothing else, a testament to perseverance. It was also somewhat anticlimactic. We were exhausted.

• • •

Whew! Finally, we got to tone it down and quit politicking. Transitioning between the November win and taking office in January was very relaxing and even productive. There was no pressure to perform yet but plenty to learn.

The outgoing commissioner and other commissioners and the entire department of transportation were very welcoming and helpful. A billion-dollar budget, many departments, applicable laws and regulations, countless federal and state programs, so many processes, and more names and people than I could remember were all introduced in a flurry of meetings, interactive presentations, and three-ring binders.

It was a crash course reminder that the wheels of government turn slowly and much too slowly for my liking.

Thanksgiving, Christmas, and New Year's passed quickly. It was time to go to work. As I picked up my government vehicle at the local maintenance shop, I heard—and had to quell—an early rumor. As I introduced myself at the shop, they shared their version of some guidance that was somewhat lost in translation.

"Good morning, y'all."

"Good morning, Commissioner. We have your truck parked out front and the keys are in it."

"So, how are things?"

"Apparently, our new governor thinks we should get rid of all our chairs so we'll quit sitting down on the job."

"Well, that's not exactly right. That word came from me in an early conversation I had with the executive director. You see, while I was campaigning I came across a shop with recliners salvaged from the roadside that were taking up workspace in the shop area.

"I advised that I wanted those recliners and lounge chairs gone by the time I took office."

"Oh, that's not us."

"No, your basic chairs and tables for drinking coffee as you arrive in the morning or eating lunch here don't hurt a thing. The crew that prompted that guidance had more than a half dozen Lazy Boys in a circle that took up an entire work bay."

We laughed and moved on to another topic. At least someone was listening, and there was awareness that I didn't want business as usual. The response, even with miscues, was positive.

Gubernatorial inauguration festivities, swearing-in ceremonies, and parties abounded in the capital city following the stressful election cycle. Our commission was joining a host of new representatives, state senators, and statewide elected officials starting our four-year terms. We were ready to change the world. Then the world really changed.

President Trump halted all travel to and from China. What? There was something going on here, and not many of us knew what it was. Speculation over the novel coronavirus ran rampant. Were we on the verge of a pandemic? Was it naturally occurring from Chinese wet markets or something more concerning, like a leak from the Chinese biological warfare facilities at Wuhan? Neither seemed to be a good option.

The biological warfare lab was plausible and fed by the lack of information coming from China. The seemingly extreme response reminded me of forest fires that are left to burn when naturally occurring, but intervention is swift when the fire is determined to be intentionally or otherwise caused by humans.

Then travel was halted to and from Europe, and we hadn't had our first U.S. confirmed case yet—unless you counted cruise ships or a few people who brought it with them from China. National Democrats mocked the president's strong response, even celebrating openly in San Francisco's Chinatown.

Uh-oh. Projections of death and disease were already off the charts. Millions of Americans projected to die . . . Reasonable numbers or hype? No way to be sure.

A novel coronavirus, Wuhan Flu, CoViD-19, China Virus . . . For some reason the name seemed to matter more than it should have.

Daily updates and news conferences fed us information and even disinformation from experts. Selectively chosen and omitted words from the mainstream media manipulated the public like few times before, politicizing it early and completely. It was obvious that this was going to be used as another chance for the Democrats and liberal media to push their liberal agenda and greater government control over our lives.

The only thing worse than free press is government-controlled press, or in this case a central party-controlled media. It was impossible to know who or what to trust as the pandemic took hold.

March Madness took on new meaning as NCAA tournaments were cancelled. The NBA season was put on hold and in jeopardy. MLB suspended its season. Pro sports of all types were reeling. Concerts were cancelled.

Two weeks of major economic shutdown and national restrictions were enacted to "slow the spread." Still there were more projections that millions of Americans would die before years end, and hospitals across the country would to be overrun in a matter of weeks. Emergency declarations and unprecedented measures were proposed for unprecedented times.

Lockdowns, restrictions, shutdowns, fearmongering, data, science, social response, and more politics . . . A quick trip to the local grocer let me know at least the panic was real. Shelves were so bare that most of us just smiled and shook our heads as we passed each other in the empty aisles.

After 15 days, another, 45-day lockdown was proposed to "flatten the curve." Lockdowns and other mitigation efforts rightly varied from state to state. Obviously, risk factors differed dramatically from New York, where tens of thousands died faster than we could count, to North Dakota, where almost no one was sick, or Hawaii to Massachusetts.

Inconsistencies from doctors, epidemiologists, politicians, media hacks, and everyone else were beyond nuts: masks/no masks, certain N-95 masks only/ any masks, homemade masks, and a new retail market for stylish masks of all sorts; handwashing; restricting crowd size at restaurants and event venues, even churches, limiting worshippers to 100, 50, then 10, then zero without regard to square footage, while places like Walmart, Lowe's, Home Depot, and grocery stores had hundreds upon hundreds, packed parking lots, and long lines. Amazon, FedEx, and UPS were rolling with everything from toilet paper and hand sanitizer to clothing and home décor. Some of it made no sense.

Truckers and online deliveries were non-stop. Essential industries ranged from the obvious like pharmacies and grocery stores to controversial ones like liquor stores and dry cleaners. Factories were staying open, then shutting down with suspected and real outbreaks.

Super Centers such as Walmart could sell clothing, toys, and crafts to hundreds crowding the aisles, but boutiques, toy stores, and hobby shops had to close. Restaurants were required to close, but gas stations and truck stops could sell chicken, burritos, hot pizza, sandwiches, and more. Large grocery stores could sell hot food, rotisserie chicken, sushi rolls, etc., but Chinese takeout restaurants were shut down.

Graduations, proms, reunions, religious services, weddings, and funerals were cancelled. Family, parents, husbands, wives, brothers, sisters were dying alone at homes and in hospitals, but mass gatherings for public protests were openly encouraged. The media script supporting liberal protests were flipped to coordinated media opposition if the protests were churchgoers and other conservatives.

If you can't keep your distance, wear a mask. Even if you can keep your distance, wear a mask. That's the same masks that were dismissed as ineffective and unnecessary by the very ones we were supposed to trust. Now the same experts said masks were imperative. (One year later the experts and the CDC had the audacity to recommend wearing two overlapping masks at once, further validating their original premise and mask critics' opinions that a mask alone would not stop the spread of the virus).

Phased reopening in the Summer of 2020 was too fast or too slow, depending on one's perspective. Three Phases, four Phases, more . . . What are we measuring today?

Essential workers like our transportation employees kept MDOT and our transportation commission functioning through it all. Some flex-time and office work from home, Zoom meetings, and conference calls were used to help navigate the craziness.

In spite of the pandemic, I was still trying to make a difference in North Mississippi. Focusing on desired improvements proved frustrating. Things inside a large organization are hard to change, and even more so during a worldwide pandemic.

Fighting a bureaucratic beast on behalf of my district wasn't much of a battle, because the people within the department of transportation were all trying to help in their own way. Still change proved difficult.

The staff and I and the other commissioners did not always agree in my first year. Some things went my way. Some didn't. Simple solutions that seemed easily doable to me were squelched by some inherent resistance of habit and posturing. Those moments were friendly reminders to me that there's more work to do on politics and infrastructure.

"Worst" roads always exist. Once that road is fixed, another one immediately receives the dubious honor. Outcries and remedies are always on the horizon. It's the same with policies and plans . . . and life. We can and should and will do better. Without continuing effort, things can and do get worse.

Worst mistakes, worst experiences, worst decisions of mine were substituted in this memoir with the worst ones *I was willing to admit in print.* There is a distinct difference between them.

What to leave in and what to leave out was especially challenging. Plenty of personal and professional failures, pains, and embarrassments were intentionally omitted. That was not done to create a false narrative but writing them all down seemed to over emphasize them on life's timeline. Including all the extremes without balancing them with countless pages of less exciting routines would have presented an inaccurately high degree of tension and turmoil. Sometimes, I have been accused of enjoying the chaos and conflicts of life a bit too much.

Events promoting our veterans and patriotism provide opportunities to wear the uniform again.

Working to make a difference as Transportation Commissioner of Mississippi's northern district

The 33-county transportation commissioner's campaign called me out of retirement.

Ready for more retirement style transportation like this ride with Crazy Horse monument behind us

Afterword

N ew conflicts arise along life's road, and those struggles can either be cursed or embraced. I mostly attempt the later. A positive frame of mind is a powerful enabler for any number of challenges.

A healthy look back allows us to learn from our past without reliving it. These personal accounts are just that. They are nothing more; They are also nothing less.

Expectations are that I will continue to leave my comfort zone and challenge myself. In fact, taking on new challenges of faith, family, and service, with all the uncertainty of success or failure, may be my truest comfort zone.

As the children's song makes full circle, I was once "too small to march in the infantry, ride in the cavalry, shoot the artillery." Now I am too old. Just as I was not too young for "the Lord's army" in that song, I am not too old to "fight the good fight of faith."

Fortunately, there are constants. Truth matters. Absolute timeless truth does not change. We just need to be careful what we identify as that kind of truth.

While some "black and white" choices exist, most of life is shaded with grays, even various hues across the color spectrum. This applies personally, professionally, politically, and even religiously; the trick is knowing the difference.

Among the many conflicts within my own belief system, I don't see grays when it comes to God, eternity or the solid core of Christianity. There are even some trustworthy principles in good government. For now, the firm foundation of the American experiment has stood the test of time. Today God, Christians and our ways of life are under attack from liberal socialists that like to call themselves progressives.

I look at it this way . . .

(1) *Eternity:* "Jesus saith unto him, I am the way, the truth, and the life: no man cometh unto the Father, but by me." From the Word of God (KJV)

(2) *Religion:* "Thou shalt love the Lord thy God with all thy heart, and with all thy soul, and with all thy strength, and with all thy mind; and thy neighbour as thyself." From the Word of God (KJV)

"I believe in God, the Father Almighty, maker of heaven and earth; And in Jesus Christ his only Son, our Lord; who was conceived by the Holy Spirit, born of the Virgin Mary, suffered under Pontius Pilate, was crucified, dead, and buried; the third day he rose from the dead; he ascended into heaven, and sitteth at the right hand of God the Father Almighty; from thence he shall come to judge the quick and the dead. I believe in the Holy Spirit, the holy catholic church, the communion of saints, the forgiveness of sins, the resurrection of the body, and the life everlasting. Amen." The Apostles Creed

(3) *Government:* "We hold these truths to be self-evident, that all men are created equal, that they are endowed by their Creator with certain unalienable Rights, that among these are Life, Liberty and the pursuit of Happiness. That to secure these rights, Governments are instituted among Men, deriving their just powers from the consent of the governed... And for the support of this Declaration, with a firm reliance on the protection of divine Providence, we mutually pledge to each other our Lives, our Fortunes and our sacred Honor." From the Declaration of Independence.

". . . that, from these honored dead we take increased devotion to that cause for which they here, gave the last full measure of devotion -- that we here highly resolve these dead shall not have died in vain; that the nation, shall have a new birth of freedom, and that government of the people by the people for the people, shall not perish from the earth." From the Gettysburg Address.

Beyond the three keystones above, it seemed only right in a political memoir to deal with more political topics. The list below encapsulates some of my views that were forged by the fires of life on a variety of national political issues:

Freedom – Live it.

Constitution – Defend it.

Economy – Liberate it.

Flag – Salute it.

Jobs – Get one.

Debt – Pay it.

Deficit – Stop it.

Military – Harden it.

War – Declare it.

Welfare – Earn it.

Social Security – Guard it.

Healthcare – Personalize it.

Law, Order and Justice – Love it.

Term Limits – Yes.

Education – Correct it.

Immigration – Manage it.

Infrastructure – Modernize it.

Environment – Conserve it.

Climate Change – Enjoy it.

Science – Prove it.

History – Learn it.

This memoir began as a way to share my untold Marine Corps story with my children in a way that my father never did with us. So, it is mostly *to* them and not *about* them. Because my Marine Corps story is predominantly a reservist version, it is intertwined in the disorder and conflicts of a uniquely impacted civilian life, including God and politics as well as other personal and professional choices. Sometimes, I look back and say, "Enough is enough." Then I question myself. "Sure you care, but do you care enough to make a difference?"

• • •

CPSIA information can be obtained
at www.ICGtesting.com
Printed in the USA
BVHW090442030721
611064BV00019B/1258